Stakeholders

ORGANISATION FOR ECONOMIC CO-OPERATION AND DEVELOPMENT (OECD)

Pursuant to Article 1 of the Convention signed in Paris on 14th December 1960, and which came into force on 30th September 1961, the OECD shall promote policies designed:

- to achieve the highest sustainable economic growth and employment and a rising standard of living in Member countries, while maintaining financial stability, and thus to contribute to the development of the world economy;
- to contribute to sound economic expansion in Member as well as non-member countries in the process of economic development; and
- to contribute to the expansion of world trade on a multilateral, non-discriminatory basis in accordance with international obligations.

The original Member countries of the OECD are Austria, Belgium, Canada, Denmark, France, Germany, Greece, Iceland, Ireland, Italy, Luxembourg, the Netherlands, Norway, Portugal, Spain, Sweden, Switzerland, Turkey, the United Kingdom and the United States. The following countries became Members subsequently through accession at the dates indicated hereafter: Japan (28th April 1964), Finland (28th January 1969), Australia (7th June 1971), New Zealand (29th May 1973), Mexico (18th May 1994), the Czech Republic (21st December 1995), Hungary (7th May 1996), Poland (22nd November 1996) and Korea (12th December 1996). The Commission of the European Communities takes part in the work of the OECD (Article 13 of the OECD Convention).

The Development Centre of the Organisation for Economic Co-operation and Development was established by decision of the OECD Council on 23rd October 1962 and comprises twenty-three Member countries of the OECD: Austria, Belgium, Canada, the Czech Republic, Denmark, Finland, France, Germany, Greece, Iceland, Ireland, Italy, Japan, Korea, Luxembourg, Mexico, the Netherlands, Norway, Poland, Portugal, Spain, Sweden and Switzerland, as well as Argentina and Brazil from March 1994. The Commission of the European Communities also takes part in the Centre's Advisory Board.

The purpose of the Centre is:

- to bring together the knowledge and experience available in Member countries of both economic development and the formulation and execution of general economic policies;
- to adapt such knowledge and experience to the actual needs of countries or regions in the process of development; and
- to put the results at the disposal of the countries by appropriate means.

The Centre has a special and autonomous position within the OECD which enables it to enjoy scientific independence in the execution of its task. Nevertheless, the Centre can draw upon the experience and knowledge available in the OECD in the development field.

Stakeholders
Government–NGO Partnerships for International Development

Edited by
Ian Smillie and Henny Helmich
In collaboration with
Tony German and Judith Randel

Organisation for Economic Co-operation and Development

Earthscan Publications Ltd, London

The information and data presented in this publication were critically reviewed for accuracy by numerous persons working in government development agencies and development NGOs. Their very useful remarks have been taken into account in the final editing. However, the opinions expressed and arguments employed in this publication are the sole responsibility of the editors and authors and do not necessarily reflect those of the OECD, the OECD Development Centre or of the governments of OECD member countries.

First published in the UK in 1999 by
Earthscan Publications Ltd

A catalogue record for this book is available from the British Library

ISBN: 1 85383 589 7 paperback

Typesetting by PCS Mapping & DTP, Newcastle upon Tyne
Printed and bound by Bell & Bain Ltd, Glasgow
Cover design by Declan Buckley

For a full list of publications please contact:

Earthscan Publications Ltd
120 Pentonville Road
London, N1 9JN, UK
Tel: +44 (0)171 278 0433
Fax: +44 (0)171 278 1142
Email: earthinfo@earthscan.co.uk
http://www.earthscan.co.uk

Earthscan is an editorially independent subsidiary of Kogan Page Limited and publishes in association with WWF-UK and the International Institute for Environment and Development

This book is printed on elemental chlorine free paper from sustainably managed forests

Contents

Acknowledgements

The present publication is the result of the effort by a team coordinated by Henny Helmich of the OECD Development Centre's External Cooperation Unit, and Ian Smillie, a development expert and writer from Canada, with Tony German and Judith Randel, partners at Development Initiatives, an independent research and information organisation specialising in aid policy, dissemination and NGO–Government relations, based in the United Kingdom. They were assisted by Frances Hill. Additional contributions for individual chapters were received from: Michelle Auld, Christian Freres, Mario Gay, Karin Küblböck, Dimitra Massoula, Mario Ribeiro, Tie Roefs and Anna Schiavoni. The overview chapter in this publication was first discussed at a second government–NGO informal experts meeting, *Stakeholders for Development: Government–NGO Dialogue on the 21st Century Partnership Strategy*, on 13 and 14 January 1998. Special thanks are due to Diana Mitlin, Colm Foy, Richard Gerster and Aye Aye Win for their contributions as rapporteurs for this meeting.

The authors and editors profited from the essential support of a large group of persons both in the development NGO community and in the governments who gave their time for interviews, provided data, made comments and provided critical assessments of drafts. Their subsequent attention to the follow-up of this project will be decisive for the impact of this study. Additional financial resources from the Government of Japan for the Centre's work on development NGOs are acknowledged with gratitude.

In compiling the book, both authors and editors have found two publications to be of great help. The first is the annual publication *The Reality of Aid*, edited by Judith Randel and Tony German and published in London by Earthscan. The second is *Searching for Impact and Methods: NGO Evaluation Synthesis Study*, published in November 1997 by the Ministry of Foreign Affairs of Finland and the OECD/DAC Expert Group on Aid Evaluation.

The team received support from Jody Kaylor in the Development Centre, who assisted in the organisation of the Stakeholders experts' meeting in January 1998, from Kristen Neymarc from the management office and from the other members of the External Cooperation Unit working on NGO issues: Vanda Legrandgerard, François Sedogo, Alice Watson and Adéle Woods.

Special acknowledgements go to Catherine Duport, Head of the Centre's Administrative Unit and her colleagues Morag Soranna and Carmen Sabbagh, who made possible the sometimes complicated arrangements needed for this project, and the Centre's Publications Unit, headed by Colm Foy.

The project has benefited from the continuing interest of Ambassador James Michel, Chair of the DAC, Bernard Wood, Director, and Richard Carey, Deputy Director of the OECD Development Cooperation Directorate.

The Stakeholders Project

The Stakeholders project, *Trends and Issues in Evolving Relationships between Donor Agencies and Development NGOs*, was initiated in 1992 by the OECD Development Centre with the support of the Government of Canada. The driving force behind the project were Jean-Guy Saint-Martin, Canadian International Development Agency Vice President, and Terrance Lorne Mooney, Senior Policy Advisor of the CIDA Partnership Branch.

CIDA provided important financial support for the project which was coordinated in the OECD Development Centre by Henny Helmich in close collaboration with Ian Smillie. In the OECD, important inputs were received by Giulio Fossi, Head of External Cooperation of the Centre and Elena Borghese, of the Development Cooperation Directorate. The project resulted in a first meeting at the OECD in Paris on 28–30 June 1993, after which the results were published in *NGOs and Governments: Stakeholders for Development*, edited by Ian Smillie and Henny Helmich.

In 1993, it was decided that the Development Centre should continue to act as a platform for dialogue between DAC member governments and development NGOs. This led to a number of thematic conferences and publications (for example, *The Challenge of Development within Conflict Zones*, edited by Terrance Lorne Mooney, 1995) and the organisation of an annual dialogue with development NGOs.

The first *Stakeholders* publication included analytical chapters on 13 DAC member countries and the European Community. In 1995 this original study was published in Italian with the Italian NGO ASAL (*ONG e governi: un tandem per lo sviluppo*), edited by Maria Stella Rognoni, who also wrote an update on the 1993 chapter on Italy.

Following this publication, additional analytical studies were jointly published by the OECD Development Centre with major NGOs in several countries: *Belgium* (Tie Roefs, 1995 published in Dutch, French and English jointly with the Belgian NGO, COPROGRAM), *Austria* (Karin Küblböck,1996 published in German and English jointly with the Austrian NGO, ÖFSE), *Ireland* (Ian Smillie,1996 published with the Irish NGO, Trócaire) *New Zealand* (Ian Smillie, 1997 published with the New Zealand umbrella NGO, CID) and *Portugal* (Mario Ribeiro, 1998 published in Portuguese and English with the Portuguese NGO, CIDAC).

Authors and Co-authors

Michelle Auld (New Zealand), Researcher, New Zealand Council for International Development

Christian Freres (Spain), Research Coordinator, Asociacion de Investigacion Y Especializacion Sobre Temas Iberoamericanos (AIETI)

Mario Gay (Italy), Consultant, Co-financing Support Program of the Liaison Committee of Development NGOs to the European Union in Brussels

Tony German (United Kingdom), Partner, Development Initiatives*

Henny Helmich (the Netherlands), Political Scientist, Administrator External Co-operation, OECD Development Centre

Frances Hill (United Kingdom), Researcher, Development Initiatives*

Karin Küblböck (Austria), Researcher, Österreichische Forschungstiftung für Entwicklungshilfe (ÖFSE)

Dimitra Massoula (Greece), Researcher, Political Scientist and Economist

Judith Randel (United Kingdom), Partner, Development Initiatives*

Mário Ribeiro (Portugal), Economist and Master in African Studies

Tie Roefs (Belgium), Historian and Political Scientist, Vredeseilanden-Coopibo, a Flemish NGO

Anna Sciavoni (Italy), Coordinamento delle Organizzazione non governative per la Co-operazione Internazionale allo Sviluppo (COCIS) Co-ordinator and Member of Italian Delegation Liaison Committee of Development NGOs to the European Union

Ian Smillie (Canada), Development Consultant and Writer

---

*Development Initiatives is an independent research and information organisation specialising in aid policy, dissemination and NGO–Government Relations

Acronyms and Abbreviations

ABOS	Belgian Administration for Development Cooperation
ACEAD	Advisory Committee on External Aid and Development
ACFOA	Australian Council for Overseas Aid
ACP	Africa, Caribbean and Pacific
ACVFA	Advisory Committee on Voluntary Foreign Aid
ADC	Austrian Association for Development and Cooperation
ADRA	Adventist Development Relief Agency
AECI	*Agencia Española de Cooperación Internacional* (Spanish Agency for International Cooperation)
AFVP	*Association Française des Volontaires du Progrès* (French Association of Volunteers for Progress)
AGEH	*Arbeitsgemeinschaft für Entwicklungshilfe* (Association for Development Aid)
AGEZ	*Arbeitsgemeinschaft Entwicklungszusammenarbeit* (Working Association for Development Cooperation)
AGKED	*Arbeitsgemeinschaft Kirchlicher Entwicklungsdienst* (Association of Church Development Service)
AIV	Advisory Council on Foreign Affairs and International Cooperation
AKM	Apostolic Church Mission
ANAO	Australian National Audit Office
ANCP	AusAID NGO Co-operation Program
ANGOA	Association of Non-Governmental Organisations of *Aotearoa* (New Zealand)
APHEDA	Australian People for Health, Education and Development Abroad
APIC	Association for Promotion of International Cooperation
APSO	Agency for Personal Service Overseas
ASI	*Associations de Solidarité Internationale* (Associations for International Solidarity)
AusAID	Australian Agency for International Development
AVA	Australian Volunteers Abroad
BBO	Christian Institute for Development Policy (Netherlands)
BDDEA	British Development Division, East Africa
BENGO	Advice Centre for NGOs working in the Field of Development
BILANCE	Catholic Organisation for Development Cooperation (Netherlands – until recently known as CEBEMO)
BITS	Swedish Agency for International Technical and Economic Cooperation
BMZ	Ministry for Economic Cooperation and Development (Germany)
BOAG	British Overseas Aid Group
BOND	British Overseas NGOs for Development
BUKO	*Bundeskongress Entwicklungspolitischer Aktionsgruppen* (Federal Congress of Development Policy Action Groups – Germany)
CAA	Community Aid Abroad
CAFOD	Catholic Action for Overseas Development
CCD	*Commission Coopération Développement*
CCF	Christian Children's Fund
CCFC	Christian Children's Fund of Canada
CCFD	*Comité Catholique Contre la Faim et pour le Développement* (Catholic Committee Against Hunger and For Development – France)

CCIC	Canadian Council for International Cooperation
CCODP	Canadian Catholic Organisation for Development and Peace
CDC	Committee for Development Cooperation
CDIE	Center for Development Information and Evaluation
CDIP	*Conférence des Directeurs Cantonaux de l'Instruction Publique*
CECI	*Centre Canadien d'Étude et de Coopération Internationale* (Canadian Centre for Research and International Cooperation)
CESO	Canadian Executive Service Organisation
CFI	*Christliche Fachkräfte International* (Christian Experts International)
CFO	Co-financing Organisation
CGAP	Consultative Group to Assist the Poorest
CID	Council for International Development
CP	Country Programme
CIDA	Canadian International Development Agency
CIDA-C	Anti-Colonial Information and Documentation Centre
CIDAC	*Amílcar Cabral Information and Documentation Centre*
CIIR	Catholic Institute for International Relations
CIPSI	*Coordinamento di Iniziative Popolari de Solidarieta Internazionale* (Coordination of Popular Initiatives for International Solidarity)
CLONG	*Comité de Liaison des ONG de Volontariat*
CLOSI	*Comité de Liaison des Organisations de Solidarité Internationale*
CNCD	*Centre National pour la Coopération au Développement*
COCIS	*Coordinamento delle ONG per la Cooperazione Internazionale allo Sviluppo* – Coordination of International Development Co-operation NGOs
CODE	Canadian Organisation for Development through Education
CONGOOD	Confederation of NGOs for Overseas Development
CORSO	Formerly Council of Organisations for Relief Services Overseas (now no longer an acronym)
CPB	Canadian Partnership Branch (CIDA)
CPLP	Community of Portuguese Speaking Countries
CPOP	*Comité Paritaire d'Orientation et de Programmation*
DAC	Development Assistance Committee
DAP	Development Assistance Programme
DCA	*Danchurchaid (Folkekirkens Nodhjelp)*
DCC	*Délégation Catholique à la Coopération*
DCD	Development Cooperation Division
DDC	Department of Development Cooperation
DEA	Development Education Association
DEC	Development Education Centre
DECJ	Development Education Council of Japan
DED	*Deutscher Entwicklungsdienst* (German Development Service)
DEFY	Development Education for Youth
DEM	Danish Evangelical Mission
DEPS	Development Education Project Scheme
DESC	Development Education Support Centre
DEV	Development Cooperation Division of the Ministry of Foreign Affairs and Trade
DFA	Department of Foreign Affairs
DFAE	Federal Department of Foreign Affairs (Switzerland)
DFI	Direct Funding Initiative
DFID	Department for International Development

DG	Directorate General
DGAP	Development Group for Alternative Policies
DGCS	*Direzione Generale per la Cooperazione allo Sviluppo* (Directorate General for Development Cooperation – Italy)
DGIS	Directorate General for International Cooperation of the Netherlands Ministry of Foreign Affairs
DIDC	Department for International Development Cooperation
D-NGO	NGO Division
DWHH	*Deutsche Welthungerhilfe* (German World Food Aid)
DZI	German Central Institute for Social Affairs
ECHO	European Community Humanitarian Office
ECU	European Currency Unit
EDF	European Development Fund
EDI	Economic Development Institute
EEDDA	Greek Committee for International Democratic Solidarity
EMW	*Evangelisches Missionswerk*
EPRD	European Programme for Reconstruction and Development in South Africa
EU	European Union
EVS	European Volunteer Service
EZE	*Evangelische Zentralstelle für Entwicklungshilfe* (Protestant Central Agency for Development Aid)
FCE	Fund for Economic Cooperation (Portugal)
FOCSIV	*Federazione Organismi Cristiani de Servizio Internazionale Volantario* – Federation of Christian International Volunteers Services
FSD	*Fonds Spécial de Développement*
FVS	Finnish Volunteer Service
GNP	Gross National Product
GOM	*Gemeenschappelijk Overleg Medefinanciering* (Co-financing Consultative Body)
GTZ	German Agency for Technical Cooperation
HEDCO	Higher Education for Development Cooperation
HIVOS	Humanist Institute for Cooperation with Developing Countries
IBRD	International Bank for Reconstruction and Development
ICCO	Inter-Church Organisation for Development Cooperation
ICNL	International Center for Nonprofit Law
ICP	Institute for Portuguese Cooperation
ICRC	International Committee of the Red Cross
IDA	International Development Association
IDEA	International Development Executives Association
IFAD	International Fund for Agricultural Development
IFC	International Finance Corporation
IIED	International Institute for Environment and Development
IMF	International Monetary Fund
IMU	Irish Missionary Union
INTRAC	International NGO Training and Research Centre
IPF	Indicative Planning Figure
IPPF	International Planned Parenthood Federation
IRCT	International Rehabilitation Centre for Torture Victims
IRS	Internal Revenue Service
ITDG	Intermediate Technology Development Group
JANIC	Japanese NGO Centre for International Cooperation

JICA	Japan International Cooperation Agency
JOCV	Japan Overseas Cooperation Volunteers
JVE	*Jeunes, Ville, Emplois* (Youth, City, Employment)
KED	*Kirchlicher Entwicklungsdienst* (Church Development Service)
KEPA	Finnish Service Centre for Development Cooperation
KFS	*Kofinanzierungsstelle für Entwicklungszusammenarbeit* (Co-Financing Office for Development Cooperation)
KOO	*Koordinierungsstelle der Österreichischen Bischofskonferenz für Internationale Entwicklung und Mission* (Coordination Office of the Austrian Bishops for Conference for International Development and Mission)
KZE	*Katholische Zentralstelle für Entwicklungshilfe* (Catholic Central Agency for Development Aid)
LO/FTF	Danish Trade Union Council for International Development Cooperation
MAE	Italian Ministry of Foreign Affairs
MCC	Mennonite Central Committee
MFA	Ministry of Foreign Affairs (Norway)
MIT	Massachusetts Institute of Technology
MoFA	Ministry of Foreign Affairs
MPA	Mini Programme Agreements
MS	*Mellemfolkeligt Samvirke*
MSF	*Médecins sans Frontières*
NCA	Norwegian Church Aid
NCDE	National Committee for Development Education
NCDO	National Committee for International Cooperation and Sustainable Development
NCOS	*Nationaal Centrum voor Ontwikkelingssamenwerking* (National Centre for Development Cooperation – Belgium)
NDRF	NGO Disasters Relief Forum
NEDA	Netherlands Development Assistance
NGO	Non-governmental organisation
NGOWG	NGO Working Group on the World Bank
NICRA	Negotiated Indirect Cost Rate Agreement
NORAD	Norwegian Agency for Development Cooperation
NOVIB	Netherlands Organisation for International Development Cooperation
NPI	New Partnership Initiative
NSS	NGO Subsidy Scheme
NVS	Norwegian Volunteer Service
NZODA	New Zealand Official Development Assistance
ODA	Official Development Assistance
ODA	Overseas Development Authority
ODI	Overseas Development Institute
OECD	Organisation for Economic Cooperation and Development
OED	Operations Evaluation Department
ÖED	*Österreichischer Entwicklungsdienst* (Austrian Development Cooperation Service)
ÖFSE	*Österreichische Forschungsstiftung für Entwicklungshilfe* (Austrian Foundation for Development Research)
OICS	*Osservatorio Interregionale sulla Cooperazione allo Sviluppo* (Inter-Regional Observatory on Development Cooperation)
OPE	Office for Planning and Evaluation
OSB	Overseas Service Bureau

OTI	Office of Transition Initiatives
PALOPS	Portuguese-speaking African countries
PL480	Public Law 480 (USA)
POSIVA	Postal Savings for International Voluntary Aid
PP	Popular Party
PSC	Project Selection Committee
PSO	Personnel Services Overseas
PVC	Office of Private and Voluntary Contributions
PVO	Private Voluntary Organisation
SAPRI	Structural Adjustment Participatory Review Initiative
SCF	Save the Children Fund
SDC	Swiss Agency for Development and Cooperation
SECIPI	Secretary of State for International Cooperation and Iberoamerica
SF	Social Fund
tdh	*terre des hommes*
SIDA	Swedish International Development Authority
TNDT	Transitional National Development Trust
UNCED	United Nations Conference on the Environment and Development
UNHCR	United Nations High Commission for Refugees
UNICEF	United Nations Children's Fund
UNIFEM	United Nations Fund for Women
USAID	United States Agency for International Development
VASS	Voluntary Agency Support Scheme
VENRO	*Verband Entwicklungspolitik Deutscher Nichtregierungs – organisationen* (a federation for all development NGOs)
VIDC	Vienna Institute for Development and Cooperation
VSA	Volunteer Service Abroad
VSO	Voluntary Service Overseas
WDM	World Development Movement
WFP	World Food Program
WTO	World Trade Organisation
WUSC	World University Service of Canada

Boxes and Tables

BOXES

TABLES

Preface

Governments and non-governmental organisations (NGOs) have made remarkable progress since the early 1990s in working together towards common development goals: OECD Development Assistance Committee (DAC) member countries have significantly increased the involvement of NGOs in their development policy-making and programmes; and many NGOs have successfully continued their efforts to improve their effectiveness as partners. Particularly striking is the progress that has been made in creating mutually respectful working partnerships. This partnership approach is needed if the objectives of the Development Partnerships Strategy, endorsed by the OECD Council at ministerial level in 1996 and since adopted internationally, are to be attained.

This publication presents the papers and discussions at an informal meeting, entitled 'Stakeholders for Development: Government–NGO Dialogue on the 21st century Partnership Strategy', organised by the OECD Development Centre in close cooperation with the DAC. The objective of the meeting was to continue to promote open dialogue between civil society and governments. British Under-Secretary of State for International Development George Foulkes delivered an opening statement underlining the important role that the strategy has played in the development community and, in particular, its central idea of partnerships. Recent OECD work has pointed to the need for continued dialogue among partners. For example, the 1997 OECD study, *The World in 2020, Towards a New Global Age,* recommends that OECD's policy dialogue activities should provide greater scope for dialogue between all relevant players to strengthen consensus building. The Development Partnerships Strategy also underscores civil society's strategic role in supporting sustainable and poverty-reducing development.

Three issues emerged from the meeting as particularly essential for stakeholders. First, an overemphasis on evaluation may be leading NGOs to evaluate their work by simply measuring output. This focus on output may have two undesired consequences: NGOs may be choosing activities that are easily accountable to donors rather than basing their activities on beneficiaries' real needs; and they may be too easily influenced by the easy 'successes' as measured by output alone and avoid a more in-depth evaluation that would permit learning from mistakes. Second, the evolution in the funding relationship between governments and NGOs – from matching grants to contracts – has had important and unexpected impacts. Current government grant-making practices mean that NGOs must increasingly compete for contracts. This trend could transform NGOs from representatives of civil society, which made them attractive partners in the first place, into service-providers and inexpensive government executing agencies. Finally, it is clear that in order to improve public commitment in OECD countries to development goals, there is growing awareness of the importance for governments and NGOs to collaborate on building public knowledge of development issues through better education.

The information contained in this volume will contribute to the further development of a constructive dialogue between governments and development NGOs. Two companion volumes are also published by the Centre: *Civil Society and International Co-operation* and *Public Attitudes and International Development Co-operation.*

I would like to dedicate this publication to my colleague, Giuilo Fossi, Head of the Development Centre's External Cooperation Division from 1960 to his retirement in 1998. He had the foresight to initiate a broad programme of work at the OECD on development NGOs and their contribution to North–South cooperation.

Jean Bonvin
President, OECD Development Centre

Part I

Government–NGO Relationships

1   Introduction

Henny Helmich[1]

This publication presents an analysis of the issues in government–NGO relationships (including, for the first time, descriptions of government–NGO relations in all OECD/Development Assistance Committee (DAC) member countries, and Greece, with additional analysis of NGO collaboration with the European Union and the World Bank) as presented at the fourth Informal Government–NGO Dialogue jointly organised in Paris from 13–14 January 1998 by the OECD/DAC and the OECD Development Centre.[2]

If the objective of reducing by 50 per cent the number of people living in absolute poverty by the year 2015 is to be achieved, one key factor should be a coordinated approach to address the needs of those living in poverty in the South. Government action alone is not sufficient. The capacities, the diverse experience and the public awareness-building activities of thousands of NGOs[3] in DAC member countries are important, if not essential, to the successful implementation of poverty reduction strategies.

In 1996, the OECD Council at ministerial level endorsed the *Development Partnerships Strategy*, elaborated by the DAC Ministers for Development Cooperation and Heads of Aid Agencies in their report *Shaping the 21st Century: the Contribution of Development Cooperation*. Following its wide acceptance by the international community, the strategy has since become an important basis for dialogue and concerted action to achieve further progress in poverty reduction. One key aspect of the strategy calls for strengthening the coordination and policy coherence among all actors (*Stakeholders*) in the development community. The *Development Partnerships Strategy* offers a platform that NGOs can fully support because it includes their own long-standing commitment to poverty reduction. It also highlights the strategic role of civil society[4] in inducing positive social change.

NGOs in general are aware of the important role of the DAC in supporting the greater involvement of NGOs within *national* policy discussions on development assistance in DAC countries. In the 1990s, in most DAC member countries, collaboration and national dialogue between governments and NGOs has been strengthened.

THE DEVELOPMENT PARTNERSHIPS STRATEGY AND COLLABORATION WITH NGOS

DAC governments promote a range of political and economic objectives in their development cooperation policies. Although many include poverty reduction in these objectives, not all consider it the primary goal. Governments in both the North and the South have recently expressed a renewed commitment to poverty reduction during the negotiations of official texts in the major UN conferences of the 1990s. This is in part due to the important involvement of NGOs. For example, they have long advocated that governments should accord higher priority to poverty reduction within their Official Development Assistance (ODA).

The Challenge of Policy Coherence for Poverty Reduction

Attaining the level of poverty eradication targeted in the *Development Partnerships Strategy* will require a major reorganisation of the efforts of both governments and of NGOs. Governments acknowledge the depth of the changes needed, and many are involved in a major effort to seek coherence with other policies affecting their relations with developing countries, and with the economic and social conditions within these countries. General economic and financial policies of OECD countries can often have a more significant impact on poverty reduction in the South than the policies and programmes of official development assistance agencies. Development ministries and agencies have a difficult task in fostering international poverty-related policy coherence with larger ministries – such as trade and finance – that have their own policy coherence priorities, for example on the relationship between trade and investment. Attracting and managing external private financial flows is increasingly important to most developing country governments, especially in the form of Foreign Direct Investment (FDI).

In particular, in an era of globalisation that fosters increasing economic interdependence, governments and NGOs are seeking ways to increase coherence between the poverty reduction policies of development agencies and issues of debt relief, trade and finance. The debate surrounding the negotiations of a Multilateral Agreement on Investment (MAI) reveals that some actors view such an agreement as a very useful instrument in liberating and attracting FDI while others, in particular some NGOs, argue that the implementation of a multilateral investment regime on the basis of equal rules for all would weaken the Southern bargaining position vis-à-vis powerful investors especially with regard to basic protection in the social, cultural and environmental fields.

The Growing Role of NGOs in the North and the South

The NGO role as contractor to official programmes, particularly in specialist areas such as emergency relief and post-conflict rehabilitation and reconciliation, has grown. ODA agencies find that they also increasingly rely on NGOs for innovation in programmes that reduce infant and maternal mortality, that promote primary health care, that spread primary education, and provide basic services such as water and sanitation. Decades of NGO experience is now increasingly tapped by governments seeking to extend the scope of their programmes in areas that are new or inaccessible to them.

The growing use of sub-contracting may encourage some NGOs to become instruments in development programmes that would place at risk their independent character. The very attractiveness of NGOs results in part from their nature as citizen-based organisations and their readiness to challenge government and private sector actors when tackling issues of poverty and promoting social justice.

DAC governments and multilateral agencies recognise that NGOs and civil society more generally (especially in the South) may have a particularly valuable role in influencing the governments of developing countries that lack commitment to poverty reduction, or do not provide adequate protection of human rights.

IMPROVING ACCOUNTABILITY AND EVALUATION

Actors in development cooperation need to be accountable to taxpayers, to private donors and especially to the beneficiaries of their activities in developing countries. A clear commitment to targets is an important basis for improved accountability and evaluation; general formulations aimed at reducing poverty are by themselves unmeasurable and unenforceable. Indicators also need to be understandable and precise, and complex systems that obscure rather than illuminate the scale of progress should be avoided.

Considerable work has been undertaken by the DAC in collaboration with the World Bank, the United Nations and bilateral agencies, to reach wide agreement on a limited set of indicators to monitor the global goals set by the *Development Partnerships Strategy*. In addition, progress has been made in reorganising statistical aid reporting systems, in order to provide better information about resource flows. Bilateral development agencies are now making an effort to make their data available in compatible ways. There is also a growing need for NGO expenditures on their poverty reduction activities to be subject to improved data reporting.

In the first half of the 1990s development NGOs in most DAC countries went through a phase of joint or individual evaluation of their impact on poverty reduction. The conclusions of these impact evaluations all showed that while the practical expertise of NGOs in poverty reduction is large, a gap needs to be closed between the setting of NGO goals and actual NGO practice. However, many of the government and NGO evaluations that do take place are not publicly available. As poverty reduction is a development process characterised by experimentation, and marked by both success and failure, this process – and the learning that must accompany it – is not well-served by practices that downplay systematic and open evaluation.

NGOs can contribute towards ensuring that poverty reduction remains 'in the realm of the possible' through increased efforts at careful and accurate measurement of their own activities. NGOs also need to be accountable for the consequences of mistaken policy advice, or the effects of advocacy, which may have weakened the capacity of the poor to improve their own conditions, or the conditions of their society, economy and environment.

PUBLIC COMMITMENT IN OECD COUNTRIES AND DEVELOPMENT EDUCATION

There is no empirical evidence for the much discussed 'aid fatigue'. In fact, available data show that public support for international development efforts has remained stable over the last 15 years in most OECD countries. However, most people lack more than a basic knowledge about development cooperation and about the differences current aid policies actually make for people living in developing societies. While there is therefore a stable level of 'compassion' for helping the poor, most people find it difficult to arrive at a judgement about present efforts of governments and NGOs in this field.

Public opinion influences government decision-making, but the degree of this influence has not yet been clearly established. It has been demonstrated that opinions of law makers and policy advisors do have an impact on government policies in favour of development assistance. Development education, therefore, should not only have a 'public' target, but should especially concentrate on the various political constituencies.

CONCLUSIONS

Both governments and NGOs have made remarkable progress since the beginning of the 1990s in improving their collaboration.[5] Most DAC governments have significantly increased the involvement of NGOs in their development policies and programmes and most NGOs have successfully continued their efforts to improve their effectiveness as partners.

As part of coordinated and coherent development efforts, not only more work on public accountability is needed, but also greater efforts and better collaboration in development information and education – in both OECD and developing countries – are necessary if the effort is to be understood by policy-makers, the media and the public at large. Public scepticism about the capacity of development policies to address the needs of the poor is a major reason that development assistance has a low political priority. This in turn has contributed to policy-makers accepting or sometimes proposing the reduction of aid resources. In this context, both NGOs and official agencies need to work towards a better quality of knowledge about, and understanding of, development efforts. This requires a wide range of complementary activities, some of which are best undertaken by NGOs, others by government agencies.

2 At Sea in a Sieve?
Trends and Issues in the Relationship Between Northern NGOs and Northern Governments[1]

Ian Smillie

They went to sea in a sieve, they did;
In a sieve they went to sea;
In spite of all their friends could say,
On a winter's morn, on a stormy day,
In a sieve they went to sea!

Edward Lear, *The Jumblies*

BACKGROUND

Edward Lear's Victorian poem about the adventurous Jumblies can be read as a metaphor for the NGO effort in international development. Many NGOs did – and still do – 'set out to sea' with little more than commitment and energy to drive them.

In 1992, the OECD Development Centre initiated an ambitious study, examining relationships between governments and Northern international development NGOs in thirteen OECD member countries and the European Union. The result, published in 1993 as *Non-Governmental Organisations and Governments: Stakeholders for Development*, became something of an OECD bestseller, going through two reprintings. In 1997 and 1998 the subject was revisited, with reviews of government–NGO relations in 22 OECD member countries and additional chapters on the European Union and the World Bank.

In the 1993 *Stakeholders* publication, there was an overview chapter on trends and issues. It described the nature and role of voluntary organisations and was organised around seven 'issues'. The first had to do with problems of knowledge, learning and evaluation among NGOs. The second issue dealt with professionalism, and the problems of competition and coordination. The third focused on funding arrangements between NGOs and donors: problems created by project funding, a decline in responsive support and the rise of special, donor-driven funding windows.

The fourth issue dealt with questions of dependence and independence, and the emergence in some countries of a contracting relationship between government and NGOs. Issue five discussed NGOs and the public: fundraising, development education and advocacy. The sixth issue revolved around the growth of NGOs in emergency programming, and the seventh had to do with roles and relationships – the direct funding by Northern donors of Southern NGOs, and the place of NGOs in the growing civil society discourse.

Most of these issues remain, and much has been written in the ensuing years about some of them. This chapter will pass lightly over those that have received the most attention, such as the civil society debate. The question of NGOs and the public – development education and advocacy – are the subject of a concurrent OECD Development Centre study and will be considered only briefly here. Some of the 1993 issues have become more acute, however, and will be examined in greater detail. A major part of the paper will deal with trends and issues in the funding relationship between governments and NGOs – the evolution from matching grant programmes to contracts, levels of dependency and the implications of the change. It will examine the problem of NGO-related statistics, and will deal with the contradictions and problems that have been created by the enduring myth that NGOs can (and must) keep their operating costs at unrealistically low levels. The rise of the 'Super NGOs' – growth, competition, child sponsorship and emergencies is then considered. The final, longest section of the chapter, deals with the increasingly urgent question of NGO evaluation – its purpose, practice and findings.

It is worth noting in any discussion about NGOs that generalisations are just that – generalisations. Describing NGOs is like describing cars on a highway. Some are old, some are new. Some have a great deal of baggage, while others travel light. Some are large, some are small. Some of the smallest ones are faster, more efficient and more dependable than the biggest, and cost is not always a factor. Most importantly, all of them are moving, and a snapshot of the highway today will be different from a snapshot of the same location tomorrow.

Great expectations

Northern NGOs have their origins in a wide variety of very different national traditions of self-help and of outreach to strangers. The international NGO movement has its roots in missionary movements that date back, in some cases, to the sixteenth century. The modern secular NGO movement had its start with the creation of the Red Cross in the 1860s. Like the Red Cross, several of today's best-known NGOs grew out of war – Save the Children in 1920, Foster Parents Plan during the Spanish Civil War (1936–39). Oxfam and CARE emerged from World War II, World Vision from the Korean War (1950–53), and *Médecins sans Frontières* from the conflict in Biafra (1967–70). All owe some allegiance for their strategies and ideas to the human rights, environment and women's movements. And all derive a considerable proportion of their ideals and human resources from the volunteer-sending organisations that developed in the early 1960s.

Until the 1970s, governments took NGOs most seriously for their emergency efforts. By the end of that decade, however, it had become apparent that Northern NGOs had development skills as well. By then, it was also becoming apparent that official development assistance was not having the desired impact on poverty reduction, and that NGOs could do more than simply reach the poor: they could help to organise and motivate successful and sustainable community self-help efforts. And they could do so in cost-effective and sustainable ways. They had special skills in primary health care, non-formal education and other forms of social development. They were pioneering new employment-generation techniques, savings, credit. They could be innovative and quick where governments could not. They could demonstrate the value of empowerment and participation in practical terms.

As the 1970s gave way to the 1980s, governments saw additional reasons for paying attention to, and supporting NGOs. NGOs could build public support for official development assistance at home. And their partnerships overseas helped to build stronger, more vibrant civil society actors that could influence local development policies, and help construct a basis for better governance and democracy. These views of NGOs – not always realistic, and not always consistent with each other – have waxed and waned over the past two decades, with governments sometimes recognising all of them explicitly, while at other times treating NGOs as little more than inexpensive contractors. NGOs have viewed themselves in different ways as well – as service providers, as agents of change, as advocates for the poor. They have acted as complements to official development assistance, as supplements, and sometimes as critics and watchdogs. However they have been viewed, they have added to the vibrancy of the development debate and have become an important part of Northern interaction with the South.

TRENDS AND ISSUES IN GOVERNMENT–NGO RELATIONS

NGOs for hire: from matching grants to contracts

There has been an almost linear evolution in government support for NGOs.[2] In the beginning, there were grants with few strings attached, and limited reporting requirements. Then came the more formalised matching grant programmes. Germany was the first to develop a matching grant scheme in the early 1960s, and by the end of the decade similar approaches had been adopted by most OECD member countries. While programme or project design lay with the NGO, the organisation had at least to fulfil a few basic government requirements. These may have required an applicant to organise itself in a certain way, or it may have excluded work in some countries, but generally, the conditions were not onerous. Then, when governments began to appreciate more clearly what NGOs could do, they encouraged new ventures. Special funds were developed for areas of greater need: Mozambique at the end of the war in mid 1994; the Philippines after Marcos, Eastern Europe after 1989. Thematic funds were also established – for gender programming, the environment, for work in areas of democratic training and peace building. These special funds, often developed in consultation with NGOs, always came with better matching arrangements. Instead of one-to-one or two-to-one funding, governments would offer as much as 90 per cent or even 100 per cent of the costs.

This 'needs-based' approach meant that an NGO could leverage its private donor income further than before, creating substantial opportunities for institutional growth. It did mean, however, that governments were beginning to set more of the parameters for where and how NGOs would work – using carrots rather than sticks. By the end of the 1980s, special funds had come to dominate government support mechanisms in many countries. In an extreme case, by 1997, the basic matching grant programme represented only 20 per cent of the Australian Agency for International Development's (AusAID) support to Australian NGOs. The rest was carrots, aimed at persuading NGOs, often very willing NGOs, to work on governmental priorities.

Beyond matching grant arrangements, there was a significant shift towards NGOs in the way governments viewed emergency assistance. By the early 1990s, 75 per cent of British food aid was being channelled through NGOs and 40 per cent of Swedish spending on emergencies and refugees was going through Swedish NGOs. By 1996, 46 per cent of French emergency funding was being spent through NGOs, and half of all the EU's European Community Humanitarian Office (ECHO) funding was being spent the same way. Between 1992 and 1997, the United States Agency for International Development (USAID) – with the biggest emergency budget in the world – spent over 60 per cent of it, not counting food aid, through NGOs.

During the heady days of these partnerships, several governments began to offer NGOs contracts for the management of bilateral programmes and projects. The practice had been common in the US for years, but Switzerland, Canada and others were not far behind and by the mid 1990s NGOs in some countries (Belgium, Denmark, US) were responsible for the delivery of over 15 per cent of all official development assistance. With the exception of the US, most contracts for the delivery of bilateral assistance were arranged on a sole-source basis, without any formal competition. Like the lengthening conditions in matching grant mechanisms, however, this too has begun to change, and in some countries (US, Canada, Finland) NGOs are being encouraged or even required to bid against each other and against private sector firms if they want bilateral contracts. The NGO's own ideas, style, capacities and innovation are becoming less important than the priorities, standards and pace of government.

One of the Clinton Administration's first efforts in the United States was a National Performance Review, which led to the passage by Congress in 1993 of a far-reaching Government Performance and Results Act (GPRA). This coincided with the appearance of the bestseller *Reinventing Government*, a book that President Clinton said 'should be read by every elected official in America'.[3] Among other things, the book devoted an entire chapter to 'results-oriented government', saying that 'if you don't measure results, you can't tell success from failure'. Soon the idea spread to other countries. The DAC Chairman's Report for 1994 spoke of the 'growing demand by parliaments, media and the public for the demonstration of tangible *results* from aid.'[4] USAID was one of the first government departments to take the new regime to heart, declaring that USAID 'is now fully committed to reinventing itself as a more efficient, effective and *results*-oriented organisation'.[5]

It was a short step from governments reinventing themselves, to a demand that NGOs should also reinvent *them*selves. In a results-oriented climate, the way to do this was clear enough: to insist that NGOs become much more focused on impact. Not in itself a bad thing, it has been accompanied in some places by a new type of arrangement between governments and NGOs: output contracting. A common feature in engineering projects – the contractor gets paid when the bridge is finished – short-term output contracting can actually work against the achievement, or at least the measurement, of longer-term impact in human development efforts, because these are often not visible within the standard project lifecycle. (This is discussed in greater detail below.)

The NGO voice

Contracting has had another effect – on the NGO voice. Most voluntary organisations are concerned with more than service provision. They are a reflection of deeply held values, and many were formed because their members wanted change and reform. Organisations working with the mentally handicapped may devote much of their time and energy to service provision, but they are also concerned with the *rights* of the handicapped, and ensuring that society and government respect these rights. Environmental organisations are concerned not only with matters of conservation, but also with the laws and the political commitment that are necessary to enforce conservation. Save the Children Fund (SCF), created at the end of World War I, began as a charity dealing with young victims of war. But one of its first acts was the creation of a document spelling out the rights of the child, a document that 70 years later formed the basis of the 1990 United Nations Charter on the Rights of the Child.

Where advocacy is concerned, there are two problems in NGO financial dependency on government, especially in a contractual arrangement. First, *all* governments are preternaturally wary of organisations with a penchant for advocacy and reform. Campaigns and crusades, even the most temperate, are not the stuff of government. In the abstract, advocacy has its place, but in the cold light of a contracting morning, it attracts little in the way of understanding and tolerance.

A 1993 study of voluntary agency contracting in the US found that many organisations had drifted far from their roots, and from their original purpose for existence. They had simply lost their voice. The study pointed out a second major problem in the contracting relationship: 'Although contracting between government and non-profit organisations may be understood as a relationship involving reciprocity, it is by no means a relationship among equals.'[6] It is usually a hegemonic relationship in which the weaker partner is obliged to accept the practices and policies of the funding agency. It is a relationship too often based on interference, containment, manipulation and limitation.

The dependency issue arises in several chapters of this book. Denials of any problem in voice and advocacy are most vociferous in the countries where the dependency ratio is highest. The argument is made that 'our organisation' or 'our country' or 'our history' is special. But most countries in both the North and the South, have a saying not unlike the old English proverb, 'He who pays the piper calls the tune'.

None of the evolution from untied grants to output contracting, of course, happened through coercion. Nobody forced NGOs to take government funds; nobody forced them to become contractors. Some have resisted the temptation or have passed byelaws restricting the amounts of government funding they will accept. Others have knowingly and willingly maximised their government income, believing that they can retain sufficient control over it to carry out their prime mandate, whether it is emergency assistance or the provision of development assistance to poor communities that governments cannot reach.

Whatever the thinking, the relationship between NGOs and governments in OECD member countries has changed dramatically in the past three decades. What began in the 1960s as a simple matching grant arrangement has moved, in many countries, through a needs-based, grant-making approach, to a sole-source contracting relationship, towards a much more competitive output-contracting arrangement. In its worst manifestations, the new approach seems determined to shift much of the risk for the most difficult aspects of aid delivery to NGOs, and in doing so, transform them from what once made them attractive, into contractors, service providers and inexpensive government executing agents.

Overheads: the low cost of running an NGO

One of the biggest problems facing NGOs is the issue of administrative overheads. With the exception of the US and Austria, all OECD member countries have established blanket percentages of their grants as a contribution to NGO overheads. These range between 5 and 10 per cent, with higher rates in a few exceptional cases. Usually there is no restriction on the use of these funds – a good thing, as most go nowhere near covering the real cost of doing business.

An understanding of the 'real cost of doing business', however, is obscured by the way NGO records are presented and this in turn is a function of the firmly held and very reasonable public belief that charities should get as much of their income to the needy as possible. This reasonable idea, however, has turned into the unreasonable demand that 'as much as possible' should equate with 'almost everything'. In practice, it doesn't scan. The most vibrant criticism of NGOs over the past two decades has centred on their lack of professionalism. NGOs are told to train more, to plan better, to monitor, report and evaluate more and better. Accounts must be professionally prepared and presented; work with partners must be handled with empathy, understanding and care; experiences must be recorded, disseminated and remembered. Reports must be done according to this standard or that.

All of this costs money. Whether its annual income is $500,000 or $50 million, an NGO must have professional accountants. To get and keep them, it must pay market rates. To keep good field staff from drifting off into higher-paying government, UN and World Bank jobs, they too must be paid reasonably. Airfares, communications and reports to donors all cost money. Finding and keeping a $50 donor also requires regular reports. These must be prepared by real people with families of their own to feed. Like administration, fundraising is not cheap. More pointedly, development is not cheap. And yet everyone involved with NGOs – institutional donors, the media and NGOs themselves – have conspired in creating the impression that it is.

One result is indecipherable NGO financial reporting. On the face of it, Catholic Relief Services in the US recorded fundraising and administration costs in 1995 of 6 per cent. The International Rescue Committee showed 7.9 per cent. Others, strangely enough, had much higher costs. World Vision Canada recorded administrative and fundraising costs of 19.8 per cent in 1996, Community Aid Abroad in Australia recorded a total of 24.1 per cent, and Childreach in the United States showed 26 per cent.[7]

The same spread can be found in the administrative costs reported by governments for their Official Development Assistance. According to the 1996 DAC *Development Cooperation* Report, these averaged a very respectable 4.5 per cent. Austria was in fact able to do it for a miraculous 1.1 per cent, while Canada, at 9.4 per cent, was the most profligate.

Was Austria actually eight times more efficient than Canada? Was Catholic Relief Services over four times more efficient in its fundraising and administration than Childreach? Hardly. But getting at genuinely comparative figures is almost impossible, as – like governments – each NGO has different ways of presenting its statements, often aimed at shedding the best possible light on overheads. Take for example, Partners International. (The name of this US organisation has been changed, but the figures have been taken from its detailed 1996 audited financial statements.) In 1996, PI had total revenues of $69.3 million. Fundraising, administration and 'sponsor ministries' (essentially reporting to donors), totalled $14.6 million, for an overall fundraising and administration charge of 21 per cent.

But $10.8 million of its income was in the form of contributions in kind, recorded at 'estimated wholesale market value'. This estimation was made by the organisation, not its auditors. In this case, a 30 per cent overvaluation of these contributions would have had the effect of reducing overheads by only one per cent, but in the case of an organisation like the Catholic Medical Mission Board, where 88 per cent of total 1995 support and revenue was in the form of in-kind contributions, a 30 per cent decrease in valuation would have had the effect of raising overheads by almost 50 per cent.

Meanwhile, deeper in the PI financial statements, there is a breakdown of the $52 million that is devoted to programmes. Of this, $45.8 million is 'direct payments to the field' along with the gifts in kind. The rest is salaries, travel, employee benefits, office equipment, professional fees. In fact, there is an additional $7 million in administrative costs buried in programmes. This brings the fundraising and administration costs up to 31.3 per cent. Stated in the most unattractive way, PI's real cost of doing business, removing all in-kind contributions and dealing only with cash, is slightly more than 37 per cent.

The point of these calculations is not to show that PI is costly, but that the real cost of doing business for PI, as it is for many NGOs, is much (and sometimes much, much) higher than appears to be the case.

Most institutional donors articulate their relationships with NGOs as partnerships. The United Nations High Commission for Refugees (UNHCR), for example, 'sees its relationship with its implementing partners as one of, precisely, partnership, and draws a clear distinction between such partnerships and contractual relationships... UNHCR [expects]... suitable agencies... at least to cover the overhead administrative costs related to the project from their own or other non-UNHCR resources'.[8]

UNHCR's commitment to partnership is an unassailable principle. But the principle falls down around the question of which elements of a project the NGO and the institutional donor should support, around the *sharing* of both the attractive as well as unattractive but necessary costs. The 'principle', in fact, assumes that NGOs have a bottomless well of unrestricted funds that can be applied to overheads. Even if they did, the expectation that private donors would foot the lion's share of administrative costs is ridiculous.

By limiting their administrative contribution to unrealistically low flat rates, governments force NGOs to cover their administrative costs in one of three ways:

1   by fudging their financial statements: allocating as much administration to projects as possible, inflating the value of in-kind contributions, and other forms of rubber mathematics;
2   by taking contracts that earn a surplus (or earning money in other ways) and applying it to the essentials that nobody wants to pay for;
3   by charging the cost to private donor income.

This latter technique can turn out to be a heavy charge on the private donation, as the two following hypothetical cases illustrate:

Case I: An NGO with a cash income of $1,000,000 and overheads (fundraising and administration) of 20 per cent, is permitted to devote 10 per cent of government contributions to these costs. The scenarios in Table 2.1 calculate the percentage of private income that must be used under varying mixes of government and private revenue:

Case II: An NGO with cash income of $1,000,000 and overheads of 25 per cent, is permitted to devote 7 per cent of government contributions to these costs:

When it places an unrealistic restriction on overheads, the institutional donor does several things:

First, it forces the NGO to cut corners on necessary and legitimate administrative costs. These include planning; the recruitment, selection and support of personnel; procurement and

Table 2.1: *Distribution of Overhead Costs. With 10% from Government for Administration*

	Private Income	Government Contribution	10% from Govt for Administration	Remaining Overheads to be Charged Against Private Income	% of Private Income Used for Overheads
Scenario 1: 25% govt	$750,000	$250,000	$25,000	$175,000	23%
Scenario 2: 50% govt	$500,000	$500,000	$50,000	$150,000	30%
Scenario 3: 75% govt	$250,000	$750,000	$75,000	$125,000	50%

Table 2.2: *Distribution of Overhead Costs. With 7% from Government for Administration*

	Private Income	Government Contribution	7% from Govt for Administration	Remaining Overheads to be Charged Against Private Income	% of Private Income Used for Overheads
Scenario 1: 25% govt	$750,000	$250,000	$17,500	$232,500	31%
Scenario 2: 50% govt	$500,000	$500,000	$35,000	$215,000	43%
Scenario 3: 75% govt	$250,000	$750,000	$52,500	$197,500	79%

shipping; programme monitoring, reporting and evaluation; financial management and report-ing; public relations with governments, other multilateral agencies and the media.

Cutting corners is not the same thing as observing efficiencies. All donors expect NGOs to be professional, to apply the best talent available to the task at hand, to be effective, to report clearly, usually in a prescribed fashion, and on time. Good planning, good monitoring and good reporting are all part of the expectation. And yet somehow, this is supposed to be achievable for 5 per cent or 7 per cent or 10 per cent of programme – usually an arbitrary blanket figure, regard-less of whether the programme relates to emergencies, long-term development, institution-building, hands-on programming or simple cheque-writing. Any cost accountant would quickly demolish the 'principle' on which such calculations are based, and any private sector CEO guilty of such amateurism would quickly find him or herself without work. If you pay for amateurs, you get amateurs, and all the talk in the world about professionalism will not make it happen.

Second, by using more and more private donor money – virtually the only source of unrestricted funds available – for administration, NGOs run the very serious risk of being charged with false advertising, and losing the very basis of their existence. A media attack in 1995 on Save the Children (US) criticised the organisation's president for saying that 'In general, we use these private funds to leverage other sources of funding, thus achieving a multiplier effect in terms of our private donations.' The article went on to say that the money SCF raises from the US public is not used for work overseas, 'Save in fact uses those funds to pay for administering the restricted money it gets from the government'.[9] This is not an attractive proposition for the $50 donor.

Box 2.1 GOVERNMENT SUPPORT TO NGO OVERHEADS
SELECTED COUNTRIES

Australia: 5%, but only for overseas work; nothing for HQ

Canada: 7.5% for matching grant projects and programmes; negotiable on bilateral projects

Denmark: 7% for development projects, 5% for emergencies, 10% for volunteers

EU: 6%

Finland: 10% (recently increased from 6%)

France: 10%

Japan: zero

Netherlands: 7.5% for co-financing, 1–3% for emergency operations

Norway: 6% for HQ overheads for development projects, 5% for emergencies; project administration costs additional

Sweden: 9.6%

Switzerland: 10% for projects; 13% for programmes; 15% for emergencies

US: Generally a 'Negotiated Indirect Cost Rate Agreement', worked out with each NGO on the basis of actuals

Note: Variations on these numbers exist within all countries, especially for bilateral projects executed by an NGO on behalf of government. There is no consistency within countries or between countries on the definition of what constitutes fair and legitimate overheads.

Third, it could be regarded as unethical for institutional donors – governments, the EU, UN agencies – to take their own overheads from the original funding source – taxpayers – and then to refuse a fair contribution towards the legitimate costs of organisations that are actually carrying out the work on the ground.

Fourth, it rewards and contributes to the growth of NGOs with unrestricted money, without questioning how they may have obtained it. Often those with the fewest financial restrictions are those most guilty of overly dramatic, 'starving baby' fundraising tactics. Widely criticised by the development community at large and by most NGO umbrella groups, such fundraising nevertheless continues apace. By encouraging such organisations, institutional donors could well, in effect, contribute to 'the pornography of poverty', reversing the development education efforts that they and NGOs have struggled with for the past three decades.

Fifth, it encourages NGOs to seek activities that can produce a surplus: contracts. Contracting (discussed above) has become more prominent, in part because it has become available. But for some organisations it has become essential. For some it has become the only way to offset the real cost of doing business without applying half or more of their private donor income to overheads.

The point of this lengthy exposition is not to suggest that NGOs should become market leaders in their salary scales, employee benefits or administrative spending. It is to suggest, however, two things. First, as in business, there are very different costs associated with different types of activity. Simple financial assistance to a Southern NGO is very different from the establishment and running of a refugee camp. In real life, overheads differ, and an arbitrary blanket rate makes little sense. Secondly, NGOs are pressed from all sides to become 'more professional', to do more evaluation, to work more with the private sector, to do more capacity-building of their Southern counterparts, to become more transparent, to learn more and disseminate more findings, to become more socially anchored at home, to become more financially independent. This simply cannot be done without appropriate budgets, and the burden cannot be expected to fall unfairly on individual donors whose primary and immediate concern is the beneficiary.

The dependency question

Several studies have sought to discover comparative levels of NGO dependency on government. Is the dependency level higher in Sweden than in Germany? Higher in Switzerland than the US? What is the appropriate norm? Ten percent? Fifteen? Efforts were made in the 1993 *Stakeholders* study to draw some conclusions, but they were incomplete, and in some countries even the roughest of estimates were impossible. The same has been true of this study.

In a few cases, a complete picture of all government–NGO financial transactions is available. Switzerland produces an excellent annual report.[10] The Government of Australia publishes an *AusAID–NGO Cooperation Annual Report* that shows clearly how much government funding has gone to Australian and international NGOs in the form of grants, contracts, support for development education, emergencies and special programmes. From this it is possible to calculate what percentage of Australian ODA goes through Australian NGOs (5.7 per cent in 1995–6). Working back from an estimate of NGO fundraising (A\$165 million in 1995), it is possible to calculate that Australian NGOs received 54 per cent of their income in 1995–6 from government. The dependency of government on Australian NGOs, therefore, was 5.7 per cent, and the NGO dependency on government was 54 per cent.

In the US, USAID publishes an annual report of contributions, contracts and food aid channelled to NGOs. The total in 1995 was \$1.9 billion. Against a total ODA figure of \$7.38 billion, this represents a 25.7 per cent level of government dependency on NGOs. In fact, however, a great deal of the \$1.9 billion was from government agencies other than USAID, for countries outside the ODA ambit. If funding from 'other government departments' is removed, the total falls to about 15 per cent. The reverse figure has not been compiled and is virtually impossible to calculate from the figures available. Beyond Switzerland, Australia and the US, calculations become more difficult. An attempt has been made in the Canada chapter to calculate the NGO dependency level on government, and the somewhat shaky figure of 47 per cent is compared with the dependency level of domestic Canadian non-profit organisations on government – 56 per cent.

Attempting to calculate the average level of NGO dependency on government may be futile in most countries, but even if it were not, the result would be more or less meaningless. All averages conceal variations, and in the case of NGOs, these are often extreme. Some NGOs (Oxfam US, for example) refuse government funding, and therefore have a zero degree of dependency. Some NGOs are not eligible for government funding or have been cut off. These too have a zero dependency level. Some have set limits on the amount they will accept from government, while others have sought to maximise their government income and may have dependency levels of 90 per cent or more.

A more useful figure might be the dependency level of government on NGOs as a delivery mechanism, but here too there are difficulties. French support for NGOs is tiny – 0.65 per cent of ODA in 1997, and yet 46 per cent of all French emergency assistance is channelled through NGOs. Overall French government dependency on NGOs is, therefore, very small, but in the emergency sector it is much higher than in many countries. In Denmark and New Zealand, the amount of government emergency assistance channelled through NGOs is approximately 37 per cent of the total, and in the US it is over 60 per cent. A significant proportion of World Food Program and UNHCR implementation is carried out by NGOs. In fact if the projects described in most government public relations material are any guide, it is likely that a very significant proportion of the health, education and poverty-related spending of most official government agencies is now carried out by NGOs. It might be said that Northern governments have become heavily dependent on NGOs for the human face of development assistance.

The quality of statistics

A chart showing percentages of government support to NGOs would be interesting, especially if it could disaggregate the amounts according to type: responsive, contracts, development education, emergencies, food aid, international NGOs, Southern NGOs. There are several problems with NGO-related statistics, however, which make them difficult, and in some cases impossible to calculate on a reliable and comparative basis.

1   The definition of non-governmental organisation varies. In its official statistics, Canada includes universities, colleges, professional organisations and trade unions. Trade unions are included in Scandinavian countries and the Netherlands, but not in other countries. In Japan, the term 'non-governmental organisation' includes many large bodies that would elsewhere be thought of as quasi non-governmental organisations (quangos) or parastatals. There are similar definitional problems in Austria. The German political foundations, virtually unique in the field of international development, are classified somewhat doubtfully as part of that country's voluntary sector.
2   NGOs may receive funding from different ministries (the official development agency, the foreign ministry, the ministries of agriculture, health, education), and from different branches within a ministry. Statistics on food aid, emergencies, special funds for things such as democracy, and matching grant funds are often not compiled together in a single report. In-kind contributions such as food, freight or government surplus may or may not be included, and the method of valuation may be very different from one country to the next.
3   The contracting of NGOs is sometimes recorded, as in the case of the US and Australia, but in many cases it is not. Figures for Germany and France, for example, are speculative or are simply not known, yet this type of relationship may be an important one. Where such figures are unknown, flows through NGOs may be significantly under-reported.
4   Funding decisions made by overseas embassies are not always included in a national calculation. Sometimes these are simply small embassy funds, but in other cases they can be significant. Funding for Southern NGOs, as grants or contracts, may be entirely omitted.
5   Several multilateral agencies depend (ie have a 'dependency') on NGOs for the delivery of goods and services. The World Food Programme channelled an estimated $580 million through NGOs in 1997, UNHCR, about $300 million.[11] Twelve per cent of UNICEF's country-level programming is directed towards NGOs. Further NGO grants, co-financing and contracts are made by UNDP, the United Nations Fund for Women (UNIFEM), the International Fund for Agricultural Development (IFAD) and other UN agencies. Increasingly, these funds go to Southern NGOs, but the bulk is still channelled through Northern NGOs. The World Bank contracts larger NGOs and some Southern NGOs for the delivery of project components. In 1995, EU allocations to NGOs totalled $1.1 billion. Taken together, these funds certainly exceed $2 billion, and may stretch considerably higher.
6   Volunteer-sending programmes can distort the apparent generosity or lack thereof in one set of government statistics as compared with another. Volunteer-sending agencies consume at least 25 percent of the NGO programme in Britain, New Zealand, Canada and elsewhere. In Japan, the United States and Norway, however, volunteer-sending is largely a government initiative and does not appear in the NGO statistics. This acts as a comparative deflator, therefore, in these countries.
7   In each OECD country where NGOs are given tax concessions, or where donors can deduct a portion of their charitable donations from their income tax, ministries of revenue undoubtedly have a very clear idea of what this costs the exchequer each year. Countries that provide tax concessions and deductions to NGOs (Germany, most of the English-speaking countries, France, Netherlands) make a real financial contribution – not included in OECD statistics – that others (such as Finland, Japan, Italy, Sweden, Norway) do not.

There is a further problem – the way NGOs record their own statistics. As noted elsewhere in this chapter, non-governmental income is rarely reported in a consistent manner from one NGO to the next, much less from one country to the next. There is virtually no reliable statistic in any

OECD member country as to how much cash is raised from the public by the international development NGO sector. Governments do not compile these statistics, nor do NGO umbrella groups. A new compulsory standardized system for NGO accounting was introduced in Australia in 1997, and this may be the first country where reliable data becomes available.

In short, differences in the treatment of NGOs, and differences in categorizing and reporting make most national statistics on NGOs and those reported to the OECD meaningless for comparative purposes. In many cases, NGO statistics are under-reported and are treated almost as an afterthought. This is an odd state of affairs, given the size of some NGOs and the enormous, multi-billion dollar scale of the overall NGO effort.

COMPETITION AND THE RISE OF THE SUPER NGO

Growth

Many years ago, several of the larger British and US NGOs began establishing branches, subsidiaries, franchises and independent partner organisations in other industrialized countries. Some, like CARE, Oxfam and World Vision, have become household names throughout Europe, North America, Australasia and, more recently, Japan. Once a rather languid process, the business of expansion grew rapidly in the 1990s for two reasons. One was money, and the other – not far removed from money – was competition.

Where money is concerned, expansion to other countries makes eminent sense. Founded in 1937, Foster Parents Plan (Plan International) had a strong US persona through the 1950s and 1960s, but by the 1970s it had begun to expand, with branches in Australia, Canada and the UK. More aggressive growth in the 1980s changed the structure of the organisation entirely. By 1996 it had national organisations in Australia, Belgium, Canada, France, Germany, Japan, Korea, the Netherlands, the UK and the US. The US enterprise had become relatively small in the general scheme of things, representing only 11.7 per cent of global income, and the headquarters of Plan International had shifted from Rhode Island to Surrey in Britain. Perhaps the most surprising developments were the growth of 'Foster Plan' in Japan (by 1996 the second largest financial contributor), and Plan International in the Netherlands, where the organisation had become one of the biggest fundraising phenomena in the country, contributing more than 44 per cent of Plan's global 1996 income of $264 million. Like other Super NGOs, by the mid 1990s Plan had begun small fundraising operations in the South – notably Korea and Thailand.[12]

World Vision has become the largest international NGO in fundraising terms, going from strength to strength in almost 20 countries and becoming by far the largest fundraising operation in the US, Canada, Australia and New Zealand. It also has significant operations in Britain, the Netherlands and Japan and, like Plan International, it has started fundraising in the South. It raises significant amounts of cash in Taiwan and Hong Kong, and has operations in Korea, South Africa and Singapore as well. The combined 1996 revenue of World Vision International was $419 million, but this masks a considerably larger capacity that is not reflected in the consolidated financial statements. In 1996, World Vision's overall US income (in cash and kind) was $303 million. In Australia it was $67.4 million, and in Canada it was $56.6 million. There is little doubt that World Vision had become, by 1998, an organisation with global annual resources of more than half a billion dollars.[13]

CARE has reached similar proportions, although the bulk of its income is still US-based, and a much greater proportion of the total is in the form of in-kind contributions, mainly food aid. The combined 1995 cash and kind income of CARE members in the US, Britain, Canada, Australia, Denmark, Germany, France, Japan, Norway and Austria was $586 million, well into the half billion dollar category.[14]

The Oxfam approach has been similar to the others in some ways, with independent members of the Oxfam family starting up – or in the case of Oxfam Quebec, splitting off – in

Canada, Belgium, the US and Hong Kong. Community Aid Abroad in Australia had a long-standing relationship with Oxfam that became more formal in the 1990s. By the early 1990s the network as a whole had begun to change. A new Oxfam was established in New Zealand, and NOVIB, one of the largest Dutch NGOs, joined the 'family', along with Intermón, a Spanish NGO. In 1995, eight of these organisations joined in forming Oxfam International (registered in the Netherlands, but based in Britain), with a view to improving and coordinating strategies in programming, research, development education and lobbying. A jointly funded advocacy office was opened in Washington. Not least among the concerns of Oxfam International is the development of 'brand strategy', to ensure that the name 'Oxfam' means something to the media, governments and donors. This, it is expected, will lead to a corporate communications strategy, international fundraising and greater cross-affiliate funding. By 1997 there were ten members, and it was expected that something between three and six affiliates would be added over the next five years. (Interestingly, a Japanese organisation declined membership in 1997, and in 1998 the Irish part of 'Oxfam UKI' became independent.) In 1995, the combined Oxfams raised an estimated $350 million.[15]

The International Save the Children Alliance (ISCA) is a loose confederation of 24 different organisations. Save the Children was founded in Britain in 1920, and over the years, affiliates were established in the US, Canada, Australia and throughout Scandinavia. In recent years, independent affiliates have been established in some countries of the South – Mexico, Mauritius, Egypt, Korea and others. Total programme spending by Alliance members in 1996 was $310 million, representing something over $350 million in total revenue. Efforts have been made in recent years to draw the Alliance closer together on priorities, organisational strategy, lobbying and coordination in emergency situations.[16]

Médecins sans Frontières (MSF) was founded in 1971 by a group of French doctors, most of whom had worked in Biafra between 1968 and 1970. By 1998 it had become a multi-faceted international network of health-related programmes, primarily in emergency situations. In 1996, MSF had 15,000 national staff, it maintained 1,131 field posts and dispatched an additional 2,400 doctors and health workers. In addition to its health programming, MSF takes a strong position on 'speaking out' – both for the provision of information and drawing attention to emergency situations, and for the purpose of 'denunciation': 'When MSF considers it to be in the interest of the victims, it will denounce massive and repeated violations of human rights and/or of humanitarian law'.[17] MSF has an International Office in Brussels and 19 'national sections' in Europe, North America, Australia, Japan and Hong Kong, whose purpose is fundraising, recruitment and public awareness. Dependent for much of its income on the institutional and private response to emergencies, MSF saw its income decline from $306 million in 1994 – at the height of the Rwanda emergency – to $252 million in 1996.[18]

Although relatively small in comparison with the others, Christian Children's Fund is another contender for Super NGO status. In 1996 its income was $114 million. The bulk of it was raised in the United States, but a growing proportion – almost a quarter of the total – was contributed by independent CCF members in Canada, Denmark, Germany, Britain, Taiwan and Australia, and by subsidiaries in France, New Zealand, Brazil and Thailand. Funding from these subsidiaries almost doubled between 1993 and 1996.[19]

Care and feeding of the Super NGOS

The Super NGOs vary dramatically in their management structures and character. Save the Children is an international 'alliance' of very loosely coordinated organisations sharing, more or less, the same general goals and outlook. In their overseas work, the different members are completely autonomous, and it is not unusual to find three or four or even more ISCA members working independently of one another in a given country.

Oxfam International and CARE International are made up of similarly independent – and often independently-minded – organisations, although concerted efforts have been made in both organisations in the 1990s to ensure better coordination, common objectives and reduced overlap in programme countries.

Unlike Save the Children, Oxfam, MSF and CARE – which might all be thought of as multinational NGOs – Plan and World Vision are transnational NGOs. The national character of the member organisations is erased at the programming level, where there is a unified approach, blended funding and full internationalisation of staff. World Vision has taken its transnationalisation much further than the others, essentially wiping out the line between North and South. Many of its offices in developing countries have been converted from programming operations to autonomous legal entities that are full members of World Vision International, participating actively at the international board and membership level. While certainly not a new approach in corporate terms, or even in non-profit terms (the Worldwide Fund for Nature has a similar approach), this is very new for international development NGOs, most of which have so far been unable to create a balanced partnership out of the traditional donor–recipient relationship.[20]

The income sources of the Super NGOs vary as well. Plan and Christian Children's Fund are relatively independent of government support and could operate without any significant change in operations if all government funding was withdrawn. Between 1994 and 1996, MSF received about 7 per cent of its income from UNHCR, a quarter from ECHO, and half from private donations raised by its affiliates. World Vision is mixed. In the US, Australia and Britain, a modest proportion of its income is derived from government – in cash and food commodities. In Canada, only a small proportion of its income is provided by government. Most CARE members, on the other hand, have maximised government income in both cash and kind, the latter mainly in food commodities. Virtually every member of the Oxfam group has a different approach. Some (Canada, Quebec, Australia) have tended to take full advantage of government funding opportunities. NOVIB in the Netherlands receives almost 70 per cent of its income from government, while Oxfam UK has traditionally limited its government income (14 per cent in 1996–7). Oxfam US refuses to accept any money from government whatsoever.

The children's hour

Among the Super NGOs there is heavy reliance on child sponsorship as a fundraising tool and as a programming device. SCF (US), World Vision and Christian Children's Fund are all based primarily on child sponsorship, as is Plan International. PI's 1996 Worldwide Annual Report states that 'Plan is an international humanitarian, child-focused development organisation without religious, political or government affiliation. Child sponsorship is the basic foundation of the organisation'. Like Plan and other child sponsorship agencies, World Vision tells donors in its literature that it takes a community-based approach to development, but there is still a strong emphasis on the direct relationship between the donor and the child. World Vision US explains it this way:

> *Caring sponsors are matched one-on-one with a child. This partnership resources a variety of community- and family-specific interventions designed to improve the child's physical and spiritual health: food and clothing, water and agricultural development, housing, education, health care, economic development and spiritual nurture. Many other children and adults also benefit through peripheral involvement in these and similar projects.*[21]

In 1982, World Vision, Foster Parents Plan and Christian Children's Fund had a combined total of 701,000 children under sponsorship. By 1996, this number had grown by a factor of more than five, to 4,479,000 child sponsorships – a remarkable growth rate of almost 40 percent each year.[22] Another half million children at least are sponsored through ActionAid, SCF (US), Compassion International, Children International, Signpost International, Global Care, Mission of Mercy, Food for the Hungry and a dozen smaller organisations.

In Australia, World Vision raises as much money from the Australian public as all other NGOs combined, and child sponsorship accounts for at least 50 per cent of all private Australian donations to NGOs.[23] In Japan, where NGO fundraising is notoriously difficult, child sponsorship has worked wonders. Japan is now Plan's second largest contributor, and World Vision had a very respectable 20,000 Japanese sponsors in 1997. Charles MacCormack, Executive Director of SCF (US), has estimated that if donations to church-based organisations are subtracted, 70 per cent of all remaining US donations to NGOs would be based on child sponsorship.[24] Half of all Canadian fundraising accrues to the four largest child sponsorship organisations, and World Vision alone raises 28 per cent of all donations in Canada.[25]

In 1982, *The New Internationalist* produced an exposé on child sponsorship: 'Please Do Not Support this Child' ran its headline, arguing that child sponsorship was, in the most precise definition of the word, paternalistic. It was costly and, the article argued, it actually created more problems than it solved, singling one child out for special attention over others.[26] Most child sponsorship organisations took the basic criticism to heart, and began – if they had not already done so – to develop community programmes, from which the sponsored child and many others could benefit. In 1998, the President of Christian Children's Fund (US) said that 'CCF maintains its focus on the one-to-one relationship between a sponsor and child.' That notwithstanding, she added, 'sponsors know the services for their sponsored children often take the form of community-based programmes when the very infrastructure of the community is insufficient. We educate our sponsors to ensure they understand that sponsorship funds are used to provide this infrastructure.'[27] Nevertheless, for the monthly donor, the approach remains essentially the same. World Vision Ireland offers sponsorships for IR£14 per month and in Britain Global Care has them available for UK£12. $22 per month is the US norm, although Christian Children offers sponsorships for $21 per month, Feed the Children and Mission of Mercy for $20 a month, and Children International is a bargain at $12 a month.

In 1995, the *Chicago Tribune* began an investigation of child sponsorship, in which reporters and editors sponsored 12 children through SCF (US), Christian Children's Fund, Children International and Childreach, the US affiliate of Foster Parents Plan. Reporters then went to visit the children they had sponsored – in Mali, Mozambique, Haiti, Colombia and elsewhere, and in March 1998, the *Tribune* published the results in a series of more than 30 articles.

While the articles contained some positive stories, by and large most were extremely negative. 'Poor as they were, none of the *Tribune*'s sponsored children resembled the desperately sick or malnourished boys and girls whose images are a staple of fundraising appeals by child sponsorship organisations... The "magical bond" between sponsor and child proved to be mostly fiction. Letters purportedly written by the sponsored children or members of their families were often composed by workers for the sponsoring organisations.'[28] The paper went on to say that 'expensive, labour-intensive and fraught with the logistical problems posed by primitive conditions and remote places, child sponsorship... is far more effective as a fundraising tool than as a reliable vehicle for delivering benefits to sponsored youngsters and their communities'.[29]

The articles sent shockwaves through child sponsorship agencies and NGO communities around the world. The story was picked up and localized as far away as New Zealand, where it quickly became a major media event. In anticipation of the stories in the US, InterAction created an advisory panel as part of its Standards Committee 'to identify best practices in child sponsorship and to make recommendations on ways to ensure that programmes are fully accountable to the public'.[30] Similar moves were initiated in Canada and elsewhere.

Supporters of child sponsorship argue that it has tremendous potential for educating the Northern public, and this is undoubtedly true. Certainly it has generated personal commitment on a very large scale. But for a taste of the way this has been handled, a half hour on the Internet under 'child sponsorship' will demonstrate that there is still a very long way to go once the basic fundraising message has been passed along. The impact of the *Tribune* stories was probably not great. One thing was clear, however: there had probably never been such a well-documented and critical attack on any aspect of development in a major newspaper up to that point in history. How the development community and the child sponsorship agencies will respond over the longer term remains an open question.

Emergencies

CARE, MSF and Oxfam do not have child sponsorship programmes. Nor do some of the SCF affiliates, including SCF UK. These organisations, however – unlike Plan and several of the smaller child sponsorship agencies – have all made a strong name for themselves in emergency relief. What they may lose in donations for sponsorship, they make up in contributions and government support for their emergency efforts. Although it engages in some long-term health-related programming, MSF is essentially an emergency response organisation. World Vision, the only Super NGO that has both child sponsorship and emergency programming, is – not coincidentally – also the largest fundraising organisation of the lot.

Implications

At a time when many NGOs talk of the compassion fatigue they see in falling donations, most of the Super NGOs are growing.[31] In some countries there have been downward fluctuations, but taken as a whole, there is little sign of compassion fatigue in their annual financial statements through the 1990s. The opposite, in fact, is true. One obvious conclusion is that they are crowding out the smaller organisations. Name-brand recognition and a mix of child sponsorship and emergency appeals has helped them make sense of the massive numbers of charitable appeals that now barrage the average individual. The Super NGOs have economies of scale, they are professional, they can provide mutual financial and political protection that is unavailable to one-country organisations. If not the way of the future, they are clearly the way of the present.

PERFORMANCE, ACCOUNTABILITY AND EVALUATION[32]

Evaluation rising

Accountability

NGOs are frequently accused of being 'unaccountable'. This charge is made most vociferously by individuals in government, in official donor agencies and by journalists whose own account-abilities are often deficient or lopsided. All organisations, including NGOs, are accountable. NGOs are accountable to different branches of government (donor agencies, revenue and taxation departments). They are accountable to individual donors, staff, the media, host governments overseas, counterpart and partner organisations and beneficiaries. The problem for many NGOs is not a lack of accountability, but *balancing* accountabilities, and keeping the ultimate impact of their work at the top of the agenda. While it is the beneficiaries to whom much accountability is pledged, the greatest effort to explain, report and justify is usually made to the donor in the North, both individual and institutional. Until recently, the Northern donor took what NGOs had to say on faith.

The gathering storm

Despite the achievements and the support NGOs receive from ordinary people, from governments and from UN agencies, today there are doubts. And many of these doubts run deep. In 1982, USAID asked Judith Tendler to examine 75 evaluations of NGO projects. Although not a hostile review, her findings were critical of what she called 'NGO articles of faith'. Effectiveness in reaching the poor, in participation, in cost-effectiveness and innovation were all open to serious doubt. While the evaluations – conducted primarily by outsiders in order to satisfy the donor – were often weak and inconclusive, questioning and self-evaluation by NGOs themselves were 'more important as articles of faith than as standards of self-assessment. That participation leads to improvement in people's lives is an article of faith for [NGOs], not a hypothesis that one is interested in testing'.[33]

A dozen years later, an Overseas Development Institute study used very similar language. 'Much of this interest in NGOs has been fuelled by a body of suppositions (what we might call "NGO-lore") about their qualities.'[34] The authors listed NGO strengths, but these were contrasted – in a four-volume study ranging across three continents – with an assortment of limitations: 'a limited capacity for research, weak links with wider policy or scientific spheres… weak interaction with other NGOs conducting similar work, the small localized nature of their efforts, and, in a wider vein, the absence of mechanisms to ensure the representativeness of NGOs and their accountability to the rural poor'.

Although USAID and CIDA have had relatively complex evaluation mechanisms in place for more than a decade, most official development agencies have come to an examination of NGO effectiveness much more recently. There are reasons for this. Originally, most NGO support schemes were small, and serious evaluation would not have been very cost effective. Several things began to change in the early 1990s, however. The end of the Cold War made the questioning of general aid effectiveness more acceptable than had been the case in earlier years, when aid was often as political as it was developmental. The domestic critique of foreign aid could no longer be warded off by strategic international considerations. Vast changes in Eastern Europe placed new financial demands on Western governments, further eroding aid flows that once ran in an exclusively southward direction. Recession and budget deficits helped fuel a growing 'aid fatigue', not just at Cabinet level where budgets are decided, but within bilateral and multilateral institutions themselves, where the effectiveness of established ways of doing things was in increasing doubt. An unprecedented number of emergencies diverted much attention from long-term development assistance to relief and peacekeeping, and led to a further questioning of what, if anything, had been accomplished in the first three 'Decades for Development'.

As government agencies became more uncertain of themselves, the NGO star continued to rise, especially among journalists and parliamentarians in search of human interest stories and at least some good news amidst the bad. NGOs were therefore poised on the threshold of two distinct trends. The first was an increasing reliance by governments on external 'agents' for the delivery of services – the private sector, parastatals and non-profits. The second was a growing political demand for accountability on the part of government departments for their spending – whether directly, or through surrogates.

Increasing NGO allocations – sometimes at the expense of bilateral and multilateral budgets – along with greater demands for transparency, accountability and effectiveness, have all combined to place NGOs under a brighter light than ever before. Evaluation has become the order of the day. Large, omnibus evaluations have been carried out by the governments of Norway (1995), Finland (1994), Sweden (1995), Australia (1995), the US (1995) and Britain (1992 and 1995). The Overseas Development Institute has conducted a series of NGO evaluations and studies: on poverty alleviation (1989–90); on NGOs, the state and sustainable agricultural development (1993); and on the changing role of NGOs in the provision of relief and rehabilitation assistance (1993–4). In 1997, Finnish International Development Agency (at present, Department for International Development Cooperation (FINNIDA) sponsored – on behalf of the OECD/DAC Expert Group on Aid Evaluation – the largest NGO evaluation synthesis yet, examining evaluation work in seven donor countries and the European Union, plus field evaluations in Bangladesh, Brazil, Chile, Kenya and Senegal. It is a safe bet that more books appeared on NGOs during the first half of the 1990s than was the case over the whole of the previous two decades.

The results reported in these books and studies – the impact of the NGO effort – are mixed. The 1995 ODA/Department for International Development (UK) study found that the majority of projects were successful and that significant benefits were received by the poor, but that there had been little change in the existing social or economic status quo, and that institutional and financial sustainability had not been achieved. The Australian review covered 216 projects and found that 90 per cent had satisfactory or better achievement of objectives, but observed that sustainability, financial viability and the involvement of women in project planning and implementation could be improved. The Swedish study found that 'the overwhelming majority [of projects] either have achieved, or are well on their way to achieving, the stated and immediate objectives for which SIDA's NGO Division provided the funds… [But] when the projects are judged against more and more of the nine broader criteria against which they were assessed, their aggregate performance rating dropped progressively. Indeed, very few of the projects examined scored consistently high marks in relation to a majority of these broader criteria'.[35]

Like Tendler in 1982 and ODI in 1993, these studies suggest that the 'articles of faith' and 'NGO lore' tend to have a fairly large myth factor built into them. (The same, of course, could be said about official development agencies.)

The NGO response: over-troubled water

The general NGO response to such findings has been two-fold. First, they say, social development is not like infrastructural development, and existing evaluation techniques are somewhat, if not wholly, inappropriate. Secondly, external evaluations – the preferred method of most donor organisations – tend to be more concerned with verification and control than they are with learning. By ignoring the participatory approaches developed by NGOs, such evaluations can result in findings that are incorrect or irrelevant, and they can also damage the project.

It is true that much NGO work focuses on social development, rather than on infrastructural projects and hardware. Evaluating participation, empowerment, self-reliance, social sustainability and political sustainability is no mean feat. Peter Oakley observes that 'we are dealing with interpretations of social development which lack the tangible parameters of social development as the provision of social services, and which confront us with a form of development which is also intangible and less amenable to quantitative measurement'.[36] This line of argument leads to a critique of the 'dominant evaluation paradigm', with its emphasis on measurement, quantity and cost-benefit techniques. Rhetorical questions then follow: How can a snapshot evaluation deal with *process*? With the dynamic as opposed to the static? Is the very concept of a structured, value-free evaluation even remotely relevant to social development? Should qualitative evaluations not be holistic, inductive, continuous, participatory, heuristic, naturalistic?

For many NGOs, attempts to develop indicators for the measurement of social development are highly suspect. A Peruvian writer suggests that choosing indicators is either inappropriate or impossible: 'Political awareness, for example, cannot be measured by collecting and analysing numerical data… [and] consciousness raising is not an objective in itself, but just one link of the chain.' In NGO literature, there is also a strong critique of *external* evaluation and evaluators; these are generally regarded as subjective, ill-informed, judgemental, political and inflexible.

Some care needs to be taken with these arguments. 'Social development' may be only one component – perhaps even a very small component – of an NGO project that intends very tangible results: agricultural extension, clean drinking water, rural credit. On the other hand, 'social development' may be almost fully related to 'conscientisation' and 'empowerment', where the *process* of development is the most important aspect, and where the more tangible benefits are almost secondary.

For NGOs, evaluation and monitoring are often synonymous – sometimes precisely because process is so important. COTA, however, a Belgian NGO service centre, stresses the importance of differentiating clearly between the two: 'Monitoring is distinct from evaluation. Monitoring is a continuous process of collecting and processing data. It is essentially done by the partners involved in the action, the community-level partners and the support NGOs. Monitoring makes it possible to detect implementation anomalies, to correct action management and effect technical reorientations… Whereas monitoring is designed to adjust the action to circumstances, evaluation is rather to appreciate the objectives set and the strategy chosen… with other eyes.'[37]

The confusion between monitoring and evaluation, and anxiety about what 'other eyes' might see often leads to dramatic conclusions about evaluation: 'Traditional forms of external quantitative evaluation have introduced new forms of status difference within the spectrum of donor–project relations, and this [has] provoked increasing unease at the project level… and an overriding sense that project staff were being tested and found deficient'.[38] Straw dogs emerge: 'Evaluation is reduced to a static and mechanical operation designed to point out irrationalities, inconsistencies, and bad practices, in pursuit of the ideal organisational form. As a result, it should come as no surprise that evaluators and evaluations are cast in a negative light and that evaluations of this type are regarded with suspicion.'[39]

It *would*, perhaps, come as no surprise, if this was the most predominant sort of evaluation that NGOs were doing themselves, or if outsiders continued to impose such evaluations in the face of good alternatives. There would be no particular reason to accept the findings of Tendler, the Overseas Development Institute and others if – somewhere in the public domain – there was a body of literature to contradict them. In all this, however, there is something rather striking: many NGOs are doing little or no evaluation. What little they do is usually kept secret (or is at least not written down), and general NGO discourse on the subject – as with the illustrations above – is defensive, confusing and not very helpful. It is unhelpful to NGO workers who want to learn from their efforts, and it is unhelpful to donor organisations, Southern governments and the public at large to whom NGOs owe at least a modicum of explanation, if not accountability.

Code words

One NGO response to concerns about quality and accountability has been the creation of codes of conduct. But first, a diversion: in 1997, an 'International Code of Ethics for Canadian Business' was unveiled, following pressure from NGOs and others on corporate employment practices, human rights abuse, child labour, corruption, and the negative role of foreign investment in countries such as Nigeria or Burma. A representative of one of the largest Canadian NGOs, the Catholic Organisation for Development and Peace, said, 'At this stage, it's interesting, but it's only a first step'.[40] The next step would be regular monitoring and verification, about which little was said at the unveiling.

In Britain, an NGO 'Monitoring and Verification Working Group' (MVWG) has been established for precisely this purpose. For them, the principal question in business codes of conduct is this:

> *What elements are key in an approach to monitoring and verification that would ensure that the information generated is accurate, complete, meaningful, and delivered to key stakeholders in a timely and intelligent manner without being unacceptably costly and without in any way penalizing workers, the very people that it is intended to assist?*[41]

One of the guiding principles for the MVWG is that 'monitoring systems incorporate verification by bodies that are demonstrably competent and fully independent from the companies involved and their agents. Any accreditation body must be competent and fully independent'. By these standards, the pot might be seen as calling the kettle black, as most NGO Codes of Conduct – of which there are now a multitude – lack any form of serious or independent monitoring and verification.[42]

In the US, the NGO umbrella group InterAction has established a set of 'PVO Standards' based on 'self-certification', a process by which each member 'accepts responsibility for following these standards'. Similar codes and standards prevail in US NGO sub-groups; for example, the 'Code of Ethics for [Child] Sponsorship Agencies', or guidelines issued by the Association of Evangelical Relief and Development Organisations.

Such codes come from two places. The first is genuine concern within a given NGO community that its members should work according to certain basic principles. The second – as in the case of the private sector codes – is external pressure, sometimes from government, sometimes

---

Box 2.2 AN AUSTRALIAN INITIATIVE

Throughout OECD member countries, there is a major problem in deciphering the way NGOs report on their finances. The definition of overheads lies with the reporting agency, and varies widely. Fundraising costs are often distributed through a number of categories, including information and development education. Over- or under-valued in-kind contributions can have a major impact on the size of overheads.

The Australian Council for Overseas Aid had a Code of Ethics to which its members subscribed but, like most others, it lacked teeth. In 1995, the Minister for Development Cooperation stepped in, insisting on a new code that would include detailed financial reporting standards, in order to 'build on the clear commitment of NGOs to greater public accountability'.[43] The new code, completed a year later, was more concise than its predecessor, but it contained an eight-page financial reporting format that all organisations would in future comply with, and which would be subject to independent verification and audit.

Among OECD member countries, this was something of a breakthrough, because for the first time there were common formats and common definitions for in-kind contributions, volunteers, donations, gifts, community education, fundraising and administration.

---

from the media, sometimes from scandal. The development of NGO codes is often long and painful, with much debate on the most critical issues – usually having to do with fundraising, financial disclosure, monitoring and publicity surrounding any negative finding. Provisions for verification and monitoring are often perfunctory, and are usually carried out in a collegiate manner (Canada) by representatives *elected* (Australia and the US) or appointed (Canada) by an agency whose board of directors is drawn from the very organisations the code is expected to monitor. Regardless of how carefully the monitoring is done, this is not the 'demonstrably competent and fully independent' mechanism that NGOs seek in the private sector. Some codes, such as the 'Code of Conduct for International Red Cross and Red Crescent Movement and NGOs in Disaster Relief', now endorsed by almost 150 organisations, contain platitudes and generalities, with no mention whatsoever of compliance, monitoring, complaints procedures or verification.

The result is that NGOs have become fair game for any passing journalist who does not understand or agree with fundraising practices, overhead costs, child sponsorship, or the hiring of security guards in refugee camps. World Vision Germany was the subject of a media attack in 1993; CARE Canada was held up to scorn by the Canadian Broadcasting Corporation in 1995, and CARE's suit against the CBC did not receive a court date until 1999. SCF (US) was attacked several times by print and television media in 1995, and in 1998 the *Chicago Tribune* presented the results of a two-year investigation into the child sponsorship activities of six US NGOs. Australian journalist Paul Cleary visited NGOs in Vietnam and spoke of high overheads, needless overlap and lifestyles that included cooks, maids, drivers, doormen and a French colonial villa.[44] Little imagination is required to know what Michael Maren had to say in his 1997 book, *The Road to Hell: The Ravaging Effects of Foreign Aid and International Charity*.[45]

In a similarly titled 1996 book, *The Charity Game: Greed, Waste and Fraud in Canada's $86-Billion-a-Year Compassion Industry*, author Walter Stewart asked this question about international development NGOs: 'Is there fraud involved in some of these foreign flings?' He answered by saying, 'We will never know. There is no effective overseer of these charities… they must be brought to heel in a systematic and open accounting.'[46] To *heel*!

Even if almost everything in these reports, articles and books, and others like them was false, the lack of NGO openness about money, about the real cost of doing business, about evaluation and about the genuine complexities of eradicating poverty, leaves the entire NGO enterprise

vulnerable to attack. Understandably, in some cases the allegations are not false, but organisations that are quick to condemn Nike, Shell Oil and Gap, say little when one of their own
stumbles.

The same, of course, can be said about official development agencies. The Pergau Dam
scandal in Britain and extensive Belgian aid scandals undoubtedly damaged public support for
development assistance in those countries. Where codes of conduct are concerned, an interesting
variation on the theme was developed by the London-based Commonwealth Foundation in 1995.
Following extensive consultation, the Foundation published *NGOs: Guidelines for Good Policy
and Practice*. This also included guidelines for governments, funders and Northern NGOs
working in the South. What is good for the goose, is good for the gander. Many Southern NGOs
have adopted national codes of ethics: Bangladesh, Gambia, Thailand – even Somalia. In 1997,
the South African National NGO Coalition ratified its own Code of Ethics, but it also developed
a draft 'Code of Conduct for Northern NGOs', which it hoped would be endorsed in 1998.

Fear of self-evaluation

In 1977, John Sommer paraphrased Mark Twain in writing about US NGO evaluations: every-
one talks about it, but few do anything about it. At that time, Sommer saw changes, a 'real trend
toward more regular evaluation', but much of what he described was taking place as a result of
pressure from USAID. Many of the evaluations were being conducted by outsiders, and many
failed to get beyond immediate project aims and objectives. Evaluations might quantify how
many jobs had been created in a particular project, but questions about the development *process*
were often ignored: What are the degree and quality of local participation? Who is benefiting?
And how? What are the costs of maintaining the benefits without continuing outside help? How
long will any programme benefits last? Have the poorest groups increased their sense of dignity,
self-reliance, and overall capacity to deal with the world around them? Did the programme
represent the best and most effective use of the particular inputs?[47]

Five years later, Tendler found that little had really changed: an 'emphasis on the number of
people trained, the amounts of equipment supplied, etc' with little real attention to processes,
sequences of action and impact. Fast-forward another half decade to a USAID study: this one
found in 1986 that NGO 'measurement of project costs and the valuing of benefits need
improvement... Unfortunately, many [NGOs had] not been very effective at documenting and
replicating their innovative experiences. Lessons learned by project managers are generally not
shared with other [NGOs], host country institutions, and others'.[48] The study could, of course,
have been describing most bilateral and multilateral donors as well.

Another half decade later, in 1990, a British study found the same thing: 'For most British
development-oriented NGOs evaluation is still very new. The vast majority of projects and
programmes funded by British NGOs in developing countries are not subject to any sort of
formal evaluation... The majority of NGOs do not carry out any evaluation.'[49] By then, part of
the problem may have been that researchers were not looking in the right places. The 1997
OECD/DAC *Synthesis Study* found many evaluations, although it also found that there was 'still
a lack of firm and reliable evidence on the impact of NGO development projects and
programmes. Most impact assessments rely on qualitative data and judgements and most are
undertaken very rapidly. The majority have been content to report on and record outputs
achieved, and not outcomes achieved, or broader impact.'[50] The report did find that NGO studies
tended to be more critical than those commissioned by donors, one reason, perhaps, why NGOs
are reluctant to distribute them.

By resisting increasingly urgent calls for evaluation over at least two decades, by mistaking
simple monitoring and reporting for something more substantive, by dodging judgement and
questions of impact, and by shrouding evaluation in a fog of complexity and jargon, NGOs have
actually encouraged the onslaught of external evaluation, much of it the very sort they most fear.

The problem, in fact, is so widespread, and so profound, that observers might be forgiven for assuming one of two things:

1   the work that NGOs do is so complex that it cannot really be evaluated, at least not in a way that would be understandable to those who are expected to pay for it; or
2   NGOs are not nearly as successful as they make out, and that is why evaluation is avoided, feared and suppressed.

There is a germ of truth in both possibilities. Social development does not lend itself readily to cost-benefit analysis any more than it does to simplistic two-year projects. The critique of the standard, time-bound external evaluation is at least partially correct. But there is something much more serious at work in the fear of evaluation, and until this is addressed, the problem is likely to continue – perhaps threatening much of what NGOs have accomplished, placing their independence in jeopardy and their future in question.

Learning systems and learning disabilities

The Fifth Discipline

In his 1990 management study, *The Fifth Discipline*, MIT professor Peter Senge wrote about the importance to learning organisations of 'systems thinking'. Systems analysis is not new, but what Senge stressed were the broad systems in which events take place, systems that are often not perceived or understood by those focusing on the issue at hand. People often cannot see the forest for the trees, but even when they see the forest, they may not appreciate its importance to the survival (or the stunting) of individual trees. Senge uses the example of dark clouds, which tell anyone with experience of weather systems that rain is likely. Rain is the event; weather is the system. But knowledge of weather systems will help those who want to predict rain before the clouds arrive – to make the connection between seasons, barometric pressure, wind, clouds and – further along in the system – groundwater, wells, rivers and crops.

In the NGO sector, seven major 'systems' work against evaluation, research, learning, transparency, and ultimately, against effectiveness. These systems combine to create a culture, an environment, a powerful mix of learning disabilities that produce the direct opposite of what those who sustain and enforce the systems hope to achieve. The first and most pervasive is the 'low overhead system', described above.

Great Expectations, Part One: charity versus development

The second revolves around the trade-offs that are made between charity and development. Whether they are raising money from the general public, a foundation or a government agency, all NGOs make promises they cannot fulfil. Take the following in a fundraising letter from a prominent British NGO: 'Just 50p a day can make a real difference to a child and her community… With our help, they could dig wells, build and equip schools, train to become health workers and work towards a brighter future'. Such appeals are sent to prospective donors every day from well-established organisations that subscribe to codes of ethics, support development education, and talk of the need for a better-informed public. They are the same sort of organisation, however, that – when faced with an imposed external evaluation – is most likely to disparage it as a 'static and mechanical operation designed to point out irrationalities…', even though these same qualities are evident in the way they describe themselves to prospective donors.

Why? Because any experienced NGO manager knows that world poverty will not be affected very profoundly by a gift of 50p a day. But having promised too much in its advertising, the

NGO is then obliged to report success stories in order to keep the money flowing. Because competition between Northern NGOs is intense, the advertising and the promises – unconnected to any serious feedback on the quality of the product or on what is being learned – must therefore increase.

The same is true of the relationship between NGOs and institutional donors. Because of the intensity of competition for institutional funding, or for marginal increases over past levels of support, NGOs generally ensure that proposals pay close attention to whatever the donor wants. Once again, however, having promised too much, the NGO finds itself in a difficult position two or three years down the road. Successes are exaggerated, and if an external evaluation is mandatory, efforts are sometimes made to deprecate the process and certainly to minimize or even hide evidence of failure and weakness. The result is that the external evaluation loses its potential as a learning exercise, and is viewed largely as a policing effort, getting only as much compliance as is necessary to keep the money flowing. In other words, doing the obvious thing to raise money does not produce the desired outcome in terms of long-term support.

The great expectations system is endemic in the financing of NGOs throughout OECD member countries. It creates a barrier between NGOs and the individuals and institutions that support them. It promises results that cannot be delivered, it buries problems, curtails any serious learning from failure, and can turn whatever evaluation there is into an adversarial control mechanism, rather than one that might promote better development. It is, in fact, self-defeating.

Great Expectations, Part Two: public ignorance

It has become fashionable among governmental and non-governmental aid agencies, especially those suffering from reduced budgets, to blame their financial problems on declining public support for development assistance. Recent studies have shown, however, that while public support fluctuates from time to time and from country to country, it is generally high, and has not suffered appreciable decline anywhere in OECD member countries.[51] A UNDP survey of opinion polls found that in 1995, on average, 79 per cent of those polled in 19 different countries supported development assistance.[52] This was one point higher than the average in 1983. This is a level of popular support that – on almost any policy – would turn most governments green with envy.

What every NGO knows, however, is that although support may be broad, it is not deep. It is based to a great extent on emotive fundraising and shallow public knowledge of what development is all about. When challenged, support for development assistance can wither.[53] So for at least two decades, many Northern NGOs have involved themselves in a range of activities – development education, advocacy, lobbying, publishing ventures – all aimed at deepening public levels of knowledge and awareness about the connections between North and South, and about the need for long-term structural change and development assistance.

Every NGO invests a significant proportion of its overheads in fundraising, but development education is optional for many, and for most it represents a tiny proportion of overall spending. Meanwhile, fundraising has become an extremely sophisticated, multi-million dollar business, with NGOs making major investments in advertising, affinity cards, direct mail, telephone solicitations, celebrity events and charity shops. Although purists distinguish between fundraising and development education, the two things are in fact, only different sides of the same coin. Both are messages aimed by NGOs at the public. And where the development education message is faint, complex and sometimes unpalatable, the fundraising message is strong, simple and emotive. Doing the obvious thing to raise money does not produce the desired, long-term results.

Little boxes: the project system

Early in the business of international development assistance, 'projects' became the preferred way of organising things. In many ways, projects make sense. In return for clear aims and objectives and a discrete set of inputs – money, technical assistance, equipment – the implementor expects to achieve clear, quantifiable results within a designated period of time. One of the weaknesses of projects, however, is that they too are subject to a range of 'systems' that the implementing organisation may not know about, and over which it has absolutely no control. These range from personalities and politics, to deeply ingrained sociological and historical factors that do not lend themselves to solutions in bite-size, two-year chunks.

Most Southern NGOs, regardless of how they are funded, and regardless of how they describe what they do, take a 'programme approach' to development. Many of their activities are not divisible, except on paper, into discrete projects. A women's income generation project may be very much related to a health programme for children, an agricultural extension effort and experiments with backyard poultry or fish ponds. Regardless of donor time frames, most Southern NGOs know that a long-term approach will be required in order to make major inroads on poverty. When programmes are subdivided for individual donors, problems develop almost immediately. One portion may be underfunded, while another may be expanded to suit a wealthier donor. One component may be funded on time, another may be approved (or turned down) long after the opportunity, or the school year, or the planting season is over. Donors have different policies on administrative costs, reporting and monitoring requirements, and these add other, sometimes irreconcilable pressures.

Many Northern NGOs have managed to convince their governmental supporters – SIDA, NORAD, DFID and others – to provide them with multi-year 'block grant' support or 'frame agreements'. This relatively important conceptual breakthrough, however, does not seem to have worked its way down the chain into the arrangements that most Northern NGOs have with their Southern counterparts. Freed of the project at home, many keep their counterparts on the leash that they have at last slipped.

Evaluating a 'project', is often like trying to evaluate a patch of water in the ocean. But there is also a problem of time. Evaluations inevitably take place a few months before or after a project's conclusion. If an extension is warranted, the evaluation will take place before the conclusion in order to allow enough time to get a second phase in place. Given the mobility of staff within most aid agencies, there is usually little interest in looking back at completed projects more than a few months after their conclusion. Out of sight (and out of money), finished projects tend also to be out of mind. The major problem with this is that the results, the impact of a social development effort, may not accrue until well after the project has finished. An end-of-project evaluation, therefore, may not capture the real results.

The partnership system

Unfortunately, far too many Northern NGOs pass on precisely the same treatment to their Southern counterparts, calling it 'partnership'. This comment may seem harsh, but in recent years there has been growing complaint and criticism from the South. In India, Kamla Bhasin observes that 'although we have been using the word partnership for a long time... project implementation has been the main thrust, and funding the main link. And with one partner giving funds and another receiving them, all the inequalities enter the relationship.'[54] Honor Ford-Smith, writing about the experience of a Jamaican NGO, says that Northern donors 'have an enormous amount of power. They are able to shape the lives of the organisations they support, not simply because they fund them, but also because of the processes and disciplines they require the organisations to become involved in. The term 'partner' only obscures what remains a very real power relation. The egalitarian label does not change reality.'[55] In Zimbabwe, Yash Tandon says that 'foreign NGOs are a secretive lot. We do not know much about them... We know little about how their heart beats in Europe or America or Canada… they work with such secrecy and opaqueness that it is right for an African to be suspicious about them.'[56]

A 1992 study found that African NGOs were much less happy with arrangements than Northern NGOs assumed. The definition of 'mutual' goals tended to be a one-way thing. Their articulation, often tortuously developed in the North, was frequently accepted without demur in the South 'for fear of losing funds'. Few Southern NGOs 'would openly express ideological difference with Northern donors'.[57] Communication revolved almost exclusively around project administration and execution, and most important decisions were made by project selection committees and boards far away in the North. Questions relating to money and accountability remained uni-directional, with enormous amounts of time spent in the South dealing with demands from the North for reports and evaluations. At a conference in Bulawayo, Southern NGOs concluded that 'in effect, more time is spent in accounting to Northern partners than in actually applying one's mind, judgement and energies to the work at hand.'[58]

The 'agency' system

An agent or an agency is a person or institution that acts on behalf of another person, group, business or government. It is no accident of language that NGOs are sometimes called 'voluntary agencies', nor that bilateral aid organisations sometimes use the word as well: United States *Agency* for International Development; Canadian International Development *Agency*, for example. Just as these institutions have delivered aid programmes on behalf of their foreign ministries, they are now – like government departments everywhere – seeking more and more sub-agents through which government services can be delivered. Sometimes disparaged by terms such as 'down-sizing' and 'out-sourcing', agency cost theory is a growing area of study in both law and economics.[59] As the phenomenon grows, at least some decision-making authority must devolve upon the agent – Northern NGOs, for example.

The Northern NGO, however, acts through agents as well: Southern NGOs. They work with groups of poor people in community-based organisations, small savings groups and so on as well. Tracing authority levels (and attributing achievement or otherwise) downward through this maze, or back up again, is difficult, if not impossible. In fact if an NGO is doing its job well, it is merely putting fuel in somebody else's tank. The NGO is a catalyst for *local* action and investment. The success or failure of a 'project', therefore, may not be attributable to an NGO in any great measure – if one takes concepts of participation and empowerment seriously.[60]

The voluntary culture

Although not exactly a 'system', there is a strong bias in the NGO culture against learning.[61] Some NGOs have developed an area of particular expertise, but the vast majority are generalists with no specialisation, and no particular desire to develop one. Is there a value-added component to what Northern NGOs do, or is it only money-added? The jury is still out on this question, but after a decade of serious deliberation, the answer cannot be long delayed. Those that *have* specialised tend also to be the ones for whom research, evaluation and the dissemination of findings through publications and seminars are most important and most evident.

One reason that NGOs work as well as they do is the level of commitment, energy and perseverance that their employees, volunteers and supporters apply to an issue. But donors aside, many NGOs themselves believe that training, evaluation, research and publications are luxuries. Smaller NGOs, which seem to abound and proliferate, may not have sufficient economies of scale to undertake serious evaluation. Too busy 'getting the job done', many have sacrificed corporate memory and learning to the exigencies of time and place. This is warranted by an underlying conviction in the rightness of the cause, and a belief that this, in turn, serves as its own accountability measure. Outsiders – often anyone beyond the *cognoscenti* on staff – are simply resented. This is partly derived from the charitable and voluntary origins of NGOs. According to one study, 'These are often coupled with a religious or other conviction that good works are valid in their own right and that to do good must be right and to challenge this through evaluation is both unnecessary and unacceptable.'[62] Simply put, they believe their own advertising, their 'articles of faith'.

Why evaluate? Learning versus control

There are two primary reasons for evaluation. The first has to do with learning – the need to learn from the past in order to be more effective in the future. The second has to do with verification and control. Both are important, but an emphasis on the latter – combined with the learning disability systems described above – will almost guarantee that the former is compromised, if not seriously impaired.

Michael Power, an iconoclastic British chartered accountant, believes that what has become a ubiquitous 'audit explosion' arises out of changing concepts of administration and governance, and from powerful but contradictory tendencies within government. On the one hand, pressures on government to decentralise, to devolve, to 'down-size', 'right-size' and 'out-source' have never been more pronounced. On the other hand, there is equally powerful pressure to exert control over the very functions that have been made autonomous. This is because private sector preoccupation with quality control and the drive for industrial competitiveness has overlapped, sometimes indiscriminately, into the public sector. 'Reinventing government' has thus become a watchword throughout OECD member countries. Bookstores everywhere are full of titles with emotive words: turbulence, quality, globalisation; they tantalise with recipes for management and leadership, for re-inventing this and re-engineering that. For government, the trend usually means less spending, but it also emphasises concepts of accountability, transparency, effectiveness *and verification*. Power believes that this accounts for the 'drift towards "managing by numbers" which in turn enables a drift towards centralized forms of control, and to the displacement of concerns about good policy by concerns about good management'.[63]

Where NGOs are concerned, the drift has been intensified by greater government funding, and by the languid NGO approach to self-evaluation. The irony is that the process leads inexorably to a shift in control from organisations that people have generally trusted (charities), to a profession that the public trusts less (civil servants) at the behest of a profession that the public today trusts least (politicians).

A further irony is that so far, there is little evidence that increasing levels of government-inspired evaluation actually *have* contributed to greater NGO effectiveness, transparency or accountability. In an effort to avoid negative findings and a concomitant funding reduction, an NGO is likely to conceal failure, reduce risk, and/or undertake things that conform to the funding agency's idea of good development. The first stunts learning, the second stunts initiative, and the third stunts independence. None enhances effectiveness.

It would, of course, be wrong to push this critique too far. Government priorities are not necessarily inimical to good development or to the work of NGOs. Government should be assured that its contributions are being spent effectively and efficiently. The problem is that current trends seem to push NGOs away from these concepts, turning them from their own strengths, values and constituencies in the process. Stressing the control and verification function of evaluation, and insisting on governmental management of the process will not foster learning and knowledge. It is likely, in fact, to be antithetical to learning. The following section will argue that the opposite, however – an emphasis on learning and self-evaluation – can satisfy much of the need for verification and control.

Possible solutions

Taking the sting out of failure

In its primary meaning, 'to fail' is to be unsuccessful in an attempt. If the attempt was an honest and honourable one, if the effort was properly researched, if the risks were calculated and judged appropriate, if the best effort was made under the circumstances, then there should be no shame in failure. This is especially true in the field of social development, where needs are so great, and where so much of what is done is experimental. Dennis Rondinelli has expounded at length on the subject in his important book, *Development Projects as Policy Experiments*.

If development was easy, straightforward and cheap, the need for development assistance would probably not have lingered much beyond the first Decade for Development. In reality, development – especially social development – is fraught with historical, situational and systemic problems that make it a difficult, sometimes painful, and often a risky business. The importance, therefore, of learning what works and what does not is absolutely critical to avoiding errors in the future. Evaluation of the control type usually focuses on the question, 'Did it work?' This is an important question, but it is only the first. The second, and much more important question (regardless of the answer to the first), is Why? Why did it work? Why did it fail?

If NGO learning is to be encouraged, funding decisions must be distanced from evaluation. In other words, if a failed project results in financial punishment, the incentives for objective evaluation and learning are effectively reduced to zero. There must be a tolerance for failure. Disciplinarians may have trouble with this – with the idea of appearing to indulge failure, but it does not mean that anything and everything goes. Failure *should* carry a stigma when mistakes are repeated or suppressed, when available lessons are ignored and basic research is avoided, and when square wheels are continuously reinvented.

This is not to suggest or promote risk avoidance. Risk is an essential component of any business, and it is important to development work because so much is experimental. Risk assessment, however, is different from risk avoidance, and getting the right balance between risk and assurance is important to maintaining support – not only from donors, but also from intended beneficiaries.

Coming to grips with overheads

As long as prevailing fictions about minuscule NGO overheads prevail, few serious changes can be expected in the way NGOs advertise themselves, or in the way they conduct their business. One way around this, especially where evaluation is concerned, is to make special funding available to NGOs for baseline surveys, project assessment and evaluation. Several governments now do this, but the amounts are usually tiny. Another is to take a realistic approach to the broader issue of overheads, and to negotiate a specific rate with each NGO, or on each project. USAID does this through its Negotiated Indirect Cost Rate Agreement. Although it is time-consuming, most NGOs find it to be satisfactory, fair and consistent.

This, of course, deals only with relationships between NGOs and other institutions. Nothing is likely to substitute for a programme of public education that will explain administration to individual supporters, including trustees and members.

Programmes, not projects

The case for programme funding, as opposed to one-off isolated project support, has been made elsewhere. In the North, block grants and framework agreements have helped to reduce the tyranny of the project. In the South, consortium funding has had some success in reducing the administrative burden on both donor and recipient, and they have allowed for institutional reviews that take into account a much wider spectrum of activities and constraints than would otherwise be the case. Frame agreements and block funding in the North permit similar sorts of institutional appraisal.

Institutional or programme funding by an external donor, however, should not necessarily lead to an institutional evaluation conducted by the donor. The dangers here are as problematic as they are for donor evaluations of the one-off project.

Rethinking partnership (or, taking civil society seriously)

Originally, individuals, governments and other institutions supported NGOs primarily because they did good work, reaching places and people that others could not. There is no evidence that this was, or is, ill-conceived, even if more and more questions have been raised in recent years about how much good work NGOs do. This chapter makes the point that it is inappropriate for outsiders, especially governments, to be the primary vehicle for these questions. This is not to say that they have no role, but it is increasingly clear that a serious re-examination is required of basic concepts such as trust and autonomy. (This is equally true of relationships between Northern NGOs and Southern NGOs.)

Such a re-examination would mean that governments that take concepts of civil society in the South seriously should do the same at home. It would mean rethinking the concept of 'agency', the validity of attempts to control from afar, and the appropriateness of standardisation, especially standardisation designed by government. On the one hand, it would mean loosening the accountability leash that is attached to the external donor, and tightening it in other ways. One way of doing this would be for institutional donors to insist that each NGO it supports commission a basic level of evaluation itself, and to insist that the results be made public. Peer pressure and public pressure can, and probably would, go a long way to ensuring greater quality control, and to educating supporters. Such a process would also help to push responsibility for results more clearly back towards an organisation's members and trustees, re-enfranchising them and reaffirming the organisation's autonomy. Poor quality evaluation (as opposed to justifiable programmatic failure) could be handled by a reduction or cessation of funding.

Donors could also foster – with financial incentives – joint evaluations. These might encompass Northern NGOs from one country or several, working in one country, or several. They might support a comparative evaluation of several Southern NGOs working in a country or a region – sectorally or institutionally. They might encourage a reverse evaluation in which Southern NGOs appraise the role and capacity of Northern NGOs and the quality of their partnerships. They might encourage joint learning exercises, such as one initiated in 1995 by the Japanese Centre for International Cooperation (JANIC), bringing together NGOs from Japan, Canada, Australia and the US, with NGOs from the Philippines, Nepal and Indonesia, to seek common ground on issues of mutual concern. Umbrella organisations in the North – like InterAction in the US, or the Council for International Development in New Zealand – could develop evaluation rosters, clearing houses, or secretariats. The same could be done by their counterparts in the South. A good start has already been made by organisations like COTA in Belgium, INTRAC in Britain and F3E in France.

There is no end to the possibilities. There could, however, be resistance to such ideas from NGOs. Change is difficult and NGOs – like any other kind of organisation – will be reluctant to engage in making what might be seen as invidious comparisons. By taking the opprobrium out of failure, however, by stressing the value of learning, by attaching financial penalties to avoidance and benefits to compliance, resistance could be reduced.

Conclusions

The rising and widespread concern for *results* within development organisations is long overdue. Because so many bilateral and multilateral development agencies are facing budget cuts, however, there may well be undue haste in government acceptance of, or in its attempt to adapt, private sector planning and measurement techniques. Of greater concern is the possibility that techniques which are useful to government may be highly inappropriate to the kind of emergent and process-oriented work that is the hallmark of much NGO success.

NGOs have been slow to grasp the nettle where results and evaluation are concerned. Defensive, obscure and sometimes obscurantist, they often give the impression that they have something to hide, or that their best achievements may not be nearly as profound as they claim. The reasons for this go well beyond the common charge that NGOs are simply anti-intellectual or that they are besotted by their own lore and articles of faith. NGOs make fundamental trade-offs every day between the needs of their beneficiaries and the opportunities created by the emotive culture of charity. They must be professional, and they must also be lean. But when 'lean' is defined and quantified without any thought to the quality or complexity of the product, danger looms. The giving–receiving dynamic adds further complexity to the contribution that evaluation could make towards improved results. By stressing control and verification, donor-led evaluations drive both failure and learning underground, hiding lessons that may be more important than those derived from success. Blueprints and a project mentality remove donors and some NGOs even further from the reality of development and from the real lives of people. Hungry for rewards in an increasingly competitive field, many NGOs can and do behave like circus lions, performing tricks in return for food. Some graduate, becoming trainers themselves, working with younger lions and calling it partnership.

Civil society is unlikely to be strengthened this way. Some fundamental changes to these anti-learning systems are necessary before there can be major change. If NGOs can be made less insecure in their donor relationships, if there are genuine rewards to be reaped from real learning, examples, tools and new models of evaluation already exist, and the work can begin.

CONCLUSIONS

Edward Lear's nursery rhyme ends with the return of the Jumblies from amazing, faraway places:

> *On a winter's morn, on a stormy day,*
> *In a sieve they went to sea!*
> *And in twenty years they all came back –*
> *In twenty years or more;*
> *And everyone said, 'How tall they've grown!*
> *...if only we live, we too will go to sea in a sieve.'*

This chapter has attempted to highlight some of the trends and issues in the relationship between Northern NGOs – how tall they've grown! – and their governments. Some of the questions have to do with the organisational life of NGOs: accountability, leadership, financial viability. Some have to do with the place of NGOs in the aid system – the quality of work, evaluation, codes of conduct, contracting, emergency response versus long-term development.

Many of the questions facing Northern NGOs, however, go well beyond the aid system. They are affected by, but they are separate from relationships with government. They have to do with the role of NGOs in society – their ideologies, their politics, their faith, their values. As previously noted, voluntary associations have been formed throughout history for two reasons. One is to help people in trouble – first neighbours, then neighbourhoods, then perhaps a wider concept such as country or 'global village'. The second reason, often closely allied to the first, has been change – a change in conditions causing the problem for which remedial action is required. The concept of change is not far removed from the concept of reform, and many of the most successful voluntary movements – the women's movement, the human rights movement, the environmental movement – have focused their primary attention on change and reform. Although perhaps less prominent in the international NGO movement, change and reform have represented a prominent thread in the relationship between governments and NGOs throughout the last quarter of the twentieth century.

Some aspects of this chapter, and some of the country chapters that follow, suggest that the idea of change and reform may be a weakening theme in the Northern NGO ethos. Development education, once actively supported by many OECD member governments, is now, for many, a thing of the past. Contracts, increasingly the result of a competitive bidding process, are more common than not. Despite these changes, or perhaps because of them, NGOs and governments are finding new harmony in long-term and emergency programming overseas. Partnerships abound and everywhere NGOs that were once hostile to the private sector are exploring the possibility of synergies and linkages. All of this may be a good thing, marking the end of what once seemed like endless acrimony and unproductive debate.

This newfound harmony coincides with an odd period in history, however, one in which there is more wealth than ever before, while – paradoxically – there seems to be less and less available for the public good, both at home and abroad. Official development assistance continues to plummet – to a 45-year low in 1998 – and much of what remains is tied to the strategic and commercial self-interest of donors. The growth in ODA to China, from $2.1 billion in 1990 to $3.5 billion in 1995 – in a declining global aid environment – is an obvious example. At something less than 15 per cent of the total, poverty spending remains a low priority in the official aid system. Despite the bright promise of increased foreign investment and the (now somewhat tarnished) example of the Asian tigers, poverty of the worst sort continues to rise. In 1998, an estimated 1.3 billion people had to survive on about one dollar a day.

Is it possible that the increasingly congenial compact between Northern NGOs and governments is not in the best interests of the poor? Is it possible that efficiency, professionalism and verbal conformism are creating an elite aid management system, run by increasingly indistinguishable experts with increasingly indistinguishable views? Some would no doubt see this compact as a problem, if not a crisis in the relationship between NGOs and governments. Canadian philosopher John Ralston Saul offers a metaphor from the field of higher education: 'We are faced by a crisis in language and communication... we are faced by a crisis of conformity brought on by our corporatist structures... we are faced by a crisis of memory, by the loss of our humanist foundation'.[64] The suggestion of a crisis of conformity will be regarded as unfair by the many hundreds of NGOs, large and small, that struggle daily with the quality of aid, and with North–South relationships that extend far beyond aid, beyond investment and beyond growth. But many others see no crisis in conformity, and that may be the crisis itself.

Part II

Country Studies, European Union and the World Bank

3 Australia

Ian Smillie[1]

Summary

Between 1995 and 1997, a number of events occurred which had a profound effect on the relationship between the Government of Australia and the Australian NGO community. The first was a public controversy over the financial management of CARE Australia. A second event was the re-examination – at government insistence – of an NGO Code of Conduct established some years earlier. A new Code of Conduct was developed in the ensuing months, with full implementation in 1997. A third event was the publication of AusAID's 'Review of the Effectiveness of NGO Programs' in July 1995. In addition to its comments on NGO effectiveness, the Review recommended major changes in the funding relationship between government and NGOs.

In 1995–6, 120 non-governmental organisations received financial support from AusAID. In 1996–7 the amount available under the government's matching grant mechanism was A$16 million (US$12.5 million). This represented 20 per cent of the government funding available to NGOs.

Government support to NGOs for emergencies, refugees and food aid grew rapidly in the late 1980s, and by 1991–2 represented 40 per cent of all Australian Agency for International Development (AusAID) funding to Australian NGOs. As a percentage, the amount had declined by 1996–7, representing 25 per cent, with a total of A$20 million. In the 1980s, AusAID began to create opportunities for NGOs to gain access to its bilateral or 'country programmes'. In 1990–1, funding through country programmes represented 23.2 per cent of the total funding to Australian NGOs, and by 1996–7 it had risen to 36.2 per cent. By 1997, however, AusAID funding for NGO development education had become increasingly constrained by budgetary and political concerns.

The Australian NGO Community

History

Australia's NGO community began with the work of Christian missions, charities and service clubs formed in the late 19th century, and with later organisations created in response to specific emergency situations. The Australian Red Cross was formed at the outbreak of World War I, and Foster Parents Plan opened its Australian office in 1970. A number of today's most prominent NGOs, including Community Aid Abroad, the National Council of Churches in Australia and the Volunteer Graduate Scheme (the precursor of the Overseas Service Bureau), were formed in the

1950s, but the major growth period came after 1960. Austcare, Catholic Relief (now Caritas), World Vision, and the umbrella organisation ACFOA — the Australian Council for Overseas Aid — were all founded in the 1960s. Later organisations include Plan International in 1970, Christian Children's Fund in 1985, and Médecins sans Frontières in the 1990s.

Greater political awareness among Australian NGOs, heightened by the war in Vietnam, by debate over sporting connections with South Africa, and by the growth of African liberation movements, drew many into the fields of advocacy and campaigning, and spawned a newer breed of organisation devoted mainly to development education. Several development education centres sprang up during the early 1970s, and Action for World Development — the outgrowth of 1970s joint campaigning by the Catholic and Protestant Churches — became an independent NGO in 1983. Aboriginal issues also started to become a focus for some NGOs in the 1970s.

Size of the Australian NGO community

In 1995–6, 120 non-governmental organisations received financial support from AusAID, down from 138 in 1991–2. While the majority of them had development assistance or development education as their primary raison d'être, there were a number of other organisations with small add-on overseas programs. Among these are the Australian Conservation Foundation, Rotary Clubs, and the Australian Council of Trade Unions. Another indication of the size of the community is membership of ACFOA, which had 92 full and consulting members in 1997.

The size and capacities of Australian NGOs vary enormously. The majority are very small. Of the 112 NGOs receiving support from AusAID, 51 received less than A$50,000 in 1996–7. The five top AusAID recipients (World Vision, UNICEF, Overseas Service Bureau, Community Aid Abroad and the Australian Red Cross) received 54 per cent of the funds available from all sources within AusAID, while the bottom 51 received 1.4 per cent.[2]

A list of the top fundraising agencies, however, is somewhat different. World Vision raises as much money from the Australian public as all other NGOs combined. Among the next in line are Community Aid Abroad (Oxfam in Australia), Plan International and Caritas.

Estimates of the amount of money raised by NGOs from the Australian public show an increase of approximately 10 per cent per annum in recent years. A 1988 estimate placed the total at A$88 million,[2] while a 1992 estimate placed the total at A$120 million. ACFOA's estimate for 1995 is A$165 million (US$129 million). If these figures are accurate, the top five fundraisers take in over 65 per cent of the donations. As much as half the donations for international development in Australia are based on child sponsorship and most of the large fundraisers (with the exception of Community Aid Abroad and Plan International) have a Church connection or a Christian orientation.

Table 3.1: *Public Fundraising: Selected NGOs (A$,000)*

	1991	*1994*	*1995*
CARE	3000	6500	18,300
Caritas	6952	9200[3]	6000
Christian Children's Fund	4600 ('92)	n.a.	8900
Community Aid Abroad	3400 ('92)	10,000	8200
Plan International	7000	8000	8200
World Vision	54,500	70,700	77,000 ('96)

Source: Annual Reports of the NGOs; US$1.00 = A$1.28

THE AUSTRALIAN COUNCIL FOR OVERSEAS AID

The Australian Council for Overseas Aid was established in 1965 as a coordinating body for organisations involved in overseas aid and development. One of the oldest NGO umbrella organisations in OECD member countries, 'ACFOA provides a forum for consultation and cooperation between its member agencies and as a means for making common representations on their behalf to the Australian Government and to overseas governments and international organisations. The council also seeks to bring the needs for, and the purposes and results of, overseas aid and international development before member organisations and the Australian community. Annual subscriptions from members, plus an annual grant from the Australian Government, sustain the work of the Council.'

The 1993 *Stakeholders* study noted a degree of controversy in the NGO community about what ACFOA should and should not be. Few NGOs feel the need to be 'coordinated', whether the need exists or not. ACFOA is thus 'a coordinating body' that coordinates information more than activities or agencies. Some of the larger member agencies resent being over-ruled by the more numerous smaller NGOs on decisions about controversial political stands and in 1993 a few talked about the possibility of creating an alternative organisation. This has now softened into the idea of creating an informal grouping of 'the big ten' – agencies with similar needs and problems that can meet informally on an as-needed basis.

The reverse of this situation also applies: smaller agencies sometimes feel left out of decision-making by the bigger agencies. The ensuing tension is common to most NGO umbrella groups. The ACFOA debates are, in fact, almost identical to debates within its Canadian counterpart, the Canadian Council for International Cooperation.

FISCAL POLICY AND REGULATION OF THE AUSTRALIAN NGO COMMUNITY

Donations to Australian NGOs for international work are generally tax deductible. The granting of charitable status to Australian NGOs is regulated by the Ministry of Foreign Affairs and the Treasurer. AusAID's NGO Program undertakes the necessary investigations on the Ministry's behalf and makes recommendations accordingly. This system prevails because the Income Tax Assessment Act normally allows deductions for activities confined to Australia alone.

The arrangement, known as the 'Overseas Aid Gift Deduction Scheme', has certain limitations. Agencies must have a sound track record and be accountable to a recognised constituency. Eligibility is confined to development or relief. 'Welfare' activities such as orphanages or homes for the elderly, are not eligible. Activities are also restricted to countries recognised by the DAC as developing countries.

A 1996 Industry Commission Report, *Charitable Organisations in Australia*, recommended that 'AusAID and the Commonwealth Treasury should introduce processes of regular review to ensure that [NGOs] and their approved funds still meet the criteria by which they were granted tax deductibility status'. In a subsequent report, the Australian National Audit Office suggested that the accreditation and review mechanisms already available be used rather than the creation of another set of procedures.

THE AUSTRALIAN AID PROGRAMME

Background

The Australian Agency for International Development, formerly known as the Australian International Development Assistance Bureau (AIDAB), is an autonomous administration within the Department of Foreign Affairs and Trade (DFAT). Except for parts of Australia's multilateral assistance, AusAID manages most of the aid programme. Until 1996 there was a Minister for Development Cooperation and Pacific Island Affairs, but with the election in March 1996 of the Liberal and National Party Coalition, this position was dropped.

Through the first half of the 1990s, Australia's ODA grew by about 2.5 per cent per annum, holding steady at about 0.34 per cent of GNP. The 1996–7 budget, however, introduced a 10 per cent reduction in ODA, and the 1997–8 budget imposed a further cut of 1 per cent, reducing the ODA/GNP ratio to 0.27 per cent, its lowest level ever.

Events of 1995–7

Between mid 1995 and mid 1997, a number of events occurred that had a profound effect on the relationship between the Government of Australia and the Australian NGO community. The first, in mid 1995, was a public controversy over the financial management of CARE Australia. A second event was the re-examination – at government insistence – of the NGO Code of Conduct that had been established by ACFOA and its members some years earlier.[4] A new Code of Conduct, described below, was developed in the ensuing months, with full implementation in 1997.

A third event, not related to the first two, was the publication of AusAID's 'Review of the Effectiveness of NGO Programs' in July 1995. In addition to its comments on NGO effectiveness (discussed below), the review recommended major changes in the funding relationship between government and NGOs. Its most prominent recommendations included:

- a simplification and streamlining of the 'complex and fragmented' approach to NGO funding, and a reduction of the 32 different mechanisms available to NGOs;
- that wherever possible, 'cost-sharing' be introduced, with a minimum 25 per cent NGO contribution, and an end to the full in-country contribution by AusAID that had prevailed in most country programmes and emergency situations.

In addition, an Industry Commission Report on Charitable Organisations, also published in 1996, identified a number of weaknesses in financial transparency and accounting in domestic community welfare organisations, and recommendations for improvement at home were incorporated into the Effectiveness Review's recommendations for improvements in the international NGO community – in part through the process that was already under way in developing a new NGO Code of Conduct.

In March 1996, a new government was elected. Although it 'supported an enhanced role for NGOs', it had a more conservative outlook than its predecessor and in May 1996 it appointed a three-person committee, chaired by businessman Paul Simons, to review the overall priorities, objectives and focus for Australia's aid programme. The new government's first budget significantly reduced Australian ODA. Data on Australian aid flows provided to the DAC indicate a decline in ODA, in real terms, of 16.5 per cent, from US$1,194 million in 1995 to US$997 million in 1996. This represents a decline in the ODA/GNP ratio from 0.36 to 0.28.[5]

In August 1996, the Australian National Audit Office (ANAO) released a report on 'The Management of Funding to Non-Government Organisations' by AusAID. Although this report found that the overall management of funding to NGOs was of a generally high standard, like the Effectiveness Review, it noted the confusing and inefficient multiplicity of guidelines. It also noted 'widespread deficiencies in the application of administrative rules, particularly in relation to contract monitoring procedures' and observed that 'NGOs as a group do not properly understand the contractual relationship with AusAID under which they operate… Within AusAID, a similar situation appears to exist. In a formal sense, AusAID contracts with NGOs are as binding as those, for instance, with commercial contractors'.

By mid 1996, therefore, the stage had been set for a series of dramatic changes in the way the Government of Australia would relate to NGOs. The first change, completed by mid 1997, involved a simplification and a tightening of the NGO accreditation mechanism for AusAID funding (described below). The second involved the development of a generic, agency-wide set of guidelines for NGO funding, reducing the confusion and multiplicity of arrangements that had existed before. A new monitoring approach has now been developed, which aims to tie funding more clearly to measurable outputs.

These changes notwithstanding, the 1997 Simons Committee Report on Australia's Overseas Aid Program said that 'there has been a lack of clarity in AusAID's NGO policies. Although a wide range of special programmes has evolved to support the work of NGOs, there has been no cohesive policy statement outlining the role of NGOs in the official programme, or the objectives for government support'.

Code of Conduct

In 1989 ACFOA adopted a Code of Ethics for member organisations that sought to ensure integrity of operations and openness in financial and programme reporting. This was very similar to the self-regulating codes of conduct adopted by NGO umbrella organisations in the US and Canada, and actually included some paragraphs that were identical to those of the US and Canadian models.

About the time of the CARE crisis of 1995, the then Minister for Development Cooperation and Pacific Island Affairs established a Code of Practice Advisory Committee to advise on possible measures to strengthen the public accountability of NGOs. With the assistance and involvement of ACFOA, the committee consulted widely and submitted its report in August 1996. The new Code of Conduct builds on principles contained in its predecessor – related to governance, organisational integrity, management and communication with the public. Its primary difference is in its establishment of a mandatory common financial reporting format to be used for all published annual reports for periods ending on or after June 30, 1997. It also includes a detailed complaints and compliance process involving a broadly-based Code of Conduct Committee which could, as a final sanction, recommend withdrawal of an organisation's 'accreditation' with AusAID. This could result in a withdrawal of government funding, and possibly a withdrawal of the NGO's ability to issue tax receipts for public donations.

Accreditation

AusAID has changed its approach to the accreditation of NGOs for government funding. Previously there were three levels, however following the studies of 1995 and 1996, it was decided that these should be reduced to two. 'Base Accreditation' now limits an NGO to grants of A\$100,000 per project per year, with a maximum duration of three years. Funding is on a one-to-one matching grant basis. 'Full Accreditation' is a more rigorous procedure. Agencies with Full Accreditation will not be subject to an upper financial limit on projects and will be given an indicative planning figure much like the block grants that are used in other countries. These agencies will be entitled to a 3:1 matching ratio based on their 'recognized development expenditure'.[6]

Because the number of organisations with a 3:1 matching ratio is likely to increase, and because the pool is not expected to increase significantly, the grants for those agencies previously on a 3:1 ratio will likely decline.

GOVERNMENT SUPPORT TO NGOS

The AusAID/NGO Cooperation Program

The basic responsive, or matching grant programme in Australia is known as the AusAID/NGO Cooperation Program (ANCP). The ANCP is administered by AusAID in consultation with the Committee for Development Cooperation (CDC). The CDC consists of equal numbers of AusAID and NGO representatives, and makes recommendations to AusAID on NGO eligibility, operation of the ANCP and the relationship between NGOs and government.

In 1996–7 the amount available under the ANCP mechanism was A$16 million (US$12.5 million). This represented 20 per cent of the government funding available to Australian NGOs and 17 per cent of government funding to all Australian and non-Australian NGOs. The ANCP budget for 1997–8 was increased by A$3 million, or 17 per cent in real terms.

Emergencies and food aid

Government support to NGOs for emergencies, refugees and food aid grew rapidly in the late 1980s, and by 1991–2 represented 40 per cent of all AusAID funding to Australian NGOs. As a percentage, the amount had declined by 1996–7, representing 25 per cent, with a total of A$20 million. Eighty three per cent was allocated to six organisations: World Vision, Community Aid Abroad, the Australian Red Cross, Austcare, CARE Australia and *Médecins sans Frontières*. The largest single recipient, World Vision, received 27 per cent of the total.

For a few NGOs, AusAID funding for emergencies and food aid has represented a significant proportion of their income. For Austcare, the National Council of Churches and Community Aid Abroad, it represented between 60 and 65 per cent of their total AusAID income. For World Vision it was more than half, and for *Médecins sans Frontières*, a relative newcomer to Australia, it was 97 per cent of the total. Of all Australian government humanitarian assistance, one third (33.5 per cent) was channelled through Australian NGOs in 1995–6.

It is expected that the amount of food aid channelled through Australian NGOs will fall dramatically in subsequent years because AusAID decided that from 1996–7 onwards, no further food aid would be channelled directly through Australian NGOs. Instead, Australia's contribution to the World Food Program will be increased, on the understanding that Australian NGOs will be used as contractors by WFP for the delivery of an equivalent value of food aid in its programmes throughout the world.

From AusAID's point of view, this will reduce its own costs, giving more responsibility for the coordination of food aid to the most logical multilateral body. From the NGO perspective, however, there are problems. They see the change as the thin edge of a wedge that might be used to reduce food aid in the years to come. For some, the reduction has meant a necessary downsizing in Australia, because the WFP contracts are now being negotiated in the field, often with an international affiliate rather than with the Australian branch. The most serious problem, however, is that like other UN agencies, WFP makes every effort to minimise the cost of delivery, sometimes – in the view of NGOs – at the expense of doing the job properly, and often at the cost of essential longer-term development investments for which WFP has no responsibility. The net result of the change, in the NGO view, will likely be less food aid overall, and less effectiveness in what remains.

Volunteer programmes

Four volunteer-sending programmes are supported by AusAID. The Pauline Association Lay Missionary Movement (PALMS) and Interserve, both Christian organisations, send volunteers mainly to Asia, Papua New Guinea and Pacific Island nations on two to three year assignments. In 1994–5, Interserve and PALMS between them had about 100 volunteers serving abroad. Australian Export Service Overseas Programme (AESOP) provides experts, often retired individuals, on short-term assignments to both public and private sector organisations, mainly in PNG, Pacific Island States and Thailand. In 1994–5, AESOP fielded 209 assignments.

By far the largest, the Overseas Service Bureau (OSB) had an average of 460 volunteers serving in 43 countries through 1995–6. Of these, about 44 per cent were working in the education sector, and more than half were over 35 years of age. In recent years OSB has also made a small number of placements with Aboriginal organisations in the Northern Territory and Western Australia. In addition to its Australian Voluntary Technical Assistance Program, OSB operates a number of projects, some co-financed by AusAID and some by other organisations. In 1996, OSB signed a memorandum of understanding with CECI, one of the largest Canadian volunteer-sending NGOs, with a view to project collaboration and cost-sharing in places of mutual interest.

A 1996 AusAID 'Review of the Efficiency and Effectiveness of Australian Volunteer Programs' found that 'in comparison with other aid donors' volunteer programmes, on the basis of the unit cost per volunteer project, both OSB and AESOP rate well, with costs of less than half the average cost of comparable agencies.' The report recommended, however, that OSB should 'reconsider the geographic spread of its programme, and focus on countries of greatest need, taking into its consideration the focus of Australia's official development assistance programme'. Specifically, it recommended that OSB close its programmes in Latin America and Thailand.

In 1996–7, volunteer-sending programmes accounted for approximately 15 per cent of AusAID funding for Australian NGOs.

Bilateral programmes

In the 1980s, AusAID began to create special opportunities for NGOs to gain access to its bilateral or 'country programmes' (CP). In 1990–1, funding through country programmes represented 23.2 per cent of the total funding to Australian NGOs, and by 1996–7 it had risen to 36.2 per cent. The procedure is both responsive and competitive. An AusAID country programmme will announce a fund and guidelines, and NGOs will submit proposals for consideration. Those that best meet the guidelines will be supported.

The Australian Red Cross is one of the best placed to submit proposals for country programmes because of its international infrastructure. In 1996–7, it was the largest recipient of CP funding, taking 20 per cent of the total. The next largest recipient was World Vision at 12 per cent. A further 22 per cent was received by four other large organisations: Community Aid Abroad, CARE, the Overseas Service Bureau and UNICEF.

The NGO windows in many cases represent uncommitted discretionary funds available to bilateral country programmes. Because of budget reductions in 1996–7, many of these windows were either cancelled or were announced late in the financial year, with severely reduced budgets. With further budget cuts for 1997–8, it is likely that these funds will be further reduced in the years ahead.

International and Southern NGOs

In 1995–6, AusAID supported five international NGOs with grants of A$2.8 million, the largest being the International Planned Parenthood Federation.

Although a 1992 study conducted on behalf of the Minister for Trade and Overseas Development recommended against it,[7] funding for Southern NGOs has increased considerably in recent years. The total recorded for 1995–6 was A$16.7 million (US$13 million), a three-fold increase over 1991–2. Slightly more than one million of this was given to international organisations such as UNICEF, CARE International, Helen Keller International and GOAL.

EVALUATION

The 1993 OECD *Stakeholders* study observed that evaluation of Australian NGO work had been limited, with periodic AusAID reviews supplementing monitoring and evaluation work carried out by NGOs themselves. The approach was regarded by many as being somewhat cursory, and changes were already being implemented. Periodic organisational reviews are now carried out by a CDC team combining NGO and AusAID representatives (although in some cases the representatives are actually consultants nominated by AusAID and NGOs on the CDC). These examine an organisation's community base, its structure, management and financial accountability, its overseas links, fundraising and development education efforts. For larger agencies, field visits are included as part of the process. In addition, a regular programme of project evaluations was instituted by the CDC in 1993. A major NGO Programs Effectiveness Review was undertaken in 1995.

The approach still lacked transparency and rigour, however. The ANAO report stated that while AusAID's approach to programme evaluation met all of the evaluation criteria established by the OECD, there was an absence of clearly stated criteria against which programme performance could be assessed. Where NGOs were concerned, the situation was worse: in many cases, 'single sentence assertions of satisfactory progress with no supporting evidence; and apparently lengthy assessments where only one or two sentences actually addressed the objectives of the project and progress towards achieving them'.

This was not universally true. Larger NGOs with economies of scale, especially those that are members of a larger international corporate body, do have systems and budgets that can accommodate a professional approach to evaluation.

Plan International, for example, has established five 'domains' or spheres of work, with indicators of achievement for each by region and by country of operation. The 'learning domain', for example, has nine indicators (number of exercise books bought, number of permanent classrooms built, etc). Inputs and outputs are tracked annually by country. A more sophisticated Corporate Planning, Monitoring and Evaluation (CPME) tool is under development that will allow the organisation to track impact-related indicators such as primary school attendance and completion rates, transition rates into secondary schools and the overall quality of a school receiving support. Plan in Australia focuses to a certain extent on environmental issues, and has contributed guidelines for environmental sustainability that can be added to the basic CPME. In the 'learning domain', environmental factors would include, *inter alia*, the inclusion of environmental and conservation awareness in primary curricula, and efforts to ensure that education systems recognise and celebrate the importance of traditional knowledge about resource use, management and conservation.

Such examples aside, however, evaluation remains an area that is likely to continue to haunt NGOs and government, pushing both towards more narrow quantitative measures of judgment unless ways and means can be found to carry out *and to fund* more qualitative assessments of achievement.

The 1995 AusAID Effectiveness Review suggested ways in which organisational reviews and project evaluations could be strengthened, but the question of cost was not addressed. As long as cost remains an issue, the initiative for evaluation is likely to remain largely with AusAID. With growing political pressure to demonstrate short-term outcomes, the focus may become increasingly narrow, emphasising short-term measurables rather than the ultimate, longer-term development impact of the NGO effort. This, of course, does not have to be the rule. ACFOA notes that several NGOs – both large and small – conduct regular, high quality evaluations. The fundamental question relates to an NGO's attitude and commitment to both evaluation and learning.

DEVELOPMENT EDUCATION

Government support for development education began in the mid 1980s with a provision that NGOs could spend up to 15 per cent of their ANCP allocation on development education. Because this was seen to place development education in competition with overseas programming, a special Development Education Project Scheme (DEPS) was made available to all NGOs that had 'a capacity to do educational work', in order to 'encourage a more informed debate on what Australians can do to assist developing countries'. In addition to supporting international development NGOs, core assistance was given to six development education centres located in different Australian cities. This fund was managed by AusAID's Public Affairs Department, as was a Global Education Project that produced teaching material for Australian schools.

The Australian critique of development education in the 1990s is similar to the debate elsewhere. From the NGO side, complaints focused on too little funding and an emphasis on public relations support for government activities; from government there was a concern that development education was little more than a recitation of concerns – sometimes ideological – about trends and issues in official development assistance.

By 1997, AusAID funding for development education had become increasingly constrained by budgetary and political concerns. A small curriculum development programme remained in place for schools, and a small amount of core funding was provided to five remaining development education centres, but the grant programme for NGOs was not offered in 1997 and its future was in doubt. AusAID's corporate plan stated that 'AusAID seeks to enhance understanding in Australia of international development issues and of Australia's development cooperation program'. But in 1997, AusAID had an allocation of A$1.64 million for its entire public affairs programme, including administration, public affairs and all development education. This was less than Community Aid Abroad spent on public policy, campaigning and education in 1996, and was one third of what World Vision spent on community education (not including fundraising). In 1997–8 the public affairs budget was reduced by a further 25 per cent.

POLICY AND ADVOCACY

Policy dialogue between AusAID and Australian NGOs occurs through formal and informal mechanisms. The most long-standing formal mechanism is the Committee for Development Cooperation, with six members elected by the NGO community and six appointed by AusAID. The CDC advises on the accreditation of NGOs and management of NGO programmes.

Other forms of dialogue take place through meetings between ACFOA and government officials, and through informal meetings arranged by individual NGOs or those with a like-minded attitude towards a specific issue, such as gender, the environment or project work in a specific country.

ISSUES

Level of support to NGOs

General

In its outline of the 1996–7 overseas aid programme, the government stated that it 'supports an enhanced role for NGOs in the aid program'. The Parliamentary Secretary for Foreign Affairs estimated that funding for Australian NGOs would reach A\$100 million, compared with A\$89.3 million the previous year.[8] In fact, while the ANCP was slightly increased in 1996–7, other windows were significantly reduced or closed. The actual total for 1996–7 was only A\$79.8 million for Australian NGOs, a reduction of 10.6 per cent. The total for Australian and international NGOs was A\$95.2 million in 1996–7 (US\$74.4 million), and this was expected to decline to A\$88 million in 1997–8, a further decline of 7.5 per cent.

In 1996–7, total AusAID support for Australian and non-Australian NGOs represented 6.6 per cent of ODA, down over two years from 7.7 per cent of the total, but up from 5 per cent in 1991–2. In future years the total is likely to be reduced. The second largest window – humanitarian relief – will perhaps fall by as much as one third because of the shift in responsibility for all food aid to WFP. And the largest NGO window, the bilateral country programmes, are likely to be reduced significantly by overall budget cuts and a proportionately larger contraction of the discretionary funds from which these have been predominantly drawn.

Table 3.2: *Summary of Official Aid Through Australian and*
Non-Australian NGOs (A\$ million)

	1991–2	1996–7
Australian NGOs		
Emergency Relief and Refugees	23.8	20.0
NGO Projects Funded from Country Programmes	9.9	28.9
Project Subsidies, Including ANCP	10.0	17.6
Volunteer Programmes	5.0	11.7
Development Education	0.6	0.5
Women in Development	0.6	0.6
ACFOA, NGO Consultancies and Other	0.9	1.0
Southern Africa & Other Special Programmes	8.7	0
Total For Australian NGOs	*59.5*	*79.8*
Non-Australian NGOs	7.1	15.2
Total	66.6	95.2
ODA	1330.3	1445.8
Support to NGOs as a percentage of ODA	5.0%	6.6%

Source: AusAID–NGO Cooperation Annual Report 1996–7

Cost sharing

The NGO Effectiveness Review suggested that cost sharing should be adopted more widely throughout AusAID's support mechanisms for NGOs, especially in the bilaterally-funded country programmes. This has been strenuously resisted by ACFOA and its member agencies, who argue that NGOs already contribute through project design and administration, the provision of infrastructure, volunteer and staff time. They argue that cost sharing would reduce the ability of smaller NGOs to participate, especially in country programmes where their specialised skills and experience currently make a positive contribution. Certainly cost sharing would radically alter the structure of AusAID funding to the NGO community.

Cost sharing was justified on three grounds. The first was to encourage greater community fundraising. This is probably naive, as some, if not most NGOs – effective or not – spend as much time and effort on fundraising as anything else. Further efforts will cost more and could deflect them from their basic *raison d'être*. It could also change the nature of fundraising, with negative effects from a development education point of view. The second justification had to do with financial independence, 'to help ensure that individual NGOs do not become heavily reliant on AusAID funds'. The third related to the willingness of an NGO to share the risks of a project with government. NGOs argue that the same concerns about dependence are not applied to private sector firms whose major (and perhaps only) client is government. Where country programmes are concerned, they argue that they are simply following rules set out by government. If a project is supported, the decision is based entirely on the quality of a competitive bid, just as it is in any tendering process where the question of dependency does not arise. These arguments have validity. Additionally, any NGO (or business) that is heavily reliant on one 'customer' is vulnerable to shifts in policy and funding. This should be a matter of greater concern to NGOs than to government.

The case for cost sharing was not supported by the 1997 Simons Committee, which said that it 'found this debate one of the most difficult areas covered by the review. After considering all the arguments, we are not convinced that the wider application of cost sharing is in the best interests of AusAID–NGO cooperation.'

NGOs and official Australian policies

The Australian Government exercises more control over NGO spending than many other member governments in the OECD. For some governments, the primary mechanism for NGO funding is a responsive, matching grant programme. These matching grant programmes began with a recognition that taxpayers were making donations, over and above their tax dollars, to support international development work undertaken independently by NGOs, and governments felt this was worthy of financial recognition. Initially, in the 1960s and 1970s, these were the only mechanisms for the government funding of NGOs, organisations that were judged to be legitimate development organisations in their own right.

In the 1980s, some governments developed additional 'needs based' funding mechanisms, encouraging NGOs to operate in sectors or countries where governments could not. Such mechanisms offered better matching terms and conditions, and were sometimes fully funded by government. AusAID adopted this path more enthusiastically than other agencies, with the result that the original matching grant programme has become one of the smaller windows available to NGOs, representing about 20 per cent of the total funding available to Australian NGOs in 1996–7.

Recent trends demonstrate an increasing effort by government to bring NGOs even more into line with the official programme and with preferred government practices. The concern of the Auditor General that AusAID contracts with NGOs be as binding as those with commercial contractors is one example, even though most projects are designed and managed entirely by the NGO in question, and even though AusAID has stated a preference for cost-sharing.

There are other examples of pressure for NGOs to ally themselves more with government priorities. AusAID recommendations that the Overseas Service Bureau align its placements more closely with government geographic priorities runs contrary to the practice of other countries, which view the volunteer and other NGO programmes as an effort to demonstrate an interest in countries where the official programme cannot reach. There is a likely introduction of competitive processes into the funding of the volunteer sending programme in order to ensure (or induce) cost-cutting contestability, a common feature in government funding across most other ministries.

Where other governments see their support to NGOs as a contribution to the building of civil society and as 'partnerships', these words are not used in government literature describing Australian NGO support programmes. Rather, NGOs appear to be seen more and more as an extension of the government programme, rather than as development organisations in their own right.

Child sponsorship

It is well known that children have great appeal in any fundraising campaign. This seems especially true in Australia, where child sponsorship is the preeminent fundraising tool. The combined sponsorship income of Plan, Christian Children's Fund and World Vision is almost A$80 million. Combined, these three agencies probably sponsor about 240,000 children, up from about 160,000 in 1992. Smaller child sponsorship organisations are also growing: Compassion, not well known among other Australian NGOs, has an estimated 16,000 sponsored children. *In all, child sponsorship accounts for at least half of the private donor fundraising in Australia.*

Evaluation

The 1996 ANAO report on government management of NGO funding noted 'widespread deficiencies... in relation to contract monitoring procedures' and the observation that 'NGOs as a group do not properly understand the contractual relationship with AusAID under which they operate'. The ANAO also recognised that there were problems in attempting to evaluate benefits and costs that may be remote in time and space, or that may be difficult to relate to a particular investment, and that in any case, many of the things related to improvements in the quality of life are not readily quantifiable. It went on to recommend that 'a suitably balanced set of performance indicators be included in the design of future grants schemes'.

The ANAO's harsher comments, combined with the absence of rigorous and conclusive evidence of NGO success (through their own or third party evaluations), may be leading AusAID into a contractual relationship with NGOs that could damage the things that make NGOs effective in the first place: flexibility, an iterative approach to development and to partnership with other developing country NGOs, and a focus on the process of community development, rather than a readily observable output. Some NGOs have matured to a programmatic approach, funding part of a larger combination of inputs to, say, adult education, income generation and community health. In an effort to demonstrate short-term outputs more clearly, a more rigorous emphasis by AusAID on identifiable and measurable projects and project outcomes could actually be a retrograde step, a reversal of international trends that now emphasise results, rather than outputs – better learning on the part of children, for example, rather than the number of teachers that may have been trained as part of the process.

In this, NGOs themselves have been partly to blame. Although most acknowledge the importance of evaluation, and many have evaluative approaches and systems through which investment decisions and course correction can be made, few of these are rigorous enough to convince the external observer – as was the case with the AusAID Effectiveness Review and the ANAO study – that careful efficiencies and effectiveness measures are actually being observed. The same points were repeated in the 1997 Simons Committee Report.

A particular problem in Australia has to do with the cost of evaluation. AusAID allows the greater of up to 5 per cent or $5000 of an NGO's ANCP grant for evaluation. For most this is inadequate for meaningful evaluation, unless the NGO uses its own private donor funds, which were raised on the basis that as much as possible will reach the intended beneficiary. Discrete funding may be set aside within an AusAID country programme grant for evaluation, but again, amounts are likely to be limited. NGOs are thus caught in a cleft stick: criticised for their inability to provide convincing evidence of success, but constrained by convention and by AusAID from spending the money that would be required to produce it.

4 Austria[1]

Karin Küblböck

SUMMARY

Secular Austrian NGOs are distinguished by the small proportion of their income that is derived from private sources. No official distinction is made between projects where NGOs act as executing agencies, and those where the government supports NGO initiatives. Several organisations are almost entirely financed by public funding and may also act as executing agencies for government. The Austrian Government, in fact, does not have an executing agency for the implementation of its development projects. Based on a principle of 'subsidiarity', bilateral projects are mainly implemented by NGOs, private and public enterprises and consulting firms, through direct cooperation with Southern governments, and to a very small extent by Southern NGOs. NGOs receive almost 50 per cent of the programme and project aid of the Austrian Department of Development Cooperation (DDC), including their work as executing agents for Austrian ODA and the responsive funding programmes.

In 1996, approximately 50 Austrian NGOs obtained government funding. Catholic NGOs dominate the scene, reflecting the fact that 80 per cent of Austrians are registered Catholics, and only 5 per cent are Protestant. Ten organisations are involved in sending volunteers to developing countries. The number of volunteers is declining, however. Apart from CARE, which divides its activities between development cooperation projects and emergency aid projects, Austrian NGOs do not on the whole regard emergency aid as a major part of their activities. The largest organisations involved in emergency aid are Caritas and the Austrian Red Cross.

Recently, there has been substantial change in NGO–government relations. Issues include the selection of priority countries; the establishment of regional offices in developing countries by the aid administration; a reduced share of the budget for NGOs; and stricter execution of budget rules. Entry into the EU has initiated a discussion on the nature and legitimacy of Austrian NGOs.

INTRODUCTION

Austria's development cooperation policies

Austria sees its development cooperation policy as an effort to enhance security and stability in the world. Debt relief is likely to increase in the programme, as debt relief agreements have been concluded with thirteen countries. Austria's ODA declined from $767 million in 1995 to $574 million in 1996, a fall of 25 per cent in real terms. As a share of GNP, ODA declined from 0.33 per cent in 1995 to 0.24 per cent in 1996.

According to the 1997 DAC Report, 'NGOs occupy a special and important position in the aid programme since they initiate and implement a large share of bilateral grant financed projects – there being no official agency for the implementation of Austria's bilateral aid. The aid administration also uses NGO personnel for local aid coordination in several priority recipient countries. This approach', according to the DAC, 'is unique among DAC members.'[2]

Austrian NGOs

The first Austrian development organisations were created in the 1950s, and were Christian in origin. The first government development activities started in the 1960s. By the beginning of 1998, over 700 organisations, with various backgrounds and different sizes, were active in development cooperation.[3]

Austrian NGOs can be roughly divided into three groups:

*   NGOs that are almost entirely financed by public funding from the bilateral aid budget, and which also act as executing agencies for government initiated development projects;
*   Church-related NGOs;
*   a variety of organisations, which self-finance the majority of their activities. Included among these organisations are alternative trade organisations, solidarity committees, self-taxing groups, groups active in town twinning.

In 1996, approximately 50 Austrian NGOs obtained government funding. The main source was the budget of project and programme aid of the DDC, referred to below as 'the PPA budget'. About half (Sch560 million or $53 million) of this budget was spent through NGOs, more than 70 per cent of it through just ten organisations.

Austrian NGOs are distinguished by two key characteristics. First, the small proportion of income that is derived from private sources in non-Church-related NGOs; second, the almost complete separation between NGOs that implement projects abroad, and NGOs active in the domestic context.

Several organisations are almost entirely financed by public funding and yet may also act as executing agencies for government. Nevertheless, they do not consider themselves 'governmental agencies'. On the contrary, they underline their NGO identity and values, and the importance of their autonomous actions and decision-making. No official distinction is made between projects where NGOs act as executing agencies, and those where the government supports NGO initiatives.

NGOs that receive public funding fall into three groups. One is made up of NGOs implementing projects abroad. In 1996 this group received approximately 66 per cent of the NGO share of the PPA budget. The other two groups comprise NGOs active in the domestic context. Those active in development education, information and cultural projects received 12 per cent of the total NGO budget in 1996. Those that administer scholarship programmes and support students from developing countries in Austria received about 18 per cent of the 1996 NGO budget. Additionally, some funds were allocated to international NGOs.

SECULAR NGOS RECEIVING GOVERNMENT FUNDING

NGOs mainly implementing projects in developing countries

The largest NGOs in this category in 1996 were:

*   ADC (Austrian Association for Development and Cooperation), which specialises in infra-structural, industrial and mining projects; in 1997 ADC merged with the relief organisation

Hilfswerk Austria;
- ÖNSI (*Österreichisches Nord/Süd Institut* – Austrian North/South Institute), specialises in democratic structure-building and promotion of civil society;
- EWA (*Entwicklungswerkstatt Austria*), focusing on vocational training and small-scale enterprise;
- CARE Austria, concentrating on rural development and small-scale enterprise;
- GÖAB (*Gesellschaft für Österreichisch-Arabische Beziehungen* – Association for Austrian-Arabic Relations), concentrating on health, education and agricultural projects.

Most of these organisations receive almost all their funds from government. There is one Church-related NGO, IIZ (*Institut für Internationale Zusammenarbeit* – Institute for International Cooperation) that also falls into this category. At the beginning of 1996, IIZ was 'privatised', and was no longer subordinated to the Bishop's Conference.

Several other organisations that are not primarily engaged in Development Cooperation also receive significant funds from the PPA budget:

- ÖJAB (*Österreichische Jungarbeiterbewegung* – Austrian Young Workers Movement) for its training programmes;
- WWF (World Wide Fund for Nature);
- Global 2000 (for rainforest and other environmental projects).

NGOs mainly active in the domestic context

There is a division of labour among development education and information organisations:
- *Südwind Agentur* (Agency for Development Education and Public Relations) concentrates on development education and public relations;
- ÖFSE (*Österreichische Forschungsstiftung für Entwicklungshilfe* – Austrian Foundation for Development Research) specialises in documentation, has a public library and, since 1996, has managed the official development aid statistics for the Ministry of External Affairs;
- VIDC (Vienna Institute for Development and Cooperation) specialises in cultural and audio visual projects and seminars on development issues. In recent years, VIDC has implemented projects in developing countries, out of a special 'rainforest' budget.

Although their presence is not always evident in the NGO community, NGOs implementing study promotion programmes for students from developing countries receive considerable amounts from the PPA budget. The largest organisation, ÖAD (*Österreichischer Akademikerdienst* – Austrian Academic Exchange Service), received about Sch47 million in 1996 ($4.4 million) for about 400 individuals from developing countries. Public funds for scholarships are also obtained by other NGOs with particular geographical associations.

CATHOLIC DEVELOPMENT COOPERATION

Church-related NGOs, established in the 1950s and 1960s, were the first development NGOs in Austria. Catholic NGOs dominate the scene, reflecting the fact that 80 per cent of Austrians are registered Catholics, and only 5 per cent are Protestant.

Many small groups and initiatives maintain direct contact with partner organisations in the South, and raise private funds to finance their projects. Most of the resources are raised in official church collections and private donations.

The organisational and funding structure among Catholic organisations is complex. Some of the charities that benefit from official church collections provide financing for other Catholic NGOs, most of which are formally controlled by the regional or national church hierarchy. KOO (*Koordinierungsstelle der Österreichischen Bischofskonferenz für Internationale Entwicklung und Mission* – Coordination Office of the Austrian Bishops Conference for International Development and Mission) is the umbrella organisation for about 30 Catholic NGOs. It was founded in 1963 and is recognised by the Austrian Bishops Conference. KOO's functions include the documentation and coordination of the activities of its member organisations, and policy dialogue with government. KOO publishes an annual report on its members, including financial data.

KFS (*Kofinanzierungsstelle für Entwicklungszusammenarbeit* – Co-Financing Office for Development Cooperation) was founded in 1992 to be a co-financing service agency for its six member organisations (which are also KOO members). Project proposals for co-financing are submitted through KFS, resulting in closer cooperation between Catholic NGOs and the government. KFS also facilitates the implementation of government-initiated development projects by Church-related NGOs. The more centralised structure of Catholic development cooperation is also advantageous in obtaining co-financing from the EU. In 1996, 22 projects from Austria were approved by the EU, of which 13 were from KFS.

Funding for Catholic Church-related NGOs

In 1996, project-executing Catholic Church-related NGOs received approximately Sch165 million ($15.6 million) from the PPA budget, about 44 per cent of official disbursements for NGOs implementing projects in the South, or 15 per cent of the total PPA budget.

Of this amount, Sch119 million was allocated to ÖED (*Österreichischer Entwicklungsdienst* – Austrian Development Cooperation Service) and IIZ. Within Catholic development organisations, IIZ has a somewhat exceptional status, as it is almost entirely financed by government. Member organisations of KFS received about Sch40 million from the PPA budget in 1996.

In 1996 the total private funds disbursed by KOO member organisations amounted to about Sch350 million ($33 million). An additional Sch247 million was spent on missionary projects.

Development education and public relations

In 1996 KOO members spent 14 per cent (almost Sch49 million or $4.6 million) of their funds on development education. Some Catholic NGOs, such as ÖED, DKA and the Diocese Commission of Graz, have development education departments. Large campaigns have been organised on themes such as 'water', with funding from the PPA budget. Several magazines and newsletters are published by Catholic organisations.

PROTESTANT DEVELOPMENT COOPERATION

On the Protestant side, three NGOs are active in development cooperation: *Brot für Hungernde, Evangelischer Arbeitskreis für Weltmission* and *Diakonisches Werk für Österreich*, which is mainly engaged in emergency aid. There are also about 15 groupings, some of which belong to international evangelical associations. Their resources cannot be estimated as there is no national data available.

EAEZ (Evangelical Association for Development Co-operation) is the umbrella organisation formed by mainstream Protestant NGOs, mainly used as a discussion and information forum, and for the coordination of the activities of its members. EAEZ is authorised to act as an official representative of the Protestant Church. The three member organisations of EAEZ handle about

Sch6 million a year ($570,000), mainly raised through private donations and church collections. Government co-financing is an exception, but there is some co-financing by municipalities.

The work of Protestant NGOs consists mainly of financing projects proposed by partner organisations – Protestant churches or Protestant Church-related NGOs – or by international Protestant bodies such as the Lutheran World Federation. Within Austria events such as seminars or conferences are organised, and a quarterly newsletter, *Die Brücke*, is published.

Although Protestant development cooperation in Austria is small in scale, and although financial relations with the government hardly exist, organisations actively participate in policy dialogue. Frequent consultations with other NGOs take place within the framework of AGEZ (*Arbeitsgemeinschaft Entwicklungszusammenarbeit* – Working Association for Development Cooperation), and representatives of Protestant NGOs also participate in NGO–government dialogue.

FOOD AND EMERGENCY AID

Responsibility for emergency aid lies with Department I of the Federal Chancellery, and activities are usually planned and implemented separately from those of the DDC.

Apart from CARE, which divides its activities between development cooperation projects and emergency aid projects, Austrian NGOs do not on the whole regard emergency aid as a major part of their activities. The largest organisations involved in emergency aid are Caritas and the Austrian Red Cross. Caritas is also active in development work. In 1996, its activities outside Austria accounted for Sch222 million ($21 million), of which about 14 per cent was for development cooperation projects.

Emergency funding benefited from *Nachbar in Not* ('Neighbour in Need'), a collaboration between Austrian national television, the Austrian Red Cross and Caritas in sending aid to the countries of former Yugoslavia. By September 1996, over a billion schillings ($95 million) had been raised. Funds are divided equally between the two organisations.

VOLUNTEERS

Ten organisations are involved in sending volunteers to developing countries. However, the number of volunteers is declining. Reasons for this lie in the increased number and effectiveness of Southern NGOs, the availability of experts from developing countries, and changing demands for volunteers with very specific skills. NGOs find it increasingly difficult to recruit appropriate candidates with the required education and experience.

ÖED regularly organises meetings and seminars for returned volunteers and encourages them to become involved in its development educational activities.

UMBRELLA ORGANISATIONS

The only umbrella organisation that links most of the different development NGOs in Austria is AGEZ. It was founded by ten NGOs in 1988 as a reaction to conflicts with the then Minister for Foreign Affairs and the aid-administration. AGEZ acts as a representative body of NGOs in relations with government, and is also a discussion-forum on development policies. Among its 29 members are all the large development NGOs. Regional branches of AGEZ have been founded in Tyrol, Vorarlberg and Styria.

In addition to the umbrella bodies for Church agencies, described above, there are other networks. WIDE/Austria (Women in Development Europe) works on gender issues and aims to strengthen gender perspectives within official bilateral development cooperation. There is also an NGO EU Platform, comprising 37 members, for the participation of Austrian NGOs in the EU NGO Liaison Committee. The 24-member KKS (*Kontaktkomittee für Studienförderung*) is a representative body for all entities concerned with students and graduates from developing countries in Austria.

GOVERNMENT FUNDING OF NGOS

The Austrian government does not have an executing agency for the implementation of its development projects. Based on the Austrian principle of 'subsidiarity', bilateral projects are mainly implemented by NGOs, private and public enterprises and consulting firms, through direct cooperation with Southern governments, and to a very small extent by Southern NGOs. NGOs received almost 50 per cent of Austrian programme and project aid of the DDC, including their work as executing agents for Austrian ODA and the responsive funding programmes.

Although the bulk of government funding for NGOs is provided by DDC, other NGO funds are provided by the Ministries of Education (development educational school projects), Science and Research (for university lectures and studies) and Environment (rainforest projects).

Domestic activities

The DDC (Division 4 – Public Relations and Development Education) is responsible for the allocation of project co-financing to NGOs active in the Austrian domestic context. In 1994 IKP (*Institut für Kommunikationsplanung*) conducted a study for the DDC, analysing the impact of public education work on development policy in Austria. As a result, major changes were undertaken to reduce the workload of the department and to establish a clearer separation between its public education work and that of NGOs.

In 1995 the DDC established its own programme for public awareness, and IKP was commissioned to implement it. In the same year, a new organisation called *KommEnt* (Association for Communication and Development), was created.[4] *KommEnt* is responsible for the appraisal of project proposals concerning public relations, development education, documentation, publications, film and cultural activities. Decisions about the funding of projects are taken by the aid administration.

Small projects

There are five 'project pools' for funding different types of small projects (for example, cultural projects, gender projects, publications) up to Sch50,000 ($4700). These project pools are administered by VIDC, ÖFSE and *Südwind Agentur*.

Budget rules

Complex budget rules regularly create problems for the execution of long-term projects for the DDC. The consequences of these rules are also born by the NGOs that receive funds from the government.

Budget commitments are made for only one year. The overall budget for a year is known only a few months in advance, and has to be negotiated each year with the Ministry of Finance.

As a result, there is a high level of insecurity in planning, as development cooperation projects usually run over several years. Some DDC officials admit that this rule is 'diametrically opposed' to the execution of an efficient and high-quality development cooperation programme.

Compounding this problem is the fact that there is no facility for unspent funds to be carried forward. They go to a reserve, and create the danger of future budget cuts on the grounds that previous year's resources were not fully utilized. As a result, at the end of the year, resources are often hurriedly spent because of time pressure.

The DDC has regular discussions with the Ministry of Finance, with the aim of obtaining a legally fixed budget, similar to fixed contributions to international organisations. Because of the long-term nature of development projects, commitments must often be made for more than a year. Although the law limits future commitments to ten per cent of the current year's budget, the aid administration usually exceeds this. This makes it very vulnerable if there are budget cuts.

The Minister of Finance can give a 'Supplementary Budget Authorisation' that allows for additional resources for expenditures that exceed the budget. The aid administration has received considerable amounts through this mechanism in recent years. However the authorisation is normally given very late in the year, which makes planning difficult.

The difficulties created by these rules were well illustrated in 1995 when the final budget for the year was decided as late as May (usually, the budget is decided in autumn of the preceding year). Because of austerity measures, the DDC budget proposal was reduced by more than 30 per cent. A large part was already committed, leaving very few resources for NGOs with annual contracts or for new projects. The Minister of Finance approved a Supplementary Budget Authorisation of Sch300 million, but it could only be arranged in November. Since this critical situation the budget has remained relatively stable. In March 1996, for the first time, a two-year budget was legislated for the year 1996–97. This procedure was repeated for the subsequent two years.

Eligibility

There are no specific criteria for NGOs to either receive financial support from the government and/or act as executing agencies. There is a provisional guideline for the selection of project-executing organisations but officials complain that these criteria could not always be applied because of prevailing national economic interests.

For many years, a very informal way of project submission prevailed between the aid administration and the Austrian NGOs. For government-initiated projects an NGO used to be contacted directly and asked to submit a project proposal. For NGO-initiated projects, the responsible person in the aid administration was contacted 'informally' before the formulation of the project proposal, and was asked whether the project had a chance. This led to a situation where almost all formally proposed projects were accepted.

Following the establishment of country programming and permanent overseas regional offices by the aid administration, changes have taken place in the mechanisms of project submission and approval. In countries where a regional office has been established, NGOs submit project proposals directly in the respective country, the project is then discussed with the responsible persons in the aid administration who will make the final decision. Project proposals for other countries are submitted with the aid administration in Austria.

The larger NGOs discuss their annual programme with the aid administration, therefore there is a certain cooperation concerning the project selection and design in priority countries and sectors. There is an increasing tendency to define projects in priority countries in cooperation with the recipient country's government and the regional offices and to put the implementation of those projects out to tender. The described changes lead to a situation where more projects are initiated by the government through the regional offices and where the proportion of project aid implemented by firms increases to the disadvantage of Austrian NGOs.

Duration and nature of government commitments

Official funding is provided on a project-by-project basis. The legal framework for contracts between NGOs and the government is a 'subsidy contract'. The official contributions given to NGOs are grants (so-called 'non-reimbursable subsidies'). There is no right of appeal in case of a negative response.

Until 1995, firm commitments for projects in developing countries were made for the whole project period. In that year, the duration of contracts for overseas projects was reduced to one year, and since then, contracts of a longer term have been concluded only in very few cases. The envisaged project period is now mentioned in the contract but is not the legal contract period. There is a wide interpretation of the meaning of 'project', however, and there are some forms of programme funding. For example, ÖED receives 70 per cent public funding for its volunteer-sending programme, and the whole programme is defined as one single project.

The largest NGOs active in the domestic context define each part of their activities as single projects, and these are submitted annually to the aid administration.

Overheads

Until 1993, four large project-implementing NGOs received a basic grant to cover their overhead costs. At present, financial resources attributed to NGOs are exclusively for their different projects. Overhead costs have to be included in the project proposals.

Following two years of discussion, a new Project Management Fee (PBA-Projektbegleitentgelt) was introduced. Overheads are assigned to different projects and each staff member in an NGO has to calculate the time spent working on each project. A fixed daily allowance is then added to the project costs.

The objective of this new arrangement is to make NGO accounting procedures more transparent. As a consequence, the aid administration expects an increase in the efficiency and professionalisation of the work of NGOs. Furthermore, the implementation of smaller projects should be made more effective, as the allowance should correspond to real administrative costs. The department intends to define different daily allowances according to the administrative requirements of different types of projects. Representatives of most NGOs basically approved of the PBA, but they object to the administrative burden (time is calculated in 15 minute segments) and the low daily rate.

Until 1992, three NGOs active in the domestic context received a basic grant for their administrative and personnel costs. Since then, they assign overhead costs to different activities. There is no fixed percentage for overhead costs.

AUSTRIAN–EU CO-FINANCING

The DDC reserves a certain amount of its budget for projects co-financed by the EU. This means that those NGOs with up to 50 per cent co-financing from the EU can be assured that the additional amounts needed (up to 35 per cent) will be provided by the aid administration. At least 15 per cent of the funds must be raised by the NGOs from the private sector.

Several statements of Austrian politicians have produced the impression in the public mind that, for the NGOs, EU funds could compensate for national budget reductions. But comparison with other countries suggests that EU co-financing is unlikely to bring in even one twentieth of the Austrian resources now being spent through the Union. A real problem for some Austrian NGOs seeking EU co-financing is that it is very difficult for them to obtain the required 15 per cent from private funding sources. In 1995 Austrian NGOs obtained ECU 2.2 million of EU co-financing, while in 1996 the amount was up to ECU 4.7 million.

EVALUATION

The Division for Evaluation, Inspection and Control in the DDC is responsible for the evaluation of development projects (co-)financed from the PPA budget. The 1996 OECD Development Cooperation Review stated that,

> *Since the beginning of evaluation activities in 1990, 14 mid-term evaluations have been carried out in developing countries and two in Eastern Europe, but no ex post evaluations... The results of each external evaluation are briefly summarized and circulated within the aid administration together with an internal annual report. The short summaries are made available to a larger audience... In general, the recommendations made by the evaluators are taken into account at the project level, but the Evaluation Division considers that the present number of annual evaluations is still too small to have a systematic impact on Austrian aid activities.[5]*

Critics refer to the need for institutional separation of the responsibilities for planning and evaluation, and to the fact that the public is not informed about success or failure of projects financed by public resources.

POLICY DIALOGUE AND ADVOCACY

On many occasions, NGOs have criticised Austrian ODA on the basis of its structures, quality, quantity and organisation. Repeatedly, proposals have been made by AGEZ urging the government to formulate a concrete and coherent development policy, to increase resources for programme and project aid, and to reserve 2 per cent of ODA for development education expenditures.

The definition of a coherent development policy, embodying stated principles covering poverty, human rights, priority regions and historical relations has not yet been realised in Austria.[6] One reason may be found in a lack of substantive development policy dialogue within government and in political party debates, due to the low importance given to development issues in Austria. As a result, there is insufficient coordination in the activities of the different departments responsible for ODA administration. Another reason may be the considerable influence that different interest groups exert on the execution of ODA.

There are various mechanisms for policy dialogue between government and NGOs, including an Advisory Board on Development Cooperation, AGEZ, advisory committees for culture, education and media at *KommEnt*, and the Parliamentary Permanent Sub-Committee on Development Policy. The Advisory Board was established in 1974 'to coordinate actions in the field of development cooperation and to advise the federal chancellor on the execution of his tasks concerning development cooperation'. While it must be convened at least three times a year by the Minister for Development Cooperation – who also appoints its members and chairs its meetings – its advice does not have to be accepted by the administration, and it is far from being a real instrument of advocacy.[7] The Board has 26 members, 40 per cent from NGOs.

Representatives of the DDC usually refer to AGEZ as their partner in discussions about development policy, and a good atmosphere is reported by both sides in formal and informal meetings. Nevertheless, according to NGOs, the discussions do not have serious implications for the execution of development policy.

The Government's Three-Year Programme states that NGOs should participate in the definition of country programmes, and NGOs are invited to participate in planning round-tables and working groups. There are no fixed mechanisms that guarantee participation in decision-making, even though NGOs are the main executers of official development projects. This leads to a question of whether or not the views of NGOs are seriously considered in official policy-making, despite DDC recognition of their know-how and experience.

ISSUES

Country programming in Austrian bilateral aid

Until some years ago, there were no predefined geographical priorities in Austrian bilateral assistance. This led to a wide dispersal of resources and constrained efficient planning. In 1992, however, the government decided to target 19 countries. In most, Austrian NGOs are the main actors in Austrian ODA. Official development projects are predominantly carried out by companies in only a few countries.

There are complaints from NGOs that the selection of some countries has been made without respecting the criteria laid out by the aid administration. NGOs with limited independent income feared that they would be obliged to withdraw from their own priority countries and to adjust their activities to official priorities. Although the aid administration has created a budget line for co-financing projects outside the priority countries (up to 35 per cent of the total), it can be assumed that this will be the case.

Cooperation with NGOs focuses on rural development, small business, democratic structures and education, and more recently on micro-credit, with each NGO tending to specialise in a few areas. The DDC used to decide which NGOs were going to be contracted for the execution of a specific project, but now, DDC is increasingly putting projects out to tender. Some sectors, such as democracy-building, were originally chosen by NGOs themselves and are now part of the official priority sectors.

Funding of Southern NGOs

Although considered desirable by the aid administration, direct funding of Southern NGOs is still an exception. Total funding for Southern NGOs is small, about Sch7 million ($660,000) in 1996. About Sch20 million was provided to international NGOs. According to aid officials, however, the new official permanent offices in priority countries will facilitate the establishment of contacts with local NGOs, and will manage cooperation between them and the government.

There are few regular contributions by Austrian NGOs to Southern NGOs. Church-related organisations and smaller organisations tend to limit themselves to financing projects proposed by their partners. The other project-executing NGOs usually exercise considerable influence in the conception and implementation of projects, stressing the value added by their own knowledge and experience.

There is a serious concern among NGOs about the intention of government to work more directly with Southern NGOs. NGOs underline the importance of their function in selecting reliable partners and maintaining partnership relations. They are concerned about the negative impact that unequal power relations could have on Southern NGOs and they question whether the government is capable of replacing Austrian NGOs in their dissemination of information and 'Southern' points of view within Austria.

Public relations and fundraising

Within the DDC there is a clear separation between (and little coordination of) responsibilities for projects abroad and for public relations. Among NGOs too, with a few exceptions, there is a clear division between project-implementing NGOs and those active in building public awareness.

NGOs active in the domestic context have been expected by the aid administration to serve as promoters of bilateral and NGO development cooperation abroad. However, they do not see this as their main function. Rather, their activities focus on disseminating information about general development issues through public campaigns, publications, information and through 'multipliers' such as teachers, journalists and the Austrian media.

In fundraising, NGOs face many difficulties. Some are relatively young and do not have a broad base in society. They find it difficult to start raising funds when well known organisations with a long tradition have essentially captured the market. There has also been a lack of real incentive for NGOs to reach out to the public because of the volume of public funding, and because there is no tax relief for donations.

Changing government–NGO relations

Informal relationships, the absence of clear criteria, a tendency to avoid conflict and to find an 'arrangement' for everything, are general characteristics of Austrian political culture. It is only in the past few years that the political climate has begun to change, resulting in more open confrontations between government and various interest groups. Relations between the DDC and NGOs are no exception to this rule. Until the beginning of 1995, relations were characterised by a relatively peaceful co-existence, due mainly to the fact that the PPA budget had increased regularly up to 1994. Close personal contacts and informal relations exist between representatives of the NGOs and the staff of the DDC, with personnel shifting from NGO to government and back again.

Recently, however, several factors have led to a substantial change in NGO–government relations and seem to have put an end to this peaceful co-existence. These include the selection of priority countries; the establishment of regional offices in developing countries by the aid administration; a reduced share of the budget for NGOs; and stricter execution of budget rules. Entry into the EU has initiated a discussion on the nature and legitimacy of Austrian NGOs. Changes in ministerial responsibility have also brought about changes in procedure.

There is a mutual dependence between government and those NGOs that receive official funding. Because it has not been possible to increase the staff of the department, many government administrative functions are effectively carried out by NGOs or consultants, leading to an NGO criticism that responsibilities and competencies are not clearly enough defined. The absence of a formal ODA executing agency and the informal nature of relations between government and NGOs has resulted in aid officials tending to interfere in the planning and execution of NGO projects.

During the first half of the 1990s, projects financed from a regularly increasing bilateral aid budget could not have been implemented without NGOs. Because they believed that this trend would continue, NGOs did not look for alternative funding possibilities, and this has led to a lack of autonomy that has now become an issue of concern.

5 Belgium

Judith Randel and Tony German[1]

SUMMARY

There are three parts to the Belgian NGO community, reflecting the federation of French-speaking Wallonie, Dutch-speaking Flanders, and a small German-speaking community. French-speaking NGOs are more numerous (around 200) and are generally small, community-based, informal and solidarity-oriented. Dutch-speaking NGOs, on the whole, are fewer, larger and more professional – raising several times more funds than their French-speaking counterparts.

The government has funded NGO activity for 20 years. New laws in 1997 redefined NGO eligibility, and introduced new funding arrangements aimed at creating incentives for NGOs to coordinate, specialise and become more professional. Clearer and more detailed criteria, along with programme funding, are meant to let the Belgian Administration for Development Cooperation (ABOS) focus on policy matters. NGOs, however, are not convinced that the new system will end problems in ABOS of weak capacity and time-consuming bureaucracy. The Government made grants to NGOs (excluding contracting and emergencies) of BF2884 million ($100 million) in 1996, about 14 per cent of the ABOS budget, and roughly the same amount as the voluntary funds raised by Belgian NGOs.

Public confidence in Belgian aid has been shaken by a series of aid crises and by the humanitarian and political crises affecting the former Belgian colonies of Rwanda, Burundi and Congo DR. Polls show public support for increased aid down to 51 per cent, the lowest level in Europe. The government response has been to introduce fundamental changes in policy (known as *Kleur Bekennen*), and a major public information campaign. The NGO stance towards ODA has changed from one of criticism to one of supportive and 'balanced' analysis.

Rather stilted 'official-style' dialogue between NGOs and government has gradually given way during the 1990s to more substantive engagement on issues such as debt relief and demographics. Joint evaluations involving NGOs and government have become standard procedure since 1991. The challenges emerging from these evaluations have led to serious discussion between NGOs and ABOS, and perhaps to a more positive NGO approach to evaluation. Changes in the ABOS evaluation service and the setting aside of 1 per cent of programme funding for NGO evaluations offers the possibility of deeper engagement, if the constructive atmosphere can be maintained.

BACKGROUND AND HISTORY

NGOs in Belgium represent almost every strand of public and political opinion. They are usually anchored in specific constituencies – the Church, popular movements or smaller communities and parishes. Just as Belgium is a federation with two main communities, a Dutch speaking part (Flanders) and a French speaking part (Wallonie), NGOs are also allied into French or Dutch-speaking coalitions. There is also a small German-speaking community.

Belgian federal government responsibility for development cooperation is also fragmented. The *Algemeen Bestuur voor Ontwikkelingssamenwerking* (ABOS – Belgian Administration for Development Cooperation (BADC)) is responsible for the bulk of Belgian development cooperation, including bilateral aid. Other ministries are also involved, particularly the Ministry of Finance. At a regional level, the Community Governments of Flanders and Wallonie also have some responsibility for development cooperation, but relations with NGOs are currently limited to support for development education work. The relations with government that are discussed in this chapter refer to relations with ABOS.

The character of all development cooperation activities in Belgium between 1995 and 1997 was strongly influenced by aid failures and crises, and by a consequent loss of public and political confidence in the aid programme. This thread runs through NGO–government relations and has led to fundamental changes outlined in a 1996 policy document: *Kleur Bekennen* ('Showing our Colours'). This was followed by an information campaign *De Tijd van Knikken is Voorbij* ('The Time of Nodding Yes is Over') in spring 1997.

According to the DAC, 'Problems and weaknesses have beset the aid programme and eroded public confidence in Belgian aid activities over the past two years. The government has been working hard on an overall reform of its aid policies and programme'. New policies were presented to a Parliamentary Commission in October 1996, and the aid administration was entirely reorganised in March 1997. Belgian ODA declined in real terms from $1034 million in 1995 to $943 million, a decline of almost 9 per cent, bringing the ODA/GNP ratio down from 0.38 to 0.34 per cent.[2]

The NGO sector

French and Dutch-speaking NGOs not only speak a different language, but also their style and constituencies are different. Official Belgian development cooperation is part of the federal government, and creating structures and strategies appropriate to both NGO communities has been an ongoing problem.

French-speaking NGOs are more numerous – perhaps as many as 200 in total, although only 57 are registered with government. On the whole, they are small. They are more likely to be community-based, more informal than their Dutch-speaking counterparts, with a strong solidarity ethos reflected in their ability to link poverty issues in Belgium and developing countries.

There are fewer Dutch-speaking NGOs. Thirty five were registered with government in 1997, and a further 27 NGOs were registered as using both languages. Dutch-speaking NGOs tend to be larger, more professional organisations. They are also much richer – raising around five times more money than the French sector. Salaries throughout the NGO community are low.

In addition to the language groupings, NGOs are allied to different social movements, to the Church, to labour and trade union movements, and many are aligned along different political ideologies.

Umbrella bodies

There are two types of umbrella body in Belgium. The first are language-based federations that represent the interests of their sector; the second are advocacy collectives.

Dutch-speaking NGOs are federated into Coprogram and French and German-speaking NGOs in ACODEV. The membership of these federations is open to any NGO that has been recognised by the government. They act as a sort of trade union for NGOs, negotiating with the government via an NGO Advisory Commission that acts on behalf of their members on funding issues. ACODEV was created in October 1997 by combining two umbrella bodies (ADO and CODEF), in response to the demands of new legislation discussed later in this chapter.

The federations are not very active on matters of advocacy. Originally, a unitary NGO umbrella body existed for Belgium, but this was separated into two bodies representing the French and Dutch speaking sectors – CNCD (Centre National pour la Coopération au Développement) and NCOS (Nationaal Centrum voor Ontwikkelingssamenwerking) respectively. NCOS has taken the lead in advocacy, government relations and communications.

A history of change

Government co-financing of NGO activities started in 1976. At that time there was discussion about whether the management and allocation of the funds should be handled directly by government, or delegated to an NGO body. Since NCOS/CNCD was an operational as well as an umbrella body, NGOs did not consider it sufficiently impartial to manage the funds, which were therefore centralised.

In the early 1990s, NGOs regarded their relationship with government as ambiguous. While ministers and officials stressed the importance of NGOs in development education and in small-scale projects, they did not appreciate being targets of NGO criticism. In the early 1980s, the environment was much more difficult than in the 1990s, when openings were created for a more constructive relationship.

In 1991, the government–NGO cooperation policy was substantially revamped following lengthy negotiations. Three Royal Decrees were issued on co-financing, development education and volunteers. These also provided for joint annual evaluations and for information exchange. Programme funding was introduced, based on five-year periods and annual plans and budgets. Only Dutch-speaking NGOs were in a position to meet the standards set for programme funding – a politically untenable situation. But the criteria were so vague that it was hard to exclude anyone and, for different reasons, programme funding arrangements were concluded with all the NGOs that applied. Even so, the vast majority of the 15 programme arrangements were with Dutch-speaking NGOs. In practice, therefore, the new standards have not been applied, and NGOs report a reluctance within government to explain funding decisions. Rather than denying funding with an explanation, the tendency has been towards a process of attrition, based on constant referrals and questions.

On the NGO side, unwillingness to reach agreement among themselves and to set goals has inhibited their ability to take a stronger role in the management of the co-financing programme, and it has inhibited substantive discussion. A series of consultative commissions was set up between NGOs and the aid administration covering projects in developing countries, field assignment of NGO staff, and development education. These were intended by government to make NGO consultation a more official process, and to cement relations between NGOs themselves. However the commissions were unable to overcome the inhibitions of both NGOs and government. The result was discussion of detail and technicalities, but not substance, leading inevitably to a loss of faith in the value of the process.

The new arrangements and their implications

In 1997, new laws were introduced. Project funding was discontinued. Existing contracts between NGOs and government became obsolete and, from 1998, any NGO became eligible to apply for programme funding. The definition of NGO was also extended to include 'service NGOs' that offer support services to the NGO community, and civil society organisations (CSO) that enter into consortia with development NGOs. Consortia must include two recognised NGOs.

At the same time, ABOS set more detailed criteria in the new laws. Normally programme funding will be offered on a 75:25 matching ratio, but 85 per cent of the costs will be provided in certain circumstances: if NGOs coordinate themselves into a consortium with one programme; for NGOs with an average annual budget of more than BF80 million (about $2.58 million) for activities eligible for co-financing; and for innovative or highly specialised programmes.

In effect this gives an incentive for NGOs to coordinate, to specialise and to become more professional. At the same time, the terms of the NGO contribution have changed. Only in-kind contributions incurred in Belgium will be counted, not those in developing countries. In very special circumstances, government will fund 100 per cent of an NGO activity. A 1997 example was the Congo DR, where bilateral aid was a political impossibility.

Changes in the management of development cooperation have been matched by a shift of administrative responsibility away from ABOS to the NGOs. The most striking change is in the management of volunteers, formerly undertaken completely by the ministry, and now the responsibility of NGOs. Positive aspects of the new laws include the extension of the programmatic approach to development education and volunteer-sending programmes.

Capacity and roles

The new structure will result in an ABOS that is focused on policy. Administrative capacity is expected to be reduced, but it is hoped that analytical and policy capacity will be increased. By moving entirely to programme support, ABOS intends to shift its role to one of engagement with NGOs on content and strategy, in contrast to the past focus on administration and budget issues.

ABOS has often been criticised for chronic structural weakness, bureaucracy and centralisation. A stronger evaluation unit and a focus on policy may create conditions where this can be overcome. However a question remains: opening programme funding to a much wider range of participating organisations will inevitably increase the demands on an organisation with historically weak capacity. As of January 1997, 80 applications had been received and processed by ABOS. Roughly one third were approved, one third were turned down, and one third were partially approved.

Criteria, coherence and concentration

Belgium's concentration policy has been a long-time matter of concern to NGOs, for two reasons. Firstly, NGOs want the freedom to operate in whatever countries they choose. Secondly, they are concerned that an unstable and untransparent policy process for countries of concentration would have repercussions on their own work. When the government introduced its 1994 concentration policy, it proposed that aid channelled via NGOs and universities should be focused on countries where they were already working (at the time, about 90 per cent of co-financed projects were in 40 countries) or that they should submit a list of 50 countries in which they intended to work, with a requirement that the list include the 19 countries of concentration. The 1996 *Kleur Bekennen* policy paper announced that there would be six concentration countries plus the Southern African Development Community (SADC) region. Political pressure added another country, and NGO pressure led to the establishment of ABOS offices in some 'new' countries in Latin America.

In 1997, the issue revolved around how much any decision on programme funding would be affected by an NGO's degree of consistency with Belgian development cooperation objectives. The answer was not clear. Two standards are to guide ABOS. One is the internal coherence of the NGO programme, and the other is the overall consistency of the co-financing programme with priorities for Belgian ODA. With its history of vague criteria, a new and transparent balance – even one allowing a set percentage of co-financing outside priority areas – is likely to help improve NGO–government relations.

NGO funding trends

Belgian government grants to NGOs reached their lowest level for five years in 1996, falling to BF2884 million, or just under $100 million. Grants to NGOs fluctuated sharply over the period, reaching their high point in 1995 at BF3305 million, $112 million. As a share of the ABOS budget (itself between 60 and 70 per cent of ODA), NGO co-financing fell back by almost a third in 1994. In 1996, NGOs received 14 per cent of the budget, and in 1997 this was expected to increase to 17 per cent. The figures are slightly distorted owing to the low disbursement rate achieved for ABOS in recent years. This led to the relatively greater share of expenditure being reported as NGO income. It is expected that following the reforms initiated by *Kleur Bekennen* ('Showing Our Colours'), the disbursement rate will increase.

A 1992 study published by Coprogram found that 25 per cent of Dutch-speaking NGO revenues came from voluntary sources. Fourteen of the larger NGOs obtained less than 25 per cent of their income from non-governmental sources, while in smaller NGOs the range was between 40 and 60 per cent. Voluntary giving has been stable at around BF3000 million or $100 million. Excluding bilateral contracting and humanitarian assistance, Belgian NGOs therefore receive around about half of their funding from the government.

In 1996 about 2 per cent of the ABOS budget was channelled to emergencies, most of it via NGOs or as donations in kind.

Regulation of NGOs

Until the new arrangements came into force in January 1998, an NGO had to be recognised by government to be eligible for co-financing. In 1997, 145 NGOs were recognised. Recognition was awarded by ABOS and was based on criteria that demonstrated that an NGO was serious and well established. Once recognition had been awarded, an NGO could opt for project or programme funding and join one of the NGO federations. Under the new arrangements, an NGO may apply for co-financing providing that:

- it is a not-for-profit organisation;
- it has development cooperation as its main objective;
- it has useful experience, proven by annual reports of activity in relevant development cooperation;
- it has a five-year strategic plan;
- it is autonomous;
- it can ensure continuity;
- it has a majority of Belgian nationals on its Board of Management;
- it has transparent accounting.

Tax relief on donations is given to Belgians who give to organisations that have been through an accreditation system managed by the Ministry of Finance. NGOs regard this tax relief as a significant incentive for donors.

Development of relations with Southern NGOs

Micro-intervention funds are available from government to support the local initiatives of Southern NGOs and are administered by aid officials in the field. Limits are set on project size – BF300,000 in 1997 (about $10,000) – but overall allocations can be large. In the Congo DR, for instance, they reached BF50 million (about $1.6 million) in 1996–7.

In 1994, NGOs reported that funding to Southern NGOs via field offices or embassies was very small, although larger sums of counterpart funds generated by debt relief had been managed by Southern NGOs. This funding was not governed by an overall policy. At the time of writing, the University of Antwerp was undertaking research on direct funding in preparation for a new Belgian policy on the subject.

Volunteers

Government support for volunteer costs is available to approved NGOs that have at least three years of experience in technical assistance. They must be able to provide adequate support for the living and working conditions of their volunteers. Government approval for postings is based on a proposal that must be endorsed either by Coprogram or the French-speaking coalition on volunteers. In 1997 there were around 800 Belgian volunteers serving overseas.

The reform of development cooperation has included two changes where volunteers are concerned. One is in administration. Formerly ABOS undertook all the administrative work, from buying air tickets to the provision of insurance. Each individual volunteer had to be authorised by an official on behalf of the minister. From 1998 onward, however, NGO federations are responsible. The French-speaking sector responded to this with a detailed proposal for the central coordination of volunteers, and at the end of 1997 was in discussion with Dutch-speaking NGOs about a shared database.

The other change is more conceptual. Now, North–South personnel (volunteers) and South–North personnel (scholarships) are to be combined into one human resource-based programme. At the time of writing, the implications of this were not clear, but it is part of a pattern giving non-governmental actors, including universities, more responsibility for achieving the goals of Belgian development cooperation.

NGO evaluation

The 1991 Royal Decrees on NGO–government relations set out provisions for annual joint evaluations. In the second half of the 1990s, these became standard procedure, operating in addition to NGO and government evaluations. Joint evaluations tend to address themes, groups or countries, and implementation by groups of NGOs.

The first of these studies, 'Credit, creditable NGOs; Summary report of a joint ACGD–NGO evaluation of credit systems for economic activities in rural areas', was conducted by South Research in 1995. It found disappointing results, particularly in terms of financial and institutional sustainability, notwithstanding the increase in income of participants. Reasons for failure included lack of skills in running the programme, poor management among implementation agencies, and over-high expectations of achievement.[3] This challenging evaluation led to serious discussion and recommendations for change. On the whole, however, evaluation is seen as a technical exercise, divorced from the process of project implementation or policy development.

Some people perceive a change in NGO culture in relation to evaluation: a greater willingness to be involved, to share information and ideas on strategy and policy, and in some areas to work to a common strategy as was the case in Rwanda and the Congo DR.

In 1996, proposals were made for *ex post facto* evaluation of NGO projects, but only BF50 million was set aside for planning and evaluation by external experts. NGOs expressed doubt that this input would be enough to enable systematic evaluation by ABOS. The big change, however, is in the management of evaluation within ABOS itself, and in the regulations for programme funding. First, 1 per cent of programme funding must be set aside for evaluation costs by the NGO. Second, the ABOS NGO Division will undertake regular monitoring of NGO programmes in order to assess the degree to which programme outputs are consistent with proposals. Third, and most significant, the ABOS Evaluation Service is to become an independent unit. Its head can be appointed from the current ABOS staff, but it is a condition of employment that s/he cannot return to work within the administration, thus encouraging objectivity. Reports will go to the

Parliamentary Committee and will cover activities under both the bilateral budget and the NGO programmes. It will be primarily geographic and thematic, rather than project-based.

Clearly the ability to communicate and learn from evaluation depends on context. If an atmosphere of trust and openness can be developed between NGOs and ABOS, then the scope for substantive discussion will increase.

Issues

NGOs and public confidence

Development cooperation in Belgium has taken a serious war battering. Former Belgian colonies – Rwanda, Burundi and Congo DR – have seen genocide and corruption on the grandest scale. This has contributed to a fundamental undermining of public confidence in the role of development cooperation. At the same time Belgian aid has been beset by a number of failures and scandals which have been exhaustively publicized in the Dutch-speaking media, particularly through the dogged activities of journalist Douglas de Coninck in the Dutch language daily, *De Morgen*.[4]

The outcome can be seen in opinion polls conducted by Eurobarometer. While the way in which polling questions are asked leads almost inevitably to an overstatement of public commitment to development cooperation, Belgian public confidence was the lowest in Europe. Fifty one per cent of the Belgian public support more development assistance – compared with 67 per cent as an average in the EU. Seventy two per cent of Belgians think aid is important, compared with an EU average of 87 per cent, and suspicion about the misuse of aid money is stronger in Belgium than in any other EU member state, with one out of every two Belgians doubting the accuracy of information provided. This finding is similar to the results of a 1993 questionnaire that looked at changes in attitude over the past decade. In 1984, the causes of underdevelopment tended to be attributed to poverty, lack of education and international forces. By 1993, corruption and weak capacity in the leaders of developing countries were considered more important. Some NGOs believe, however, that the scandals did not have much effect on already meagre public support.

The controversies were investigated by a Parliamentary Committee, which demanded more transparency and a new culture of evaluation. In addition, the major changes discussed above aim to improve the overall approach to development cooperation and its management.

NGOs have not been immune from the drop in public confidence, but the effect on them has been fairly small. In the French-speaking sector, the crises failed to make the news. Dutch-speaking NGOs did detect some fall in unsolicited donations, but it has not lasted and humanitarian agencies have been wholly exempt. Some commentators see this as a reflection of a public attitude that regards structural change and long-term development as being too difficult, leaving humanitarian assistance as the only reasonable response to overseas need.

NGOs have been implicated in some of the criticism. A series of press articles questioned NGO activities; the Parliamentary Commission raised issues about NGO work, and three NGOs were audited to see whether funds had been spent in accordance with the declared purpose. The upshot of this has been a shift in attitude. NGOs are not given quite as much credibility as in the past, and are no longer seen as being above the fray. Assumptions of higher quality aid in the NGO sector are no longer automatic. None the less, NGOs retain strong parliamentary links, and their representation across a wide swathe of Belgian society – through churches, trades unions and social organisations – gives them a depth of public support that is denied to the official sector.

NGOs have dealt with an environment that is highly critical of aid by changing their own stance. Formerly critical, they have started providing a counterweight to the media's pursuit of scandal, and have attempted to provide a more balanced analysis. NCOS, the lead agency on advocacy, is perceived as constructive in this, and has offset some of the more extreme press comment.

Development education

NGO campaigns on development education suffer from the usual criticism that they are preaching to the choir and that they fail to stimulate real interest from new constituencies. Attitudes and approaches to development education differ in Flanders and Wallonie. The French-speaking NGO community is much more firmly anchored in small organisations and community groups. It also has to battle against greater public unwillingness to spend money on overseas aid, because of real pressure on basic services. In Flanders, there is a more professional style of development education that focuses more on global issues.

Development education has become a pillar of Belgian development cooperation policy, and the federal government has concluded conventions with the provinces for an education programme on *Kleur Bekennen*.[5] This has not been translated into financial resources, however. The budget for government initiatives in development education had by 1997 been frozen for several years at BF56 million ($1.8 million). Government support to NGOs was a further BF2.45 million. A simulation enabling people to get a taste of village life in a developing country, combined with workshops to help interpret the experience, was being staged in each province during 1997, funded by ABOS. In Brussels ABOS has also taken proactive steps, planning an International House for Education as a centre for organisations and as a focus for North–South relations.

NGOs and the community governments

In development education there is a relationship between NGOs and the community governments of Wallonie and Flanders – arising from community government responsibility for education, and from the fact that the social organisations in each community differ.

Further decentralisation of development cooperation to the community governments is a concern for many NGOs, who fear that decentralisation could marginalize them from international issues and limit their capacity to bring Southern interests to the attention of decision-makers at the federal level. For the community governments however, it would have the advantage of adding to their portfolio of responsibilities.

Government-sponsored debate

At the time of writing in 1997, the government response to public concern about development cooperation centred on reform of the administration of Belgian aid. Earlier in the decade, however, when there was less talk of aid scandal and more focus on the disastrous situation in the Great Lakes – an area with strong historical links with Belgium and a major focus of the aid programme – the government and NGOs both reacted to and initiated public debate. At the end of 1994, Parliament held a major debate on Africa with good media coverage and support from NGOs advocating specific policies. With its stress on shared responsibility and on the importance of African countries leading their own development policies (with appropriate support from Belgium), the discussion reflected the character of the Development Goals outlined in *Shaping the 21st Century* – the objectives to which all OECD/DAC members agreed in 1996.

In general, however, government information campaigns are seen as outdated and uncritical. They are not useful ammunition for a ministry trying to defend itself against media attack or against pressure from business and other ministries.

Consultation and the role of the advocacy federations

There is some friction within and between the advocacy-based federations – seen both as umbrella bodies but also as competitors for programme funds with their members. CNCD has clear links to political parties and has found it more difficult to organise the French-speaking NGO sector on a pluralistic basis. In practice, because of the difficulty in the French-speaking sector in coming to consensus on policy, NCOS has become the main NGO interlocutor with government on policy. Its annual report on Belgian aid is influential and it has a number of significant Belgian NGOs among its members. It has, however, suffered from its own rapid growth and, in common with most NGOs, financial support has dropped. Some people attribute this to its visible engagement in the debates on Belgian development cooperation, and to its consequent association in the public mind with the complexities and failures of aid. NCOS also has problems with a very diverse membership. Building consensus on topics such as conditionality or military intervention is extremely difficult and makes it hard for NCOS to fulfil its role as principal interlocutor with the government.

Consultation between government and the NGO sector improved over the 1990s. In 1992, NGOs requested and were offered opportunities for consultation with government on debt relief. This led to an agreement with the commercial banks on private debt relief. NGO views on demographic issues have also been sought by the minister. Although this has been broadly welcomed, some NGOs have had reservations, fearing being coopted to the government position.

In 1996, government proposed the establishment of a foundation in order to begin a policy dialogue between government and NGOs on information and development education issues such as funding, responsibilities, initiatives and results. At the time of writing (late 1997), progress on the establishment of the foundation was being held up, partly because of discussions over whether development education should be a federal matter or one for the communities. In general, there is evidence that change is taking place and that mutual confidence is growing, based on trust between individuals in NGOs and government, rather than on institutional relationships.

6 Canada

Ian Smillie[1]

SUMMARY

Canadian NGOs vary in size from the very small, to a handful of very large organisations. About half of all fundraising is derived from child sponsorship appeals. Serious reductions in Canadian ODA have been the order of the day for several years, and were projected to continue through 1998–9. Proportional reductions have been passed on to Canadian NGOs.

The Canadian International Development Agency (CIDA) has a matching grant programme for NGOs and also makes funding available on a contractual basis through its bilateral programmes. Roughly 14 per cent of Canadian food aid and 12 per cent of CIDA's spending on emergencies in 1996 was channelled through Canadian NGOs. Evaluating the impact of NGOs is difficult, in part because measuring impact has not often been a priority, and because baseline data and monitoring information are weak or absent.

The dependency ratio of Canadian NGOs on CIDA varies dramatically. The overall ratio is about 47 per cent, but for some it is as high as 80 per cent. The overall ratio compares favourably with the Canadian domestic sector, where an estimated 56 per cent of all income is received from government. The quality of the international NGO dependency is changing, however. Government support began in the 1960s with a simple matching formula. CIDA's responsive programme has become more pro-active in deciding how money should be spent, and how recipients should organise themselves to do so. Changes in government support for development education have effectively muted much of the NGO voice. For several NGOs, the responsive mechanism is now the smaller part of their CIDA income representing, overall, only 50 per cent of governmental income for the largest. Contracts, overshadowed by a new competitive bidding process, are becoming the order of the day.

THE CANADIAN NGO COMMUNITY

Background

Canadian NGOs have their roots in 19th-century missionary movements and relief activities following the World Wars I and II. In the 1940s and 1950s, a number of relief and refugee agencies – often branches or offshoots of British and American organisations – were established. Among these were CARE Canada, Oxfam Canada, Save the Children and Foster Parents Plan.

The 1960s was a period of rapid expansion in the number of home-grown NGOs, a phenomenon encouraged in part by the establishment of a CIDA matching grant programme. A 1988 study estimated the number of Canadian NGOs at 220, although the number fluctuates according to the description that is used. In 1997, CIDA provided support to 275 NGOs, of which 33 were environmental organisations, and 50 were international NGOs based in Canada and elsewhere. Because CIDA provides funding to a broad range of other players in the non-governmental sector (labour unions, cooperatives, community colleges, universities), the number of organisations it deals with is estimated at approximately 400.

World Vision Canada is the largest NGO, with a total cash income in 1996 of more than C$89million (US$65 million), C$77 million of it derived from the public. Almost three quarters of Canadian NGOs are secular in nature, and one quarter – among them the largest NGOs – are branches or parts of larger US or European organisations. Although programming independence within these organisations has developed rapidly in recent years, their origins led to a slower development than in other countries of direct Canadian overseas programming expertise.

The Canadian Council for International Cooperation

CCIC is an umbrella council of approximately 100 Canadian NGOs, ranging from small development education centres to large institutions with a dozen or more overseas offices. CCIC has a core budget of approximately C$2 million, although in the 1980s and early 1990s, this was augmented by several million dollars in additional CIDA funds aimed at specific countries or thematic areas. The last of these CCIC-managed funds, an Indonesia–Canada Forum and a fund for projects in Haiti, were scheduled for conclusion in 1997–8. Like most Canadian NGOs, CCIC has been affected in recent years by heavy CIDA cutbacks, and in 1997 it instituted a 'summer layoff', closing the office entirely for three weeks in order to save money.

CCIC operates three policy-related working groups – one on the Americas, one on Asia and the Pacific, and one on the Horn of Africa. Much of CCIC's work in recent years has centred on efforts to protect the aid budget and to improve working relations between the NGO community and CIDA. CCIC officials have appeared before parliamentary committees and the organisation has worked to ensure that a focus on poverty eradication is maintained within government aid programmes, despite budget reductions. With the end of federal government budget deficits being predicted in 1997, CCIC's attention began to shift to the possibility of increasing ODA. In addition, CCIC initiated a 'Ten-Point Development Agenda for Poverty Eradication' in 1997. Topics of focus include reforming Canadian ODA, building ecological sustainability, enforcing human rights, and the promotion of gender equity. 'To be blunt', said the organisation's president, 'we have to become more politically engaged... it requires an across-the-board acknowledgement by each and every NGO that direct policy engagement with our elected officials is a *sine qua non* of our mandate as NGOs'.[2]

Training and learning have been a feature of CCIC activities in recent years. A six month 'learning circle' on micro-enterprise development, based on action research in the South, found that 'without minimizing the importance of credit... [it] is not a panacea for leading the most under-privileged out of poverty...In the absence of simultaneous progress in other areas such as primary education, health care, clean water and sanitation, basic infrastructures, and peace and security, microenterprise offers few sustained benefits for the poor'.[3]

CCIC developed an NGO Code of Ethics in 1995, and an Ethics Review Committee was established in 1997 to conduct an annual compliance review of all members, and to work on issues relating to the inclusion of minority groups within the Canadian NGO community. As a means of recognising good development work, learning from and publicising it, CCIC inaugurated International Cooperation Awards in 1996, awarding the first three to a Central America human rights monitoring group, a small development education initiative in Quebec and a project matching Canadian teachers' unions with counterparts in the South. The work of the three organisations and the 1997 and 1998 winners are described in bilingual 1997 and 1998 CCIC publications, *Profiling Development Practice: Innovation in Canadian International NGOs*.

Provincial councils

In the 1970s and 1980s, provincial councils of international cooperation were established by NGOs in the Atlantic provinces, Quebec, Ontario, and all of the western provinces. In some cases they were designed to attract or manage provincial government funds, particularly in Quebec and the western provinces. They also served as a local forum for development debate and development education in a large country where travel to national meetings can be prohibitively expensive. By the early 1990s, all of the provincial councils were receiving a significant proportion of their administrative and programming income from CIDA. Two types of CIDA cutback have severely damaged the capacity of these councils. The first was a 1995 cancellation of development education funding for organisations without overseas programmes. The second was the cancellation of decentralised funding arrangements. These are discussed in greater detail below. The net impact, however, was most severe for provincial councils and for some of the smaller development education organisations that they supported. In Manitoba, the staff of the council was reduced by more than 50 per cent. The IDEA development education centre closed immediately, and other development education efforts were seriously curtailed. In Saskatchewan, the Council cut its staff by more than two thirds, and two development education centres closed. In British Columbia, the council was reduced from five permanent staff to none.

FISCAL POLICY AND REGULATION OF THE CANADIAN NGO COMMUNITY

The legal incorporation of voluntary organisations is regulated through Part 2 of the Canada Corporations Act (administered by the Department of Consumer and Corporate Affairs), which deals with non-profit organisations. In addition, voluntary organisations may apply for charitable status to the Department of Revenue, which authorises the issuance of tax receipts. In 1997, new measures were introduced to increase the annual limit on charitable donations eligible for tax credits to 75 per cent of yearly income, up from 50 per cent. This was expected to cost the federal government about C$95 million (US$70 million), and to encourage an estimated C$200 million (US$147 million) in new donations to the charitable sector as a whole.

Eligibility for CIDA funding requires that an organisation be legally incorporated in Canada and accountable to a Canadian board of directors. It must also be non-governmental and non-profit, although charitable registration is not required. In addition to regular project information and reports, NGOs must provide CIDA with annually audited financial statements and must permit CIDA to inspect and examine financial records and accounts if required.

CANADIAN OFFICIAL DEVELOPMENT ASSISTANCE

Background

In 1994, the Government of Canada conducted a wide-ranging foreign policy review under the auspices of a Special Joint Parliamentary Committee. The committee held over 70 meetings, received more than 550 briefs from 500 witnesses across the country, and commissioned several expert studies. A comprehensive report was issued at the end of 1994, and a 'Government Statement', *Canada in the World*, was issued in 1995. This document outlines the government's overall approach to foreign policy, and includes a chapter on international assistance:

The purpose of Canada's ODA is to support sustainable development in developing countries, in order to reduce poverty and to contribute to a more secure, equitable and prosperous world.

To achieve this purpose, Canadian ODA was to concentrate on six programme priorities:

- basic human needs: including primary health care, basic education, family planning, nutrition, water and sanitation, and shelter. The government undertook to devote 25 per cent of ODA to basic human needs. Food aid, emergency and humanitarian assistance are included in this category.
- women in development;
- infrastructure services;
- human rights, democracy and good governance;
- private sector development: to promote sustained and equitable economic growth by supporting private sector development in developing countries;
- the environment.

Canada in the World also rededicated Canada to the 0.7 per cent of GNP ODA target: 'Recognizing the importance of ODA, the Government remains committed to improving its effectiveness and to making progress towards the ODA target of 0.7 per cent of GNP when Canada's fiscal situation allows it.'[4]

Serious reductions in ODA, however, have been the order of the day for several years. From an average of 0.45 per cent of GNP in the early 1990s, Canadian ODA fell to 0.32 per cent in 1996, its lowest point in 30 years. It was projected to fall still further through 1998–9, to less than 0.30 per cent.[5] The drop is more precipitous if the imputed costs for first-year Canadian government expenses for refugees from developing countries are removed from ODA totals after 1993–4, when they were first introduced.[6] The 1997 DAC Aid Review noted that 'the Government's intentions with regard to future funding levels… will be announced in early 1998 when the Minister of Finance tables the federal budget in Parliament. As the government has restored stability to its fiscal situation, this will be a critical moment for the future of Canada's ODA programme, and for Canada's valued international role'.[7] When the 'critical moment' arrived in February 1998, Canada had its first balanced budget in 30 years, but there were further ODA cuts. These were, however, not as deep as planned.[8]

The Secretary of State for Foreign Affairs has overall responsibility for Canadian foreign policy. With a brief exception in 1979, Canada did not have a cabinet minister responsible for development assistance until the election of a Progressive Conservative government in 1984. With the election of a Liberal government in 1993, the position was downgraded to non-cabinet rank and divided between two individuals with representative duties and no financial authority. A full Cabinet position was re-created in 1995, and over the next two years was held by three different individuals.

The Canadian International Development Agency

The Canadian International Development Agency is responsible for the management of approximately 75 per cent of Canada's development assistance budget. The Department of Finance manages Canadian relations with the international financial institutions and the Department of Foreign Affairs manages relations with about two dozen other multilateral organisations, including the World Health Organisation, the Organisation of American States and the Commonwealth Foundation.

CIDA is headed by a president and eight vice presidents, each of whom manage a branch of the agency. The Canadian Partnership Branch (CPB) is responsible for programmes with NGOs, business, and institutions (universities, colleges, and volunteer-sending organisations).

The budget for Canadian Partnership Branch in 1997–8 was C$258.5 million (US$190 million), a reduction of 8.5 per cent from the previous year, and a 25.3 per cent reduction since 1994–5. Funding for humanitarian assistance and food aid are the responsibility of separate CIDA branches, although operational management of some of the funds provided to NGOs by these branches is handled by the NGO Division.

GOVERNMENT SUPPORT TO NGOS: CANADIAN PARTNERSHIP BRANCH

Background

CIDA's Canadian Partnership Branch (CPB) 'seeks to foster sustainable development in developing countries by encouraging and supporting the establishment of ties between partners in these countries and Canadian for-profit or non-profit organisations'. To this end, CPB has articulated several objectives. Among them:

- capacity building in developing countries: to strengthen the capacity of Southern organisations and institutions to make a significant and sustainable development impact among disadvantaged communities;
- support for Canada's official development assistance priorities (as stated above);
- leverage: to invest CPB resources where they will have the greatest strategic impact;
- benefits to Canada and engagement of the Canadian public: to provide opportunities for Canadians to better understand development challenges and become involved with development activities;
- good governance and sound project management and administration among the organisations that CIDA supports.[9]

Contributions to NGOs: the 'Responsive Program'

Like most official development agencies, CIDA originally funded NGOs on a project-by-project basis, but by the early 1980s the agency was moving towards multi-year programme grants for larger organisations. CIDA's proportion of a project or programme varies. For professional and membership associations, the CIDA contribution may not exceed 80 per cent of all Canadian resources. For programme NGOs, cooperatives and colleges the amount is 75 per cent. For universities and trade unions it is 70 per cent. Volunteer-sending agencies are capped at 67 per cent, but in-kind contributions can make up to 90 per cent of the organisation's total. For one-off projects, the total is 67 per cent (a two-to-one match). In addition, there is a capping mechanism that prevents a single NGO from taking more than 10 per cent of the overall CIDA allocation for NGOs. Although it is rarely invoked, the Canadian Catholic Organisation for Development and Peace (CCODP) reached this ceiling in 1997.

Following experiments in the 1980s, a decision was made in the early 1990s to devolve the funding of smaller NGOs to regional funding bodies, often a coalition of NGOs or a provincial NGO council. The aim was to reduce bureaucracy and the amount of time required to process small grant applications, both for CIDA and for applicants. The system was in place for less than two years, however, when a ministerial decision reversed the direction, recentralising all funding in CIDA headquarters.

CIDA handled this, in part, by expanding the number of organisations receiving multi-year programme contributions. There were 59 of these in 1996–7, with annual allocations ranging from C$121,000 to C$8.8 million. New mechanisms were put in place to reintroduce project-by-project funding for smaller NGOs (see below), but a number of special umbrella funding bodies were caught without a home in the changed policy environment. Partnership Africa–Canada, for example, which assisted African NGOs and African umbrella bodies, and the South Asia Partnership which did the same in South Asia, lost virtually all their CPB funding and survived, either as shadows of what they once were, or by seeking funds from bilateral programmes within CIDA.

In 1992 CIDA began developing NGO institutional assessment criteria in order to allocate funding. The criteria cover management and governance, national identity, fundraising, constituency development, development education, the NGO's policy role, its relevance to overall CIDA objectives, and its programme impact. It was intended that CIDA's 'cost-sharing' of NGO projects would then be determined according to these criteria, rather than solely on annual increments related to the historical relationship. The criteria were used in 1995 and 1996, and even though CIDA's overall support to NGOs was being reduced because of budget constraints, some NGOs actually received increases, based on CIDA's assessment of quality. Despite CIDA's desire to continue with the approach, a ministerial decision returned the agency to across-the-board reductions in 1997.[10]

In order to deal with the many small organisations that had been farmed out to regional funds in the early 1990s, CIDA created an 'NGO Project Facility'. This is open to Canadian NGOs with a minimum of two years' experience in overseas development activity. CIDA will not consider applications of less than C$25,000, and the upper limit for a CIDA contribution to a single organisation under this facility is C$350,000 in a given year. One third of the cash costs must be met by the NGO, although for an organisation with an annual budget of less than C$50,000, as much as 25 per cent of the organisation's contribution may be in-kind donations. As of December 1996, CIDA had allocated C$12.7 million through the NGO Project Facility.

As with other CPB mechanisms, funding will not be provided for child sponsorship, humanitarian and emergency relief (which is funded from another branch; see below), fundraising and other self-promotion, political advocacy in Canada and abroad, or the promotion of religious beliefs.

Universities, professional and membership associations

In the 1970s, CIDA began to provide support to a category of non-governmental institution that in many OECD member countries does not have ready access to ODA support. This includes professional institutions, trade unions, cooperatives, community colleges and universities. Among the professional institutions receiving support are the Federation of Canadian Municipalities, the Canadian Bar Association, the Canadian Nurses Association and the Canadian International Immunisation Program, operated by the Canadian Public Health Association. In recent years, several trade unions have begun to raise funds from their membership for international activities, and these have become eligible for matching CIDA support.

Unlike most OECD member countries, CIDA also makes grant funds available from its Canadian Partnership Branch to Canadian universities and community colleges. In 1996–7, these institutions received C$32.4 million (US$23.8 million), a drop of 12 per cent over four years.

Volunteer programmes

Canada has an unusually large number of volunteer-sending NGOs. From CIDA's perspective, there are five major organisations (Cuso, World University Service of Canada – WUSC, Oxfam Québec,[11] Canadian Executive Service Organisation (CESO), Centre Canadien d'étude et de coopération internationale (CECI)) and five smaller ones. For most of the larger organisations, volunteer placements are not the sole preoccupation, several having diversified into project support as well. In addition, personnel placement on volunteer-like terms and conditions plays a large part in the work of several other organisations. The Canadian branch of the Mennonite Central Committee, for example, had 98 volunteers serving overseas in mid 1997 (13 of them in the 18–24 age group), compared with about 200 serving with CECI, 100 with WUSC, and 240 with CUSO.

There is an eleventh organisation, the British volunteer-sending organisation, VSO, which began operations in Canada in 1994, and which, by mid 1997, was said to be the third largest volunteer sender, with approximately 140 Canadian personnel serving overseas. Although increasingly Canadian, it received no CIDA support. In 1993–4, CIDA allocated C$48.7 million to ten volunteer-sending organisations; by 1995–6 this had fallen by 8.7 per cent to C$42.8 million.

These organisations consume a relatively large portion of the overall funding available for NGOs, and remain exempt from the matching requirements that apply to other organisations, in part because raising funds for high-cost volunteer programmes is very difficult. In 1995, WUSC raised approximately C$775,000 from the Canadian public, less than 5 per cent of its total cash income. It maintained a degree of financial independence from CIDA, however, by raising offshore contributions amounting to 35 per cent of its income from, for example, the governments of Botswana, China and Indonesia. In 1996, CECI raised C$613,000 from the Canadian public against a cash income of C$31.1 million (about 2 per cent of the total) although approximately 38 per cent of its cash income was derived from non-CIDA sources.[12]

International NGOs

CIDA provides support to some 50 international NGOs, of which approximately 20 are based in Canada. These include the International Council for Adult Education and the International Council on Social Welfare. CIDA-supported international NGOs based elsewhere include the International Ocean Institute, the Society for International Development, Women's World Banking and the Population Council. Disbursements in 1996–7 for international NGOs totalled C$10 million (US$7.3 million), down from C$20.2 million in 1994–5.

FOOD AID

Along with other cuts to Canada's ODA, food aid has been dramatically curtailed in recent years, falling from a value of C$400 million in 1991–2, to an estimated C$260 million (US$191 million) in 1995–6. In the mid 1980s, most Canadian food aid was channelled through multilateral institutions or was handled on a bilateral basis. Today, a significant proportion is programmed by the NGO community. This occurs in one of four ways:

1   Through direct food aid grants to NGOs. This is a relatively small proportion of the overall food aid programme, representing about 12 per cent of all food aid in 1991–2, and 14 per cent in 1996–7. More than half of this is channelled through the Canada Food Grains Bank, a consortium of 12 Church-based NGOs that raise an additional support in cash and grain, mainly from prairie farmers.
2   Through bilateral country programmes. NGOs are used as executing agencies by CIDA, in both development and emergency situations.
3   Through multilateral agencies. Canada allocates roughly half its food aid to the World Food Programme. In emergency situations where governments have limited capacity, a multilateral agency such as WFP will subcontract the delivery of food to NGOs. These NGOs may or may not be Canadian.
4   Through special monetized food aid initiatives. For example CARE in Bangladesh has operated a large rural road maintenance programme for several years. The wages of about 39,000 women are paid from local currency generated from the sale of Canadian wheat. This project is somewhat unusual in size and scope, but represents a food value of roughly C$13 million annually.

Although the nominal value of CIDA food aid being channelled through NGOs is small, unofficial estimates place the net value at something between 30 per cent and 50 per cent of the total.

NON-FOOD EMERGENCY ASSISTANCE

In the late 1980s and early 1990s, CIDA expenditure on humanitarian assistance grew dramatically, to a 1992–3 high of C$118 million. Amounts remained relatively static through 1994–5, and then dropped in 1995–6 to C$86 million, a reduction of 27 per cent. Of the total, C$2 million was allocated to the International Committee of the Red Cross, and C$25 million was allocated to UNHCR.

Of the balance, an estimated 10–12 per cent is channelled through Canadian NGOs. Consideration is given to the 'Canadian content' of any proposed NGO programme, and to the options available. In some emergency situations, funding may be channelled primarily through NGOs; in others it could be mainly a UN operation. In a given year, no more than a dozen NGOs receive funding, with the largest amounts being channelled through CARE Canada, World Vision and *Médecins sans Frontières*. Lesser amounts have been made available to Inter Church Action, Adventist Development and Relief Agency–Canada (ADRA), Oxfam Québec and Oxfam Canada. As with food aid, however, some of the funds channelled multilaterally through UNHCR would inevitably find their way to NGOs, though not necessarily Canadian NGOs.

BILATERAL/COUNTRY PROGRAMMES

In the early 1980s, CIDA made a decision that the choice of delivery channel for aid in a given country should be based upon the objectives of the programme. If CIDA was involved in, say, the transportation sector, it would likely depend heavily on Canadian private sector firms for the supply of equipment and the management of programmes. If it was involved in poverty alleviation and human resource development, NGOs might be the most appropriate programming channel.

The approach was called 'country focus', and it opened a number of new opportunities for NGOs with programming and management capacities. Technically, it meant that CIDA would approach an NGO to become a sole-source executing agency on a particular project. In actual fact, however, NGOs approached CIDA country desks with proposals of their own that fitted within CIDA's aims and objectives. For several years, this proved to be the most common way for NGOs to gain access to bilateral funds. A 1993 survey of CARE Canada, the Canadian Organisation for Development through Education (CODE), OCSD (now part of Oxfam Québec), Inter Pares and the Aga Khan Foundation Canada found 20 'country focus' projects in force, all of which had been initiated by the NGOs.

There were always concerns about the country focus model. NGOs complained that there was no consistency of approach, planning, reporting or evaluation among CIDA country programmes. CIDA's acceptance and administration of one project might run very smoothly, while another might be in constant difficulty. CIDA knowledge and understanding of NGOs and of grass-roots development was, in the NGO view, patchy. In CIDA's view, NGO delivery and administrative capacities were uneven. CIDA was forced on more than one occasion to help an NGO that had become over-extended on a country focus project. The private sector also voiced concerns about unfair competition from NGOs that did not pay taxes and were already subsidized by CIDA through matching grants and other arrangements.

Essentially the debate had three strands. First, who should initiate bilateral programmes, CIDA or outsiders? Second, were the sole-source country focus contracts providing CIDA with the best value for money, regardless of whether they went to NGOs or the private sector? Third, was the non-profit sector crowding out the private sector?

On the last question, a CIDA review found that in 1994–5, the non-profit sector took 63 per cent of all bilateral service contracts, essentially indicating that the private sector was, indeed, being crowded out. The figures, however, were somewhat disingenuous, as the definition of 'non-profit' included multilateral agencies, colleges, universities, cooperatives and crown corporations. Some NGOs believed that the calculations were deliberately presented in a way that would put them in bad odour with a minister who was strongly oriented towards the private sector. In fact the NGO share of 'country focus' commitments had declined from 91 per cent of the total in 1983–4 to 27 per cent in 1994–5.[13]

The conclusion of the CIDA review helped to answer the second question about value for money. A decision was made to allow open competition between non-profit organisations and the private sector over a 15-month experimental period between 1997 and 1998. In order to make the playing field as level as possible between the business sector and non-profits, it was decided that the cost component of any bid would not count for more than 20 per cent of the total number of points allocated in a competition. A much reduced sole-source option would remain available, and would be open to the private sector as well, levelling the playing field further.

It is uncertain what this change will mean. A handful of NGOs have welcomed it. For most it will make little difference to their relationship with CIDA. Some of those that benefited from the country focus mechanism will lose out because the possibility of making their own proposals to CIDA will be severely reduced. In essence, the new approach also answers the question about where most bilateral programmes are expected in future to originate: within CIDA.

Allocations for Canadian NGOs from bilateral programmes in 1996–7 were C$49.5 million. Twenty-two organisations had bilateral contracts, with more than half of the total going to three – CECI, CARE and the Aga Khan Foundation Canada.

DEVELOPMENT EDUCATION

The development education work of Canadian NGOs was supported by CIDA through a matching grant programme known as the Public Participation Program. By 1995, CIDA was disbursing C$11 million to approximately 100 organisations for development education work, making Canada one of the largest supporters of development education in the OECD. CIDA's development education budget was, for example, about ten times higher than that of USAID – in actual rather than relative terms.

There were always doubts about development education, however – its heavy reliance on government support, worries about effectiveness, quality and the problem of talking to the converted. In 1995, the Minister of Foreign Affairs cancelled the programme without warning or debate. It was decided that henceforth, learner centres and others focusing exclusively on development education would no longer be eligible for CIDA support, and many of these quickly folded their tents and disappeared. CIDA stopped using the expressions 'development education' and 'public participation', and adopted a new term, 'public engagement'. 'Public engagement is based on the idea of global citizenship, a broader concept that CIDA encourages Canadian NGOs and their constituents to adopt.'[14]

While cutting off a fragile domestic development education network, CIDA encouraged NGOs with overseas programmes to become more active in the field, and announced that they could use up to 10 per cent of their CIDA allocation for public engagement if they saw fit. A description of eligible and ineligible themes and activities was drawn up and circulated.

The decision removed C$11 million from the CIDA pool and seriously damaged a number of existing organisations, but theoretically it opened up a wider window of opportunity for larger NGOs to become more active in the field of development education. Many of them, however, have not traditionally been very active in development education. In addition, most have – along with CIDA – been cut back. To expect that they might then add an entirely new development education effort and fund it out of on-going programme obligations was probably unrealistic.

At the time of writing (January 1998), it was unclear whether many NGOs were taking advantage of the new possibility for development education, or whether the general programming cutbacks would relegate development education to a lower priority than in the past.

Table 6.1: *Amount of Canadian ODA Channelled through NGOs*[15]
(millions of Canadian dollars)

Year	Bilateral Aid through NGOs	% of Total Bilateral	Responsive Support to NGOs	Total Support to NGOs	% of Total ODA
1984–5	24.8	2.8%	121.0	145.8	6.9%
1991–2	91.3	8.2%	200.4	291.7	9.2%
1995–6	96.1	11.2%	165.4	261.5	10.8%

ISSUES

Evaluation

In 1997, in conjunction with a wider OECD/DAC study,[16] CIDA commissioned a review of Canadian NGOs and evaluation.[17] The purpose was to analyse and report 'on the extent and quality of evaluations conducted on the activities of Canadian NGOs, to provide an assessment of the impact of NGO development interventions, and an assessment of evaluation methods and approaches used'. The focus was on larger Canadian NGOs, but a number of smaller organisations were included for reference. The study discussed four broad sets of evaluative material on NGOs:

- institutional assessments carried out by CIDA's Canadian Partnership Branch (CPB);
- evaluations of CIDA bilateral projects managed by NGOs;
- CIDA corporate reviews;
- evaluations carried out by Canadian NGOs and/or their overseas partners.

'The report began with a discussion of the evolution of institutional assessments carried out by CIDA's Partnership Branch. By 1994, the Branch policy on evaluation was articulated as follows:
An institutional assessment will be defined as a broad review of the financial, managerial and technical capacities of an institution or organisation funded by CIDA in collaboration with the organisation being assessed and based on terms of reference established jointly between CIDA and the organisation... The main thrust of these institutional assessments should, therefore, be to assess: 1) financial, technical and managerial capability to achieve the desired results; 2) relationship with their partners in developing countries, including the latters' overall performance and 3) actual observable results'.
This represented a gradual shift over the previous decade, away from interest in a Canadian NGO's development impact, and was based on the idea that the Partnership Branch mandate was to promote *partnerships* for development rather than development itself. The policy went on to state that 'CPB is accountable for ensuring the eligibility of the organisations receiving support. It is also accountable for assessing the financial, managerial and technical capacities of partner organisations. CPB is not accountable for the realisation of individual projects and programmes developed and implemented by these partners'.
A 1991 corporate review found that the impact of NGO programming was generally positive, but the report was imprecise. The most recent review of the NGO evaluation function within CIDA was completed in 1997. This is a considerably more sobering report than others. It noted that CIDA's NGO Division completed 89 institutional evaluations with 50 organisations between 1989 and 1996 at a cost of C$4.7 million – about C$50,000 each on average. Although they present a great deal of information on the management of each organisation, they provide little, if any, information on programming issues in general, or on results in particular. This would not be problematic if NGOs themselves were focusing on results. Many recent reviews suggest, however, that this is not the case. Most assessments focus mainly on institutional issues – as is

their purpose. While almost all include some field visits and do attempt to address questions of programme delivery, the effort is usually cursory. Findings are based on anecdotal evidence, brief (if any) site visits, and informal discussions with project participants and managers, rather than an examination of data that might reveal solid indicators of impact. Comments abound in virtually all the reports about vague objectives, lack of baseline data and weak reporting. In short, institutional assessments do not focus on the achievement of results, and this function is not being adequately addressed by NGOs themselves.

Over the past decade or more, some Canadian NGOs have served as executing agencies for projects managed by CIDA's bilateral programmes. A significant proportion of these projects have been evaluated, and the findings tend to be more impact-related than those in institutional assessments. In addition, corporate reviews of food aid programmes and the role of NGOs in CIDA's human rights and democratic development projects also reveal deeper insight into NGO effectiveness and impact.

NGOs themselves were asked if they carried out their own evaluations and if there were distinct or important features in the way these are done. Several provided examples of independent evaluations, manuals and methodologies that had been developed by themselves or by another member of their wider international organisation. These were often thoughtful and innovative, and were no less critical of weaknesses than any other evaluations. Such examples notwithstanding, the comments in CIDA's institutional assessments about lack of adequate monitoring and evaluation were borne out by the lack of *any* evaluative material from many of the NGOs surveyed. What was available was often patchy, and with a few exceptions, it is evident that evaluation is not a systemic part of the Canadian NGO culture.

There are both cost and professional reasons for the paucity of NGO impact evaluation, including the difficulty of assessing social development and some of its components, such as empowerment and participation. Social development can be more a process than an end in itself, further complicating measurement. These problems notwithstanding, there is evidence in the available impact evaluations that Canadian NGOs can be effective and efficient development organisations, that they can create and maintain effective partnerships with organisations in developing countries, that they can develop and manage effective and sustainable *technical* programmes and projects, that they can be important and effective in the delivery and management of food aid, and that they can play an important role in issues of human rights and democratic development. Ways *have* been found to evaluate and measure a wide range of activities, processes and social change projects.

The evidence for generic conclusions on Canadian NGO impact, however, is uneven. Institutional assessments have become lengthy and often contentious affairs, with CIDA officers and NGOs sometimes engaged in lengthy debate over terms of reference, selection of evaluators and the drafting of final conclusions. The process is unwieldy, the timing can be erratic, and there is a fairly high degree of dissatisfaction within CIDA and the NGO community, and among evaluators, with both the process and the results. Most importantly, however, institutional assessments provide little assurance apart from indirect evidence, that good development is actually taking place.

Overall, evidence of NGO impact is sketchy, in part because 'impact' has not often been a priority in evaluation, and because baseline data and monitoring information are weak or absent. Cross-cutting issues such as poverty reduction, environmental impact or gender have rarely been addressed outside CIDA's own corporate reviews, and these tend to be infrequent and sometimes subjective.

The report concluded by saying that government priorities were not inimical to good development or to the work of NGOs. Government *should* be assured that its contributions are being spent effectively and efficiently. CIDA's emphasis on institutional management, however, may be pushing NGOs away from these concepts, and away from their own strengths, values and constituencies in the process, to an emphasis on good management rather than development *results*. Stressing the verification function of evaluation is not likely to foster learning and knowledge, and it could do the opposite.

An entitlement mentality

CIDA's lack of knowledge about the quality of an NGO's programming has created what some observers call 'an entitlement mentality'. Unless a major problem arises, each NGO receives more or less what it received the year before, with adjustments for decreases or increments in CIDA's own income. The historical relationship is what counts most, making it difficult for newcomers to become serious players unless they have political connections. This makes good NGOs as well as weak NGOs defenceless in the face of across-the-board cuts and it discourages (or at least does not reward) excellence in programming.

The permission that was given early in 1997 for NGOs to compete openly against each other and against the private sector through the government's Open Bidding System may change this somewhat. But only the largest NGOs will have the ability to compete for large contracts, and many – large or otherwise – will not be interested. Those primarily concerned with their own programmes rather than those of CIDA, may find themselves increasingly relegated to a backwater of diminishing resources and across-the-board cuts that bear no relationship to the quality of their overseas programming.

An unbalanced NGO community

This historical and philosophical problem has helped to create an unbalanced NGO community. Table 6.2 ranks Canadian NGOs by size. This ranking is misleading for a number of reasons. First, many of the annual reports of NGOs do not present a clear or consistent picture. The most distorting factor has to do with in-kind contributions. The largest in-kind amount registered in 1996 was for CARE Canada. Much of this was counterpart funds, derived from the sale of Canadian food grain by the government of Bangladesh and paid directly by the government to beneficiaries working in CARE projects. Christian Children's Fund of Canada recorded the next highest amount, described by their auditors as 'donated goods, which include such items as used clothing, grain, medical supplies, baby food, agricultural supplies and seeds... reflected as revenue and expensed at their assessed values when shipped'. How these values are assessed in CCFC or any other organisation is not usually explained.

As a category, the most uncertain values assigned to in-kind costs are those among the volunteer-sending organisations. The five on this list report in-kind contributions of C$28.33 million. In Canada, as in other countries, the imputed value of foregone volunteer salaries is accepted as a valid in-kind contribution, although few organisations explain how this amount is calculated. In short, in-kind contributions for Canadian NGOs are reported in a highly inconsistent and ad hoc manner, and reveal very little about an organisation's real size or income.

If the 17 organisations listed opposite were ranked according to public fundraising, the order would change dramatically, with the exception of World Vision, Foster Parents Plan and the Aga Khan Foundation Canada. If they were ranked by CIDA income, the ordering again changes dramatically.

Figures in CCIC's *Who's Who in International Development* show that Canadian NGOs raised an estimated C$275 million (US$200 million) from the Canadian public in 1995. Assuming this amount to be more or less the same in 1996, the 17 largest NGOs listed here raised about 73 per cent of the total. The remaining 27 per cent is therefore being raised by an estimated 200 organisations. Half of all Canadian fundraising accrues to the four largest child sponsorship organisations, World Vision, Foster Parents Plan, Christian Children Fund and Canadian Feed the Children. World Vision alone raises 28 per cent of all donations for international work in Canada.

Where cash is concerned, the 'matching' concept provides little in the way of explanation for CIDA's contributions to NGOs. Among the 17 largest organisations, CIDA's Partnership Branch provided an average of one dollar against each C$3.34 raised from the public – a match of roughly one to three. The four child sponsorship organisations, however, raised C$28.75 for each CPB dollar received, a 'match' of one to 28. Volunteer-sending organisations had a ratio of one CIDA dollar for every 21¢ raised, but the ratio reaches almost 10:1, or $1 for every 11¢ when the two largest fundraisers are removed from the calculation.

The dependency ratio of Canadian NGOs on CIDA, therefore, varies dramatically. Using the numbers in Table 6.2, below, total CIDA support for NGOs in 1996–7 was C$138.3 million, and NGOs themselves raised an estimated C$300 million from the Canadian public. The dependency ratio overall, therefore, was about 47 per cent. For CUSO, however, it was 78 per cent (excluding in-kind contributions), for CECI it was 65 per cent, and for World Vision it was 18 per cent.

Are Canada's international development NGOs more financially dependent on government than domestic NGOs? A 1980 study of domestic voluntary organisations found that in the fields of education and welfare, government support averaged 93 per cent. In health care, the figure was 80 per cent and in culture, broadly defined to include recreation, religion and the arts, the

Table 6.2: *Largest Canadian NGOs Ranked by Total Income 1996 (C$ million)*

Organisation	Public	In Kind	Other	CIDA Total	CPB	Other	Total
1. CARE	3.74	21.7	3.06	9.62	12.68	56.5	96.75
2. World Vision	77.10	7.20	1.81	13.97	15.79	0.75	96.31
3. Foster Parents Plan	32.52	0	2.91	0	2.91	1.17	36.60
4. Aga Khan Fdn Canada (95)	12.39	8.85	2.59	8.15	10.73	2.03	36.06
5. CECI	0.61	4.92	6.85	13.84	20.68	10.71	36.04
6. Christian Children's Fund	10.80	16.52	0	0	0	28.14	
7. CUSO	4.00	4.90	14.00	0.18	14.18	0.50	23.90
8. MCC	7.36	9.80	1.94	0	1.94	3.00	23.37
9. Cdn Feed the Children (95)	6.29	15.51	0	0	0	22.23	
10. CESO	1.98	10.23	3.00	1.997	4.96	1.51	19.90
11. CCODP	9.23	9.34	.33	9.66	1.65	18.68	
12. UNICEF Canada	12.48	2.88	15.12	18.00	1.51	18.62	
13. WUSC	0.57	2.94	4.04	2.88	6.92	7.38	17.98
14. Oxfam Québec (95)	0.93	5.28	0.63	5.91	8.74	16.37	
15. Canada World Youth	0.46	5.24	7.48	1.35	8.83	0.94	16.17
16. Oxfam Canada	5.03	3.36	1.92	5.28	1.60	12.48	
17. United Church	6.48	1.06	0	1.06	1.81	9.34	

Sources: Oxfam Québec figures are from CCIC's Who's Who in International Development. With the exception of CIDA figures, all others (unless otherwise noted) are taken from the 1996 annual reports of each NGO. CIDA figures represent 1995–6 disbursements and were supplied by CIDA. Because financial years and reporting practices differ, the totals are those shown in an NGO's Annual Report, and are not a total of the figures in each row.

figure was slightly over 50 per cent.[18] More recent studies show that donations of all types, corporate, foundation and individual, represent a relatively small proportion of the overall income of Canadian charities. Roughly 56 per cent of the income of all Canadian charitable organisations is received from government, and 84 per cent of this comes from provincial governments. In short, international development NGOs are on average, considerably less dependent on government than their domestic counterparts.[19]

The quantitative dependency of international NGOs on government may be no higher than other parts of the charitable scene in Canada, but the quality of the dependency is changing. Government support began in the 1960s with a simple matching formula. It moved through various stages over the years to a point where CIDA's 'responsive' programme has now become more pro-active in deciding how money should be spent, and how those who spend it should organise themselves to do so. Changes in government support for development education have effectively muted much of the NGO voice. For several of the largest Canadian NGOs, the 'responsive' mechanism is now the smaller part of their CIDA income. For the 17 largest NGOs as a whole, it represented only 50 per cent of their governmental income in 1996 and 1997. Contracts, overshadowed by a new competitive bidding process, are becoming the order of the day, and may become even more important over time.

Longtime Canadian NGO worker, Brian Murphy makes a point and issues a plea:

> *The role of Canadian NGOs in the Third World is a very limited role, essentially to accompany our counterparts in their own struggles to bring about lasting change. This means providing funds, when it helps and can be given freely. More important is our solidarity and friendship, our political protection and the visibility of our solidarity. Probably most important is our role and obligation to learn, and to honour that learning in our activity in Canada. Of all this, providing funds is the easiest, the most lucrative for ourselves, and the least important. In our work in Latin America, Africa, Asia, we do not give only. We receive. That is why we love the places we have worked, and why we love to return there. It is in Canada that we must give, to honour what we have received... The work in Canada should include vigilance, advocacy and education. We should be promoting justice and human rights, not aid... The future for Canadian NGOs is political and economic activism in Canada for profound social change. And our relevance and credibility ten years from now will depend upon how we meet this challenge.[20]*

7 Denmark

Judith Randel and Tony German[1]

SUMMARY

The Danish NGO community is regarded as an important part of the resource base upon which Danish development assistance is based. Danish NGO work overseas has its origins in missionary efforts and in post-war relief and rehabilitation. Prominent concerns of Danish society – labour rights, international friendship, the Church, children's rights and fair trade – are clearly reflected in the NGO community today.

NGOs helped shape the beginnings of Danish ODA, and along with business and the academic community, they continue to have an input into aid strategy. The Danish aid programme – with its high volume and its strong poverty orientation, thus reflects a degree of consensus – not only within the aid community itself – but also, according to opinion polls, among the broader Danish public.

In 1987 a decision was made by government to increase NGO involvement in the delivery of Danish aid, and NGOs now deliver about one sixth of Danish bilateral assistance. The growth in funding has been accompanied by a rise in the expectations placed on NGOs (by DANIDA, the arm of the Danish Foreign Ministry that manages development cooperation, and by NGOs themselves) and by a greater emphasis on professionalism.

The generous funding of overseas projects by DANIDA (up to 100 per cent funding is available) means that official funding forms over 90 per cent of the income of some of Denmark's largest NGOs. While NGO advocacy does not appear to be inhibited by this level of financial dependency, some observers question whether the accompanying professionalism might distance NGOs from their grassroots both at home and overseas.

BACKGROUND

The origins of Danish NGO development activity can be traced back to the work of missionary and relief organisations in the 19th century, and to post-war humanitarian assistance in Europe following World War II. Danchurchaid for example, 75 years old in 1997, expanded beyond Europe in the late 1940s and early 1950s. The 110-year-old Danish Red Cross began working in developing countries in the early 1960s and *Mellemfolkeligt Samvirke* (MS), the Danish Association for International Cooperation – founded in 1944 and focused initially in Europe and the Middle East – had by the 1960s begun to work in India and Africa.

THE SIZE OF THE DANISH NGO COMMUNITY

A detailed 1988 survey of development NGOs found 194 organisations based in Denmark, of which 137 were Danish.[2] These NGOs represented 300,000 members (6 per cent of the population), but their members were unevenly distributed, with a small number of NGOs having a large membership and two-thirds having fewer than 500 members each. In 1996, 191 NGOs were listed under Denmark in the OECD *Directory of NGOs Active in Sustainable Development*, suggesting that the size of the NGO community has remained stable.

As in many other donor countries, Danish NGOs can be divided into two categories, those for which relief and development is a primary concern, and those for which development is secondary to their main purpose, such as trade unions. The NGO community in Denmark is involved in a wide range of activity: development programmes; disaster relief; volunteer programmes; development education and solidarity activities.

A few examples will illustrate the diversity of Danish NGOs. Danchurchaid (DCA or *Folkekirkens Nodhjelp*) is the largest of the organisations with a framework agreement. Operating in 80 countries, including the former Soviet Union, DCA has an income of approximately DKr400 million (over $60 million) and around 120 staff, of whom a third are based in developing countries. DCA is engaged in relief and a wide range of development activities, as well as fundraising, development education, campaigning and advocacy. Approximately one fifth of DCA funds come from private sources. DCA is a member of the European Protestant NGO network, APRODEV.

Ibis, which received the second largest allocation of framework funding for the period 1995–9, was established in 1966 as a solidarity organisation linked to liberation movements such as FRELIMO, the MPLA and SWAPO in Southern Africa. It became involved in development work during the 1980s and its turnover trebled between 1988 and 1992. Of more than 155 salaried staff, 130 are in developing countries. As well as Southern Africa, Ibis works in South and Central America, focusing on human resource development, health and agriculture. In Denmark it is extensively involved in information campaigns, formal education, publishing and advocacy. IBIS is 99 per cent government funded. It is a member of EUROSTEP, the secular EU NGO network.

Denmark has many small NGOs focused on just one country such as Gambia (*Dansk-Gambiansk Forening, Gambias Venner*), Mongolia, (*Dansk Mongolsk Selskab*) and Ghana (*Agoro I Danmark*). The list of organisations involved in friendship activities or country-specific development interventions is long, extending beyond the 20 programme countries on which Danish ODA is concentrated. Organisations with their origins in missionary work are also well represented: the Danish Evangelical Mission (DEM), the Apostolic Church Mission (AKM), the Danish Baptist Union.

Some NGOs specialise in alternative trade: *Butik Salam, Butik Papaya, U-Landsimporten*. Others focus on a range of specific issues, from the Danish Gymnastics and Sports Association, which works in seven countries, to Internationalk Rehabilitation Centre for Torture Victims (IRCT), which engages in research and rehabilitation work with torture victims in 37 countries. The environment, workers rights and children also provide the focus for several organisations.

A relatively high proportion of Danish NGO funding comes from DANIDA. Many NGOs collect only modest contributions from their constituencies, and DANIDA will now provide 100 per cent funding for most NGO activities overseas. The three agencies receiving 80 per cent of framework funding between 1995 and 1999 – DRC, DCA and Ibis – derive 92 per cent, 82 per cent and 99 per cent of their funds respectively from government. Other large NGOs also derive a high proportion of funds from official aid: *Red Barnet* (Danish SCF), over 90 per cent; CARE Danmark, 90 per cent; Caritas Danmark, 94 per cent.

UMBRELLA BODIES

There is no single umbrella body coordinating Danish NGOs or providing a central point of contact with government. But as in many other European countries, several informal networks exist that enable NGOs to collaborate on specific issues – for example trade, exchanges and new technology. These groupings often provide a point of dialogue with government on specific issues. NGOs in Denmark frequently participate in several networks, although smaller NGOs are less likely to do so because of limited capacity.

The Danish Platform of the EU NGO Liaison Committee has over 30 members, including NGOs focused on children, labour, women's rights, the environment, refugees, handicapped people and torture victims. The platform facilitates cooperation between member NGOs on issues relating to the EU, and maintains a dialogue with the Foreign Ministry on Danish aid and Denmark's role in EU development cooperation. During 1996, the platform was also active around Danish participation in the World Food Summit.

NGOs concerned with the environment and development issues meet under the umbrella of the '92 Group', which began prior to the Earth Summit and which is now concerned with issues such as monitoring Denmark's commitment of 0.5 per cent of its Gross National Income (GNI) to International Environmental Protection and Emergency Assistance.[3]

DANIDA coordinates a contact group on humanitarian issues that involves development NGOs and others involved in relief activities, including the military.

NGOS AND DANISH DEVELOPMENT COOPERATION

The Danish ratio of ODA to GNP is one of the highest among DAC member countries. Having reached 1.03 per cent in 1994, it fell back to 0.96 per cent in 1995. In 1996, however, with an increase of 10.5 per cent, Denmark led the DAC group again at 1.04 per cent of GNP, or $1.79 billion. Danish ODA is evenly divided between bilateral and multilateral aid, and since 1989 has consisted entirely of grants. The strategy is aimed at improving coherence among Denmark's international policies. While confirming fundamental cross-cutting themes such as poverty alleviation, women in development, the environment and good governance, the strategy introduced population, trade and debt relief as additional priority themes.[4]

Danish NGOs have been involved from the outset of Danish development cooperation – helping to shape DANIDA's predecessor organisation in the early 1960s. NGO partnership with DANIDA accelerated rapidly following a decision by government in 1987 to increase cooperation between DANIDA and NGOs. An important principle underpinning Danish development cooperation today is the close involvement of NGOs and other elements of civil society in both the formulation and the implementation of official assistance programmes. The presence of NGO personnel on the board of DANIDA illustrates this collaborative approach.

The legal basis for Danish aid envisages a five-year planning framework. Current policy is enshrined in a 1994 paper, *A Developing World: Strategy for Danish Development Policy Towards the Year 2000*. NGOs, businesses and academic institutions all contributed to this document. A key concept in Denmark's aid programme is that of the 'resource base'. Along with the business community and the academic institutions that contribute experience and know-how, NGOs are seen as an important part of the resource base upon which Danish development assistance is founded. NGOs help to foster the social and humanitarian consensus that underpins Denmark's traditionally high level of development aid. They provide links to civil society in the South as well as a depth of geographic and technical expertise.

DANIDA'S NGO STRATEGY

In 1993, following a period of consultation with NGOs, the government adopted a new NGO strategy. The strategy recognises the comparative advantages of NGOs in terms of skills and networks, but it also makes demands on organisations receiving public funding for development efforts. DANIDA attaches particular importance to:

- the NGO constituency and support base in Denmark;
- NGO contacts with implementing partners and target groups in the South;
- NGO ability to facilitate relevant contacts and cooperation between its constituency in the North and target groups in the South;
- NGO experience in project implementation, both sectorally and geographically.

The NGO strategy aimed to simplify management procedures, to help NGOs strengthen their own capacity, and to consolidate their involvement in the delivery of Danish assistance. Large NGOs with framework agreements (see below) were to be given greater operational responsibility for project selection and implementation. They would then be monitored to assess their capacity to design and implement projects successfully. The professional dialogue between DANIDA and NGOs would be expanded to include NGO participation in the formulation of DANIDA's sector and country strategies.

The strategy introduced twice-yearly assessments of individual projects submitted by smaller organisations. Using simplified procedures and clearer criteria, DANIDA hoped to reduce its administration. Amended funding rules kept DANIDA's contribution to NGO administration at 7 per cent, but scrapped the requirement that NGOs contribute 10 per cent to overseas project costs.

Framework agreements

In 1988 DANIDA commissioned a major study of Danish NGO activities, which recommended the establishment of four to five year framework agreements with major NGOs.[5] Following parliamentary approval, DANIDA entered into framework agreements with four agencies in 1991–2: Danchurchaid, the Danish Red Cross, Ibis and LO/FTF (the Danish Trade Union Council for International Development Cooperation). In 1995, CARE Denmark became the fifth NGO with a framework agreement.

The intention was that the agreements should enable agencies to take a programmatic approach to their work, giving them flexibility in their implementation. The expectation was that frameworks would reduce the administrative burden on both NGOs and on DANIDA, leaving DANIDA more time to devote to working with other NGOs. In 1993 a review of the framework agreement was carried out, with the active involvement of both DANIDA and NGOs. This review focused on the administrative side of the framework agreements, rather than on policy issues.

In 1994 DANIDA commissioned a further study, this time evaluating the extent to which framework agreements had achieved their objectives.[6] A mixed picture emerged.[7] The frameworks did not appear to have ensured the application of a coherent approach to planning and implementation. Nor did they ensure NGO–DANIDA dialogue on their respective comparative advantages and approaches. The focus for discussions had remained on administration. Comprehensive capacity assessments were not made, however, of the NGOs' professional and administrative capacity as required in the enabling Act.[8] On the other hand, frameworks were found to have assisted NGOs with long-term overseas planning, and less documentation was needed than under previous arrangements.

As the framework agreements became more established, NGOs benefited from the security of long-term funding, but have not enjoyed as much freedom as some expected. They still feel that the administrative burden is substantial. Paradoxically, some argue that ending the 10 per cent financial requirement has also reduced their freedom to act. Some wonder whether the more formalised approach to development may actually be an obstacle to focusing on poverty.

Volume of official funding for NGOs

During the early 1990s, there was a rapid rise in the percentage of Danish aid channelled through NGOs. From 5 or 6 per cent in the late 1980s, aid channelled through NGOs had doubled to 11 per cent by 1991–2, a figure that remained steady during the first half of the decade. In 1995, overall funds channelled through NGOs amounted to DKr1000 million ($178.5 million) or 16.5 per cent of bilateral assistance. Of this,

- just over half (DKr530 million or $95 million) was responsive funding, allocated to development projects under framework agreements ($43 million), for single projects ($50 million), or mini-programme agreements (less than $2 million);
- around 17.5 per cent was spent on volunteer-sending ($31 million);
- almost 29 per cent was devoted to humanitarian interventions ($51 million).

Since the Danish government is seeking consolidation in the NGO use of DANIDA funds, NGO assistance is likely to stabilise, as planning figures for 1996 and 1997 show:

Table 7.1: *DANIDA Responsive NGO Funding[9] (US$ million)*

	1995	1996	1997
Framework Agreements	42.9	46.6	55.5
Mini Programme Agreement	1.7	2.2	3.2
Single Projects	49.9	41.7	36.0
Volunteer Programmes	31.4	30.9	33.0

Use of official funding by NGOs

The geographical focus of NGO assistance differs significantly from that of Danish official aid, maintaining a substantial link with Latin America. NGOs allocate 49 per cent of their funding to Africa, 30 per cent to Asia and 18 per cent to Latin America (3 per cent being spent on international activities). DANIDA's bilateral activities concentrate primarily on Africa and Asia, although Bolivia and Nicaragua are among Denmark's 20 concentration countries. In line with Denmark's intention to focus on poverty, after September 1996, official support for NGO activities was not available for countries with a GNP of over US$2000 per capita.

In terms of sectoral distribution, 79 per cent of NGO disbursements in 1995 related to social infrastructure, 17 per cent to the productive sectors, and 4 per cent to economic infrastructure.

Details of funding and taxation

In the case of responsive funding (whether under frameworks or single projects) 100 per cent of the overseas project costs are met by DANIDA. The same 100 per cent availability applies to emergency work and volunteer programmes. For responsive funding 7 per cent may be charged for administration purposes. For emergency funding, 5 per cent is allowed for administration, and for volunteers, 10 per cent.

Before DANIDA scrapped the rule that NGOs should contribute 10 per cent of their own funds to overseas project costs, some NGOs felt that experimentation might be inhibited if they were not using their own resources for more innovative work. Some NGOs still feel they might have more freedom if they reverted to making a 10 per cent contribution.

Mini-programme agreements (MPAs)

Aimed at networks and medium-sized NGOs, the aim of MPAs is to ensure flexible funding arrangements for organisations that deal with small projects and multiple local partners. A mini-programme agreement covers a two-year period. Under an MPA, projects of up to DKr250,000 ($44,600) can be initiated by an NGO without prior approval from DANIDA. As Table 7.1 shows, MPAs are not yet a major NGO funding channel, but their importance is likely to increase.

Single projects

Organisations with insufficient levels of development activity to qualify for a framework agreement or an MPA can apply for assistance on a project-by-project basis. Table 7.1 shows that DANIDA expects single project funding to decline over time. None the less, DANIDA is strongly committed to a policy of funding for smaller organisations.

Denmark offers assistance to a number of countries undergoing restructuring following armed conflict, a shift to a democratic political system or a change to a market economy. About $15 million a year between 1995 and 1997 was allocated to NGOs for 'transitional assistance projects'.

Emergency funding

In 1995 Denmark spent a total of DKr783 million ($140 million) on humanitarian aid, of which DKr287 million ($51.2 million) was spent via NGOs. There have also been steps to facilitate the use of the Danish Defence Forces and Civil Defence in emergency situations. In 1995 the International Humanitarian Service (IHB) was established and this has increased Denmark's capacity to contribute personnel to international conflict prevention operations, and to support democracy and human rights.

Volunteer programmes

The official volunteer programme is run by the NGO *Mellemfolkeligt Samvirke* (MS). Volunteers are posted to a number of countries, mainly in Africa and Central and South America. The number of volunteers decreased from 349 in 1993, to 234 in 1995, with a corresponding drop in person-months from 4,476 in 1993, to 3,333 in 1995. However, there was a marginal increase in the number of women volunteering, up from 46 per cent in 1993, to 48 per cent in 1995.

MANAGEMENT OF RELATIONS WITH NGOS

DANIDA has an NGO unit with a staff of six. It does not handle emergency activities, and development education is managed by the Information Department. Southern NGOs are handled by Danish embassies abroad.

Embassies

Eighty per cent of Danish bilateral ODA is concentrated on 20 'Programme Cooperation Countries', and much responsibility for country specific cooperation rests with Danish embassies in these countries. An increased emphasis on securing local participation has meant that greater importance is being placed on cooperation with local NGOs, which in turn are more involved in implementation as well as in the formulation of ideas, project design and evaluation.

Danish embassies can fund projects presented by southern NGOs or local enterprises up to a value of DKr3 million under a Local Grant Authority (LGA). Embassies cannot fund Danish or international NGO projects. Only DANIDA in Copenhagen can fund Danish NGO activities – and in a few exceptional cases, the work of international NGOs.

Dialogue between government and NGOs

Denmark's strong performance on aid volume in recent years has been underpinned by a consensus within society in favour of Danish development cooperation. A 1995 poll, for example, showed that 75 per cent of the public supported aid levels at 1 per cent of GNP. Relations between NGOs and the government reflect this consensus. There are shared values on aid volumes and on Denmark's poverty focus. NGOs and DANIDA also have a common approach to policy.

Despite this broad agreement, Danish NGOs take the view that an important part of their role is to challenge government and DANIDA, to be an independent voice and to provide an alternative approach. Danish NGOs feel they have a significant role to play in areas such as protecting Danish aid from over-commercialisation, and balancing ODA between bilateral and multilateral spending.

There are many opportunities for NGOs and DANIDA to discuss policy on an *ad hoc* basis and through more formal mechanisms. An NGO Contact Committee meets twice yearly and involves representatives from the NGO community and the Ministry for Development Cooperation. NGO personnel (in their personal rather than their organisational capacity) are appointed as members of the DANIDA Board, and NGOs appoint members to the DANIDA Council for International Development Cooperation. DANIDA often engages in discussions with NGO networks, and consults NGOs on both its country and sector strategies.

Coordination of policy discussions between NGOs and the administration is a responsibility shared among DANIDA's NGO Unit, the Policy Department and the relevant regional departments. In recent years, the main subjects of discussion have been poverty orientation, the environment, Danish bilateral country strategies and EU development assistance. Denmark's policy of active multilateralism, announced in 1996, calls for the Danish development community to be proactive on multilateral policy issues (for instance within the EU). And in areas such as the 1995 Copenhagen Social Summit, DANIDA has encouraged NGO involvement by providing financial support for follow-up activities. Concern has been expressed, however, that the high levels of financial support from DANIDA mean that NGOs have not been very active in developing a broader dialogue, not only with the EU, but also with other partners in the donor community.[10]

DEVELOPMENT EDUCATION AND PUBLIC AWARENESS

According to a 1995 opinion poll, 75 per cent of the Danish public favoured maintaining development assistance at its present high level of 1 per cent of GNP. Only 17 per cent were in favour of a reduction. There has clearly been a dramatic change in attitude since 1960, when polls showed only 35 per cent support – this at a time when Danish aid was around 0.1 per cent of GNP. It is widely believed that this strong public support owes a lot to the activities of NGOs.

Many development NGOs have made development education their sole or major purpose, and almost all NGOs see awareness-building as an important part of their function. Larger NGOs such as MS have very extensive information and awareness-raising programmes, involving research, publishing, formal and non-formal education, lobbying and campaigning.

Denmark allocated DKr32.4 million ($5.9 million) to DANIDA's Department of Information in 1995, with the twin aims of raising public awareness of Southern issues in general, and of Danish development cooperation in particular. These funds were split between the Development Information Programme, which received DKr19.9 million ($3.6 million) and miscellaneous activities costing DKr12.5 million ($2.2 million). These included publications on Southern issues, and cooperation with journalists and the media, usually on broader development themes rather than on specific projects. The programme has also worked with Denmark's School of Journalism and the Institute of Post Graduate Journalism.

Under the Development Information Programme, 100 NGOs were given financial support of approximately DKr10 million ($1.76 million) for their information and education work in 1995. Travel grants are also used to promote understanding, and in 1995 179 such grants were given to help representatives from developing countries participate in information activities in Denmark.

Professionalisation, which has been a strong theme in overseas programming, has also been applied to the area of information and development education. During 1995, six major NGOs employed a development information consultant, financed by DANIDA, to assist in their aware-ness work. There are NGO concerns that a more professional and formalised approach in dealing with the public could weaken the grassroots NGO base. This parallels similar fears that profes-sionalism could become an obstacle to working closely with the poorest.

EVALUATION

In 1996 DANIDA released an evaluation on 'Poverty Reduction in Danish Development Assistance'.[11] The evaluation noted that NGOs and civil society organisations played a signifi-cant role in implementing development assistance, but it commented on the fact that DANIDA's NGO strategy was inadequate as a policy paper, because it dealt almost exclusively with the mechanisms of cooperation between government and NGOs. The lack of explicit policy guidance on NGO poverty interventions was thought to have delayed improved targeting and the develop-ment of good practice in poverty reduction.

The evaluation noted that there was no a priori guarantee that NGO interventions contributed more to poverty reduction than projects managed by others. Because of this, and because of increasing strains on NGO capacity and capability, it was deemed important to review the role of NGOs, both Danish and Southern, as a channel for development assistance. Following the evalu-ation, Danish NGOs started in 1997 to plan a study of their own. The study will involve Southern partners, and the aim is to make a constructive contribution to the debate on about Danish assis-tance, including its impact on the poorest.

ISSUES

Funding

As noted above, a relatively high proportion of Danish NGO funding is provided by DANIDA, while a minor share originates from voluntary sources. Donations of more than DKr300 are tax deductible for gifts to humanitarian and non-profit NGOs. The NGO community engages in a standard range of fundraising activities, but the overall effort is relatively modest. Some people argue that the Danish climate for voluntary giving has been difficult in recent years – one reason being competition from a lottery operated by the Ministry of Finance (NGOs receive some Lotto funding).

Danish NGOs have found that obtaining funding from the EU for projects and development education activities is both complex and time consuming – particularly given the readily available DANIDA assistance. In 1995, just 0.73 per cent of EU assistance for development interventions went to Danish NGOs.[12]

Dependency and concentration

Danish NGOs are aware of the potential dangers in their high levels of dependency on government. Given the shared commitment on volume and the relatively strong Danish focus on poverty and social development (particularly following the Copenhagen Social Summit), the scope for major disagreement is said to be limited. In spite of the high dependency level, NGOs do not feel that they are in any sense inhibited from commenting on Danish aid policy.

In the early 1990s, following the introduction of framework agreements, government support became more heavily concentrated on a half-dozen NGOs – those with framework agreements and the volunteer sending agency MS. In 1993, for example, DANIDA supported the overseas development work of more than 30 NGOs, and supported the development education work of 100. But 75 per cent of the funding went to just four agencies. This concentration is seen, in part, as a reflection of the government demand for increased NGO professionalism.

Professionalism

The need for increased professionalism in the work of NGOs has been a recurring theme in Denmark. Along with the increase in government funding there has been an increase in expectations. A 1993 MS report raised questions about the growth in NGO professionalism, and these remain highly relevant. The report noted that Danish NGOs make a much larger contribution to cooperation activities than they did in the early 1980s. But it suggested that while strengthening NGO technical capacity, professionalisation also tended to divorce an NGO from the public and its sources of support and legitimacy. The report noted that major aspects of the work once carried out by an active NGO membership in Denmark had been shifted overseas. Demands on NGOs to professionalise make it more complicated for them to ensure the active involvement of their membership. 'The more specialized and professional the organisations become, the higher the risk that they are regarded as interest organisations and lobbyists, and not as voluntary member organisations speaking out on the basis of involvement and self-organisation.'

Linked to this issue is the question of whether a more professional and programmatic approach will result in NGOs losing their image as an alternative to official development assistance. Generous funding from government, however, does not seem to inhibit NGOs from taking advantage of Denmark's liberal tradition of free speech and dissent. NGOs in Denmark believe their role as ODA critics is significant. But if NGO interventions start to resemble those of DANIDA how long will it be before this role is undermined?

8 Finland[1]

Compiled by Frances Hill

SUMMARY

Finnish aid rose steadily each year from the mid 1970s until 1991, when it reached 0.8 per cent of GNP, making Finland one of the most generous donors in the OECD. Within three years, however, it dropped to 0.3 per cent of GNP and seemed to be in freefall. However, in 1996 the government published a 'Decision-in-Principle', based on a policy review that set out priorities and options for Finnish ODA. The 'Decision-in-Principle' represented a new commitment to development cooperation and was a break with the years of decline. Reductions in ODA as a percentage of Finnish GNP were reversed, and a target of 0.4 per cent was set for the year 2000, with a long-term commitment to the UN target of 0.7 per cent. In 1996, Finland's net ODA grew by 9 per cent in real terms – to $408 million – and its ODA/GNP ratio rose from 0.32 per cent in 1995 to 0.34 per cent the following year.[2]

Aid to Finnish NGOs amounted to approximately 6 per cent of ODA in 1996, and is heavily concentrated on five organisations with framework agreements. According to the Decision-in-Principle, the goal is 10 per cent, and this amount was expected to be surpassed in 1998. About three-quarters of Finnish aid to NGOs is in the form of project support, with the remainder divided between development education and information, and funds distributed through Finland's embassies.

Information and advocacy activities are important to Finnish NGOs, which, through a 'Percentage Movement', have been active in building political and public commitment to aid, and in making a case for better quality development assistance. Government support for information activities was particularly hard hit by budget cuts in the early 1990s.

Evaluation has been a feature of Finnish aid. In 1993–4 a major evaluation of NGOs recommended increased funding for NGOs and a more coherent policy framework.

BACKGROUND AND HISTORY

Finnish NGOs have been active in development for a relatively short time. Prior to the 1970s, missionary societies carried out development activities along with their church work, but without government support. Secular NGOs became active in the 1960s, in part through their involvement in Vietnam anti-war protests and their support for Southern African liberation movements, and in part through increased general interest in the problems faced by the developing world.[3]

The Finnish government's support for NGOs can be divided into five phases:

- 1960s to early 1970s: marked by the emergence of, and thinking through, the basic notion of NGO support;
- 1974–84: government started to fund Finnish NGOs' development efforts on a regular basis. This was a 'maturing period' for the NGO Support Programme (NGO-SP);
- 1984–92: rapid expansion of the NGO-SP, with notable changes in structure and mechanisms, and a growing emphasis on the developmental role and impact of the funds provided;
- 1992–5: characterized by deep cuts in funding for both projects and information activities (although more moderate than cuts to the overall aid programme);
- 1996 the 'Decision-in-Principle' announced an increase in NGO support to 10–15 per cent of the development cooperation budget (as opposed to ODA), and the encouragement of new forms of NGO activity.

Since 1974 the number of government-funded Finnish NGO projects has grown from six to over 420, and the geographical spread of NGO activities has widened from six to 69 developing countries.

Finland joined the EU in 1995. This had an impact on aid policy in that Finland, while keen to maintain priority objectives in line with its foreign policy, is also keen to harmonize with EU development objectives. To this end, the government produced 'Guidelines for Programme Design, Monitoring and Evaluation'. The guidelines are based on EU project management principles and are considered an important step in the coordination of Finnish ODA with EU practice. This document says, *inter alia*, that,

> *'Finland is active in seeking new forms of cooperation which support human rights, equality and democracy and encourages an open dialogue with partner countries, international organisations and NGOs.'*[4]

NGOS AND CIVIL SOCIETY

The 1994 ODI Evaluation, *Strengthening the Partnership; Evaluation of the Finnish NGO Support Programme*,[5] suggests that Finnish NGOs can be divided into roughly three groupings with regard to their objectives and development orientation:

- organisations for which development and other international activities are the main fields of work. These include such NGOs as the Finnish UNICEF Association, solidarity organisations, 'Third World Shops' and friendship organisations;
- those for which development work forms a part of their overall activity, such as Church-related organisations, trade unions, women's and youth organisations, and NGOs working with the disabled;
- those organisations that concentrate on raising public awareness in Finland on development and other international issues. The gap between this group and the other two is closing, because most NGOs are involved in some form of information dissemination in Finland.

Government support for NGOs has also served as a means of channelling assistance to countries and target groups that are difficult to reach through the official aid programme. Examples have included organisations such as the African National Congress, the Southwest Africa People's Organisation of Namibia and the Palestine Liberation Organisation.[6]

UMBRELLA GROUPS

In 1982, linked to the 'Percentage Movement' (see below), some 40 NGOs established a cooperation forum, the NGO Advisory Board on Development Cooperation. It promoted cooperation between NGOs, worked on advocacy and served as a main forum for NGO discussions concerning the role of a new organisation – KEPA. The Finnish Service Centre for Development Cooperation (KEPA)/Finnish Volunteer Service (FVS) was established in 1985 to do two things. It acts as an NGO umbrella organisation and forum for NGOs, and it implements the government-funded volunteer programme.[7] In 1997 it had 180 member organisations and was coming to the end of a major renewal and reorientation process. KEPA considers itself a melting pot for different organisational and political cultures, providing professionally competent services to NGOs and creating space for voluntary participation in campaigns and other activities.[8] KEPA's influence in the development NGO community is substantial and multi-faceted. Its activities are described in more detail below.

In 1986 the Trade Union Solidarity Centre of Finland (SASK) was established to promote trade unions in developing countries. It has over 30 member organisations and funds several dozen development projects. The Finnish Disabled People's International Development Association (FIDIDA) was founded in 1987 and serves as a network and information forum for NGOs working with the disabled.

HOW GOVERNMENT FUNDING IS ORGANISED

Recognition

In 1993, new guidelines were introduced for legally registered and developmentally competent Finnish NGOs. Their projects must be consistent with the objectives of Finland's official aid programme. The government has stressed the need for Finnish NGOs to place particular emphasis on strengthening the capacities and competence of their local counterparts and target groups, whose self-reliance should be a programming objective.[9] The guidelines are intended for projects aimed at long-term development impact, however, in the absence of separate guidelines for non-project humanitarian aid, they have also been applied to emergencies, where suitable.[10]

The government requires NGOs applying for funds to have been actively working in Finland for two years (after 1997, one year), and to have been working with an NGO or a group of citizens in a developing country for at least one year. The Southern counterpart must have been active for at least a year before the funding application. The Finnish NGO must have clear development objectives, expertise and resources, and must have demonstrated planning, assessment and monitoring skills.[11] An NGO's capacity is assessed by desk officers in the NGO Division (D-NGO). According to the 1994 ODI evaluation, however, this assessment has been minimal in practice.

The share of project costs that must be provided by the NGO has been declining. Before 1990, 40 per cent had to come from an NGO's own resources. In 1990 this was reduced to 25 per cent, and in 1997, following the 'Decision-in-Principle' it was further reduced to 20 per cent. The allowance for administration costs was also increased to 10 per cent from 6 per cent.

Besides supporting the work of Finnish NGOs, the Government of Finland also supports international NGOs (INGOs) through direct and indirect bilateral support. In 1996, Mk5 million ($1.09 million) was allocated to international NGOs. Direct bilateral support has largely been channelled through the Department for International Development Cooperation's (DIDC) humanitarian aid budget, and indirect support through the Finnish affiliate of the INGO in question. In addition, some of Finland's multilateral assistance funds have been channelled to INGOs.[12]

Trends in government support

A 'One Man Committee' was appointed by the government in September 1995 to review the Finnish Aid Programme.[13] The report was the basis for a ministerial working group that prepared the 'Decision-in-Principle' on development cooperation. The report emphasised the role of NGOs, both as independent development and relief actors, and as potential experts with know-how that should not be ignored in government projects.

Finnish ODA has been used to support NGOs since 1974. It reached 5 per cent of ODA in 1992 and 6 per cent of ODA in 1996. In the 'Decision-in-Principle' put to Cabinet in 1996, the government agreed to,

> *Gradually increase the assistance funnelled through NGOs to 10–15 per cent of the budget for development cooperation proper and to encourage NGOs to partic-ipate in bilateral assistance projects and humanitarian aid and, together with these organisations, investigate the adoption of new forms of support and financ-ing.*

Support is provided in the belief that NGOs play a vital role in strengthening the sense of global solidarity among the Finnish people, and that they contribute to building civil society in devel-oping countries.[14] A special mechanism for funding NGO activities, the Non-Governmental Organisation Support Programme (NGO-SP), is administered within DIDC by the Division for NGOs. In 1995, 144 NGOs received ministry funding for 360 projects in 60 developing countries, mostly in sub-Saharan Africa.

Most support to NGOs is project based. In 1996, Mk96 million ($21 million) or 76 per cent of NGO support was allocated to projects. Mk2.6 million ($566,500) was allocated to informa-tion and development education, and the same amount went to Finnish embassies for small projects.[15]

Table 8.1: *Government Support by Type of NGO, 1996*

Religious Organisations	60%
Social Service Organisations	13%
Political Organisations	9%
Trade Union Organisations	7%
Cultural Organisations	6%
Friendship and Peace Organisations	4%
Environmental Organisations	1%

Table 8.2: *Sectoral Distribution of NGO Projects, 1996*

Education and Training	40%
Health	33%
Other Social Services	6%
Environment	9%
Agriculture and Forestry	4%

Source: Kyllonen, T., 'The Finnish Case Study' in NGO Evaluation Policies and Practices, for DAC/OECD NGO Evaluation Synthesis Study, IDS, Helsinki, 1997

The NGO Support Programme concentrates on the largest organisations but most projects are small. Average allocations in 1996 were Mk270,000 (about $50,000) per project.[16]

In terms of financial importance to the Department for International Development Cooperation, there are five major NGOs:

- The Finnish Evangelical Lutheran Mission;
- The Finnish Free Foreign Mission (Pentecostal), with 16 projects and 21 per cent of ODA/NGO funds in 1996;
- Finchurchaid, with 15 projects and 8 per cent of ODA/NGO funds;
- The Finnish Red Cross, with 20 projects and 5 per cent of ODA/NGO funds;
- Trade Union Solidarity Centre of Finland, with 31 projects and 6 per cent of ODA/NGO funds.

Since 1992, these five NGOs have worked under individual framework agreements. In 1992, 50 per cent of NGO-SP development project funds were allocated to these organisations; by 1993 the amount was closer to 60 per cent.[17] Under a framework agreement, an NGO is not at liberty to allocate funds at its own discretion. DIDC requires funds to be used for specific projects that have been submitted, and the NGO Division approves each project in the agreement according to its general project criteria. While this may appear the same as funding on a project-by-project basis, it differs slightly, in the sense that an NGO must contribute at least 20 per cent of its own resources to the overall programme, but not necessarily to each individual project.[18] Up to 25 per cent of a project's costs may be transferred to another project (up to Mk 100,000) without DIDC approval.

Bilateral projects

Since 1988 it has been possible for Finnish NGOs to implement official bilateral projects. For bilateral projects entirely funded by DIDC, initial screening and project preparation are carried out by DIDC. Thereafter, project responsibility normally lies with the implementing agent and its project director overseas.[19]

DIDC's decision to open the bilateral programme to NGOs was based on a desire to enlarge the pool of bilateral project implementing organisations at a time when the aid programme was expanding. It was felt that NGOs would enhance the quality of bilateral projects. Thus far, however, only a few NGOs have shown an interest, and few have engaged in the competitive bidding process. This is attributed partly to the fact that NGOs want to safeguard the independence, integrity and image of their organisations, and also to the fact that few NGOs have the administrative and professional capacity required.[20]

Emergencies

The largest part of Finnish bilateral aid spent through NGOs is channelled through DIDC's humanitarian aid budget, administered by the Division for Humanitarian Assistance. This is because the Government has been using some of the biggest NGOs as channels for such assistance, especially for emergency aid.[21] NGOs, nevertheless, spend a small share of Finland's humanitarian assistance – less than 5 per cent in the mid 1990s.

An evaluation carried out in 1995 suggested that the inter-departmental Working Group for Humanitarian Affairs should focus more on its main function – developing Finnish humanitarian policies and strategies. This evaluation questioned the way in which government under-utilized NGOs in emergency situations, but it also pointed out that NGOs themselves have done little to promote their profile within humanitarian assistance, preferring to involve themselves in development work and more general Southern issues. The evaluation advocates that 20 per cent of the yearly humanitarian budget be channelled into NGO projects and that a consultative group be established to include relevant NGOs, research institutes, the Humanitarian Unit, Political Department, civil defence/national disaster teams and military personnel earmarked for peace-keeping duties.[22]

In the 1996 Decision-in-Principle, the government agreed to 'keep the proportion of humanitarian aid at 10–15 per cent of the budget for development cooperation proper... and to encourage NGOs to participate in... humanitarian aid and... investigate the adoption of new forms of support and financing'.[23]

Volunteer programmes

In the 1970s, DIDC supported Finnish NGOs sending volunteers overseas as Technical Assistance Personnel (TAPs), and Finnish support for the United Nations Volunteers dates back to 1971. After 1986, support was provided to KEPA/FVS for a volunteer programme in Mozambique, Nicaragua and Zambia. The architects of the renewed volunteer programme envisaged that even if it reached 100–120 volunteers, its developmental impact would be modest. It could be justified, however, by its importance for Finnish development information and education.[24]

A 1995 evaluation of Finland's volunteer programme found that it,

> *Suffered from a mix of (vague) objectives, lack of clarity in numerous aspects and little result orientation. The management of the programme switches between the aims identified by KEPA and its member organisations in the North, and the aim to serve interests of the host organisations and their development course in the South... This mix of objectives is being governed by a complicated organisational structure of over 150 member NGOs, the majority of whom have nothing to do with the volunteer programme.*[25]

Partly in response to this, KEPA began a major reorientation and restructuring. One part of this was a gradual move to diversified partnership programmes. Much was done to develop new arrangements, with both old and new partners, leading to a substantial decrease in the number of long-term development workers.[26] In 1996 KEPA received Mk20 million ($4.36 million).

GOVERNMENT STRATEGY TOWARDS NGOS

Government support for NGOs is the responsibility of DIDC, and since 1986 it has been administered by the NGO Division (D-NGO). The division has a number of inter-related responsibilities: it provides funds to NGOs for development projects and for information work (in cooperation with the DIDC Unit for Information); it also provides funds for the Finnish Volunteer Service and for international and Southern NGOs. The staff of the division consists of a director, five desk officers, one person responsible for NGO information support, a financial assistant and a secretary.

PRIVATE FUNDRAISING

There is no comprehensive information on NGO fundraising in Finland, although KEPA plans to begin collecting such data. Based on the 25 per cent self-financing ratio with government, Mk60 million ($13 million) would be a rough 1996 estimate.

A 'Percentage Movement' was established in the 1980s in response to a demand for Finland to increase its aid volume to 0.7 per cent of GNP. The Percentage Movement aimed to raise public awareness by encouraging Finns to contribute one per cent of their salaries to development efforts through NGOs. In 1985, the number of regular donors to the Percentage Movement was estimated at something between 150,000 and 200,000. However, the movement ended, partly because government support for NGOs was increasing rapidly, and partly because the NGO matching requirement decreased, significantly easing the financial pressure on NGOs. As a result, private fundraising initiatives declined.

With the economic recession of the early 1990s this changed. Severe cuts in ODA, and growing difficulties among NGOs in raising their required match, provided new fundraising impetus. A New Percentage Movement was launched in 1992 by over 70 NGOs, again calling on citizens to contribute 1 per cent of their salaries to support development efforts of NGOs.[27] The 1996 Decision-in-Principle 'unfroze' the aid budget, however, and the new ODA target was within one year of the demands of the Percentage Movement. The campaign was therefore disbanded again. It indicated, however, that should government fail to meet its commitment, the Percentage Campaign would be reactivated.[28]

With the reform of the tax system in the early 1990s, tax concessions for NGOs were abolished.

DEVELOPMENT EDUCATION AND PUBLIC INFORMATION

Government support for Finnish NGO development education began in 1975. The 1980s witnessed a steady growth in funding, rising from Mk300,000 in 1981 to a peak of Mk4.5 million in 1992. During that period, the number of applicants doubled from 73 to 144, and over 80 per cent of the applicants received some funding. NGO development education funding, however, was particularly hard hit by ODA cuts. The first decrease in 1993 saw funds cut by almost one third, and by 1996 it had still not recovered.

Government support to NGOs for information activities reached only Mk2.6 million ($570,000) in 1996. Funding is provided to registered Finnish NGOs that have been active for at least two years. They do not have to work overseas in order to qualify for an information grant, but they must make a contribution of their own to the project costs. This can be in the form of voluntary work. According to a 1989 survey (the latest carried out), one quarter of Finnish NGOs finance their information work mainly by themselves.

A renewed KEPA focus is the strengthening of global awareness in Finland. KEPA aims to encourage NGOs to expand development education and information activities. Another focus – the Partnership Programme – encourages volunteers from the South to come to Finland to work in development cooperation, serving as a further vehicle for information exchange. KEPA produces a quarterly *International Bulletin*, which publicizes major development issues, such as the future of the Lomé Convention. An event directed to the broader public during 1997 was the second annual 'World Village in Helsinki', which attracted some 50,000 participants over a weekend in May.

ADVOCACY

Since the early 1980s many Finnish NGOs have been actively engaged in public debate on development issues, and have often acted as pressure groups, lobbying government. At the beginning of the decade, the main effort was to have government increase the volume of Finland's ODA to 0.7 per cent of GNP, and this led to the establishment of the Percentage Movement.

The movement shifted focus to the quality of Finnish aid, demanding that the poorest people – and Southern governments, emphasising the poor – be targeted. Other issues included the separation of aid and trade objectives, a shift to an integrated programme approach, the use of alternative technologies, and a reduction of support to international financial institutions – in favour of NGOs.

A more recent example of NGO advocacy has to do with the development by government of a new World Bank Strategy. Finnish NGOs have wide and efficient e-mail networks with the international NGOs monitoring the World Bank. These, along with their good contacts in Finnish political circles are likely to enable them to play an influential role.[29]

DEVELOPMENT OF RELATIONS WITH SOUTHERN NGOS

Into the late 1980s, DIDC provided support to Southern NGOs in exceptional cases. However, in 1988 this changed. The Finnish embassies in six developing countries were given special funds on an experimental basis to support the projects of indigenous NGOs and other local institutions. This initiative, called the 'Small Project Fund', was intended to expand and deepen government understanding of Southern NGOs. Special priority was given to self-financing and income-generating activities. By 1992, the volume had increased to Mk3.2 million, disbursed from 22 embassies but concentrated largely in Ethiopia, India, Kenya, Mexico, Namibia, Zambia, Tanzania and Thailand. At the end of 1992 this funding was halted because of the deep ODA cuts, but it was reinstated in 1994, with funds reaching Mk2.6 million ($566,500) in 1996.

1996–7 was designated as a period of transition, re-examination and restructuring for KEPA. KEPA feels that it requires a strong concrete presence in the South in order to have a credible message for Finnish NGOs. One new aim was to widen involvement in southern Africa, South and South-east Asia and Central America, and to focus especially on countries in which Finnish NGOs are active or about which they needed better information and contacts. Another was to develop new financing initiatives, such as the creation of micro-funds for environmental and human rights projects. One option being explored was a new micro-financing structure to be run by NGOs. To increase flexibility in Finnish–Southern exchange, volunteers from partner countries are being encouraged to visit Finland to work on development projects.

Finnish activity for global responsibility includes new forms of campaigning and a revamping of information services and education work. Effective North–South partnerships and building a sense of global responsibility in Finland are closely intertwined. This mirrors a similar development among many European NGOs, where there is also recognition of a need to build partnerships and to revamp relations with the South.[30]

EVALUATION

Many evaluations have been carried out on various aspects of Finland's aid programme. A 1992 study, combined with the views of different DIDC staff, found that NGO work was too scattered, haphazard and narrow in its focus.[31] The Volunteer Programme was examined in 1995, Humanitarian Assistance in 1996, and a comparison of EU and Finnish aid was carried out in 1995. The NGO-SP was evaluated by the Institute of Development Studies at Helsinki University and the London-based Overseas Development Institute (ODI). Work began in 1993 and findings were presented in 1994. Based on project performance in four countries, the evaluation was generally positive. As a result, one of the report's recommendations was that government should allocate more funds to the NGO- SP.

> *The thrust of the recommendations made in this Report is that in general FINNIDA should increase the support it gives to NGOs for their development work. It should do this by raising the share of aid funds allocated to the NGO Support Programme. The basis for this particular recommendation is the evidence of project performance obtained during the evaluation. Overall, it is judged that the NGOs funded are doing development work that is fulfilling a need and having a positive impact on the poor people assisted. Some projects have performed exceptionally well and the problems identified are neither insurmountable nor any more severe that those found in studies undertaken by other donors* [32]

Negative aspects of the evaluation highlighted poor planning, insufficient understanding of the local project environment, poor costing estimates, inadequate sustainability of projects and the need for more time than planned in reaching objectives.

The 1994 evaluation highlighted the fact that the majority (95 per cent) of NGO projects focused on a more-or-less specifically defined target group and that it was a rare exception for a Finnish NGO to attempt to influence national policies, even where these were considered unjust, undemocratic or unsustainable. Very few Finnish NGOs – notably some trade unions and more radically-oriented NGOs – focused on these wider issues.

In 1995, DIDC, in conjunction with the OECD/DAC Expert Group on Aid Evaluation, acted as a sponsor in initiating a broad international study on NGO evaluation – whether carried out by donor agencies or NGOs themselves. The two-volume report covered seven donor countries and the EU, and looked at evaluation work that had been carried out in five developing countries, synthesizing lessons on methods and effectiveness from a wide range of existing material. The study, *Searching for Impact and Methods: NGO Evaluation and Synthesis*, was published in 1997.[33]

The evaluations have influenced the restructuring of the Finnish aid programme, including an increase in NGO support and an 'unfreezing' of the aid budget. They have also influenced KEPA, and this will have an impact on the way NGOs work in the future.

9 France

Judith Randel and Tony German[1]

SUMMARY

In France, NGOs are increasingly known as ASIs (*Associations de Solidarité Internationale*) in order to stress the idea of cooperation between people. Numbering around 1000, the French ASI community is large, but many of them are small and local, and many of the larger ASIs do not have resources on the scale of comparable organisations in other EU countries. French humanitarian NGOs in particular figure prominently as recipients of multilateral emergency assistance.

Responsive government funding for long-term ASI development programmes is modest – currently less than 1 per cent of ODA – so dependency is not a significant issue. But the French government seems to be interested in increasing cooperation with NGOs. Government funding for ASI humanitarian work is significant, and direct support through bilateral programmes also takes place.

Dialogue between ASIs and government tends not to focus on political or global issues, but it is growing. Several subject- or region-specific networks, as well as more formal mechanisms (such as the CCD – *Commission Coopération Développement*) provide opportunities for increasing dialogue. Issues-based advocacy has been limited. A contributing factor is the fragmentation of the ASI community. But more important is the nature of French aid and aid management. Development cooperation policy is closely integrated with French foreign policy and involves many government departments. Its complexity appears to have inhibited the development of ASI advocacy activities.

In 1997, discussions took place at a national *assise* (conference), on the possible creation of a *Haut Conseil de la Coopération*. This would be a major new forum for dialogue between government and the broader development community. The *Haut Conseil* could increase transparency and thus create opportunities for more effective dialogue and deeper ASI understanding of French development assistance.

BACKGROUND

There is a very large number of non-governmental organisations in France dedicated to international solidarity – at least a thousand – of which fewer than 100 have a national profile. Even the national ASIs that work on international development are relatively small. But among the larger organisations are several with a strong international reputation: *Médecins Sans Frontières*, Handicap International and *Action Contre La Faim*.

A recent study of 330 ASIs by Coordination SUD (Solidarité, Urgence, Développement) found that more than half had an annual budget of less than FF250,000 ($50,000).[2] The 1997 directory published by the *Commission Coopération Développement* shows a similar picture – see Table 9.1.

Table 9.1: *Number of ASIs According to Levels of Income*[3]

Income in 1996 French Francs	Number of ASIs
More than 300 million	2
Between 50 and 300 million	16
Between 15 and 50 million	27
Between 10 and 15 million	16
Between 3 and 10 million	57
Between 1 and 3 million	86
Between 250,000 and one million	126

Source: Coordination Sud. US$ 1.00 = FF 5.12.

Many ASIs are local, solidarity-based groups, sometimes founded on individual initiatives, or based on a link to a particular place in a developing country. Although the theme of solidarity is reflected in a number of ways, not least in the name given to French NGOs, in general there is little linkage between local and national organisations.[4]

COALITIONS AND UMBRELLA BODIES

The larger ASIs have formed a number of associations and coalitions. As with French official ODA, these reflect a certain fragmentation, and there has been much discussion about the possibility of creating one body representing the sector as a whole, thereby wielding greater ASI influence in dialogue with government. At the time of writing the prospect of the formation of a *Haut Conseil pour la Coopération* was under active consideration (see Issues, below). In late 1997, however, the larger ASIs were grouped into nine government-recognised federations, and these in turn were grouped into two coalitions. *Coordination SUD* represented 70 ASIs, and the *Comité de Liaison des Organisations de Solidarité Internationale* (CLOSI) represented 100 ASI members grouped in three federations. Of CLOSI's 100 members, only 30 have international programmes.[5]

These groupings represent their federations to government, conduct information campaigns, mobilise public opinion and stage debates on development issues. CLOSI spans ASIs active in France as well as in the South. *Coordination SUD* includes only development ASIs, but has among its members most of the larger ASIs, as well as many of the mid-sized and emergency organisations. The government funds both *Coordination SUD* and CLOSI.

There are many other groupings. Under the *Comité Catholique Contre la Faim et pour le Développement* (CCFD) there is a body of Church-based ASIs, organised in local branches. Another active federation is the *Peuple Solidaire*. Volunteer-sending agencies are grouped in *CLONG-volontariat*. The *Programme Solidarité Eau* is one of several sectoral groupings. It brings together specialists and professionals on water issues from relevant government departments, ASIs, municipalities. A similar group, the *Program Solidarité Habitat* was set up in 1988 and disbanded in 1996. The Ministry of Cooperation is usually represented in these bodies. There are also geographical committees – on Mekong countries, South Africa and Palestine – giving ASIs a further opportunity to network.

GOVERNMENT STRATEGY TOWARDS ASIS

The French government is giving increased priority to relations with ASIs and, through decentralised cooperation, to relations with local authorities. The government is interested in the potential for ASIs to become substantial development cooperation partners. ASIs, however, are wary, not wanting to be seen as contractors implementing French aid. Politicians are also recognising that ASIs have something to contribute to the debate and, in their role as citizens' organisations, helping to build public involvement in French development assistance.

The government takes a broad view of the NGO sector, and does not make sharp distinctions between research institutes, study groups and other bodies. According to the *Mission de Liaison auprès des ONGs* in the Ministry of Foreign Affairs, its job is to choose the most competent organisation for each operation, regardless of its legal status. Many French ASIs – for example Solagral and GRET – combine research and operational work. One consequence of this is a great difficulty in documenting ASI funding for development purposes alone.[6]

Channels of communication

There are various channels for government liaison with ASIs, reflecting the interests of different ministries. The work of these bodies is largely about the implementation of French aid, rather than the policy that guides it. This is not surprising: the bulk of French aid is spent through the Ministry of Economy and Finance, but relations with ASIs were, at least until 1998, the province of the State Secretary for Cooperation in the Ministry of Foreign Affairs (see Issues, below).

ASIs do have a place in French diplomacy, however. In 1989 instructions were issued to ambassadors to listen to the perspective of French ASIs, and to keep them informed. In Africa and the Caribbean there have been meetings with ASIs and government representatives from more than one country to build interstate liaison and learn lessons from shared experience. The Ministry of Foreign Affairs also has formalised longer-term understandings with particularly important ASIs, including the *Croix Rouge Française.*

Bodies for dialogue

Chaired by the prime minister, *Le Conseil National de la Vie Associative*, is made up of around 60 federations of associations, covering all aspects of voluntary activity. It participates in the formation of national and European legislation related to association and foundations.

The *Commission Nationale Consultative des Droits de l'Homme* relates directly to the prime minister and meets every Monday. Included in this group are the most important human rights ASIs. The commission assists the government in preparing its position on international human rights issues.

The *Commission Coopération Développement* (CCD) is a joint body of all the ministries involved in both development and humanitarian assistance. It was started in 1984 and revamped in 1996 when its mission was redefined to give greater attention to information, particularly in relation to issues related to the implementation of development cooperation. It includes groups interested in public awareness, voluntary engagement and international institutions. ASI members are invited to suggest priorities for annual voluntary sector budgets.

The CCD provides the best opportunity for ASIs to engage with the government on policy, but the scope of the dialogue depends on the Minister of Cooperation. Currently the CCD is the forum where ASIs discuss the future of the Lomé Convention.

CCD has had a role in coordinating ASIs since the *Comité Paritaire d'Orientation et de Programmation* (CPOP) was set up in 1995 – partly as result of ASI requests. CPOP includes representatives of both government and ASIs, and while it is still in its early stages, there are signs that it will be a useful forum for ASIs and government in working together on substantive and practical issues.

The CPOP mandate includes:

- 'Priority Intervention Programmes', which are eligible for 75 per cent government funding. A 1996 example was ASI collaboration on the implementation of an FF8 million ($1.6 million) three-year programme in Burkina Faso;
- programmes of partnership between government and ASI experts in particular fields. Known as 'Goals Agreements', the first one, worth FF8 million ($1.6 million) over three years, was established in 1997 for the development of livestock farmers' associations;
- block grants for micro projects. These were established to deal more efficiently with small applications. Block grants to a value of FF6 million (US $ 1.2 million) were agreed in 1995 and 1996.[7]

The *Secretariat d'Etat a l'Action Humanitare d'Urgence* (Humanitarian Aid) has as part of its mission the prioritisation of collaboration with ASIs, and allocates just under half of its budget to this collaboration.

In the *Ministère des Affairs Etrangères* there are several departments where partnerships with ASIs are the norm:

- the emergency unit (*La Cellule d'Urgence*);
- *le Service de l'Action Humanitaire*;
- the section for decentralised and non-governmental cooperation within *La Direction Générale des Relations Culturelles, Scientifiques et Techniques*, which co-finances a number of ASI projects each year;
- the department for human rights and relations with the UN and international institutions, which prepares the annual French contribution to the Commission of Human Rights in collaboration with major French ASIs;
- the department for economic affairs, which works with ASIs in advance of the major UN summits;
- *Mission de Liaison auprès des ONG*, which, as part of the *Direction Générale des Affaires Politiques et de Securité*, is the main interface between French ASIs and the Ministry of Foreign Affairs.

FUNDING

The management of French aid is split between a large number of ministries and technical units, many of which have their own small programmes with ASIs. The bulk is managed by the State Secretary for Cooperation in the Ministry of Foreign Affairs. The French government does not combine these efforts to produce a global figure showing aid to ASIs, but it is estimated that the average government contribution represents about 8 per cent of an ASI's income. If the French share of EU support is included, the average would rise to about 15 per cent.

According to a 1996 CCD survey, ASIs mobilised FF3.2 billion ($640 million) for their activities in 1994, up from FF2.8 billion ($550 million) in 1993. The single largest source of funds was public donations, followed by support from multilateral agencies – primarily the UN and the EU. The French government, primarily the Ministry of Foreign Affairs and the Ministry of Cooperation, supplied 8 per cent. Approximately 60 per cent of these funds was for emergency assistance, and 40 per cent was for development projects.

French ODA began to decline after 1994, falling more than 11 per cent between 1995 and 1996 alone – from $8,433 million to $7,510 million.[8] Nevertheless, in 1996, France held fourth place for the total volume of ODA among DAC donors, following Japan, the United States and

Germany. Its ODA/GNP ratio was 0.48 per cent. ASIs, however, increased their government allocations in both volume and percentage terms. Their share of ODA has been tiny, but until 1998 it was increasing – from 0.42 per cent in 1994, to an estimated 0.65 per cent in 1997.

In addition, French ASIs receive government support from the *Fond d'Urgence Humanitaire* – FF50 million ($10 million) in 1996.

Table 9.2: *Government–ASI Co-financing, 1994, 1995 and 1997 (FF millions)*

	1994	1995	1997
ODA to ASIs through the Ministry of Foreign Affairs	34.2	37.0	
ODA to ASIs through the Ministry of Cooperation	162.8	195.7	
Total ODA to ASIs	197.0	232.9	269.0
Percentage Increase		+18.2%	+15.9%

Source: Lire et comprendre le Budget Français d'aide publique au developpement 1996

Co-financing

Seven of the ministries and departments involved in funding ASIs produced a joint set of *Conditions Générales de Co-financement* in 1994, which govern conditions and eligibility for official funding. Co-financing is handled by the *Bureau de la Vie Associative*, which, at least until 1998, reported to the State Secretary for Cooperation in the Ministry of Foreign Affairs (see Issues, below). After receiving a request for funding, the bureau's assessment process includes reference to two steering committees, advice from the technical services of both ministries, and advice from missions and embassies overseas. In the mid 1990s it was handling around 300 requests per year.

In 1995, the bureau received 279 proposals from 138 ASIs. Forty three per cent was spent on co-financing development projects, 53 per cent was spent on volunteers, and 4 per cent was for development education.[9]

Funding is available from government under framework agreements, or as matching grants to French ASIs, or to Southern NGOs linked with a French organisation. Funding is multi-annual for up to four years, with payments in annual tranches. Matching grants offer up to 50 per cent of project costs, including 6 per cent for administration. An ASI seeking funds must provide a minimum of 15 per cent of project costs from private resources. The remainder can come from any source, provided the ministry is satisfied that it is reliable.

In addition to individual projects, there are *Programmes Concertes*, coordinated by one ASI but involving several others, for either a specific region or sector. Examples are the *Fleuve Senegal*, based on the Senegal River Basin, or the *Jeunes, Ville, Emplois* (JVE) programme – a youth and employment initiative based in urban areas. These programmes run over several years and applications can be made for smaller projects within the broad parameters of the programme. This is designed to allow some autonomy and to ensure continuity.[10]

Legal status and fiscal benefits

There is no legal definition in France of an NGO/ASI, but non-profit organisations, from football teams to environmental organisations and ASIs, do have legal status. There are no taxation schemes that benefit ASIs as such, although tax can be recovered by the donor on donations to ASIs. An association must be recognised as performing public duties in order to qualify for this relief.

BOX 9.1 MÉDECINS SANS FRONTIÈRES

Established in response to the Biafran emergency, in 1995 MSF received income from 19 donor countries totalling $265 million – more than ten times the total French support to NGOs for emergency work in 1994. MSF does much in establishing the way humanitarian assistance is perceived in France and elsewhere. It regards itself as morally independent – a position that it feels is guaranteed by its financial autonomy. Almost two million people donate regularly to MSF, 800,000 of them in France. MSF will not accept more than 25 per cent of its income from any one donor, and accepts nothing from agencies with any political involvement in an area.

HUMANITARIAN ASSISTANCE

Until a government reorganisation in May 1997, the *Secrétariat d'Etat à l'Action Humanitaire d'Urgence* dealt with emergencies, and liaised closely with many NGOs. In the year before it was disbanded, 46 per cent of its total disbursements were distributed via NGOs. Its executive arm – the *Service de l'Action Humanitaire* – was housed within the Ministry of Foreign Affairs. There is also an emergency unit within the Ministry of Foreign Affairs (see above).

France was the first country to have a secretary of state for humanitarian action, and links between this ministry and NGOs are strong – not least through Bernard Kouchner, who has held high-profile posts as director of *Médecins sans Frontières* and as Minister for Humanitarian Action. The senior staff of the ministry have been drawn in part from NGOs. French NGOs are prominent in international humanitarian assistance and emergency assistance has captured French public imagination. Sixty per cent of total ASI disbursements are spent on emergency assistance. French ASIs are more strongly represented than any other country on the list of ECHO's main partners for 1996, numbering 13 out of a total of 56.[11]

VOLUNTEERS

French aid in the 1980s was characterised by the large number of volunteers.[12] Over the period 1994–7, more than half of all government co-financing was for volunteers, and with the Ministry of Cooperation, the proportion averaged more than 60 per cent.

Thirteen ASIs specialise in volunteer work and are organised into an umbrella organisation – *CLONG Volontariat* (*Comité de liaison des ONG de volontariat*). The two most important organisations are the DCC (*Délégation Catholique à la Coopération*) with 623 volunteers overseas in 1997, and AFVP (*Association Française des Volontaires du Progrès*) with 444 volunteers in 1997. The volunteers are posted on contracts of up to two years. They do not receive a salary but all their expenses are covered and they are given training, a subsistence allowance, an equipment allowance and a return ticket. These expenses are met by the sending organisation, which in turn receives matching government or private donor funds.

DEVELOPMENT EDUCATION AND PUBLIC INFORMATION

Government views the raising of public awareness as part of the responsibility of the voluntary sector, and development cooperation with Africa is part of mainstream political life. The political framework within which development cooperation is managed, however, ensures that the usual issues of concern to ASIs – solidarity, sustainable development, poverty reduction, social inclusion – do not figure highly in discussions with government.

Funding

In 1994 3 per cent of all official funding to ASIs went towards information and educational activities in France.[13] Up to 15 per cent of a project's cost can be devoted within France to educational activities directly linked to the project. The Ministry of Cooperation targets three areas for development education:

*   French youth, especially teaching materials that bring Southern issues into the classroom;
*   areas of research in which the ministry has an interest – sectoral (such as rural development, health, credit, micro-enterprise) or thematic (women, the environment, youth);
*   information and communication – the creation of arenas for the dissemination of research and lessons learned from experience.

The government feels that the impact of a project should be nationwide, if not European, and it should reach a public beyond the constituency of the ASI concerned.[14]

Links between ASIs and the academic community are increasing and a number of ASIs have their own research capacity. Because of its long-term research in the Sahel, *Solagral*, for instance, became a major contributor to a Europe-wide campaign against EU beef dumping. An association of academics on development cooperation was formed at the Sorbonne, and ASIs are using academic inputs to an increasing extent in their training, evaluation and policy work.

An interesting development education innovation is a programme of 'Social Integration through Humanitarian Aid'. This is designed to link disadvantaged young people in France with young people in developing countries. More than 2000 young people from France have taken part in work schemes to build schools in Africa, for instance. It has been a popular programme, and an evaluation of the results suggests that for the French youth it has helped achieve the goal of greater social integration. The benefits to developing countries were much less clear.

EVALUATION

F3E

In 1994, two funds[15] that had been established to support feasibility studies and to carry out evaluation were merged into a new organisation, 'F3E' – the Fund for the Promotion of Preliminary Assessment Surveys, Inter Programme Surveys and Evaluation Surveys.

F3E was established both by ASIs that were operational and some that were research-oriented. In 1997 it had 40 members, and was co-financed by government. Its tasks include both assisting with evaluation and promoting it. It offers technical assistance to ASIs, including the definition of appropriate terms of reference, the identification of external evaluators, and funding – 85 per cent of the costs. Its advocacy role is equally important. The results of its work are made public and evaluation summaries are published four times a year. Workshops are also organised to discuss results.

By late 1997, F3E had co-funded 36 Preliminary Assessment Surveys at a total cost of FF5.9 million ($1.1 million). It had also arranged 18 evaluations and two inter-programme thematic surveys, one on savings and credit in West Africa, and the other on the volunteer programmes of 11 ASIs.

The evaluations are seen as aids for decision-making, not as external audits. Commentary from ASIs suggest that F3E has been successful in this. A main finding of the evaluations is the need to disseminate ASI experience. To capitalise on their expertise, F3E has requested ASI participants to identify specifically what they learn from an evaluation. A year after a report has been completed, the ASI is questioned about evaluation follow-up and about the implementation of recommendations.

F3E intends to work with traditional ASIs and with local authorities that have development cooperation activities. They see a further strategic benefit from this work: 'in the field, the aid work carried out by the authorities and ASIs tends to intertwine, thus helping, at least partially, to dissolve the separation between State and private approaches, methods and programme contents. This is the reason for F3E's attempts to promote consultation in matters of co-funding of surveys and exploitation of their results.'[16]

Those taking most advantage of F3E have tended to be development ASIs with an interest in research – including those that do evaluation work for government. Emergency NGOs have been less interested, and have not felt that evaluation has much to offer them. The government, however, is very positive towards F3E because it recognises the value of the process and finds that the evaluations provide a more informed starting point for discussion with ASIs. Evaluations of the official aid programme, in contrast, are confidential.

Support for Southern NGO evaluations

The *Fondation de France* has also been active in promoting the concept of evaluation. In 1995 it published a 'Charter for Evaluations Made During Development Work'[17] with a view to using its experience both in France and in developing countries to promote an ethical framework and practical approaches.

The *Fondation* also developed a programme of institutional support for evaluation in Southern NGOs. The first evaluation project was financed in November 1996. Support can be offered both directly to NGOs in the South or through NGOs in France, but is limited to three countries in Africa: Mali, Senegal and Chad, and to some islands in the Indian Ocean. The *Fondation*'s conditions for support stress participation, involvement with a local NGOs and the use of professional evaluators.[18]

ADVOCACY

Advocacy on specific issues

CFA devaluation

In January 1994, the French government ended a 46-year-old system that had formed the basis of its historical relationship with 14 countries of the 'franc zone' in Central and West Africa. The franc zone guaranteed currency convertibility, with a fixed exchange rate against the French franc, free movement of capital within the zone, and the centralisation of reserves in a French public revenue account. The 50 per cent devaluation of the CFA franc divided both ASI and French political opinion. ASIs argued that the Special Fund for Development should be adequately financed as a safety net, and that there should be a long-term French commitment to these countries.

Lomé and the alliance with government on the EDF

French ASIs were, on the whole, as one with their government on the 1996–2000 replenishment of the European Development Fund, which finances aid to 71 African Caribbean and

Pacific countries under the Lomé Convention. France took a strong stand, speaking up for Africa and for the partnership character of the Lomé Convention. In doing so it became the largest contributor to the EDF, and earned the praise of French ASIs.

Armed conflict

Rwanda has been an issue of major public debate in France, where emergency assistance in general has captured the public imagination. NGOs have worked with the military in peacekeeping situations, and media attention has helped to enhance NGO credibility. French ASIs were among the first to call attention to the genocide.

The French government and Handicap International have worked together to promote the international convention against land mines.

The limits to advocacy

There are no legal restrictions on what French ASIs can say in terms of advocacy, but there remains, none the less, a range of obstacles that have resulted in limited impact:

- the public has perceived ASIs as technical specialists rather than advocates, particularly as those ASIs with a mandate for advocacy have had a low profile;
- the ASI community is fragmented – the large number of small ASIs do not add up to a critical mass with a significant or even noticeable voice. In addition, a number of ASIs regard themselves as 'apolitical';
- the highly fragmented nature of French aid makes it difficult for ASIs to focus their efforts. ASIs do have a dialogue with government departments – but not with the Ministry of Finance, which controls over 50 per cent of French aid;
- it is difficult to draw a line between French development cooperation and the rest of French policy towards the developing world. French relations with Francophone developing countries have a long history and are highly political. There has always been a close economic relationship between France and its former colonies. Political responsibility for relations between France and the 'ambit' countries in Africa[19] has rested at the highest level of State and has also involved party political links;
- the complexity of French relations with developing countries makes it difficult for ASIs to inform and involve their supporters. This is not helped by a low media profile on North–South Relations and development cooperation. Scrutiny of French overseas policy has been seen as an academic issue, rather than a subject for campaigning. In recent years there has been some change. Issues such as Rwanda and the landmines campaign have achieved a higher public profile, and ASIs have started to gain credibility with the media;
- the French government gives less than 1 per cent of aid through ASIs. Some people argue that because the proportion is so small, there is no basis for a dialogue based on partnership.

Issues

Development of relations with Southern NGOS

Data on support to Southern NGOs is not available, but it is reported that strengthening local structures and organisations is a concern of both government and French ASIs. The government is also interested in diversifying the range of Southern organisations that can be regarded as partners, involving new civil society actors in development. The Special Social Development Fund (*Fonds Spécial de Développement* – FSD) was set up in 1994 to alleviate the detrimental impact of devaluation on the poorest in CFA countries. Most of the projects supported through the FSD are put forward by local associations or municipal governments. The FSD is used to support projects that will have an immediate impact on the living conditions of the most severely disadvantaged. In practice, the FSD is the main mechanism for French support to private organisations in the South.[20]

Decentralised cooperation

Decentralised cooperation has become a major issue in French aid – encouraged by the Minister of Cooperation and reinforced by a general interest in decentralisation in French public life. Since 1992, local authorities have been able to make agreements with their counterparts overseas. The primary aim has been to support local authorities in developing countries, but an additional goal is to increase popular interest and involvement in development cooperation. Decentralised cooperation operates in three main fields:

* municipal cooperation in relation to issues such as public transport, water and housing;
* the mobilisation of local populations through trade unions, organisations and professional groups to support development cooperation, particularly with Africa;
* the mobilisation of local businesses and associations to build industrial or commercial partnerships.

Up to 50 per cent of decentralised cooperation is co-financed by a joint office of the Ministries of Foreign Affairs and Cooperation. Most projects submitted in the mid 1990s were funded, but a more discriminating approach is said to be pending. This notwithstanding, overall funding for decentralised cooperation was expected to increase in 1998. Funding from the Ministry of Cooperation in 1995 amounted to FF27 million ($5.4 million), and FF37 million ($7.2 million) in 1996, with a slight reduction in 1997.

A 1994 assessment by the Ministry of Cooperation, covering the years 1982–92, commented on the useful complementarity of decentralised cooperation: it can do things the State cannot, but the imprimatur of French official assistance can also be useful in some circumstances.[21] The study suggested that the programme had helped in building French public opinion in favour of developing countries. However some ASIs suggest that in most cases this is limited to elected officers and officials.

As in other parts of the European Union, the involvement of a wider range of organisations in development cooperation – fire brigades for instance – raises issues for more traditional ASIs about their own distinguishing characteristics. This issue becomes more heated as community organisations begin to enquire about access to the co-financing that ASIs have traditionally enjoyed on an exclusive basis. ASIs report that grants from decentralised cooperation bodies in support of their work remain small, reaching FF49 million in 1994 for overseas work with a further five million francs for activities in France.

Les Assises and the *Haut Conseil*

Two major issues for French ASIs have been coordination among themselves, and improvement in the transparency and management of official aid. Over 1996 and 1997, nine regional assises were held on French development cooperation. The *Assises Nationales de la Coopération et de la Solidarité Internationale*, held at the Sorbonne in Paris in October 1997, was the culmination of these, bringing together 1,600 participants. Speakers included the Minister of Cooperation, the Chair of the Development and Cooperation Committee of the European Parliament, the

Director General of the IMF, the Secretary General of a major French trade union, regional political leaders and representatives of the major ASIs.

The meeting took place in a context of anticipated change. The new government was expected to redefine its approach to development cooperation before the end of 1997, and decentralised cooperation was growing in importance, particularly through regional councils and large municipalities. At the same time, the disadvantages of ASI fragmentation were evident and there was interest in forming a single coordinating body. It was recognised that a regrouping of ASI umbrella organisations would give French ASIs a much needed voice and greater political impact.

The main outcome of the *Assises* was the creation of the *Haut Conseil de la Coopération*. This was intended to be a permanent structure for dialogue between the official sector on the one hand, and a cross-section of public and private non-profit bodies on the other (ASIs, trade unions, research institutions, local authorities). Open dialogue was expected to enhance both transparency and public support for development cooperation. The *Haut Conseil* was expected to operate through a series of colleges that would group members according to various categories. In November 1997, a working group was set up to prepare proposals for the organisation of the *Haut Conseil*.

The effectiveness of the *Haut Conseil* will depend not just on itself, but on the way government organises itself. There have been improvements in the coordination of French aid since 1995. A deputy minister responsible for development cooperation has been appointed in the Ministry of Foreign Affairs; an Inter Ministerial Committee for Aid and Development has been set up to define the orientation of French ODA and to ensure coordination. In addition, Local Committees for Aid and Development have been set up in ACP countries to harmonize and monitor development programmes.

10 Germany

Judith Randel and Tony German

SUMMARY

In 1962, Germany became the first DAC member to introduce NGO co-financing. Today, the German NGO sector is very large: nine of its 2,000 organisations are amongst Europe's 25 largest NGOs. The NGO sector has three categories: Church-based NGOs, political foundations and private non-denominational agencies. Each category has a separate budget line. Until recently large NGOs dominated the NGO scene and dialogue between government and smaller NGOs was negligible. With the 1995 formation of the Verband Entwicklungspolitik Deutscher Nichtregierungs-organisationen (VENRO – Association of NGOs in Germany), a federation for all development NGOs, small organisations gained new opportunities for information exchange and dialogue with the Ministry for Economic Cooperation and Development, BMZ.

In 1996 and 1997, Germany allocated roughly DM680 million ($450 million) or 9 per cent of the BMZ budget to NGOs. This represented about 40 per cent of their income. Church agencies and political foundations were allocated 89 per cent of the total, split fairly evenly between the two groups.

NGOs receive little official support for development education, but BMZ has a public education and information programme, and this may increase as a priority. Dialogue between NGOs and government is quite formal. NGOs are invited to comment on country planning documents, and VENRO contributes to public debate.

Following the 1996 Copenhagen Social Summit, German NGOs collectively analysed both BMZ and – recognising their need to be accountable – their own approach to poverty reduction. The resulting suggestions for improvement in both BMZ and in NGO performance offer a constructive basis for a positive future dialogue that is less sensitive to criticism than in the past.

BACKGROUND

Development policy-oriented NGOs have a substantial impact on German development assistance. Besides planning, financing and implementing aid projects, they contribute to better public understanding of development issues and put pressure on the government to keep the traditional commitment to allocate 0.7% of GDP to foreign aid and to improve the quality of German aid by untying it and by increasing the allocation of funds to promote poverty alleviation.[1]

In 1962, Germany became the first DAC member to introduce co-financing for NGOs. The NGO sector is large with over 2000[2] active NGOs and nine of the 25 largest NGOs in Europe: Misereor; Friedrich Ebert Foundation; Hermann-Gmeiner-Fonds Deutschland; Bischofliche Aktion; Adveniat; Bread for the World; Churches Development Service; German Committee for UNICEF; Konrad Adenauer Foundation.

The German NGO sector is structured distinctively, with three categories of NGO:

- NGOs related to the Protestant and Catholic Churches;
- five political foundations related to each of the major national parties;
- private organisations: these consist of secular and community-level organisations.

At the national level some are purely development-oriented, while others are part of German civil society with a partial interest in developing countries.

Each of these three sectors has a separate budget line and its own arrangements with the Ministry for Economic Cooperation and Development, but the lion's share of the funding goes to the Church agencies and the political foundations. The Minister for Economic Cooperation is responsible for aid, and handles about 70 per cent of the ODA budget. The two other ministries most involved in development assistance are the Ministry of the Economy and the Ministry of Foreign Affairs.

UMBRELLA BODIES

Until recently, larger NGOs have dominated the NGO scene. As the 1995 DAC Aid Review points out: 'official cooperation with private aid institutions is characterized by the special role played by the large institutions and the virtual absence of a structured dialogue with smaller ones'.[3]

In 1995, negotiations took place on the formation of a single NGO federation for information exchange and dialogue with the government. NGOs argued that the government should strengthen its institutional support to NGOs, particularly to national networks and federations. As a result, all of the development NGOs have now formed VENRO. This body superseded the Bensheimer Kreis – a coalition of around 80 NGOs.

While the VENRO umbrella is open to all NGOs, and now incorporates the platform for the EU NGDO Liaison Committee, there are many additional alliances. At the federal level there is the Bundeskongress entwicklungspolitischer Aktionsgruppen (BUKO). There are also State or Länder networks and a series of networks focused on particular developing countries.

CHURCH-RELATED NGOS

Church-related NGOs can be divided into Catholic, (mainstream) Protestant and 'evangelical' groupings. The Catholic and Protestant NGOs have each created a Central Agency for Development Aid (Katholische Zentralstelle für Entwicklungshilfe – KZE; and Evangelische Zentralstelle für Entwicklungshilfe – EZE). The two central agencies were created for the purpose of receiving government funds for Catholic and Protestant activities in development cooperation. In addition to government funding, the two central agencies receive income from Church tax.

Although possessing many similarities, the two central agencies maintain significant differences for historical and organisational reasons.

The Catholic Central Agency (KZE) is a legally independent entity, but it shares a location and is organisationally linked to Misereor, the largest Catholic NGO. This leads to considerable integration of the activities of both organisations, with economies of scale in evaluation, policy planning and integration of policy approaches vis-à-vis the government.

The German Protestant Churches, which are a pluriform group, relate to government in different ways from the Catholic Church. The Protestant Central Agency (EZE) is legally independent of the other Protestant NGOs, but is also logistically and organisationally separated from them. Partly because of the logistical integration of KZE and Misereor, this combination forms the largest German Development NGO. Misereor receives voluntary contributions from its own constituency and part of the taxes paid to the Catholic Church. The German Catholic Caritasverband is mainly active in emergency and relief activities in developing countries (in addition to its charitable activities in Germany). The Arbeitsgemeinschaft für Entwicklungshilfe (AGEH – Association for Development Aid) is the Catholic organisation for volunteer and expert assistance. There are an estimated 70 to 90 other Catholic NGOs with development activities; included among them are Missio, Adveniat, and Päpstliches Missionswerk der Kinder in Deutschland.

On the Protestant side, Brot für die Welt/Diakonisches Werk (Bread for the World) is the largest development NGO. The Protestant volunteer and expert organisation is Dienste in Übersee (Services Overseas). These two NGOs, the Protestant Central Agency, Kirchlicher Entwicklungsdienst (KED – Church Development Service), and Evangelisches Missionswerk (EMW) form the Arbeitsgemeinschaft Kirchlicher Entwicklungsdienst (AGKED – Association of Church Development Service). Within this federation, Diakonisches Werk deals with emergency relief activities.

The funding relationship within the Protestant group is complex. EZE receives government funds and Church tax. Brot für die Welt receives part of the Church tax and voluntary contributions. Dienste in Übersee receives funds from all three sources. KED is funded by Protestant churches from the various regional churches (Landeskirchen). EMW receives funds from the various member missionary societies of the individual Protestant churches. The five Protestant organisations work together in the AGKED, where policy coordination takes place through meetings of the directors and project coordination is carried out at a regional desk level.

In addition to the AGKED group, other major Protestant NGOs in a community of 40 to 50, are Kindernothilfe (Children Relief Aid), and Christoffel Blindenmission (Aid for the Blind).

Beyond the mainstream Protestant churches, there are a number of evangelical development NGOs. One of the larger of this category is Christliche Fachkräfte International (CFI – Christian Experts International).

Project partners of the churches in developing countries are usually local church authorities (dioceses, state churches, missionary societies) but may also be NGOs without ties to churches. Projects focus largely on social justice and participation. In addition to fulfilling material needs, projects dealing with human rights issues are actively pursued. About a third of NGO spending is devoted to educational projects. Other important areas are health, rural development, the establishment of 'social infrastructure', and community development. Integrated projects covering several sectors are becoming more common. Projects aiming to strengthen local institutions and executing agencies as well as establishing networks are also gaining in importance.

In 1991, after almost 30 years of experience of Government–NGO collaboration, the Church-related central agencies started receiving funds through new and much simpler administrative procedures, which were concluded in close collaboration with the central agencies. Under the new procedure, the central agencies receive a global allocation for approximately 80 per cent of their project proposals. The balance is still supported through project-by-project procedures.

The budget line is established once a year. The central agencies present their proposals for the use of funds in a joint paper to the government. They also report annually on the use of funds. The total funding (in 1997 DM286.5 million, about $190m) was divided equally between the agencies. In addition, the agencies receive funds for projects in Central and Eastern Europe (in 1997 DM2.9 million, just under $2m).

POLITICAL FOUNDATIONS

The political foundations of the major parties are the Konrad Adenauer Foundation of the CDU, the Friedrich Ebert Foundation of the SPD, and the Friedrich Naumann Foundation of the FPD. In addition there are foundations linked to the CSU and the Greens – the Hanns Seidel Foundation and the Heinrich Böll Foundation.

The political foundations started as part of a process to support the building of democracy in post-war Germany. Today they have a continuing role in promoting participation and political engagement. Although linked to their relevant political party, they are supposed to be autonomous. They may not receive any funding from party budgets and they are not under the direct control of party bodies. Most of their governing bodies include a high ranking political figure, however, and there are informal party contacts. In their international work, they tend to focus on political and institutional issues, with typical partners being trade unions and political parties in developing countries.

Funding for political foundations is decided by a Parliamentary Budget Committee and comes from three ministries. For development cooperation work overseas, it comes from the BMZ; for political education in Germany it comes from the Ministry of the Interior and for Central and Eastern Europe and for scholarship programmes it comes from the Ministry of Foreign Affairs and BMZ.

Funding for development programmes is given on the basis of projects funded for three years, rather than in block grants. Even after projects are approved, they remain under the control of BMZ and are subject to external audits. Allocations to the political foundations are made according to a parliamentary agreement that broadly reflects each party's percentage of the vote on a medium-term base. Funding covers administration as well as project costs and the political foundations do not fundraise.

Relations with the Ministry of Foreign Affairs are somewhat different. The Ministry of Foreign Affairs may ask for the assistance of a particular political foundation in its work. If the foundation wishes to take on the work, it will submit a management proposal and, if it is funded, it must submit regular reports and accounts.

The political foundations have suffered from public criticism based on concern about their development work and their links with political parties. They have been subjected to increased financial scrutiny and they are making greater efforts to demonstrate transparency and to explain that their party links are based on common and shared social and political values.

The foundations establish partnerships with democratic bodies in developing countries and try to inject the concerns and aspirations of their partners into German sectoral and national policy discussions. As part of the foundations' emphasis on democracy, there is a focus on peace building. For example, meetings have been organised between representatives from the North and South of Sudan. In post-war Mozambique, the Friedrich Ebert Stiftung has been working with the two main political parties – Frelimo and Renamo – and with groups outside parliament, helping them to engage in the political process.

Although the projects of the political foundations are distinct from the official aid programme, there are increasing efforts at coordination. In Mozambique, for example, work on decentralisation that was initiated by political foundations has now been taken over by GTZ (German Agency for Technical Cooperation). In the early stages it would have been too sensitive for an official German aid programme but the political foundations have the freedom to establish their own direct relations with governments and partner organisations.

The political foundations are not members of VENRO but some cooperate with it and participate in NGO campaigns. Some are very active in adult development education.

PRIVATE ORGANISATIONS

BENGO (Advice Centre for NGOs working in the Field of Development) was set up in 1988 on the initiative of NGOs and BMZ to act as an advice centre for NGOs classed as private organisations – in other words those which are not part of the Protestant or Catholic churches or political foundations. It acts as a clearing house, advising NGOs on project applications, ensuring that those that go forward for decision meet government criteria.

BENGO has about 1000 German organisations on its database – but reckons that there are three times that number in existence. Around 200 NGOs apply for funds from BMZ via BENGO each year. These range from large, national organisations like Deutsche Welthungerhilfe to specialist organisations based on a link between communities. About 130 organisations received government funding, and over 340 projects were financed in 1997. BENGO is run as a project and attached to an umbrella organisation for German non-denominational welfare NGOs, the PARITÄTISCHE wohlfahrtsverband.

Conditions for eligibility are stringent. NGOs must have been registered locally as an association for three years and are required to have a democratically elected board. They must be engaged in project work. They must submit financial reports covering a three-year period and they must spend no more than 20 per cent of their income (net of fundraising costs) on administration.

DM32 million (about $21.3 m) was available for co-financing private organisations in 1997 and was expected to increase in future years. Private organisations have a strong group of supporters in parliament and although their allocation is much lower than Church organisations it has been protected from budget cuts. BMZ intends to increase the co-financing of non-denominational NGOs by 10 per cent a year, even in the face of general cuts expected in the coming years.

Co-financing is offered on a 75:25 ratio and is only available for project funding, not for general or programme support. Up to 15 per cent of the cost may be met from developing country inputs, but most NGOs finance the full 25 per cent from fundraising in Germany. NGOs in eastern Germany are in an especially difficult situation. Therefore, in most cases they are required to finance only 10 per cent of the costs themselves. Furthermore, a foundation has been established – the North–South Bridge Foundation – that assists eastern German NGOs with part of their proportion of project costs.

VOLUME OF SUPPORT TO NGOS

In volume terms, German government and voluntary public support to NGOs was the second highest in the DAC in 1995, exceeded only by the US. As a percentage of the BMZ budget in 1995, Germany allocated 9 per cent to support for NGOs. This represented 40 per cent of their total income. Funding is also available from German embassies to local organisations up to a project limit of DM15,000 (about $10,000).

Non-denominational NGOs have in the past been very critical of their small funding share and have argued that it should be increased. They have also argued that the administrative requirements attached to project applications should be streamlined and simplified. They also objected to a double standard, which funds administrative costs for projects under the political foundations and not for them. The BMZ took the latter argument very seriously and convinced the Federal Ministry of Finance to finance administrative costs for non-denominational NGOs as well.

Table 10.1: *BMZ Allocations to German NGOs in 1996 and 1997*

NGOs[4]	Allocations from BMZ in 1997 in thousand DMs	Allocations from BMZ in 1996 in thousand DMs
Church NGOs	286,500	296,000
Political Foundations	312,000	317,000
Non-denominational NGOs	32,000	32,000
NGOs supporting the building of social structures	41,000	42,000
Total	671,500	687,000

REGULATION

NGO finances are monitored by the German Central Institute for Social Affairs (DZI). NGOs that meet defined standards are certified. The DZI also monitors performance of NGOs that have been recognised and it has the sanction to withdraw approval – a sanction that has on occasion been used.[5]

FISCAL INCENTIVES AND PRIVATE GIVING

Private contributions are a major (and sometimes the only) source of income for many NGOs. Government fiscal policies are supportive of this fact and donations are eligible for tax relief up to 10 per cent of taxable income. In 1992 private fundraising exceeded government funding by a factor of almost two to one.

HUMANITARIAN ASSISTANCE

Humanitarian aid is disbursed by the Federal Foreign Office. German aid for humanitarian assistance has been constant over the last few years, with a budget of DM70–80 million a year (about $47–53 m). Only four out of the 56 NGOs described by ECHO in its 1996 annual report as 'main partners' were German. Since then the relationship between German NGOs and ECHO has improved considerably.

The Federal Foreign Office is not operational in disaster situations, working only through German embassies, international agencies and NGOs. With the two latter ones it discusses strategy, but not management or tactics. A key role is played by the Committee of Coordination, which brings together the more important humanitarian organisations along with the relevant federal ministries, including the Federal Foreign Office, Ministry of Economic and Development Cooperation, the Ministry of Defence and others such as the Ministry of Transport, as well as representatives of the Länder (Federal States). The committee was established in 1991 when operations in Iraq demonstrated the need for better coordination. It was then formalised in 1994. Non-government members include German humanitarian organisations and international bodies with German affiliation.

The committee exists to define a course of action and then to identify what resources different agencies can apply to it. Important among these are their partner organisations and their links to civil society. This is seen as part of the guiding philosophy and raison d'être for the involvement of NGOs: the opportunity to work with different groups and support pluralism in an emergency situation. Thus while the focus is on humanitarian assistance, there is a role for NGOs in supplying information about the broader political scene and in positioning their own work in a wider political context.

The allocation of funds of the Federal Foreign Office to NGOs and international organisations varies according to the location of the disaster. In former Yugoslavia, for instance, around one third of the funds went to international organisations and two thirds to German-based NGOs. In the Great Lakes, a much lower proportion went to NGOs.

NGOs have welcomed the introduction of a new BMZ budget line, which integrates emergency, food and refugee aid. It is hoped that this will lead to a more consistent approach to the linkages between short-term and long-term aid. A VENRO working group is coordinating NGOs also involved in humanitarian assistance.

VOLUNTEER PROGRAMMES

There are six volunteer sending agencies in Germany. The two Church-related agencies send three to four hundred volunteers each, but the largest, Deutscher Entwicklungsdienst, has about 1000 volunteers in the field at any one time. DED is a private company in which the Federal government holds 95 per cent of the shares with an association of NGOs holding the remainder. It is fully financed by government, including all running costs. The 18-member board of directors includes government officials and deputies from the federal parliament as well as representatives from associations of small businesses and other groups.

Volunteering through a German agency is open to anyone in the EU, but volunteers must bring at least two years of professional experience and currently the average age is 38. Because of the importance of returned volunteers in development education, DED resources are allocated to this. DED is in contact with almost 10 per cent of the 11,000 volunteers it has placed over the last 30 years and 300 of them are active in development education.

EVALUATION

BMZ evaluates the effectiveness of official German development cooperation while implementing agencies evaluate their own work. Wiemann reports that in 1993, '50 efficiency control measures were carried out, including 40 evaluations of individual projects or programmes, five thematic serial evaluations and five thematic cross sectoral analyses.'[6] He observes, however, that findings remain confidential except for condensed cross sectoral analyses, which are submitted to parliament.

The BMZ has started a process of thematic evaluation in addition to project evaluation. The aim is to tie evaluations to a process of improving the quality of project work. The two completed by mid 1997 were on housing and credit.

DEVELOPMENT EDUCATION AND PUBLIC INFORMATION

Very little government support is offered for development education: just over DM6 million (about $4 million) from the BMZ budget in 1997. This was less than in 1996. More money is spent by the churches than by the State for development education. The most active development education organisation is the Ausschuss für Entwicklungsbezogene Bildung und Publizistik (the Committee for Development Education and Publications of the Protestant churches), which exists to promote, fund and coordinate development education in Germany. Funded completely from Church taxes it covers a wide range of topics and maintains a staff person in each German state.

BMZ produces a regular flow of public information, including a magazine which places development cooperation in a mainstream economic and political interest framework. Wiemann describes BMZ as 'a relatively open ministry, aware that it has to education the public on development issues and provide a realistic assessment of both the problems and the limited capacity to solve them with the present aid volumes, in order to enhance public support for development cooperation'.

There are indications that public education is becoming a greater priority for BMZ and that it is trying to reach out to new public constituencies. Part of this outreach has been through a television drama series set in South-east Asia. NGOs support the concept of development education that is more than preaching to the choir, but many felt that the use of soap opera as a medium, while innovative, did not convey its messages clearly enough.

There is good potential for NGOs and governments to work together on development education around international summits. These have been vehicles for promoting new ideas about international cooperation, but so far they have not been part of a strategy to energize public opinion about development cooperation.

German attitudes towards development cooperation are broadly supportive. Over 87 per cent of Germans – equal to the EU average – consider development assistance to be important. A 1997 Eurobarometre survey,[7] however, notes that compared with the EU average, German knowledge about development is low, and there is a higher than average overstatement of the volume of aid. A 1994 survey found that 75 per cent of people in western Germany and 69 per cent in eastern Germany were in favour of development cooperation, but at that time only 34 per cent considered themselves to be well informed on aid spending.

ADVOCACY AND ENGAGEMENT

Dialogue on policy issues is relatively formal in Germany. NGOs are invited to comment on country concept papers before negotiations with the recipient country take place, and VENRO now has the task of ensuring that NGOs with appropriate expertise are engaged in these discussions. Sectoral policy papers are reviewed by the political foundations, churches and specialised NGOs. NGOs are also represented on key working groups such as one on poverty alleviation.

The churches use some of their block grant money to support advocacy and policy work among their partners overseas. Striking examples include work on child labour, particularly in the carpet industry; support for the NGO advocacy body *Third World Network* and activities to form a network on economic justice in Zimbabwe. German NGOs have been very active on trade issues – the handloom carpet industry, environmental issues, bribery, and the use of mixed credits for export promotion.

German NGOs have also been concerned about the share of German aid that should go through multilateral agencies. NGOs have reacted strongly to parliamentary suggestions that a ceiling should be set on multilateral contributions, and that they should be explicitly linked to returns to Germany. NGOs, which in Germany have a particularly global perspective, argue that multilateral aid is often more effective and more appropriate than bilateral assistance.

Debt has also been a key issue, led by the 25 member organisations of the Debt Crisis Network (Initiativkreis Entwicklung braucht Entschuldung). At the end of 1996 a petition with 13,000 signatures was presented to the German Parliament requesting a cancellation of all of Germany's debt claims with the 30 poorest countries. This was turned down by the Parliamentary Budget Committee despite strong support from development-oriented politicians.

ISSUES

NGO collaboration on social issues

The German NGO community has been characterised by its segmentation into churches, political foundations and non-denominational groups. The sectors do work together, most notably in the founding of VENRO, but also in other ways. For many years there has been a close and fruitful cooperation between German development NGOs and BMZ on the issue of poverty reduction. The ministry's concepts are based on this cooperation. Following the World Summit on Social Development, German NGOs established a forum. This has proved to be a strong collaborative venture resulting in both policy positions and a drive towards reform and change within NGOs themselves. In addition to analysing BMZ approaches to, and expenditure on, poverty reduction and above all the 20:20 issues,[8] the NGO Forum also looked at NGO efforts, recognising that 'the general public expects a higher degree of transparency and accountability with regard to priorities of NGO programmes.'[9]

Interestingly, NGOs cite the process of discussion about ODA as actually having been a challenge to them. 'Discussions over poverty issues between NGOs on the one side and bilateral as well as multilateral donors on the other side have deepened NGO understanding of their own deficiencies.'

SENSITIVITY TO CRITICISM

BMZ appreciates the support of NGOs for development questions in the public discussion. Because of mergers between other ministries, BMZ has been engaged in a process of building support for its continuation as a separate ministry and for the maintenance of its funding. NGOs represent both public and parliamentary constituencies and receive substantial government co-financing. NGOs – in common with many others, including the DAC – want BMZ to remain as a separate ministry and to be strengthened. In these circumstances, it is not surprising that BMZ has been sensitive to criticism from NGOs.

Criticism was expressed through an annual report on German aid led by two non-denominational NGOs, terre des hommes (tdh) and Deutsche Welthungerhilfe (DWHH). This is not always critical of BMZ but it caused a forceful reaction from the Minister for Economic Cooperation in 1994 and 1997. Some NGOs see a benefit for the sector as a whole if particular agencies go out on a limb in their critiques. They feel that it may move the debate ahead and create opportunities for progress in less public advocacy. Others see it more as a matter of style. As far as substance is concerned however, there is probably not a great deal of difference between the NGOs. While government always reacts to criticism, it also recognises that it needs NGOs. The noise they create helps focus attention on issues and raises awareness of the importance of development cooperation.

COMPARATIVE ADVANTAGE

BMZ and German NGOs are close to each other in their policy positions and approaches to development. With the formation of VENRO, the common ground has become more marked. Some NGOs are concerned that this may mask the need to highlight the comparative advantage of different actors in development assistance. They question whether NGOs are overstating their own strengths and obscuring the need for State action. One example is in the area of conflict prevention, where NGO bullishness about their capacities may be undercutting public understanding of the need for a strong government role in working towards peace.

11 Greece

Dimitra Massoula

SUMMARY

The population in Greece has suffered from many natural catastrophes, and people are sensitive and willing to help others in need. Because the economy was fragile for many years, development assistance was largely a government activity until recently, and the arrival of NGOs in civil society in Greece is a relatively new phenomenon. Greek NGOs have participated in EU co-financing since 1981, the year of Greek accession to the European Community. Nevertheless, the further development of NGOs will depend on further interaction between Greek public opinion, government, and the NGOs themselves. Until recently they acted more or less independently, in a limited and informal context. At present, the governmental aid structures are at a crossroads, with NGOs posing a dilemma for the government. The government opted for change (the Five-Year Programme, the elaboration of a legal framework for cooperation with NGOs), and is inaugurating a new era in Greek international development.

Greek NGOs are still in a learning process. Much has yet to be done on official registration procedures, record keeping, evaluation, development education, and the evolution of longer-term development programming, as opposed to short-term emergency activities. Greek NGOs will have to work harder on private fundraising in order to avoid an over-dependence on government. Both the government and NGOs have many programmes and interests in common and they are already collaborating to establish closer cooperation on a long-term basis.

INTRODUCTION

In 1833, Greece became an independent state after four hundred years of Ottoman rule. At the crossroads of East and West, of Asia and Europe, Greece is a Balkan, a European and a Mediterranean country. Greece was seriously damaged by both World Wars and the two civil wars that followed. This meant that Greece was mainly, until recently, a recipient of foreign aid, and at the same time did not enjoy the take-off experienced by other countries in Europe.

Despite economic difficulties, Greeks have been strongly motivated from the early 1950s to assist in humanitarian causes and development work, initially through Greek Orthodox Church missionaries in Asia and in Africa. Greece has deepened and strengthened her civil society through membership in international organisations, and through the domestic evolution of multi-interest religious and political institutions, NGOs, think tanks, and lobby groups.

The Ministry of Foreign Affairs is the principal determinant of Greek priorities in official development assistance, exercising a preference for emergency situations over long-term development. Data on NGOs and development assistance in Greece dates mainly from the early 1990s. Systematic research and record keeping only began in 1995.[1]

The Motivation and Legal Framework of Greek ODA

In the establishment of an aid programme, 'At first Greece acted cautiously, mostly through multilateral aid programmes financed or supported by international organisations. Gradually, however, as experience was gained and the amount of available funds increased, bilateral assistance programmes were initiated and have become ever more important.'[2] Greece's motivation for official development assistance is fundamentally humanitarian. Enlightened self-interest is a second reason for development assistance, and development cooperation is seen as a way of helping people from both industrialised and developing countries to work together in addressing common problems and to pursue common aspirations. Greece is interested in alleviating social problems and in developing acceptable living conditions in countries receiving official development assistance, and in encouraging the respect of receiver governments for basic human rights and freedoms.[3]

> 'Greece tends to favour small scale projects targeted to the solution of specific problems. At the same time, Greece feels that it is important to develop close partnerships with non-governmental organisations in the receiving countries with the aim of increasing the efficiency of the assistance programmes, developing local skills and encouraging self-reliance.'[4]

Because of the absence of a central agency for the administration of Greek aid, official development assistance on a multilateral or bilateral basis is supplied by various Ministries, primarily the Ministry of Foreign Affairs and the Ministry of National Economy, but also the Ministries of Industry, Agriculture, Labour, Health, Education, Commerce and National Defence. Traditionally and historically, the Ministry of Foreign Affairs is the principal governmental institution dealing with development assistance. In particular, according to Presidential Decree 11/1992, it is competent to:

*   grant foreign aid and development cooperation together with the other jointly competent ministries, agencies and organisations and non-governmental organisations;
*   study and administer matters concerning development cooperation in all sectors, in cooperation with other ministries;
*   grant aid to developing countries from the budget of the Ministry of Foreign Affairs;
*   evaluate programmes of development cooperation with other ministries;
*   suggest the adoption of general principles of development, such as the concentration of Greek foreign aid in certain countries;
*   support non-governmental organisations dealing with development cooperation.

Within the framework of this Presidential Decree, a law was prepared by the Ministry of Foreign Affairs, and at the time of writing was being discussed in the Greek Parliament. This law 'will readjust and clarify all matters relating to the supply of development aid, as well as the relevant jurisdiction of the Ministry of Foreign Affairs. In particular, the role of the Ministry of Foreign Affairs will be determined in the formulation of development aid policy, as well as [in] the establishment, operation and follow up of the activities of non-governmental organisations.'[5] Furthermore, this law will enable and facilitate closer relations between different development aid actors, and will end the absence of a legal framework for such cooperation.

The five-year programme

A five year development assistance programme was prepared in 1996 by the Ministries of Foreign Affairs, National Economy and Finance. This programme puts the development co-operation policy on a new basis and widens possibilities concerning both the number of sectors and the total sum of allocations. It provides for:

*   an increase in total Greek bilateral ODA to US$90 million (0.08 per cent of GNP) for the five years 1997–2001;
*   the adoption in the State Budget of a specific line on the necessary funds, with the aim of gradually attaining the level of 0.1 per cent of GNP for bilateral ODA, so that total multilateral and bilateral assistance will amount to at least 0.2 per cent of GNP;
*   the establishment of a Special Committee on Development Cooperation composed of representatives from relevant ministries and agencies for the coordination, monitoring, following and evaluation of bilateral development assistance.

The main goals of the five-year programme are:

*   economic well-being; the reduction of poverty;
*   social development; progress in education, gender equality, basic health services;
*   environmental sustainability;
*   reinforcement of locally planned development strategies, by financing public expenditure through the budget of the developing countries and economies in transition.[6]

Geographical priorities for bilateral ODA for the years 1997–2001 are the Balkan states, countries of the former Soviet Union, Black Sea countries, Asia and Africa.

THE GREEK NGO COMMUNITY

Domestic non-governmental organisations are a rather recent phenomenon in Greece, compared with their long history in other European countries. Even more recent and more limited are the international development NGOs. Development NGOs firstly appeared at the end of the 1980s and early 1990s, and Greek branches of international NGOs have also been established, mainly in the areas of human rights and environmental protection.

Founded in 1981, the Greek Committee for International Democratic Solidarity (EEDDA) was the first Greek NGO,

> *'to contribute to the consolidation of friendship and solidarity among the peoples, to plan, promote and implement development programmes in developing countries, in partnership with local NGOs, to inform and mobilize the Greek people to offer moral, political and economic support to the peoples struggling for national independence, freedom, democracy, social progress and peace.'*

In 1986 following the creation of the Committee of the Initiative for Hunger in Africa, which organised two large solidarity concerts at the end of 1985, the Hellenic Institute of Solidarity and Cooperation with developing countries (HELINAS) was founded. Its objectives are,

> *'to relay the message of solidarity of the Greek people to the people of the Third World and of Central – Eastern Europe, with the supply of urgent humanitarian aid to the victims of natural disasters and war, and with the implementation of*

> *long-term development projects in agriculture, health, education, employment, environmental protection, etc.'*

It also implements educational programmes in Greece which aim to inform, mobilise and sensitise Greek public opinion on the problems and needs of developing countries and the countries of Eastern Europe, and to disseminate information about the basic principles of cooperation and interdependence of North–South/East–West and the necessity of collaboration between them.

In 1991, KESSAP DIMITRA was founded to carry out development and educational programmes, as well as humanitarian aid. These three are the principal Greek development NGOs. There are also Greek branches of international medical and humanitarian aid NGOs (*Médecins sans Frontières*, Doctors of the World, the Hellenic Red Cross, Save the Children).

For their fundraising, NGOs appeal to public and private sources. The largest part of their projects is financed by government (Ministry of Foreign Affairs, Ministry of National Economy). As no legal framework exists for norms and conditions, the financial contribution of government is handled on a project-by-project basis. For the balance, NGOs depend on private donations, member subscriptions and in certain cases, on commercial activities (concerts, publications). As noted below, they also receive co-financing support from DG VIII of the European Commission.

Most NGOs work through volunteers; HELINAS has the largest number of permanent salaried staff. In terms of strategy, Greek NGOs have tended to support mainly medium-term programmes. Lately, however, they are working towards a longer-term development approach. The medical and humanitarian NGOs are concerned mainly with emergency and short-term projects.

The Greek Orthodox Church

The Greek Orthodox Church undertakes important development initiatives. Under its Holy Synod, the *Apostoliki Diakonia* of the Church of Greece is responsible for the planning, organisation and execution of the missionary and educational work of the Church. The *Apostoliki Diakonia* was founded in 1936 and undertook its first missionary work in Africa and in Asia in 1970, establishing medical, health and educational programmes. Their development tasks include teaching and education, school construction and organisation, potable water, hospital construction and equipment, and the amelioration of living and sanitary conditions. Their programmes are long-term.

Funds are provided from the budget of the *Apostoliki Diakonia* and from public collections once a year during the first Sunday of Lent.[7] Only volunteers are engaged in the missionary work, receiving their travelling expenses and a monthly allowance of US$200 to cover personal expenses. They live in missionary settlements. Missionary work does not benefit from government assistance, but the government or local authorities (regional, prefectoral) can cooperate with the Church in some initiatives, such as emergency aid programmes.

Due to the decentralised structure of the Orthodox Church, there is no institutionalized 'umbrella organisation'. Each Church acts independently in its development and emergency aid. Though, acting independently did not exclude cooperation among several churches in assistance programmes, as happened, for example, in the former Yugoslavia.

The European Community Development Programme

Greek NGOs have participated in EU co-financing since 1981, the year of Greek accession to the European Community. Seventy two programmes had been implemented by 1996, with a total cost of ECU 13,575,856. Greek NGOs usually provide 15 per cent of the total cost required.

Nine Greek NGOs participate in these programmes but two are more involved than others. Of 54 projects between 1981 and 1996, EEDDA participated in 44 and HELINAS in ten. For

Greek NGOs, the biggest problem is covering their 15 per cent of the budget. The EU demand for professionalism is also problematic, as most Greek NGOs are new and work largely with volunteers. Moreover, Greek NGOs are still very attached to emergency aid, although this is changing.

THE GOVERNMENT AS PARTNER IN DEVELOPMENT

The government position on ODA:

> '*At present, Greece, with the level of economic development that it has achieved and the economic policy that has been applied in recent years, has become an industrialized country and has found itself in a position to be able to grant official development assistance with the view of deepening existing relations of friendship and trust with developing countries*'.[8]

Through different ministries, the government has also inaugurated a policy of cooperation with NGOs. In the absence of a distinct institutional government umbrella for this, in 1996 government took the initiative of elaborating one. Following consultation within government and with NGOs, a bill was drafted, and at the time of writing was before Parliament.

The Greek government allocates the greater part of its total development and humanitarian aid to the Balkans and the former Soviet countries for three reasons:

- good neighbourliness;
- Greeks live in these countries;
- their proximity decreases aid delivery costs.

The B5 Directorate on Development, Cooperation and Special Economic Affairs in the Ministry of Foreign Affairs co-finances NGO projects, requiring the participation of a local partner as a precondition to approval. Other factors include the work and operational background of the NGO, and the project itself. There is no ceiling on allocations but the total grant depends on the nature of the programme and budget restrictions in the Ministry. In 1995, for example, the Ministry met approximately 30 per cent of the total cost of the programmes that were approved.

Greek authorities confirm the emphasis on emergency programming. Since 1990, of 36 NGO programmes co-financed by different ministries, 17 were development or non-emergency aid with a total cost US$7 million. During the period 1993–1995, development or non-emergency assistance totalled US$2.8 million, while emergency and humanitarian aid totalled US$84.7 million.

Table 11.1: *Greek Humanitarian Aid Allocated between 1993–95 (US$)*

Humanitarian aid allocated by governmental institutions	Humanitarian aid allocated by NGOs	Year
11,295,534	5,967,079	1993
25,781,715	11,671,840	1994
22,838,871	7,174,613	1995

Source: Ministry of Foreign Affairs B5 Directorate – Development cooperation & special economic affairs

The Ministry of National Economy has also worked with NGOs. During the period 1990–1996, eight programmes were implemented, mainly in the field of education, medical services and infrastructure, institutional support and training. Other Ministries that have supported NGOs include the Ministry of Agriculture, the Ministry of Health and Welfare, the Ministry of Social Security and the Ministry of Defence. A number of municipalities, in cooperation with the Greek Orthodox Church, provide emergency assistance, and educational institutions (universities and secondary schools) also work with NGOs.

Separately from the development activities undertaken by the different ministries, important initiatives are also undertaken by state-funded and state-supervised organisations. The 'Greek organisation of small-medium manufacturing and handicraft enterprises' (Eommex) promotes small-medium enterprises and development infrastructure in cooperation with the EU, NGOs, local and public authorities. The 'Greek Organisation of Export Promotion' focuses on investments, trade, training and support of development programmes especially in Eastern Europe and the former Soviet Union. The 'Greek Productivity Centre' 'aims the promotion of productivity in various sectors' through training, development and the application of advanced technology and know-how, especially, since 1980, in the Eastern Mediterranean, Central and East European countries within the context of EU programmes and in cooperation with several organisations.

DEVELOPMENT EDUCATION

Some development education in Greece is undertaken solely by government, and some is undertaken by NGOs with government support. Government works primarily through the school system, dealing with subjects such as relations with other countries and peoples, economic growth and development, international trade, and protection of the environment. These are presented for the first time in primary school, to children between the ages of nine and twelve in text books (*Emeis kai o kosmos, Erevno to fisiko perivalon*) published under the aegis of the Ministry of National Education and Religions.

A second approach is through projects undertaken by the Ministry of National Education and Religions and NGOs, in the domains of environment and health education. In 1996, the Ministry informed school directors that NGOs could submit proposals that were complementary to school curricula. These proposals might include mobile educational programmes, environmental excursions, live presentations, pilot programmes, distribution of information and contests. The General Secretariat of Youth also works with NGOs. Projects deal with racism and xenophobia, ecology and environment, and employment issues.

On the environment, activities are carried out by NGOs on the basis of bilateral protocols with other countries. From 1990 to 1997, 110 programmes were carried out in cooperation with 37 NGOs (35 Greek and two branches of international NGOs). Expenses are covered by the NGO, the General Secretariat of Youth and private sponsors. The European Union may also contribute. A principal target for this department is the development of a European orientation for youth networks on the environment, culture, civilisation, employment, and the creation of local youth councils.

In the field of development-environmental education, important initiatives have been undertaken by the Goulandri Museum of Natural History in Athens. In cooperation with several ministries, the Museum organises and promotes educational programmes and public awareness activities on environmental issues.

12 Ireland[1]

Ian Smillie

SUMMARY

Many Irish NGOs are very small, but Ireland's largest are as large as those in almost any DAC Member country, despite Ireland's relatively small population.

Irish Aid operates a co-financing mechanism, providing grants for projects in health, education, water supply, sanitation, employment creation, agriculture and rural development. Although multi-year funding is not excluded, most projects tend to be one-off efforts. In 1994, a block grant mechanism was created for NGOs that 'have demonstrated a significant track record in development projects and involvement in the Official Aid Programme'.

With 70 to 80 personnel-sending organisations, some of which are very small, Ireland's volunteer-sending efforts differ markedly from those of other DAC countries, in part because of the country's long tradition of missionary outreach. As with other DAC Member countries, Ireland's expenditure on emergency and humanitarian assistance has increased dramatically in recent years, with at least half of the government's expenditure being channelled through Irish NGOs, and more than one third through the three largest, Concern, Trócaire and Goal.

A formal development education programme was initiated in 1985, 'aimed at promoting a better awareness and understanding among Irish People of development issues'. One estimate placed independent NGO spending on development education at more than Ir£1.5 million in 1994, or about double government expenditure. The issue of human rights has risen on the agenda of both the Government of Ireland and the Irish NGO community in recent years, partly because of increased numbers of asylum seekers in Ireland, and partly because of the 1997 appointment of the then Irish President, Mary Robinson, as United Nations High Commissioner for Human Rights.

BACKGROUND

Ireland's international non-governmental outreach has its roots in the missionary movement which dates well back into the eighteenth century. It has perhaps deeper roots in the devastating famine which struck Ireland in the middle of the last century, the 150th anniversary of which was commemorated throughout the country in 1995. A 1995 Pastoral Letter of the Bishops of Ireland observed that,

> *In the years following 1845, a million people died and millions emigrated... We need to draw lessons from our famine experience in a world which still knows*

> *famine and hunger. There is plenty, yet over 700 million people do not have enough to eat each day; 40 million people die annually from hunger and related diseases; one third of all African children are malnourished. Moreover, the presence of a sizeable Irish emigrant community, much of which arises from famine times, reminds us of refugees and displaced people in many parts of the world today.*[2]

Although not as strong in relative terms as it was two or three decades ago, Irish missionary activity – which increasingly emphasises development work in addition to its pastoral outreach – is still very strong. In 1994 there were over 4000 Irish Catholic missionaries serving in 90 countries, representing 90 congregations of religious sisters, 34 societies of priests, 10 congregations of religious brothers, 21 Irish dioceses and two Lay Missionary organisations.

Size of the NGO community

A 1992 NGO publication put the number of voluntary organisations at approximately 50,[3] but the figure depends to a certain extent on the definition used. A 1992 directory listed 43 organisations involved in development education, and a further 21 groups involved in solidarity and campaigning work. A 1996 OECD Directory listed 56 Irish NGOs.[4]

Many of these are very small, some operating entirely on a voluntary basis. Ireland's largest NGOs, however, are as large as those in almost any DAC Member country, despite Ireland's relatively small population. Concern,[5] founded in 1968, is the largest and fastest growing, with 1994 cash revenues of Ir£31.3 million (US$46.7 million), an increase of 24 per cent over the previous year. In recent years it has established offices in Britain and the United States, and its private donor fundraising in these three countries represented approximately 45 per cent of its total cash income. Trócaire, established by the Bishops of Ireland in 1973, recorded a 1994–5 income of Ir£17.2 million (US$27.5 million), and Goal, established in 1977, recorded a total 1994 expenditure of Ir£6.8 million (US$10.2 million).

A handful of larger 'transnational' NGOs operate in Ireland, among them ActionAid, Christian Aid and Oxfam. World Vision, by far the largest fundraising NGO in the United States, Canada, Australia and New Zealand, began operations in Ireland in the 1980s, but became the centre of controversy because of its child sponsorship funding base, and has not grown in Ireland as it has elsewhere.

There are a variety of formal and informal NGO networks in Ireland. The Confederation of NGOs for Overseas Development (CONGOOD), founded in 1974, merged with the Irish National Assembly in 1994 to form Dóchas ('Hope'), a grouping of 24 NGOs aiming to help its members 'speak with a single voice on development issues', to elect a member to the EC/NGDO Liaison Committee, to conduct research and to carry out development education activities. Dóchas and its predecessor agencies have published a variety of materials, including a *Guide to Development Education Resources-Activities in Ireland* (1992), and *75:25; Ireland in an Increasingly Unequal World* (1996). Dóchas takes adherence to its values and its code of conduct seriously, and in 1995 turned down applications for membership from two of Ireland's larger NGOs because their fundraising was based in one case on child sponsorship, and in the other on overly emotive emergency-based appeals. Dóchas played an active role in advocacy on development issues during the Irish presidency of the EU (July–December 1996), highlighting the importance of coherence between development and other policies – arms, food security, security policy and gender.

Some Dóchas members represent a broader constituency of smaller organisations. The Irish Missionary Union (IMU), for example, represents over 80 church-based organisations. There are other networks that involve Dóchas members and non-Dóchas members. NODE, a 'Network Outreach in Development Education' project, links a number of development education resource centres and NGOs around common themes, while DEFY – Development Education for Youth – is a partnership between a number of NGOs and youth organisations. The Network of Irish

Table 12.1: *1994 Sources of Income of Selected Irish NGOs (Ir£ 000)*

	EU	Irish Govt	Public	Other	Total
Concern	3529	3806	13,491	24,552	45,378
Trócaire	1312	1463	13,306	1176	17,234
Goal	462	1320	3221	3104	8107
Oxfam Ireland		250	◄——— 1570 ———►		1820
Self Help Dev'ment	◄——— 585 ———►		293	44	922
Action Aid	86		738	10	841
World Vision		72	650		723

Source: Irish Times, 22 November 1995. Notes: Figures for public giving in 1994 were unusually high because of the Rwanda crisis; 'other' Concern income includes Ir£ 14 million.

Environment and Development Organisations issued a 1995 Directory, which included the names of 124 Irish organisations, ranging from Greenpeace and World Vision to Cuba Aid and Badgerwatch Ireland.

Regulation of NGOs and tax status

There is no charities legislation in Ireland, but an official advisory group was established in 1996 to advise government on the establishment of charities legislation, and possibly a code of practice. In order to qualify for assistance from government, NGOs are required to register with the Revenue Commissioner for Charitable Status. This mechanism is regarded by some as rather permissive, and is only loosely administered. The possibility of a provision for making charitable donations tax deductible was mentioned in Irish Aid's 1993 *Strategy Plan*, but this was overtaken by a rather unique scheme to encourage greater philanthropy for international development: starting in 1995, all donations between Ir£200 and Ir£750 are permitted a 27 per cent refund on donations by the Ministry of Finance.

This means that a donation of Ir£200 to an NGO results in a net value of Ir£274, and a donation of Ir£511 is worth Ir£700. It is unclear what volume of new donations the scheme will attract in the long run. The bulk of Irish donors probably give less than £200 per annum. Will the scheme encourage higher levels of giving? Or will it actually yield very little in the way of new money? Because the scheme has been made available only to international development NGOs, there is pressure to expand it, and this would likely dilute the potential value for international development.[6] In December 1997, a new mechanism was established, giving tax relief to corporate donors on donations of more than Ir£10,000, complementing the scheme for individual donors.

IRELAND'S OFFICIAL DEVELOPMENT ASSISTANCE

Before 1975, Ireland's ODA was based almost entirely on mandatory contributions to multilateral organisations such as United Nations development agencies, and its development assistance image was derived primarily from the work of Irish missionaries and a handful of small NGOs. Following Ireland's entry into the European Community in 1973, official development assistance began to grow, and a formal bilateral aid programme was established within the Department of Foreign Affairs (DFA) in 1975.[7]

Throughout the 1980s, Ireland's ODA remained small, focusing heavily on multilateral agencies, and on the sending of technical assistance and volunteers. As a percentage of GNP,

Irish Aid fell from 0.28 per cent in 1986 to 0.16 per cent in 1990 and 1992. Soon after the 1993 formation of a coalition government between Fianna Fáil and Labour, a new Strategy Plan, *Irish Aid: Consolidation and Growth* was released, outlining profound changes in the quantity and approach to official development assistance. It was announced that ODA would be returned to 'a position of prominence in terms of international issues facing the Government' and that as a percentage of GNP, it would rise to 0.4 per cent by 1997. In fact the totals fell somewhat behind target, increasing from Ir£54 million in 1993, to Ir£179 million in 1996, representing an increase of 15 per cent in real terms in only one year, but an ODA/GNP ratio of 0.31 per cent.[8]

Much of the growth has been absorbed by relative increases in bilateral assistance, and by adding Ethiopia and Uganda to the four priority countries that have consumed most of Ireland's bilateral assistance in the past – Tanzania, Zambia, Lesotho and Sudan. The new *Strategy Plan* stated that 'The first priority of Irish Aid is to provide assistance to poorer developing countries... to meet basic needs, particularly of the more disadvantaged... and to contribute to long term economic and social development... The objective of Irish Aid is to leave behind structures which enable our development partners to manage the future themselves.' The strategy also noted that 'sustainable development is possible only when adequate attention is paid to the particular role of women in development and to environmental issues.'[9]

A joint Oireachtas (Parliamentary) Committee on Foreign Affairs was established, with a sub committee on development cooperation. An independent body – the Irish Aid Advisory Committee – was also established to advise the Minister on broader issues relating to development assistance. And in 1994, the first annual National Forum on Development Aid brought together high level government officials, NGOs and others involved in international development to exchange views on the aid programme and on Ireland's development policies. The 1997 Forum examined issues related to multilateral assistance.

Since 1997, the Minister of State with responsibility for ODA has the title of Minister of State for Overseas Development and Human Rights. Irish Aid is administered by the Development Cooperation Division (DCD) of the Department of Foreign Affairs. An Assistant Secretary is responsible to the Minister of State, and DCD is divided into four branches:

- Multilateral Institutions and Aid Policy;
- Bilateral Aid I: Southern, Eastern and Horn of Africa; NGO Co-financing Scheme;
- Bilateral Aid II: Other Countries, Emergency Aid, Refugees, Volunteers, Administration, Liaison with Advisory Committee;
- Audit and Evaluation Unit.

Irish Aid provides support to NGOs through several mechanisms. The most prominent is a co-financing arrangement for development projects designed and managed by NGOs. Funding is made available for volunteers and other overseas workers through the Agency for Personal Service Overseas (APSO), and in recent years, increasing amounts of support have been available to NGOs for their work in emergencies. Government supports the development education work of NGOs, and has initiated a special fund for human rights and democracy.

THE NGO CO-FINANCING SCHEME

Irish Aid operates a co-financing mechanism (The NGO Co-Financing Scheme), providing grants for projects in health, education, water supply, sanitation, employment creation, agriculture and rural development. Until 1994, there was an upper limit of Ir£50,000 per project, towards which Irish Aid would contribute up to 75 per cent. The upper limit was raised that year to Ir£75,000, although most projects tend to be much smaller. The average grant size in 1994 was approximately Ir£14,000.

Table 12.2: *Irish ODA, 1985–95 (Ir£ million)*

	1985	1994	1995	1996	1997
Total ODA	39.0	75.2	88.9	105.8	122.2
Bilateral	15.4	38.1	53.3	65.0	79.4
Multilateral	23.1	29.6	33.8	36.8	38.6
ODA as % of GNP	0.25	0.24	0.27	0.29	0.31

Source: DFA (1995); O'Neill, 1995a; *Reality of Aid 1996*; Department of Foreign Affairs. 1996 and 1997 figures are allocations.

Although multi-year funding is not excluded, most projects tend to be one-off efforts, with funding criteria placing a heavy emphasis on 'hardware', rather than 'software': wells, buildings, vehicles. The rationale for this is that recurrent costs should be met by the NGO, and that government support should be provided mainly for capital investments that are beyond the NGO's normal reach.

Submissions are made to Irish Aid for consideration at four meetings during the year. Decisions on grants are made by an NGO Co-Financing Committee, chaired by the Bilateral Aid Counsellor, and comprising senior Irish Aid officials, a representative of APSO and a representative of the Irish Aid Advisory Committee.

In 1994, a block grant mechanism was created for NGOs that 'have demonstrated a significant track record in development projects and involvement in the Official Aid Programme'.[10] Currently available to Trócaire, Concern, Goal and Christian Aid, the block grant scheme aims to reduce the amount of paper work required for the bigger agencies. Organisations with a block grant arrangement are not precluded from approaching Irish Aid for additional, one-off projects once their allocation has been depleted.

Although the biggest NGOs tend to take the lion's share of the matching grant funds in most DAC countries, this is not the case in Ireland. The three largest agencies combined have never consumed more than a quarter of the fund, although their fundraising capacity would suggest a larger potential. Allocations in the early 1990s reveal no pattern, with projects approved only on the basis of the criteria at hand, rather than on any historical record.

Table 12.3: *NGO Co-Financing as % of ODA (Ir£ 000 000)*

	ODA	NGO Co-financing	As % of ODA
1992	40.3	1.7	4.2%
1993	54.7	2.5	4.6
1994	75.2	4.0	5.3
1995 (Budget)	88.9	4.3	4.8

Source: DFA, O'Neill 1994, 1995a

OVERSEAS WORKERS AND VOLUNTEERS

General

With 70 to 80 personnel-sending organisations, some of which are very small, Ireland's volunteer-sending efforts differ markedly from those of other DAC countries, in part because of the country's long tradition of missionary outreach. The first formalisation of Irish Aid was, in fact, the 1974 creation of the Agency for Personal Service Overseas (APSO), a year before the start of the bilateral Irish Aid programme. APSO is an incorporated company receiving a grant-in-aid from the Department of Foreign Affairs. Its Chair and Board are appointed by the Minister of Foreign Affairs, and although it has charitable status and may receive donations, it is a 'Semi-State Body' fully owned by the government.

Originally, APSO was to be a temporary phenomenon, an arms-length body that would handle the details of co-financing the many different NGO personnel-sending efforts. When the hoped-for consolidation of these efforts did not occur, APSO became a permanent organisation, and in addition to supporting Irish NGOs, began sending its own personnel in 1986.

The government's 1993 *Strategy Plan* aimed to expand APSO's scope of activity from approximately 440 volunteers in 1992, to 2,000 by 1997, and APSO consequently received significant levels of additional support after 1993. In 1994–5 the organisation supported 1,143 assignments, and the number had risen to 1,247 by the end of 1995. The growth targets have been somewhat controversial among NGOs, some of whom – although benefiting from it – see it as a supply-led effort that could sacrifice quality to quantity.

In addition to its own direct assignments, APSO supported assignments arranged by 78 Irish NGOs in 1994–5. The largest individual NGO recipients of support were Concern (196 assignments), Goal (86 assignments), AWEPA (European Parliamentarians for South Africa – 54 assignments) and Trócaire (30 assignments).

In the mid 1990s, APSO consolidated its package of support to NGOs into a single all-inclusive rate (Ir£460 per month in 1996) for each worker. With this amount, the NGO is free to set (and augment) its own package of support. Limited only by the DAC list of ODA recipient countries, there are no restrictions on where personnel may be sent, and increased amounts are available for individuals who extend their contracts, or who bring previous overseas experience to their assignment. In an effort to attract and keep more experienced people, APSO's own 1996 allowances ranged from a low of £300 per month for an individual with no prior overseas experience, to £880 for a person with eight years of experience.

In addition to its support for secular NGOs, APSO provides a kind of 'block grant' to the Irish Missionary Union (IMU), an umbrella body dealing with approximately 80 different church organisations. In 1995, the IMU accounted for 232 assignments through 42 different bodies, or approximately 20 per cent of APSO's total, and included both missionaries (on development rather than pastoral assignments) and lay personnel.

NGOs and mission organisations consume approximately 60 per cent of the overall APSO budget. In 1994–5, 743 of the 1143 assignments supported by APSO were managed by NGOs, rather than by APSO itself.

Returned development workers

Where APSO acts as a consolidator or 'wholesaler' for NGOs at the sending end of the personnel spectrum, Comhlámh acts as a consolidator at the returning end of the spectrum. Established as a membership-based NGO in 1975, Comhlámh undertakes three types of work: its offers re-integration and counselling service to returning development workers, it provides employment advice, and it undertakes a programme of development education in Ireland. Comhlámh emphasises overseas development work as a serious professional commitment, working with employers to recognise its validity upon return, and working with returnees on longer-term development education efforts in Ireland. Although there is a high turnover in its membership, Comhlámh has been instrumental in setting up a vibrant network of development education workers and more than a dozen development education centres around Ireland. Several of these have staff of their own and are now free-standing bodies.

HUMANITARIAN ASSISTANCE

As with other DAC Member countries, Ireland's expenditure on emergency and humanitarian assistance has increased dramatically in recent years, with at least half of the government's expenditure being channelled through Irish NGOs, and more than one third through the three largest, Concern, Trócaire and Goal. Government contributions, however, are dwarfed by the public fundraising done by NGOs themselves. One estimate places the total emergency spending of the three largest NGOs in 1994 at Ir£31.7 million, of which Ir£29 million was raised from sources other than the Irish Government. This resulted in a remarkably high (and remarkably generous) figure of £10.57 per capita contributed by Ireland to emergencies that year.[11] It should be noted, however, that the Rwanda crisis makes 1994 figures unusually high, and these may not represent a trend.

Emergency spending has resulted in some major changes within the NGO community. Much of the growth in NGO fundraising has been a result of emergency appeals, and NGO programming has consequently changed as well, as has the relationship with Irish Aid. Government contributions to Concern for emergency spending increased from Ir£192,000 in 1992, to Ir£1.7 million in 1994, an increase of 876 per cent in two years. During the same period, contributions to Goal for emergencies increased by a factor of ten, and Trócaire's government emergency funding increased almost five-fold.[12] More remarkable, however, organisations which spent very little on emergency assistance during the 1980s, were by 1994 devoting more than half their budgets to such interventions.

Government contributions to NGOs for emergencies have been relatively free of constraints and criteria. Emergency spending is not as constrained by the restrictions that guide the co-financing scheme, and in 1995 a separate Irish Aid budget line for rehabilitation assistance was established at Ir£3.5 million. Expenditure has been made through Irish NGOs, international organisations and developing country governments.

No matching financial component is required by government on the part of the recipient NGO. This is not an issue in the case of the larger NGOs, whose spending far outstrips that of government, although there are concerns about the pace of expansion. Smaller NGOs, however, may have grown – or even come into existence – on the basis of government support, rather than on the basis of their ability to raise funds from the Irish public for emergencies (or, for that matter, for longer-term development).

Table 12.4: *1994 Emergency Expenditure: Concern, Trócaire & Goal (Ir£ 000 000)*

	Total Expenditure	Emergency Expenditure	Irish Aid Contribution	Emergency as % of Total
Concern	45.0	23.0	1.683	51%
Trócaire	9.2	4.8	0.479	52%
Goal	6.8	3.9	0.746	57%

Source: O'Neill, 1995b.

DEVELOPMENT EDUCATION AND ADVOCACY

Although Irish Aid has been supporting development education officially since 1985, small grants to NGOs and universities over the previous decade would also fall under this heading. The university-based Higher Education for Development Cooperation (HEDCO), for example, established in 1975, promotes links with developing countries, and enhances teaching and research on development issues in Ireland.

A formal development education programme was initiated in 1985, 'aimed at promoting a better awareness and understanding among Irish People of development issues'.[13] Among the initiatives at that time was the establishment of a government-financed Development Education Support Centre (DESC) to provide professional support to organisations working in development education. A 1988 review resulted in the establishment of a national committee to administer development education funding. A National Development Education Grants Committee (NDEGC) was established in 1990, with ten members from the NGO and education sectors, serving in a personal capacity and appointed by the Minister. A second review in 1993 resulted in the creation of the National Committee for Development Education (NCDE). More broadly representative, its role is to administer a larger development education fund, to formulate development education policy, to support and to evaluate the work of those involved in the field.

A 1994 DAC Review of Ireland's ODA remarked on the strong general support for the Irish Aid programme, both at the political level and among the public at large, with Ireland particularly noted for the generosity of its people towards those in distress. It commented, however, on the limited public understanding of the need for longer-term development assistance, and recommended 'a more active information policy on Irish Aid and a new approach to development education'.[14] Several of the recommendations have now been implemented (a decision to make evaluations public; the creation of an information unit within Irish Aid), and the volume of funding available for development education and information has been growing at a considerable pace.

Table 12.5: *Government Expenditure on Development Education (Ir£ 000)*

Year	Amount	As % of ODA
1985	290,000	0.74
1990	370,000	1.07
1992	460,000	1.14
1994	675,000	0.90
1995	1,100,000	1.24
1996	1,200,000	1.13

Source: O'Neill, 1995a; DFA Statistics; Trócaire; figures for 1995 and 1996 are budgeted amounts.

Approximately 15 per cent of these funds are consumed by the Department of Foreign Affairs itself, but the balance is mainly devoted to co-financing arrangements with NGOs and educational institutions. Dóchas, the NGO umbrella organisation, has called for development education spending to be increased to 5 per cent of bilateral spending by 1997. (The 1995 estimate represents about 2.8 per cent of bilateral spending.)

One estimate placed independent NGO spending on development education at more than Ir£1.5 million in 1994, or about double government expenditure. This figure is probably on the low side.[14] While the bulk of NGO spending may be done by the two largest Irish NGOs – Trócaire and Concern – a 1992 *Guide to Development Education; Resources-Activities in Ireland*, lists 43 NGOs doing development educational work, along with 21 solidarity and campaigning groups. Dóchas maintains a Development Education Working Group which organises seminars, lobbying efforts and provides a support, advisory and coordinating service for member agencies and others.

Criticism and calls for greater government spending notwithstanding, the Irish Government probably spends more of its ODA budget on development education than any other member country in the DAC, and combined government–NGO spending would be of a similar high nature.

Ireland has taken a strong position on its participation in the structural adjustment programmes of the IMF. In 1996, the IMF was informed by government that 'participation by Ireland in ESAF would need to follow rather than precede implementation of the Highly Indebted Poor Country (HIPC) initiative'.[15] Some credit for this position can be taken by the Debt and Development Coalition, Ireland – a group of over 70 NGOs and community groups – which initiated a 'No to ESAF' campaign in 1995. A bill to support ESAF for the first time, however, went to Parliament in December 1998.

OTHER FORMS OF GOVERNMENT–NGO INTERACTION

Contracting

The contracting of Irish NGOs for the delivery of bilateral development assistance, well developed in some DAC Member countries (Switzerland, Canada, the United States), has so far been undertaken only on an experimental, case-by-case basis in Ireland. The approach has been used in countries where Irish Aid does not have a presence, and where NGOs are either already on the ground, or are able to move on short notice. So far, such initiatives have been largely limited to rehabilitation projects in Somalia, Cambodia, Mozambique and Vietnam.

Support to Southern NGOs

Support to Southern NGOs from Irish Aid is mainly handled through embassy funds for small, one-off projects. Each mission has an allocation of Ir£75,000 per annum for this purpose.

EVALUATION

In January 1997, Irish Aid published a document entitled *Irish Aid Partnership with NGOs* which outlined the arrangements which apply to the funding of NGO development activities. It included the developmental criteria used for appraising funding applications submitted to Irish Aid: reaching the poor, levels of participation, reaching men and women, relevance, efficiency, effectiveness and sustainability.

In the summer of 1997 Irish Aid organised a seminar with NGOs on the results of their evaluation of the co-financing scheme and how this is being fed back into the decision-making process in Irish Aid. A number of points emerged:

*   Irish Aid NGO co-financing increased from Ir£0.729 million in 1991 to Ir£5.53 million in 1995; as a percentage of the bilateral aid programme between 1991 and 1995, NGO co-financing rose from 7.3 per cent to 14.34 per cent;
*   in 1991 70 projects were funded and in 1995, 411 projects were funded;
*   the top 10 countries for co-financed projects over the five years covered were Zambia, Kenya, Nigeria, Ethiopia, Lesotho, South Africa, Uganda, Tanzania, India and Cambodia.

Initial conclusions were that the co-financing scheme provides value for money, that 99 per cent of projects satisfy all the development criteria, that the projects are responding to the felt needs of people, that the success of projects is enhanced by an openness to explore and refine them, that projects benefit from multiple linkages with other initiatives, and that projects originating from indigenous or indigenised organisations demonstrate enhanced success rates.

ISSUES

General

Although something of a late starter in the field of official development assistance and in its evolution of an NGO community devoted primarily to international cooperation, Ireland's philanthropic roots and its international outreach have strong origins in its widespread missionary movements and in its long-standing generosity towards those in distress. Recent changes in Ireland's aid policy make it one of the few DAC Member countries that is strengthening an aid programme. While the growth in Irish ODA may be starting from a relatively low base, it has already surpassed some much wealthier DAC Member countries as a percentage of GNP.

Growth in Ireland's ODA reflects, in part, a strong commitment on the part of the Irish public – demonstrated by expanding donations to NGOs through the 1980s and into the 1990s – towards those in distress. Today's Irish NGO community is strong, and its private income base is growing. A 1994 opinion poll, however, showed a decline in public interest between 1992 and 1994 in overseas charities as compared with domestic organisations, and an overall decline in the percentage of people making donations to any charitable organisation (from 89 per cent to 84 per cent).

The growth of Irish NGOs in recent years has been based almost entirely on emergency appeals. Despite an unusually high level of investment by Irish Aid and by many NGOs in development education, public understanding of the need for longer-term development investments is relatively weak. There is a real danger that NGOs which once concentrated almost exclusively on longer-term development, will be transformed into agencies whose greatest effort is on short-term emergencies. The trend is not a product of the NGO–government relationship, as government contributions for emergency work represent a relatively small part of the income of Ireland's largest NGOs. It is more a conjuncture of need on the one hand, and on the other, opportunities provided by a generous public response to NGO appeals.

A relatively high, and possibly disproportionate share of Irish Aid, and of Irish Aid support to NGOs, is focused on personnel-sending efforts. There is concern that quality may be endangered by a continuing emphasis on quantity.

The rapid expansion in Irish Aid in recent years has been accompanied by many changes in procedure where NGOs are concerned, but there have been a number of anomalies and lacunae. The single-year, one-off project support provided by Irish Aid for most NGO development projects is bureaucratically time-consuming, and developmentally narrow. The annual list of government-supported NGO projects was, until recently, a catalogue of buildings, bore holes and vehicles. While support for one-time capital expenditure is, no doubt, a genuine NGO need, the list of government-supported projects reflected few of the hallmarks that have made NGOs successful worldwide: group formation, public health programmes, non-formal education, savings and credit, job creation. This has recently changed, however, with the addition of support for projects in the areas of human rights, democratisation and capacity building. At the 1997 launch of the Irish Mozambique Solidarity book *Peace Without Profit*,[16] the Department of Foreign Affairs Minister of State noted the link between capacity building and the ability of country programmes to absorb funds. This view coheres well with much of the work done by Irish NGOs.

Human rights

The issue of human rights has risen on the agenda of both the Government of Ireland and the Irish NGO community in recent years, partly because of increased numbers of asylum seekers in Ireland (4,000 cases were waiting to be heard at the beginning of 1998), and partly because of the 1997 appointment of the then Irish President, Mary Robinson, as United Nations High Commissioner for Human Rights.

A 1996 Government White Paper on foreign policy stated that,

> *Contact between the Department of Foreign Affairs and the NGO community on the human rights aspects of foreign policy is now so intense that it has been decided to establish a formal framework for the regular interchange of views between the Department and representatives of the NGO community. A Joint Standing Committee representing the department, NGOs and experts in the human rights field will therefore be established.*[17]

The Standing Committee's inaugural meeting was held in June 1997, and while the intended focus was human rights in foreign policy, much of the early debate centred on refugees and asylum seekers in Ireland. NGO and expert members of the Committee have argued that the issue represents an important interface between domestic and foreign policy on human rights.

13 Italy[1]

Mario Gay and Anna Schiavoni

SUMMARY

In the late 1980s and the first part of the 1990s, Italian NGOs experienced a severe crisis that became worse with each passing year. In 1996 this trend changed, thanks to a more stable political environment. Even though funding procedures for NGOs remain limited and difficult, the new environment of stability exerts a positive influence on the NGO community.

Italy's development cooperation has been characterised by long-standing problems affecting the disbursement of bilateral ODA. However, at the time of writing, a political debate on reform was taking place that could result in new ODA-related legislation by mid 1998. Also, the ODA administration is being improved through the approval of decrees, regulations and new procedures for rationalising aid management. These changes are expected inter alia to facilitate aid disbursement.

Despite the reduction in official co-financing, the Italian NGO world as a whole does not seem to be weakening, and is in fact showing signs of recovery. This observation is based on general trends including the following:

- the importance of Europe has increased significantly, not only in terms of funding possibilities, but also in terms of increased awareness of the European dimension in aid. There has been greater participation in the EU NGDO Liaison Committee (CLONG) and other European NGO bodies, as well as coordination with other European NGOs and networks, including the establishment of offices or focal points in Brussels. This trend is likely to continue and increase in the years ahead;
- in Italy, decentralised cooperation and the relationship with regional, provincial and local authorities have also increased in importance. This has resulted in a diversification of funding sources, but also in the establishment of deeper roots throughout the country. This trend is likely to be increasingly important in future, and matches a perceived need by NGOs to increase their advocacy and campaigning activities;
- a trend towards improved coordination has resulted in three initiatives:
  a) the establishment of a new NGO association with self-regulating membership;
  b) the establishment of platforms with the participation of all NGOs in certain sectors or countries; the first of these were for Palestine and Albania;
  c) greater use of consortia for project implementation, both in Italy and in the South.

BACKGROUND AND HISTORY

The Italian voluntary movement for international solidarity and cooperation has existed for over 40 years. Research carried out in 1992 for *Coordination of Popular Initiatives for International Solidarity* (CIPSI) in cooperation with Labos, an Italian research centre, found almost 1300 organisations working on development-related issues, employing around 300,000 people.[2] In Italy there are also a number of International Solidarity Associations that work on campaigning, advocacy and lobbying. They do not implement projects like NGOs, but they do undertake some specific emergency relief activities.

At the end of 1997, 150 Italian organisations were involved in CLONG, and 129 NGOs were recognised by the Italian Ministry of Foreign Affairs (MAE) under Law number 49/87,[3] which has regulated Italy's cooperation activities with developing countries since 1987. The procedure for recognition started being applied again by the ministry as from August 1996. In 1996 and 1997, 30 additional NGOs asked for recognition from MAE, and five of them had obtained this recognition at the time of writing.

In recent years, Italian NGOs were categorized as either Church-related or secular, a division that was entrenched by three umbrella bodies: *Coordinamento di Iniziative Popolari di Solidarietà Internazionale* (CIPSI – Coordination of Popular Initiatives for International Solidarity), *Coordinamento delle onti per la Cooperazione Internazionale allo Sviluppo –* Coordination of International Development Cooperation NGOs (FOCSIV) (*Volunteers in the World*) for Church-related NGOs, and *Federazione Organismi Cristiani de Servizio Internazionale Volontario –* Federation of Christian International Volunteers Services (COCIS) (*Coordinamento delle Organizzazione non governative per la Cooperazione Internazionale allo Sviluppo*) for secular organisations. In 1997, CIPSI had 27 members, FOCSIV had 56 and COCIS had 27.

During the 1990s, the division between Church-related and secular NGOs became less significant. Changes that NGOs have made in their methodologies and political perspectives have contributed to this. In particular, lobbying work in Europe has become increasingly important over the last few years. The main cause, however, seems to be changes in the Italian political environment. This has created conditions for better dialogue between NGOs.

In the mid 1990s, a new trend resulted in the establishment of local or national groups of NGOs under new umbrellas, or NGOs under no umbrella. At the national level, the *Associazione delle ONG Italiane* (Italian NGOs Association) was established in 1997, and the process of membership was still in progress at the time of writing.

The main characteristic of the *Associazione delle ONG Italiane*, compared to the previous *General Assembly of Italian NGOs*, is the membership itself. While membership in the assembly was accorded on the basis of an NGO's relationship with the two main official contributors (Italian Ministry for Foreign Affairs and European Commission), in the new association, membership is based on acceptance by the founding members. This has opened up membership to associations other than traditional development NGOs, on condition that they have been committed to international cooperation activities for at least three years; that their request for membership is accepted by the assembly; that they pay the annual fee; and that they accept and are committed to the 'European NGOs' Charter'.[4]

THE ESTABLISHMENT OF PLATFORMS

A significant trend that has increased coordination among NGOs has been the establishment of platforms to improve cooperation and/or campaigning on a specific issue. A Platform for Palestine was established in 1996 and included several development NGOs from different umbrella organisations, as well as some international solidarity associations. The organisation of the platform is informal. It has no secretariat of its own, and relies on the goodwill and support of each member organisation. Its activity is therefore limited, but it is perceived very positively and could eventually result in a bridge between NGOs and solidarity associations.

A Platform for Albania was also established in 1997, with similar characteristics, but with the ambition of a unified NGO voice on cooperation with the country and increased ODA for Albania. While this objective was reached, overall Italian cooperation with Albania began more slowly than expected. In the autumn of 1997 a local coordination group was established on Angola, but with a more limited scope than the other two platforms.

THE CHARACTER OF NGO–GOVERNMENT RELATIONS

After several years of serious decline, Italy's aid volume improved considerably in 1996. Net ODA increased by 35 per cent in real terms to $2.4 billion.[5] The sizeable increase highlights the recent volatility of year-to-year flows. Multilateral ODA was unusually low in 1995 because of the timing of subscriptions to multilateral agencies, and the shortfall was made up in 1996.[6]

In its 1997 report, the DAC states that in addition to regions and municipalities 'NGOs make a major contribution to Italy's overall aid effort. Their activities enhance the 'people-to-people' aspect of Italian cooperation, and mechanisms have been established to ensure that they are well coordinated within the official programme'.[7]

The character of NGO–government relations has nevertheless changed radically since the crisis of the early 1990s, and NGO funding from government has not yet increased to earlier levels since the aid cuts during the 1990s.

In 1995 no new NGO projects were financed, and only six were approved by the Directional Committee of MAE. In 1996, 26 new projects were financed and 20 others were approved, but 11 of them were asking only for 'recognition' status. In 1996, half of the approved projects were for Latin America, 40 per cent for Africa, 8 per cent for the Mediterranean Basin, and 4 per cent for Asia. In 1997, 20 new projects were approved.

Table 13.1: *Summary of Italian ODA (billions of lire)*

	1992	1993	1994	1995	1996
ODA as % of State Budget	0.84	0.46	0.37	0.37	0.23
ODA as % of GNP	0.34	0.31	0.27	0.14	0.20
Grants	2.417	0.450	0.806	0.691	0.590
Disbursements	4.122	3.043	2.705	1.521	2.397

Source: MAE, Annual Report 1996; 1994 $1 = L1613; 1995 = L1629; 1996 = L1543

The total payments for NGO projects approved in 1996 amounted to L14.2 billion ($9.2 million), distributed among 25 projects. In 1996 the payment of second and third tranches to ongoing projects was resumed, after an interruption in these payments due to insufficient staff capacity in DGCS. In 1997, the disbursement of previous commitments increased again to L14.6 billion for 20 NGO projects. The evolution of ODA grants for NGO projects since 1989 can be found in Table 13.2.

The impact of the crisis is also demonstrated by the decline in the number of volunteers and experts registered by MAE. In 1990–91, volunteers and experts registered by MAE numbered over 1200. In 1995 there were 348 volunteers and 323 experts. The following year the numbers had further declined to 235 and 220 respectively.

Where funding is concerned, Italian NGOs have performed a remarkable turnaround during the 1990s. At the start of the decade 80 per cent of their funding came from government. By the middle, 80 per cent was derived from other sources, some of it private, but most of it from the

Table 13.2: *NGO Projects Approved and Amount of Contributions (billions of lire)*

Year	Number of Projects Approved	Amount of Contributions Approved	Total ODA Grants	ODA Grants to NGOs as Percentage of Total ODA Grants
1989	not available	122.0	1617	7.54
1990	169	117.1	2078	5.63
1991	140	102.4	2435	4.20
1992	39	26.9	2417	1.11
1993	63	57.0	450	12.66
1994	29	25.3	806	3.13
1995	6	6.5	691	0.94
1996	25	14.2	590	2.40
1997	20	14.6	519	2.81

Source: MAE Annual Reports to Parliament. Development Education Projects are not included.

European Commission. Partly because of the crisis in Italian aid policy, NGOs intensified their relationship with the EU, and Italian NGOs are now more visible within the EU arena. NGOs report that the expansion of programmes co-financed by the European Commission (particularly DGVIII) has meant a shift in operations towards more emergency and humanitarian relief.

All Italian NGOs receiving co-financing from the commission are eligible to take part in the *Platform of Italian NGOs in contact with EU*, to vote on issues concerning the EU, and to elect one delegate to the CLONG, as well as eight experts to the CLONG Brussels General Assembly. The platform is quite active. It is divided into different areas of competence and meets every two months to define Italian positions on EU policy.

During the Italian Presidency of the EU in the first half of 1996, the Italian delegation to the CLONG set up a special secretariat and implemented two different projects, both involving the entire Italian NGO community. The first was a campaign on some of the main issues of the presidency from an NGO point of view: the Mediterranean, the EU Intergovernmental Conference, Development Education, Decentralised Cooperation, and Emergencies and Rehabilitation. The main aim of the campaign was to lobby the Italian government to place certain issues on the agenda for the presidency. The Italian NGO team worked in close collaboration with Spanish NGOs, in an effort to follow up on some of the issues that they had raised.

The second project was an education campaign targeted at the general public, through photographic exhibitions shown in nine Italian cities, and capitalizing on local events in some way related to the presidency. These projects were implemented in cooperation with, and were funded by, ECHO.

In July 1997, the platform organised an Italian Co-financing Programme – increased NGO involvement in the monitoring of NGO applications for EU funding – a process taking place throughout the EU.

How Government Funding is Organised

Mechanisms

The Italian government funds NGO activity in five areas:

- development projects;

- selection, training and employment of volunteers;
- training of citizens in developing countries;
- information activities in Italy;
- development education in Italy.

Official eligibility

The problems of official eligibility for government funding have been widely discussed amongst Italian NGOs for years, and became a major issue in 1996. Regulation, based on a system of public recognition for NGO eligibility, was sharply criticised by international solidarity organisations, who argued that they were entitled to the same legitimacy as NGOs when applying for government project funding. NGOs disagreed with this 'project approach', stating that the criteria for the assignment of public funds must be strict and transparent, and that an organisation should show evidence of at least three years experience in developing countries to obtain recognition from the Ministry for Foreign Affairs.

During 1997 the debate became less intense. The two parties agreed that rules were necessary, and that some changes were needed in the regulations in order to increase both flexibility and accountability. It was agreed that the European Charter would be a suitable model.

Starting in 1995, a reform process was set in motion that involved government, Parliament and the NGO community. A Parliamentary Inquiry Committee on Development Cooperation worked through 1995 and 1996 with a view to reforming legislation governing development cooperation. The main suggestion from the review team – that aid should move away from bilateral governmental programmes to small-scale 'people to people' assistance – was highly significant for NGOs. Although this was symptomatic of a lack of confidence in governmental structures and the decentralised nature of much Italian cooperation, it did envisage a strategic role for Italian NGOs in the country's aid programme.

The report on 'Guidelines for a New Development Cooperation Policy' issued by the 1995 Inter-ministerial Committee for Economic Planning affirmed future support to Italian NGOs on the basis of:

- their deep roots in Italian society;
- the moral values that inspire their activities;
- the contribution which they have always provided to Italy's presence abroad in countries where there is no official cooperation;
- the role they play in educating and informing Italian society on development problems.

The financing system

The main characteristic of the relationship between NGOs and government is that NGOs do not receive core funds of any kind. They are entitled to apply only for programme or project contributions, and these are subject to compliance with stringent and lengthy procedures. In principle, government contributions to NGOs are of two different kinds:

1. *Progetti affidati:* ('*entrusted projects*', comparable with the en régie projects in Switzerland) agreed between the Italian and host governments. In such cases, the NGO has no responsibility for appraisal and design, but is in charge of implementation and receives 100 per cent of the project budget. The number of these projects has decreased in recent years, and this is now a marginal activity. The main reasons for the decline are scarce resources and administrative constraints. This is the only way in which NGOs actually implement part of the official Italian aid programme.

2. *Progetti promossi* (*'private projects'*): agreed between Italian NGOs and their local partners. Projects are submitted to the Ministry for Foreign Affairs with a request for a contribution that cannot exceed 50 per cent of the project budget as a general rule although there are projects which may receive up to 70 per cent. The remaining 50 per cent must be provided in part by the NGO in cash (minimum 5 per cent) and in kind (minimum 10 per cent), and also by the local partner and/or other donors. The procedure in this case is as follows:
   - project presentation to the NGO Office (Office XI) in the DGCS-MAE on a 'first in, first out' basis;
   - in the case of a positive appraisal by Office XI, the project document is referred on to the Technical Unit in DGCS-MAE;
   - once approved there, it then goes to the Directional Committee for approval;
   - if approved there, the project is transmitted to financial control for disbursement of the first tranche of funds.

Although the procedures state a specific time scale for each step, it is rarely respected, largely because at every step the NGO in question can be asked to modify the project. The real timetable can vary from six months to a few years. The reasons for this may include, according to views within the government, inadequate formal perfection in the formulation of project submissions by NGOs.

DECENTRALISED COOPERATION

A significant and interesting feature of Italian development cooperation is the growth of development programmes among regional, municipality and other local governments. Known as 'decentralised cooperation', it has benefited from an environment that values non-State activity and increased local autonomy. *Foro delle città per la cooperazione decentrata* (Forum of Cities for Decentralised Cooperation) was formed in 1995, and by mid 1997, 26 cities were members, including Venice, Rome, Milan, Genoa, Turin and Naples. Another 40 or so are reportedly keen to join. At the regional level, the *Osservatorio Interregionale sulla Cooperazione allo Sviluppo* (OICS – Inter-Regional Observatory on Development Cooperation) based in Rome, coordinates the activities of regional governments. The interest in decentralised cooperation is not confined to expressions of intent. Significant financial commitment has been shown by numerous local authorities at various levels as shown in Table 13.3.

Table 13.3: *Local Government Development Cooperation Spending, 1996*
(millions of lire)

Region	
Emilia Romagna	1183
Liguria	548
Lombardia	1686
Marche	40
Piemonte	500
Toscana	476
Valle D'Aosta	180
Veneto	1
Municipality	
Bergamo	313
Florence	87
Milan	977

In 1997 Bergamo earmarked one billion lire ($588,000) for development cooperation, while Milan gave L800 million ($470,000). Municipalities are allowed to earmark 0.8 per cent of their first three budget items for development cooperation activities. This has enabled municipalities to go beyond generic twinning and ad hoc development programming.

Shared experience of fighting poverty is seen as a building block for cooperation between Italian communities and those in developing countries. There is a strong solidarity element that seeks to link between policies that counter social exclusion in Italy and policies for sustainable development in the South. By its nature, this type of cooperation is closer to the NGO movement than ODA, and encourages the participation of the Italian public – and not only in giving money. NGOs are also being brought in to supply expertise in community relations, offering training and providing technical support.

NGOs are developing more intense relationships with municipalities, but it is unlikely that municipalities will replace NGOs as a focus for public interest and identification, nor can decentralised cooperation replace official cooperation at national level. Municipal activities can be seen as part of a broader, decentralised approach to development cooperation, marked not only by the growth of Italian NGOs since the early 1980s, but also by the increased activity of universities and research institutes.

While it is argued that this decentralised approach is an organic one, growing from various strategies to promote social development adopted in Italy through its aid programme, there is a danger that it will result in a series of ad hoc activities, reinventing the wheel and bringing in little benefit from previous experience. This has to be balanced against the possibility that ordinary people in Italy can become much more engaged in development cooperation through local community involvement.

Local approaches do not have to result in incoherent activity, as evidenced by Italian assistance for reconstruction in Bosnia, which originated with ad hoc citizens' groups often in liaison with municipalities. This was coordinated through *Tavolo di Coordinamento*. This committee was set up in 1993 to coordinate assistance to former Yugoslavia, bringing together government officials, NGOs, local and regional authorities. A point is made in the 1996 DAC Aid Review that such initiatives, which draw on the moral resources and organisational talents of Italian regions and cities, voluntary organisations and NGOs have resulted in an,

> *Italian approach to emergency and reconstruction efforts in conflict zones which demonstrates the importance of going beyond material assistance to the recognition of social issues. Italy has made important advances in finding practical ways of tackling this complex dimension.*[8]

Although this was a very positive experience, it had peculiar characteristics that made it unique, and difficult to recreate in other situations.

DEVELOPMENT EDUCATION AND PUBLIC INFORMATION

Italian NGOs are eligible for government funding for information and development education projects in Italy. Co-financing is managed on a project-by-project basis. Each year, generally between January and March, NGOs are invited to present projects to the MAE. In the 1980s, between 7 and 10 per cent of the NGO budget was reserved for development education and information. In 1991, according to the annual report of the MAE, the equivalent of $8.5 million was allocated to this category.

Information and development education have long been an issue of contention between Italian NGOs and government, particularly during the period of acute crisis that started at the end of the 1980s. In 1993 all funding for previous and new development education activities was blocked because of an interpretation of the rules that suggested that information and development education activities could only be funded retrospectively.[9] In the uncertain environment of the time, few NGOs felt able to take the risk of investing funds that might never be reimbursed.

In the report of the 1995 Interministerial Committee mentioned above, the role of NGOs in development education was specifically recognised: 'They (NGOs) represent an asset in themselves due to the role they play in educating and informing Italian society on development problems'. The report went on to state that funding would be supplied for activities in Italy as well as in developing countries: 'Their activity in the field of information and training of the public on development issues will be supported'.

As a result, after three years of interruption of funding for NGO projects, the MAE started to approve new programmes in the first month of 1996. NGOs presented 133 projects, 100 of them totalling L6.5 billion ($3.8 million) including L2.3 billion for development information and education projects. In 1997, 64 projects were approved, for a total of L6.3 billion ($3.7 million).

The main issues for development education projects in 1996 included:

* immigration and development;
* decentralised cooperation;
* human development, women and partnership in NGO projects;
* voluntary service;
* cooperation in the Mediterranean basin.

PUBLIC OPINION

After the difficult period in the first half of the 1990s, in 1998 interest towards voluntary and solidarity activities was increasing again. The experience of cooperation with former Yugoslavia and Albania, and in particular the initiatives of citizens' groups for Bosnia, mentioned above, demonstrated to the public that cooperation can be helpful and transparent, allowing citizens to act together. These experiences also highlighted a perceived need to promote higher standards of living in other countries, in order to prevent mass immigration to Italy.

Decentralised cooperation has not been very influential in changing public opinion so far, despite the increasing 'multicultural' character of the country. However, development education activities have contributed substantially to a better understanding of other cultures.

ADVOCACY AND ENGAGEMENT

Most advocacy campaigns are carried out by development NGOs in association with non-development NGOs (usually referred to as 'associations' in Italy).

Successful campaigns were carried out in 1997 on:

* child prostitution allied to tourism – the Italian Branch of ECPAT (End Child Prostitution in Asian Tourism) had support from a number of NGOs;
* anti-personnel mines, led by the Development NGO Mani Tese;
* World Bank reform, supported by a group of development NGOs;
* debt relief, still in its initial stages.

DEVELOPMENT OF RELATIONS WITH SOUTHERN NGOS

Direct funding of Southern NGOs is still not permitted, however Italian NGOs are becoming increasingly active in the areas of institutional strengthening, capacity-building and advocacy in working with their local counterparts.

NGO EVALUATION

For overseas projects, evaluation remains at the discussion stage, despite a debate on the subject having been initiated many years ago when resources were abundant. By the time the discussions moved towards implementation, resources had become so scarce that it was impossible to execute anything of value.

Evaluation of development education was being discussed in 1998, and will be a key topic for the newly created Platform for Development Education within the framework of the Association of NGDOs.

14 Japan

Judith Randel and Tony German[1]

SUMMARY

Before the government-led modernisation that began in the mid 19th century, mutual support groups existed throughout Japan. Historically, however, beyond the Buddhist tradition of charity, Japan has a limited tradition of philanthropy, related mainly to the building of temples and private schools for classical and special education. Government has traditionally provided leadership, and has organised the delivery of most social services. A dominant bureaucracy left very limited space for non-governmental action. Figures published in 1993 show that in Japan less than one third of the public had participated in voluntary activity in the previous year.[2] Sixty percent of those surveyed said they were 'too busy', while 45 per cent said they had no opportunity to become involved.[3]

Since 1991, Japan has been the world's largest aid donor, contributing $9.4 billion in official development assistance in 1996 to some 160 countries and territories. In 1997, however, it was announced that ODA would be reduced over the next three years, beginning with a reduction in 1998 of not less than 10 per cent.[4]

Where NGOs are concerned, there is a problem of definition. Many legally incorporated non-profit organisations are private foundations or have quasi-governmental origins. Many citizen-based non-profits are not legally incorporated. Prior to 1989, the Japanese government had few NGO support schemes, and the NGO community was small. But during the 1990s the government placed increasing emphasis on the role of NGOs, and there has been rapid growth in the availability of official funding. There has also been an establishment of regular NGO–government dialogue.

At 1.2 per cent in 1993–4 and rising to 1.8 per cent in 1995, the proportion of aid from Japan given to NGOs of all types has been modest by DAC standards.[5] But events such as the 1995 Kobe earthquake, in which NGOs played a critical role, have led to a new perception of the importance of NGOs within Japanese society. During 1997, the Japanese parliament considered measures to make the registration of non-profit organisations easier, and there are hopes that the tax treatment of NGOs may also be improved. Such steps would reinforce an NGO sector that is growing in both size and confidence, and becoming an increasingly significant partner to government in the delivery of development assistance.

DEFINING NGO ACTIVITY IN JAPAN

In Japan there are a wide variety of organisations that fall into the broad non-governmental category. Not all of these are NGOs in the sense that the term is understood internationally. Rather they are 'public interest corporations' – known in Japan as *koeki hojin*. Many of these public interest corporations, while legally independent, are closely linked to government by subsidy, by their implementation of entrusted projects – largely defined by government – as well as by their acceptance on staff of former civil servants, and by their approach to policy and programme implementation. In some countries the term 'quango' – quasi-NGO – would apply to these government-inspired organisations.

Other public interest corporations include foundations and associations established by corporations and prominent individuals (often former government officials). According to data from the Prime Minister's Office, there were 13,471 foundations in Japan as of October, 1996. Of these, there are three types:

- those engaged mainly in project implementation, with very small endowments;
- grant-making foundations (about 10 per cent of the total);
- those engaged in a combination of the above.

The Foundation Centre of Japan lists 800 of the 13,471 foundations as large ones established by business corporations. Aside from these foundations, there are 12,618 membership-based 'associations'.[6]

Organisations that more closely resemble the generally accepted idea of an NGO are known as *minashi hojin*. Mostly these are citizen-initiated, unregistered and generally taxable. They are nevertheless eligible for support from the government NGO subsidy scheme and the post office savings scheme (see below).[7] These organisations are what the Japanese NGO Centre for International Cooperation (JANIC) refers to as 'NGOs' and they are, by and large, what is described in this chapter.

Legally, Article 34 of the Japanese Civil Code places formidable obstacles in the way of those wanting to establish and register an NGO. In order to become incorporated, NGOs must have a substantial endowment. Those foundations whose legal status has been approved by the Foreign Ministry in recent years have endowments of Y300 million ($2.4 million) and corresponding annual budgets. Other forms of *koeki hojin* are membership-based associations. In practice, the requirements here are for endowment funds of Y50 million and an income of Y35 million from members. Even if an NGO crosses this sort of threshold, government approval of incorporation remains at the discretion of the relevant ministry.

In spite of the advantages that incorporation offers in terms of recognition, fundraising and taxation, a great many NGOs are discouraged from applying because the process is laborious and opaque, and once registered, the reporting requirements – originally designed to combat tax evasion – are onerous.[8] A 1995 survey of 373 NGOs by JANIC (the Japanese NGO Centre for International Cooperation, the main NGO umbrella group – see below) described a legal environment that was not favourable to citizen-based voluntary organisations. Of 247 NGOs examined in detail, only 25 – about 10 per cent – had legal status.

The Kobe effect

Even before the January 1995 *Hanshin-Awaji* earthquake (known outside Japan as the Kobe earthquake), government budget deficits and a growing recognition of the societal contribution that voluntary activity could make, were encouraging a re-examination of attitudes towards NGOs. But the impetus for change, and for government removal of obstacles to voluntary action, were given a real stimulus by the prominence of the work done by volunteers and development NGOs in response to the Kobe earthquake.

In February 1995, the government indicated to the Diet – the Japanese Parliament – that it intended to study measures that would encourage volunteer activities and citizens' organisations. It established a Volunteer Activity Coordination Conference, comprising representatives from 18 ministries and government agencies, to explore ways of reducing obstacles and of increasing support for voluntary action.

The bill to support citizens' organisations

As a result, by June 1997, a bill to promote citizens' organisations (the NPO Bill) – intended to improve the climate for non-governmental action – had been passed by the lower house. At the time of writing in late 1997, however, it was unclear whether the parliamentary timetable would allow the bill to become law.

Development NGOs saw the NPO bill as a compromise. If passed, it would simplify registration, removing the discretionary element and much red tape. It would also underscore government recognition of the legitimacy and importance of NGOs. On the negative side, the bill did not address taxation issues. Another NGO concern was a clause allowing the government to investigate and cancel a group's legal status. NGOs were confident, however, that if passed, the bill would be followed by positive measures on taxation within a couple of years.

THE SHAPE OF THE DEVELOPMENT NGO COMMUNITY IN JAPAN

Number of NGOs

The Ministry of Foreign Affairs (MoFA) divides the development NGOs in Japan into four categories:

- organisations mainly involved in providing assistance to developing countries;
- organisations for which assistance to developing countries constitutes only part of their activities;
- international NGOs that maintain an office in Japan;
- organisations whose activities are largely carried out in Japan, but which include development education and advocacy.

According to JANIC statistics, since the late 1960s, when the Ministry of Foreign Affairs (MoFA) estimated the number of international development NGOs at around a dozen, there has been a substantial growth in numbers – spurred in part by the Indo-Chinese refugee crisis of the late 1970s. From 27 NGOs in 1975, numbers grew to 100 in 1984 and then to 200 in 1990. During the 1990s (with government funding now available), the number of NGOs increased rapidly to some 350 by the middle of the decade. When other, smaller organisations are added to the list, estimates put the total number of NGOs involved in development work at between 300 and 400.

A 1995 JANIC survey identified 380 organisations (of which 247 had accessible data) involved in international cooperation, each spending at least a million yen ($8000) annually. These organisations had combined revenues of Y18 billion ($176 million) in 1994, and they had 1234 paid staff (687 in Japan and 547 overseas). They also engaged 4191 individuals as completely unpaid volunteers – 367 full-time in Japan, and 206 overseas (full- and part-time). The organisations had an aggregate membership of almost a quarter of a million people. Approximately two thirds of the income of these organisations came from voluntary sources, 18 per cent came from government, and 4 per cent was derived from private foundation grants.

Figures from a March 1996 MoFA survey are also illustrative. Of the 211 private organisations that were examined, 14 provided aid worth more than Y100 million ($920,000) each. These 14 agencies accounted for about three quarters of all NGO contributions. More than 60 per cent of the organisations surveyed contributed less than Y10 million ($92,000).

These statistics show the relatively small size of the international development NGO sector in Japan. Very few organisations are large by international standards. The modest size of the sector means that there are clear limits to its capacity and therefore limitations on the extent to which government can channel ODA through them.

Umbrella bodies

The main umbrella body for development NGOs in Japan is JANIC, founded in 1987 to improve working relations among leading Japanese NGOs and to provide services to strengthen the NGO community. JANIC is an important source of information to its 52 members. (The combined budgets of the JANIC members constitute an estimated 70 to 80 per cent of all Japanese NGO income.) JANIC also provides its information service to about 400 NGOs. At the same time, JANIC represents the NGO community to the outside world, and acts as a point of contact with government. JANIC provides training in human resource development and accounting; it houses a resource centre used by an estimated 1500 people annually; it organises study tours and NGO placements; and gives advice to local governments, economic organisations, labour unions, junior chambers of commerce and others interested in NGO activities. JANIC provides the secretariat for an All-Japanese NGO forum that takes place about every two years. It has compiled a directory of Japanese NGOs and it publishes a newsletter, *Global Citizens*, and an English-language periodical, Kokoro.

Approximately 55 per cent of Japanese NGOs are concentrated in the greater Tokyo area, but some are active in Japan's regions. Umbrella organisations such as the Kansai NGO Umbrella, the Nagoya NGO Centre, the Hiroshima NGO Network, and the NGO Fukuoka Network facilitate regional exchange. In Japan, as in other countries, there are also NGO networks focused on particular overseas regions – the Nippon NGO Network for Nepal, the People's Forum on Cambodia, the Japan NGO Network on Indonesia and the Africa–Japan Forum. While the Nepal network focuses on information exchange, others emphasise advocacy. There are also issue-based groupings on, for example, ODA reform or the welfare of migrant and foreign workers. The 'People's Forum 2001 Japan' developed out of the UNCED process and continues to focus on environment and development advocacy.

GOVERNMENT SUPPORT FOR NGOS

The rationale for government support to NGOs

The involvement of citizen-based NGOs (ie those without legal status) in Japan's official aid programme is a recent phenomenon – with funding only becoming available within the last ten years. The strengthening of cooperation with NGOs was an important theme in the Fourth Medium-Term Target for Japanese ODA, approved in 1988. Since then, substantial efforts have been made by MoFA to increase links with NGOs.

The Ministry of Foreign Affairs gives several reasons for supporting citizen-based NGOs. First, it notes the NGO capacity to work at the grassroots level and to respond directly to local communities, particularly in the area of basic human needs. It regards NGOs as flexible and values their participatory approach to development, noting that small-scale NGO efforts complement Japan's official development assistance.

Another key consideration for government is that NGOs give aid a human face. This is important in two respects. First, it counteracts the historical perception that Japanese aid is too concerned with economics and infrastructure. In the past, Japanese aid was seen as too commercially oriented, but the DAC has noted major steps to untie aid and to make procurement more open and transparent. Secondly, NGO involvement is seen as being important to an increase in public appreciation of Japan's official aid programme.

Government structures

The environment for Japanese NGOs is complicated. Some 19 ministries and a range of agencies are involved to some degree in international development activities. The principle focus for

NGOs is the Ministry of Foreign Affairs, which regards development cooperation as inseparable from Japanese diplomacy, and vital to the enhancement of friendly and cooperative relations with recipient states. Since MoFA is responsible for development cooperation policy, its Economic Cooperation Bureau is naturally a key point of contact for NGOs. Within the Economic Cooperation Bureau, an NGO Assistance Division was created in 1994 to manage the funding relationship with NGOs.

While MoFA deals with aid policy, the implementation of grants and technical cooperation is undertaken by the Japan International Cooperation Agency (JICA). One of JICA's responsibilities is expansion of the domestic support structure for aid. Local government and recently NGO personnel are seen by JICA as important resources, helping to extend the results of aid to a wider community within recipient countries. JICA's Joint Cooperation Promotion Division is responsible for the coordination and promotion of cooperation with both local government and NGOs.

Overseas, JICA has growing contact with Japanese, international and local NGOs. JICA uses NGO experts in sectors such as social forestry and primary health care, and taps NGO expertise on issues such as technology extension. NGOs are increasingly consulted on project formulation, and NGO staff are sometimes used in JICA training courses.

How government funding is organised

The MoFA has two principle mechanisms for supporting NGOs, the NGO Subsidy Scheme and Grant Assistance for Grassroots Projects. Both were started in 1989.

The NGO Subsidy Scheme (NSS)

Designed to subsidise project costs of Japanese NGOs in developing countries, the NSS offers assistance in areas such as agriculture, fisheries, manpower development, women's self reliance, health and hygiene, medical care, improvement of local industries, environmental conservation, appropriate technology extension, and the dispatch of experts. In 1995, projects related to women in development (WID) were added to the eligibility list. In 1996, integrated local development projects became eligible for support.

The subsidy amount for each project can be up to 50 per cent of the total project cost and ranges from half a million yen to a ceiling of Y15 million ($138,000). MoFA decides on the level of subsidy and whether or not a particular expense can be considered as part of the project.

The number of projects financed under the NSS grew tenfold, from 23 in 1989 to at least 230 in 1997, and the value of projects funded increased from Y112 million to Y1.2 billion ($11 million) over the same period.

Grant Assistance for Grassroots Projects (GGP)

Previously known as Small Scale Grant Assistance, this support, handled principally by Japanese embassies and consulates, is available to any non-profit organisation working at grassroots level, including Southern and international NGOs as well as local governments. If an organisation is non-profit and shows a degree of competence its nationality is of little consequence under the GGP. Funding for Southern NGOs has increased dramatically from Y455 million in 1993 to Y1868 million ($17.2 million) in 1996, doubling in one year between 1994 and 1995.

In general, grants per project will not exceed Y10 million (approximately $80,000), although in exceptional cases the total may rise to Y20 million (approximately $160,000). Grants are for one year only. Funding is not available for administration costs or for recurrent costs such as fuel, salaries and per diems. In principle any grassroots activity may be funded, but the priority for assistance is still hardware costs. Special attention is given to primary health care, primary education, poverty relief, public welfare and the environment. WID activities and vocational training for the handicapped are also given special focus, but funding for micro-finance is not available. From Y300 million in 1989, funds allocated under GGP grew to Y5 billion ($46 million) in 1997, with the number of projects assisted rising from 95 in 1989 to 969 in 1996.

Other sources of government funding

Other government departments and agencies, including the Ministry of Construction and the Ministry of Agriculture, Forestry and Fisheries also have NGO assistance budgets, but the amounts involved are small. In 1993, the Environment Agency established the Japan Fund for the Global Environment, which provides funds for NGOs.

Disaster relief does not feature prominently in Japanese assistance, and there is no specific funding available to NGOs seeking emergency funds. However, MoFA says it can act quickly when NGOs present applications for funding if the need is urgent. Under a 1992 law on relief activity, Japan does dispatch teams to assist with emergencies, drawing on expertise registered with JICA. This can include personnel in aid agencies, local government and domestic services such as municipal fire departments.

Overall, between 1991 and 1997, official Japanese support for NGOs increased by 380 per cent, with annual increases of 62 per cent and almost 39 per cent respectively in fiscal years 1995 and 1996. In June 1997, facing a huge budget deficit, the Japanese government announced a 10 per cent cut in aid for fiscal year 1998, with further unspecified cuts in the following two years. But MoFA officials aim to minimize the impact of these cuts on NGOs, proposing no reduction in the GGP and cuts of only 4.1 per cent in the NSS.

Local government

Municipal authorities have become involved in international development activities, with JICA drawing extensively on them for technical expertise. In 1995 about 6 per cent of the JICA experts sent overseas were from local government. The involvement of local authorities is seen as a way of drawing on Japanese know-how, and of increasing public participation in Japan's international development assistance effort. Local participation and awareness are seen to be critically linked to broad public support for aid.

In 1996 the government earmarked Y39 million to support the sending of local government experts to overseas projects, and prior to the announcement of aid cuts in 1998, there was an expectation that this kind of assistance would increase.

Local government also hosts trainees in areas such as agriculture, medical treatment and environmental protection. Since 1992 all cities in Japan have been eligible for subsidies to assist in technical training, and in 1993 the retraining of past trainees was made eligible for subsidy. Y1.23 billion was available from government in 1996 to promote this local government training. The extent to which local authority involvement in international development is based on the availability of funding, and the extent to which it represents a deepening local interest in overseas issues, should become clear with the forecast aid cuts.

The voluntary savings scheme

In 1990 the Ministry of Posts and Telecommunications (MPT) established a scheme through which the public could donate 20 per cent of the interest earned on postal savings accounts to a fund, managed by the MPT, for the support of NGO activities. The Postal Savings for International Voluntary Aid scheme (POSIVA) has been extremely successful, with over 20 million people registering as donors for the POSIVA funds between 1990 and 1996. In 1995 the

POSIVA scheme generated Y2.8 billion ($29.8 million) for 305 projects run by 235 NGOs working in 61 countries and regions.

Reductions in interest rates after 1995 substantially reduced the availability of POSIVA funds. From Y2.8 billion in 1995, contributions to NGOs fell to Y1.57 billion in 1996 and Y1 billion in 1997. These reductions have been significant for NGOs, some of which received more from POSIVA than from government. In 1995, POSIVA funding was four times larger than MoFA's NSS and almost as large as the GGP scheme, but by 1997 the picture had changed dramatically. POSIVA was roughly the same size as the NSS and was about one quarter the size of the GGP.

VOLUNTEERING

Japan Overseas Cooperation Volunteers (JOCV) is the government agency promoting volunteering. In 1996, 2354 volunteers were working in 55 countries, and the JOCV budget that year was Y17 billion. By 1997, 16,647 volunteers had served since 1965. Japan Silver Volunteers, an NGO founded in 1977 by retired experts, also sends volunteers in response to specific requests. Recent changes have improved the system of volunteering, enabling local government officials to take leaves of absence in order to participate in ODA projects without losing their jobs. This system has led to a growing number of teachers joining JOCV. Of the 1118 volunteers sent abroad in FY 1995, 86 (7.7 per cent) came from local governments.

In 1994, Japan introduced a system in which the government shares the cost of insurance premiums for development volunteers working abroad. In fiscal year 1995 this scheme paid Y7.8 million in subsidies through JANIC for a total of 288 volunteers in 14 NGOs.

MUTUAL LEARNING AND EVALUATION

The MoFA has had, since 1982, an ongoing programme of evaluation, conducted in accordance with DAC evaluation guidelines. Its 1997 Annual Evaluation Report on Japan's Economic Cooperation covers 167 projects that were evaluated in fiscal year 1995. Two evaluations looked specifically at NGO project subsidies. The Annual Report notes that other evaluations looked at grassroots interventions, and country or thematic evaluations also included discussion of the role of NGOs.[9]

Amongst the lessons emerging from the 1997 report were the need for assistance to extend beyond one fiscal year for grassroots poverty projects, given the deep-rooted nature of poverty. It also noted that Japanese embassies had to be able to process NGO applications more speedily – one official in Bangladesh was reportedly dealing with 200 applications a year. A survey of NGO projects in Cambodia, Malaysia and Myanmar (Burma) identified specific weaknesses, but overall the report argued that 'as experimental ventures, all the projects were within acceptable bounds', with NGO assistance making a 'serious contribution, provided there is suitable after-care'.

An important outcome of the regular NGO–MoFA consultations was a 1997 agreement to explore mutual learning and evaluation through NGO and ODA-funded projects. Following this agreement, a working group arranged a joint study of three projects in Bangladesh, two funded by Japanese official aid and the third involving the NGO *Shapla Neer*. The activity was meant to be a joint study rather than an evaluation, and it was hoped that the exercise would yield valuable lessons from which both government and NGOs could learn.

PUBLIC INFORMATION AND AWARENESS

In recent years, the government of Japan has taken a proactive approach to the promotion of public awareness on aid, believing that wider public understanding and support are essential to its further expansion and improvement. This commitment to public awareness is in line with Japan's ODA Charter, adopted in June 1992. Noting that aid projects are implemented in recipient countries – and are therefore not very visible to the public – the government feels that it is important to provide the public with information, and to implement aid in ways that increase its visibility and encourage public participation.

The 1996 MoFA Annual Report makes an explicit linkage between NGO cooperation and public support: 'It is essentially impossible to bring the public into direct contact with a form of activity that is essentially carried out overseas... the Japanese government therefore has an obligation to try even harder to inform the public... [this is] one reason why it is so important to pursue various forms of cooperation with NGOs'.

The government carries out annual opinion polls on the level of interest in ODA. According to an October 1995 poll, 36 per cent of respondents thought Japan should step up its economic assistance, and 43 per cent thought it should remain at the current level. The 1994 poll showed that 33 per cent were in favour of more aid and 46 per cent supported current levels – results that suggest that the intervening Kobe earthquake did not actually have a significant impact on public attitudes to aid.

Aid cuts announced in mid 1997 did not produce a major outcry from parliament or from NGOs. This seems to reflect in, part, weak parliamentary support, and in part the limitations of the NGO community itself – sections of which had, in the past, been quite critical of Japanese ODA. But it also reflects widespread awareness of the Japanese budget deficit and a growing preoccupation with domestic problems. By mid 1997, both NGOs and MoFA were stressing the need for increased efforts to reinforce public and parliamentary support for aid.

Initiatives and spending on public awareness

The government undertakes a range of initiatives – both directly and through intermediaries such as JICA and OECF – to increase public awareness. A variety of publications (some in English) include a very comprehensive annual report, a series of information pamphlets and publications on specific aspects of ODA such as women in development and Japan's role in emergencies. There is a range of teaching materials, comic book presentations on ODA, videos, and wall posters for use in schools and lecture meetings. University teach-ins, an Internet site and a new logo for Japanese aid are all aimed at increasing public awareness.

Several initiatives involve NGOs. For example, each year since 1992, MoFA has sponsored an International Cooperation Festival in Tokyo. In 1995 over 150,000 people attended. The two-day festival, which coincided with Japan's International Cooperation Day in 1997, involved a range of NGOs and government departments, and included a concert, a symposium and displays by some 170 organisations involved in cooperation activities.

The Development Education Council of Japan (DECJ) was established in 1982 and in 1997 had a membership of more than 50 organisations and 700 individuals. With two full-time staff, one part-time and one volunteer, DECJ coordinates education activities and disseminates information to NGOs, local groups, academics and teachers. It organises lectures and symposiums, and in 1997 produced a development education directory. In 1993 the Association for Promotion of International Cooperation (APIC), a non-profit foundation, opened a 'Plaza for International Cooperation' in Tokyo to provide a showcase and a point of information on Japanese aid. In 1995 10,000 people used the plaza, including many school students.

Total ODA spent on information, public relations and development education has been rising, from Y219 million ($1.7 million) in 1993, to almost Y389 million ($3 million) in 1996.

Of this, the average spent exclusively in development education has been around 70 per cent. The amount channelled through NGOs, however, has remained steady at about Y47 million ($375,000). In addition to these amounts, APIC, JICA and OECF also have budgets for development education and public information.

GOVERNMENT–NGO DIALOGUE

In April 1996, a quarterly NGO–government dialogue was initiated by JANIC, comprising eight NGO participants and eight from MoFA. The forum has become a key opportunity for NGOs and MoFA to exchange ideas. Initially the dialogue focused mainly on practical matters such as funding. NGOs, for example, voiced concern that government support is overly focused on hardware-type inputs and is not concerned enough with the human elements of development. NGOs have also asked government to consider multi-year funding. MoFA has expressed a willingness to be more flexible on funding issues, but some of these issues must be addressed by the Ministry of Finance, rather than MoFA.

As these meetings become better established, both MoFA and NGOs feel that past disagreements between government and NGOs can be replaced by a more mature dialogue on a wider range of issues concerning development cooperation policy. Japanese NGOs were, for the first time, included in Japan's official delegation to ICPD Cairo in 1994, and NGO involvement in delegations has continued through the Copenhagen Social Summit (1995) and the World Conference on Women in Beijing (1995). Since 1994, when Japan launched its Global Issues Initiative on population and AIDS, MoFA and NGOs have met regularly to discuss such issues. By July 1996, 12 meetings had taken place, resulting in practical collaboration on things like NGO staff training, and NGO participation in population and HIV/AIDS project feasibility missions.

These examples suggest that dialogue between government and NGOs has developed rapidly, in parallel with increased government funding for NGOs – particularly since 1994. From a resource point of view, NGOs and government operate on a vastly different scale, but a new sense of partnership seems evident. The involvement of NGO personnel in MoFA evaluations and project identification missions is indicative of the growing confidence and collaboration between the two.

ISSUES

NGOs and ODA reform

Against a background of economic recession and criticism of the aid budget – not least from a business community arguing that Japanese aid does not adequately reflect domestic interests[10] – a variety of proposals were put forward on ODA reform in 1997. MoFA established a group of aid experts, including the managing director of JANIC, to make recommendations. The Ministry of International Trade and Industry, the Economic Planning Bureau, *Keidanren* (a business organisation) and a coalition of some 50 NGOs all submitted proposals for reform.

The NGO proposals included recommendations for a less fragmented Japanese ODA structure under a single ODA agency. They also recommended that greater priority be given to social development, and they recommended the establishment of a policy conference with NGOs on ODA issues. NGOs felt that their proposals had been fairly well taken into account by the MoFA expert group, and the proposal was submitted to the Ministry of Foreign Affairs in January, 1998.

Funding crisis

Despite an increased Japanese awareness of development activities and greater public interest in the activities of NGOs, in 1997 Japanese NGOs faced a funding crisis. After the Kobe earthquake, funding from the general public was diverted away from NGOs operating abroad towards reconstruction initiatives in the Kobe area. In addition, funds generated through the POSIVA scheme dropped by 50 per cent in 1996 due to a decrease in interest rates. NGOs also suffered from difficulties in expanding the number of supporting members.

In early 1997, JANIC conducted a survey on the financial condition of 100 NGOs involved in development activities. Of the 68 that responded, two thirds described their financial situation as difficult, and 62 per cent said their position was worse than the previous year. Over 40 per cent recognised the need to strengthen their fundraising in order to improve the situation.

Dependence

Whilst the availability of official funding for NGO activity has increased very quickly, so far there is little evidence that Japanese NGOs are becoming dependent on government funds. In fact government funding as a percentage of income remains modest by international standards. A 1994 JANIC survey of 250 NGOs put the proportion of government income at 18 per cent. More recent figures for specific organisations suggest much the same: Save the Children Japan, 13 per cent in 1996; *Shapla Neer*, 5.6 per cent; JVC, 7.9 per cent (1995); World Vision Japan, 3.3 per cent – with a maximum target for government funding set at 10 per cent.

There are several factors behind this. First, Japanese NGOs themselves seem clear that they do not want government support to be a large proportion of their income. Second, the terms on which funding is available – 50 per cent maximum for project costs, no provision for overhead or administration, no multi-year funding, an exclusion of personnel costs – work against the development of a government-funded NGO bureaucracy. Government's limited funding of NGOs for humanitarian relief also means that NGOs are not receiving the kind of sudden funding inflows that have dramatically affected the overall income of some NGOs in other countries.

Institutional capacity

While NGOs and government have managed to avoid the potential for dependency that is inherent in a rapid rise in official funds, there is not much evidence that government funding has contributed to the institutional strengthening of Japanese NGOs. The non-availability of recurrent and core funding makes it difficult for NGOs to find basic resources for training and capacity building.

Even JANIC – which is well positioned to act as a resource on NGO institution-building – has a constant struggle to fund its programmes. Press criticism of project shortcomings among government-supported NGOs underline the need for greater NGO professionalism. NGOs and MoFA are discussing these issues, and seem to be agreed in principle on the need for greater flexibility in funding arrangements. But with NGO activity still a relatively new phenomenon, it may be some years before the wider government bureaucracy is flexible enough to accommodate the needs and approaches of the NGO sector.

15 Luxembourg

Tie Roefs

SUMMARY

There are 73 NGOs registered with the Government of Luxembourg and eligible for government financial support. Government grants to NGOs show gradual growth in recent years, from LF295.7 million in 1994, to LF464.3 million ($15 million) in 1996. In percentage terms, government support for NGO activities represented 17.6 per cent of total ODA in 1994 and 18.2 per cent in 1996. In 1994, Luxembourg NGOs raised about 60 per cent of their total turnover themselves.

Both government and NGOs have difficulties in finding enough qualified staff to manage their development cooperation programmes. On the government side, staff shortages create difficulties for the *Direction des Relations Economiques Internationales et de la Coopération* in handling both the administration of technical matters, as well as larger issues in its relationship with NGOs.

Luxembourg public support for development cooperation is high, but there is a general feeling among NGOs and government that the public does not understand what development and development cooperation are about. As a result, in concert with NGOs, government agrees that more resources are required for development education, along with better collaboration with institutions such as the Luxembourg media.

INTRODUCTION

Luxembourg continues to expand its aid programme with a view to reaching 0.7 per cent of GNP in net aid by the year 2000. It is also strengthening its legal and administrative capacity. In order to increase the coherence of Luxembourg's aid activities, an interministerial development cooperation committee was set up in August 1996. And in 1996 a regulation was adopted determining thresholds of co-financing and block grants for NGOs. In 1996, Luxembourg's net ODA increased by 29 per cent in real terms, rising from $65 million in 1995 to $82 million in 1996, and reaching an ODA/GNP ratio of 0.44 per cent, compared with 0.36 per cent the year before. Luxembourg ranks sixth among DAC members in its ODA/GNP ratio.[1]

At the beginning of 1998, about 73 NGOs were recognised by the Luxembourg government. More than two thirds were members of the *Cercle de Coopération des ONG de Luxembourg*. The *Cercle* is the umbrella organisation of Luxembourg NGOs, and it has a double mission. It represents NGOs with national and international public authorities, and it coordinates the internal activities of the Luxembourg NGO community.

The *Cercle* was founded in 1982 and groups NGOs from all ideological backgrounds. In addition to Catholic Church-related organisations, the *Cercle* counts among its members NGOs that have links with the scouts movement, traditional social movements and political parties.

GOVERNMENT

Governmental recognition of NGOs dates from 1986, and this provides NGOs with eligibility for government financial support. According to the Development Cooperation Act of 6 January 1996, an NGO can obtain official recognition provided that it has serious experience in development cooperation. In fact every NGO seeking recognition must provide government with a dossier that outlines its capacities, competencies and experience in development cooperation activities, with details on programmes and projects in developing countries.

Applications for recognition and other information required for government grants are processed by the *Direction des Relations Economiques Internationales et de la Coopération of the Ministère des Affaires Etrangères, du Commerce Extérieur et de la Coopération*. In 1996 the ministry was responsible for spending LF2.5 billion ($82.5 million) or 78.1 per cent of total ODA. For the execution of ODA, the ministry relies largely on *Lux-Development*, a private corporation.

FUNDING TRENDS

In absolute figures, government grants to NGOs show gradual growth in recent years, from LF295.7 million in 1994, to LF464.3 million ($15 million) in 1996. In percentage terms, government support for NGO activities represented 17.6 per cent of total ODA in 1994 and 18.2 per cent in 1996.

In 1994, Luxembourg NGOs raised about 60 per cent of their total turnover themselves – representing about LF450 million ($13.4 million). In 1996 this percentage fell back to about 50 per cent, with fundraising accounting for about LF500 million.[2] Donations to officially recognised NGOs benefit from tax relief.

Under the 1996 Development Cooperation Act, NGOs can apply for co-financing and subventions. *Co-financing* refers to grants of 100 per cent, 200 per cent or 300 per cent of an NGO's own contribution, and is meant to support well-defined and long-term projects. Annually every NGO is automatically entitled to receive two 200 per cent grants and two 300 per cent grants. Projects submitted by a consortium of two or more NGOs are always co-financed at a ratio of 200 per cent, while projects executed in a 'country of concentration' automatically obtain 300 per cent co-financing. In 1996, co-financing reached a total of LF331.8 million.

In the same year, LF7.6 million was spent on support for mini-projects which, for reasons of size or time span, did not qualify for co-financing. Subventions of LF11.9 million ($384,000) were provided for activities in development education.

In 1996, government provided programme funding or block grants to nine NGOs that had received the bulk of government funding in 1995. Criteria for programme funding included having been recognised by government for five years, and having received support from government for at least 20 co-financed projects. LF33.2 million was allocated to this purpose.

In the same year, LF11.8 million was granted to NGOs as a contribution to their expenses for scholars and *stagiaires* (trainees), and LF14.3 million was spent on volunteers. Finally, about LF43.7 million ($1.4 million) was granted to NGOs for emergency operations and LF9.8 million for food aid.

ISSUES

Faced with a growing ODA budget, the *Ministère de Affaires Etrangères, du Commerce Extérieur et de la Coopération* is requiring a better organised and more structured collaboration with NGOs. In fact, *Lux-Development*, which executes a large part of the ODA budget under the control of the ministry, is also starting to look for NGOs for subcontracting.

Human resources and professionalism

Both government and NGOs have difficulties in finding enough qualified staff to manage their development cooperation programmes. On the government side, staff shortages create difficulties for the *Direction des Relations Economiques Internationales et de la Coopération* in handling both the administration of technical matters, as well as larger issues in its relationship with NGOs. NGOs confirm that the handling of their applications for recognition, co-financing and subventions takes a long time. While they understand the problem, they feel that their Southern partners suffer the consequences.

A partial answer to this problem is found in the *Accord Cadre*, introduced by the 1996 Act, mentioned above, providing for long-term contracts between government and NGOs, including co-financing arrangements, subventions, block grants and subcontracting. The *Accord Cadre* system could lighten the work of both government and the NGOs, as an NGO will have to apply only once instead of many times for as many different projects. The government would then be able to speed up applications. NGOs and government agree that with the *Accord Cadre* they could also invest more in ex-post project evaluation, but the new system will only come into force after a two or three year experimental phase.

The problem of building a permanent staff holds true for NGOs as well. There are only about 40 permanent staff working in Luxembourg NGOs, an average of half a person per NGO. Government and NGOs foresee the evolution of a two-tier NGO landscape: on the one hand NGOs with permanent staff, on the other, NGOs whose work relies exclusively on volunteers. While recognising the importance of volunteers, both government and some NGOs believe that with growing budgets, NGOs without permanent staff will quickly reach a ceiling in their management abilities.

The government is willing to contribute to NGO investments in administrative structures. In principle, unspent funds for mini projects and development education can be used for this purpose,[3] and NGOs are allowed to include a figure of 8 per cent in their project applications to cover general administrative charges.

Dialogue between NGOs and government

Questions relating to management capacities were to be raised in 1998 in the *Groupe de Travail ONG–Gouvernement pour la Coopération au Développement*. This group includes three representatives of the *Direction des Relations Economiques Internationales et de la Coopération* and nine NGOs. Six NGOs are mandated by the *Cercle de Coopération*, and three are non-*Cercle* NGOs. The *Groupe de Travail* replaces a *Comité Consultatif* which, because of doubts concerning the representativeness of the *Cercle*, welcomed all Luxembourg NGOs and turned into an inefficient debating forum.

The aim of the *Groupe de Travail* is to deal with questions of a technical nature relating to granting mechanisms, but it may also become an instrument for discussing more general policy matters. The *Groupe de Travail* could become a forum where NGOs officially meet members of *Lux-Development* as well as representatives of the *Comité Interministériel* – an interministerial consultative body established by the 1996 Act in order to formulate policy advice on Luxembourg's ODA.

Some Luxembourg NGOs are likely to be pleased with a more structured arrangement for their involvement in policy matters. They would like to broaden their dialogue with government and address questions such as Luxembourg's aid concentration policy. For example, some NGOs regret the absence of a forum in which they can discuss the policy, say, of concentrating aid on Mauritius, which, as an upper-middle-income country is, according to the 1998 DAC Report, Luxembourg's fifth highest ODA recipient, with receipts in 1996 of $1.2 million.[4]

Development education and lobbying

Luxembourg public support for development cooperation is high, as evidenced by a generous average donation of about LF1000 ($32) per person per year, but there is a general feeling among NGOs and government that the public does not understand what development and development cooperation are about. As a result, in concert with NGOs, government agrees that more resources are required for development education, along with better collaboration with institutions such as the Luxembourg media. In the same vein, government has started discussions in the *Comité Interministériel* regarding development education in the schools. Some ten NGOs already work regularly in schools on development issues. For them, schools are becoming a more demanding consumer of NGO development education, especially in the framework of the yearly *Journées Tiers-Monde* ('Third World Days') in the schools.

For influencing policy-making on development cooperation, NGOs also have their own instruments. The magazine *Brennpunkt Drëtt Welt* of the *NGO Action Solidarité Tiers-Monde*, regularly publishes analytical and critical articles on development cooperation in general and Luxembourg's ODA in particular. Among the estimated 1000 subscribers are several politicians who, according to NGOs, refer frequently to the magazine in their regular parliamentary interventions.

In recent years, development education has been a major parliamentary issue. While the 1996 Development Cooperation Act was being drafted, the *Commission des Affaires Internationales* – in concert with NGOs and the *Secrétaire d'Etat pour la Coopération au Développement* – introduced an amendment to integrate development education into the co-financing system. The Luxembourg government, however, opposed it. Because of doubts about possibly questionable activities under the cover of development education, the co-financing system is not applied to development education.

As mentioned above, however, development education activities are eligible for subventions, but in contrast with co-financing, the subventions can only be assigned for one year. In general, government and NGOs recognise the low level of development education funding. In 1996, LF12 million was spent on subventions for development education, but this represented only 2.5 per cent of the total government funding for NGOs that year, and was not much higher than in 1994, when development education grants represented 2.3 per cent of the total.

COLLABORATION

Working on better public understanding of development cooperation, several NGOs also collaborate in consortia or umbrella groups. Five organisations joined with the NGO *Aide à l'Enfance de l'Inde* to work on the textile trade. Other NGOs are involved with the organisation *Transfair-Minka*, which campaigns for fair trade. Some NGOs are members of the *Collectif des Refugiés* and of the *Alliance pour le Climat*. In the latter, 13 municipalities are also involved. Like several other municipalities these 13 have in recent years had their own budget for development cooperation, to which NGOs can apply for support.

The Luxembourg government tries to stimulate collaboration between NGOs through its 200 per cent co-financing for all projects that involve joint action between two or more NGOs. However, government has developed doubts about the sincerity of the collaboration in some of the projects presented, and plans to review the system and the underlying selection criteria. Some NGOs also have doubts about such collaboration, and about the aim of greater coherence between governmental and non-governmental interventions in Luxembourg's countries of concentration. Government automatically grants 300 per cent co-financing for NGO projects in concentration countries, but some NGOs question the reality of collaboration in the field.

Finally, collaboration takes place, through the *Cercle*, in the NGO Liaison Committee of the European Union, and other international NGO activities. In humanitarian assistance in particular, several Luxembourg NGOs take part in activities that are organised internationally. For example Caritas Luxembourg works extensively through Caritas Switzerland.

Control and evaluation

It was in the framework of such international collaboration that Caritas Luxembourg engaged an external expert to undertake an evaluation. Because members of the international consortium were having an evaluation, Caritas Luxembourg joined. In general however – and NGOs and government agree on this point – a culture of evaluation does not exist. NGOs can include the costs of evaluation in their project applications, but they are not obliged to do so. From time to time government organises *ad hoc* missions to the South in order to check NGO projects, but there is no budget specially allocated for evaluation purposes.

A beginning has been made, however, with the auditing of several NGOs by external experts. Due to the misuse of funds by one NGO, government decided to commission a financial audit of the 12 NGOs that receive the majority of government support. This was to begin in 1998 with five organisations. The government sees this as the first step in a process of deeper examination. It feels that this is necessary, given the recently introduced block grant system and other features that will come into force in the near future. The new systems of support for NGO activities imply and require trust in the capacities of an NGO. NGOs agree with this view, but point out the difference between control and evaluation. Given the desire for high quality development cooperation, which they share with government, they stress the importance of evaluation as a learning instrument.

16 The Netherlands

Judith Randel and Tony German[1]

SUMMARY

Two principle features give NGO–government relations in the Netherlands a distinctive character. The first is that while more than 300 NGOs are concerned with international development, the NGO scene tends to be dominated by four organisations that have a special co-financing arrangement with the government: the Inter-Church Organisation for Development Cooperation (ICCO), the Catholic Organisation for Development Cooperation (BILANCE – until recently known as CEBEMO), the Netherlands Organisation for International Development Cooperation (NOVIB) and the Humanist Institute for Cooperation with Developing Countries (HIVOS). The second is the consensual nature of NGO–government relations – seen by many as a clear reflection of Dutch society.

While Dutch NGOs do not have an overall umbrella body for coordination and dialogue with the government, a variety of networks and coalitions enable NGOs to work together, and with the government, on matters of mutual interest.

Government funding for NGOs has risen substantially in recent years. Allocations for the co-financing organisations (CFOs[2]) have gone up from 6 per cent of total aid at the start of the decade to more than 9 per cent in 1996, with the allocation for 1999 reaching 10 per cent of Dutch ODA. With aid spending set at a norm of 0.8 percent of GNP and a buoyant Dutch economy, the co-financing organisations are experiencing a rapid growth in resources.

In 1995, the government embarked on a major programme of decentralisation. This has transferred responsibility for the management of much of Dutch aid to embassies. At the end of 1997, NGOs were still adapting to this change.

BACKGROUND

The strength of the development NGO community in the Netherlands and the way that it is organised reflect important aspects of Dutch society, particularly the public and political consensus supporting Dutch development cooperation. Dominating the NGO scene is the Co-financing Programme (CFP[3]) started in 1965. There are four major co-financing organisations, ICCO, BILANCE, NOVIB and HIVOS, each of which represents constituencies that have traditionally been strong within Dutch society. The majority of government funding for NGOs is channelled through the CFOs which in 1997 received Gld529 million or 9.5 per cent of Dutch aid and 86 per cent of government support to NGOs.

Beyond the CFOs, more than 300 other organisations, local and national, undertake a wide variety of development activities.[4] Some organisations are distinguished by their approach, others by their sectoral or geographical interest, and others by virtue of their support within the Netherlands.

A third major category within the Dutch NGO community covers organisations involved in development education – supported by NCDO, the National Committee for International Cooperation and Sustainable Development.

As well as those agencies whose principle focus is international development, many other organisations have some involvement in international work and receive government co-financing. Examples are Dutch trade unions, which have a programme financing agreement for support to counterparts in developing countries; employers' programmes through which former managers offer their expertise; the association of Dutch local communes, the Organisation for Cooperation in Development Research and Education (NUFFIC), and expert and volunteer sending organisations.

The government produces a booklet listing all the Dutch organisations that are, in one way or another, involved in international development. Taking into account NGOs, groups involved in development education and a wide variety of other organisations with an interest in international action, the list extends to over 600 addresses.

NETWORKS AND UMBRELLAS

The NGO community does not have one uniting umbrella body. Rather there is a wide range of coalitions, committees and several single-issue bodies that enable participants to network as well as to focus on particular concerns. There appears to be no significant feeling, either within the NGO community or the government, that an overall umbrella is needed. This is partly because the existing groupings provide adequately for exchange between NGOs, and between NGOs and government. But it also reflects the fact that existing groups and coalitions each have their own dynamic and sense of continuity.

The four have established the Co-financing Consultative Body (*Gemeenschappelijk Overleg Medefinanciering* or GOM) for coordination and dialogue with government on both policy and funding matters. GOM describes the co-financing programme as 'a form of cooperation between private initiative and government'.[5] The CFOs are accountable to the Minister for Development Cooperation who holds political responsibility for the Co-financing Programme, for the policies they pursue and their management of the funds provided for projects.[6]

GOM is chaired on a rotating basis by one of the CFO directors. It meets monthly, and has extended its activities to promote wider dialogue between CFO staff on evaluation, training, regional programming and other issues. Regular meetings between the GOM and government provide a channel through which the government can directly communicate its policy preoccupations – and through which the CFOs (and indirectly their constituent organisations) can pass on their views to government.

Coordination on matters of public awareness and support is addressed through the National Committee for International Cooperation and Sustainable Development (NCDO), whose board has 21 representatives from different sectors of civil society and independent experts. Originally established in 1970 as NCO (the National Commission for Development Education), NCDO was formed in 1996 following a merger with the Platform for Environmental Education (PDO).

Around 30 NGOs involved in personnel assistance have an umbrella body called PSO (Personnel Services Overseas), which covers NGOs sending out 'experts' (formerly called 'volunteers'), and those providing training for workers operating in different cultural contexts. PSO is financed by the government under a programme similar to that of the CFOs.

Food security matters are handled through the VPO Platform, comprising Caritas Neerlandica, NOVIB and SOH/Dutch Interchurch Aid. Ten NGOs involved in emergency aid work together through SHO (*Samenwerkende Hulp Organisaties*). When an emergency occurs, an *ad hoc* working group is formed. SHO elects a president on an annual basis. In 1997, the Catholic agencies established a new organisation for emergency response: Coordination for Relief and Development Aid (CORDAID). This aims to ensure coordination and a sensible division of labour between agencies. Similarly, non-religious agencies have established the DRA (Disaster Relief Agency).

Following the 1996 integration of development cooperation and Foreign Affairs, the Advisory Council on Foreign Affairs and International Cooperation (AIV) replaced other councils that had advised government on development cooperation.

International networks are increasingly important, particularly within the EU. Over 50 organisations belong to the NGO–EU Network, which is the Dutch affiliate of the EU–NGO Liaison Committee. This network provides information to its members on EU policy and funding. It also acts as a forum for discussion, and as a vehicle for collective lobbying on European issues.

In addition, each of the CFOs is a member of a European advocacy umbrella: ICCO belongs to the Protestant coalition APRODEV, BILANCE to the Catholic CIDSE, and the secular organisations, NOVIB and HIVOS, to EUROSTEP. NOVIB's 1995 decision to become a member of Oxfam International, and its prominent role in supporting both *Social Watch* and *The Reality of Aid* illustrate its growing engagement in international advocacy.

FUNDING

General

The Netherlands has traditionally been one of the most generous of DAC donors. Following a major foreign policy review in 1996, the government set a new norm for aid spending of 0.8 per cent of GNP on ODA. In 1996, the Netherlands' aid volume rose by 4 per cent in real terms, reaching $3.2 billion, or 0.81 per cent of GNP.[7] The government allocates a set proportion of aid for spending through NGOs, and since 1991 has increased this percentage by 0.25 per cent of ODA each year.

The NGO programme has four categories:

* the Co-financing Programme (Gld543 million or about $314 million in 1997): 86 per cent;
* programme for Personnel Cooperation (Gld35 million or about $20 million in 1997): 5.5 per cent;
* the Programme for Food Security and Nutritional Improvement (Gld30 million or about $18 million in 1997): 4.8 per cent;
* the Trade Union Co-financing Programme (Gld22 million or about $13 million in 1997): 3.5 per cent.

Table 16.1: *Dutch Aid to NGOs 1995–97 (Gld million)*

Year	Governmental support to NGOs	Total ODA	Support to NGOs as a % of total ODA
1995	532	5663	9.39%
1996	575	5849	9.83%
1997	630	5963	10.56%

Source: Ministry of Foreign Affairs Budgets 1996 and 1997

Table 16.2: *Dutch Support to Four CFOs 1995–97 (Gld million)*

Year	Government support to the four CFOs	Annual growth
1995	451	7.6%
1996	490	8.7%
1997	543	10.8%

Source: Ministry of Foreign Affairs Budgets 1996 and 1997

With the Dutch economy growing, aid increased each year from 1994 to 1996, in both cash and real terms. Funds earmarked for NGO use are therefore increasing significantly.

The terms of co-financing

Since 1980, the four CFOs have worked under formal financing agreements with the Directorate General for International Cooperation of the Netherlands Ministry of Foreign Affairs (DGIS). In 1997, the name of DGIS was changed to Netherlands Development Assistance (NEDA). Under the agreements, each CFO manages its own programme independently, reporting annually to government, with responsibility for its own financial management, evaluation and policy.

Through their programmes, the CFOs fund numerous Southern NGOs active in the field of development cooperation. In total, the CFOs assisted around 2800 organisations and 6000 projects in 1994.

The CFOs themselves, through GOM, agree upon a formula for apportioning government funding between themselves. This was reviewed in 1997, and under the 'Catharijne Agreement' the shares of BILANCE and ICCO are to decline, and the shares of HIVOS and NOVIB are to increase as shown in Table 16.3.

Table 16.3: *Anticipated Percentage Shares of CFO Income 1998–2001*

CFO	1998 Share	1999 Share	2000 Share	2001 Share
Bilance	29.25	28.18	27.84	27.5
Hivos	13.83	14.55	14.78	15.0
ICCO	29.25	28.18	27.84	27.5
NOVIB	27.66	29.10	29.55	30.0

In addition to this major co-financing effort, the Dutch government also provides co-financing for three other programmes. The programme for Food Security under VPO was allocated Gld30 million in 1997. The trade union co-financing allocation was Gld22 million and Gld34 million was set aside for personnel cooperation (including volunteering) under PSO.[8]

Under the co-financing programme, NGOs can use up to 7.5 per cent of the government contribution for overheads. For other direct funding of NGOs, allowable administration costs vary up to 7.5 per cent.

Tax can be recovered by individual taxpayers on donations made to NGOs that are appropriately registered with the taxation authorities. Additional tax concessions like those available in other OECD member countries, such as VAT exemption, are not available to Dutch NGOs.

The increasing proportion of the ODA budget being channelled through NGOs reflects a generally positive view of the potential of NGOs within government and Parliament. The 1990 Dutch policy document, *A World of Difference*, states that the importance of poverty reduction and democratisation make NGOs a natural channel for funding.[9] The emphasis on social development, participation and the strengthening civil society in a more recent foreign policy review suggests that government's commitment to funding through NGOs remains strong. A key challenge to the NGO community in recent years – and in the foreseeable future – is therefore how to cope with this expanding role.

Funding for emergency relief

Government responsive funding of NGOs for emergencies remained fairly static in the mid 1990s, at around Gld130 million (about $77 million) in 1993, with a dip to Gld100 million in 1994. The costs met by government vary, but they can be anything up to 100 per cent of the cost. Between 1 per cent and 3 per cent may be charged as administration costs. Within the Ministry of Foreign Affairs, responsibility for NGO emergency cooperation rests with the Crisis Management and Humanitarian Aid Department, Humanitarian Aid Division (DCH/HH).

Over the years, NGOs have become more and more involved in conflict prevention and resolution, but experience has led the Ministry for Development Cooperation to believe that there are only limited opportunities where NGOs can operate at the highest level of political negotiations. NGOs and the military do not work together on a formal basis, however there have been cases, such as in Northern Iraq and Goma, where they have done so on an *ad hoc* basis.

De-pillarisation and funding

In recent years, there is said to have been a significant secularisation within Dutch society. Traditional religious allegiances are less strong and the pillars of Dutch society that supported, for example, politics, schools and labour relations, have become less significant. A reflection of this 'de-pillarisation' of society can be found in changes in the division of funding between the four CFOs. As religious ties have loosened, there have been calls within the social democratic and liberal parliamentary groups for a reallocation to reflect the new balance between Church-based and secular CFOs. The substantial beneficiaries of this change have been NOVIB and HIVOS, which are receiving a growing share of a growing budget.

Private fundraising

Reliable information on private donations for international development is not readily available, but NCDO estimates that annual support for development NGOs has risen from Gld450 million in 1986 to twice that figure in 1997. This represents an average contribution of Gld150 (almost $90) per household. These figures do not include exceptional appeals; the 1994 Rwanda campaign raised Gld77 million, for example.

As a whole, the four co-financing organisations received more than 85 per cent of their income from the Dutch government. ICCO has no private donations; HIVOS receives only 5 per cent from the public and BILANCE 8 per cent. About one third of NOVIB's income is self financed. About 5 per cent is derived from book and product sales, and the remainder is derived from the general public – half through donations, and half through a Postcode Lottery. Despite significant levels of dependence on government, the CFOs have, in their own view, managed to maintain a high degree of autonomy in their activities. This notwithstanding, the CFOs are all attempting to increase their private income.

Among the top ten Dutch charitable fundraisers in 1995, there were four development NGOs: the Red Cross, *Artsen zonder Grenzen* (*Medecins sans Frontières*), NOVIB and Foster Parents Plan. Through extensive media coverage, Foster Parents Plan Nederland had by 1997 recruited an estimated 400,000 supporters. Its total income of almost Gld200 million ($120 million), makes it about the same size as NOVIB, the largest of the CFOs. Its only significant government support, however, is Gld9 million (over five years) for a programme in the Philippines.

VOLUNTEER PROGRAMMES

SNV is the official Dutch volunteer sending programme of the Netherlands. While SNV is established as a separate foundation, it is 100 per cent government funded – and by far the largest organisation sending experts on a voluntary basis. SNV prefers to use the term 'professional' rather than 'volunteer' to describe the people it recruits.

SNV is active in 30 countries, cooperating with 300 partner organisations and employing 460 development workers. Personnel from SNV are involved in large projects under the Dutch bilateral programme, and SNV also provides consulting services for organisations such as the EU, UNIFEM and IFAD, as well as NGOs such as Save the Children Fund (UK). SNV has been engaged in a major effort to improve its monitoring and evaluation, with the aim of shifting from a management culture based on inputs, to one focused on results.

PSO is the Association of Dutch NGOs for Personnel Overseas. It has 30 member organisations that recruit volunteers funded by PSO with money from the government. A total of 760 volunteers were financed through PSO in 1995. Funding covers travel costs, insurance, pension contributions and may supplement the salaries that are provided locally in developing countries.

ADVOCACY AND ENGAGEMENT

Dialogue with government

There is no shortage of opportunities for NGO–government dialogue in the Netherlands. Apart from formal exchanges at senior level at least twice a year through GOM, officials can meet with the NGO community through the other groups and coalitions that draw together particular areas of interest or expertise. SCO, for example, brings together people with an interest in overseas communications projects, while FMO is concerned with enterprise development.

The Directorate of Social and Institutional Development within the Ministry of Foreign Affairs is responsible for liaison with NGOs and for involving NGOs in policy discussion with the aid administration. In general, discussions have involved programme administration, policy reviews, and specific issues such as major international conferences and individual emergency situations. For emergencies and special situations, other departments have direct contact with NGOs. The Department for Emergency Aid, for example, meets with the 12 emergency NGOs four times a year. In spite of the close relationship between the CFOs and government, Dutch NGOs do not appear reticent in terms of advocacy. Both NGOs and government seem to feel that the relationship is mature and non-confrontational.

NOVIB has a well established profile on policy issues, and a Christian Institute for Development Policy (BBO) has been established jointly by ICCO and BILANCE, bringing together 11 Church-based NGOs for advocacy purposes. During the 1994 election, BBO analysed the positions of political parties so that their members could raise development issues during the campaign. BBO has undertaken lobbying on major issues such as those raised in the Rwanda crisis, and attempts to keep civil servants and Parliamentarians briefed on key issues.

The smallest, but possibly the most radical of the networks on advocacy is the South– North Federation, which comprises HIVOS, SNV, fair trade organisations and solidarity committees. In addition to advocacy, the federation undertakes campaigns and development education initiatives.

NGO advocacy on trade, the private sector and the market

In recent years there has been a change in the nature of NGO relations with business. NGOs acknowledge the role and significance of the market, and many have initiated a constructive engagement with companies on issues such as environment, income generation and small-scale enterprise. This approach now seems more characteristic of the relationship than the confrontational disagreements of the past over such issues as Dutch involvement in South Africa. Under Development Minister for Development Cooperation Jan Pronk,[10] private sector involvement in the aid programme has been encouraged, and NGOs seem comfortable with the idea of 3 per cent of ODA being earmarked for (and expressly limited to) expenditure that is expected to bring benefits to Dutch business.

One example of practical engagement between NGOs and the private sector is ICCO's dialogue with wood importing and processing interests. HIVOS has become involved with the banking sector, allowing people in the Netherlands to use their money in support of rotating credit funds in the south. And fair trading initiatives for products such as coffee and textiles are now well established as an important element of Dutch NGO activity.

Development education and public information

The Netherlands Government has a strong tradition of support for public awareness activities on development cooperation issues. In 1996, 0.56 per cent of ODA or Gld31 million was allocated to information work on development cooperation, of which Gld27 million was earmarked to NGOs in the Netherlands for development education.

Since 1970, NCO (National Commission for Development Education) – now renamed NCDO following its merger with the PDO environment and sustainable development platform – has been an independent foundation whose role is to stimulate, support and channel government funds to a wide range of organisations working on development awareness. NCDO is responsible for drawing up a four-year rolling programme for development education and public awareness activities in the Netherlands. This is based on an analysis of the prevailing development context and activities currently in progress. The NCDO programme defines guiding principles, priority issues and key targets for awareness raising work. These are the criteria against which NCDO assesses funding applications.

During the period between 1994 and 1998, NCDO priorities included Africa, sustainable development, human rights, population and armed conflict. With the aim of stimulating a broad range of activities, 80 per cent of NCDO grants are allocated to large projects, 7.5 per cent go to small projects and 12.5 per cent are reserved for innovative projects.

NCDO identifies five sectors covering a broad spectrum of society:

- national organisations (eg trade unions, churches);
- local and regional organisations (including long term support for development education or cooperation centres);
- solidarity groups (which foster ongoing links and exchange);
- the media;
- educational organisations (schools as well as non-formal activities such as adult education).

A noteworthy initiative is the KPA (*Kleine Plaatselijke Activiteiten*), which promotes the direct involvement of the Dutch public in development. It supports local and regional groups in raising funds for a particular project overseas, and this is used as the basis for stimulating further interest, understanding and commitment amongst the public. If the project is participatory in nature and addresses basic needs, NCDO will meet 50 per cent of the costs, and will provide funding for promotional and educational work.

Development education and fundraising

By total income, Foster Parents Plan Nederland is the sixth largest NGO in the Netherlands, but using voluntary donations as a measure, it is the largest by far, raising more than one fifth of all the voluntary income for development NGOs in the Netherlands. Government support represents less than 5 per cent of its overall income, and is not provided on a regular basis. *Foster Parents Plan Nederland* raises funds through television advertising programmes, which each generate tens of thousands of enquiries about sponsoring a child. Almost 7 per cent of Dutch households now sponsor a child through FPP – about one person in forty. In terms of generating involvement amongst the Dutch public, FPP has a major impact, and the organisation believes that it makes a major contribution to development education through the project profiles, reports and magazines it sends to supporters, and through educational material for schools. Unlike other large NGOs, however, *Foster Parents Plan Nederland* does not take a leadership role in formal development education. An explanation for this isolation is the initial hostility to FPP's arrival in the Netherlands by other NGOs.

In a way, the growth in fundraising by the Dutch section of *Médecins Sans Frontières* (*Artsen zonder Grenzen*) is even more spectacular. Starting from nothing in the 1980s, the organisation managed to attract more than 200,000 paying supporters in less than a decade. Greenpeace has 600,000 members in the Netherlands – 10 per cent of Dutch households.

EVALUATION

Support for development cooperation amongst the Dutch public has traditionally been high, with 84 per cent in favour of maintaining or increasing aid in 1994.[11] While the principle of helping seems to enjoy sustained support, public confidence that funds are being used properly is less strong.[12] In 1989, following press criticism and closer public scrutiny, the CFOs initiated a major evaluation.[13] It included six country case studies and 19 field studies, undertaken by a commission that comprised a number of prominent development experts and critics.

The evaluation included the following observations:

1. That it was extremely difficult to measure the impact of the CFO programme because:
   - policy objectives were imprecisely defined;
   - data was lacking;
   - disaggregating the impact of CFOs from other influences was highly problematic.
2. Smaller projects seemed more successful than multidimensional programmes.
3. Welfare services seemed successful, but few economic support projects were sustainable and replicable.
4. NGOs in Asia and Latin America had achieved positive results in influencing local and national policy.
5. The Co-financing Programme had increased support for Southern NGOs acting as catalysts by:
   - improving access to employment and stimulating income-generation and productive opportunities;
   - increasing the capacity of the poor to access government services and to participation in civil society.

The outcomes of the evaluation were interpreted in different ways. Comment from the media and from critics focused on NGO limitations. For some, the fact that the assessments were subjective, impressionistic and based on interviews with interested parties, meant that the evaluation was skewed in favour of a positive outcome. For others, the evaluation concentrated on implementation and immediate outcomes rather than long-term impact – something which can be said of most NGO evaluations in other DAC countries in recent years. The CFOs themselves pointed to the generally positive overall outcomes of the field studies, and stressed steps being taken to improve their effectiveness.

The questions about NGO effectiveness that surrounded the evaluation may now be less intense, but they have not disappeared. In September 1997 for example, an article in the newspaper *De Volkskrant* took up the findings of a doctoral thesis that compared 12 projects supported by ICCO, and 12 supported by government. It put large question marks against a number of claims made by NGOs.[14] Evaluations of the official Dutch aid programme have also received significant press coverage. In 1994, the Evaluation Service started a programme of country evaluations focusing on Tanzania, India and Mali. It was, however, the most critical evaluation that received the bulk of press coverage. This led NOVIB to comment that,

> *'It is a sad fact in the present political climate, that evaluation reports are not considered first and foremost as an instrument to improve the aid programme, but rather as a means to question the relevance of development cooperation.'*

The ongoing efforts of NGOs to improve their own effectiveness reflect an awareness of the need to account for their performance on a continuing basis, and to make effective use of resources. All of the CFOs have evaluation units and each year the government Directorate for NGO Cooperation and the CFOs organise seven or eight Joint Programme Evaluations (JPEs), examining both programmes and strategic issues. About 75 such evaluations had been carried out by late 1997. The JPEs are also intended to contribute to institutional learning and memory – a weakness highlighted in the 1991 evaluation. And they are used by government to provide justification for continued funding.

For each of the CFOs, evaluation is now well established as part of the normal routine of accountability and learning. A 1997 study undertaken on behalf of the DAC Expert Group on Aid Evaluation found, however, that Dutch NGOs are not finding it easy to establish systems which enable them to measure outcomes and impact – and which use evaluation to improve long-term organisational planning.

ISSUES AND KEY DEVELOPMENTS

NGO restructuring

Since the early 1990s, the CFOs have made major efforts to improve their management systems and to address recommendations that were made in a 1991 evaluation. These are outlined in a 1995 GOM publication, 'With Quality in Mind'.

> *For a long time the special value of the CFOs' contribution to poverty alleviation was unchallenged. In the mid eighties academics began to query development cooperation's effectiveness and reach. Both within the CFOs and outside, calls for tangible results grew stronger. In 1989, the CFOs decided to commission an independent study of the programme. ... The study showed that NGOs in the developing countries make a contribution, albeit modest, to the building of a more open, democratic society and to a gradual increase in the knowledge, incomes and political influence of poor sections of the population. But the Steering Group also pointed to a number of shortcomings, and it made specific recommendations for improving the programme.*

As a result of this evaluation, the CFOs have undertaken a number of changes in the way they operate:

- by choosing partner organisations more carefully in relation to their effectiveness with their target, and their relationship to poverty-related policy priorities. The idea is that CFOs should not just continue funding organisations because of established relationships. Rather they should look for partners that can help them address their priority concerns (such as human rights) by providing, for example, skills in management and financial control;
- by stressing policy dialogue as a means of deepening the relationship with partner organisations and by attempting a better balance between 'donor centrism and partner autonomy';
- by decentralising and through greater delegation to partner organisations;
- by reducing activities, partners and countries, with a view to enhancing quality;
- by strengthening the extent to which evaluation contributes to implementation and to policy by compiling and comparing results.

Focusing on professionalisation, there was emphasis on:

- engaging more experts in human rights, women and development, environment and financial management;
- making more funds available for the professionalisation of partner organisations;
- improved cost consciousness and better financial management.

Another outcome was the so-called 'New Directions', which made a case for increased resources for non-governmental cooperation based on a recognition of the importance of civil society in any development effort. With this in mind the CFOs stressed three areas:

- social development through local organisations;
- building and strengthening a pluralist civil society;
- advocacy in both the North and the South.

The CFOs are considering how to strengthen their links with social organisations in the Netherlands and how to create joint ventures between them and counterpart social organisations in the South.

Absorptive capacity

The combination of a rising Dutch official aid budget and increasing relative allocations to NGOs presents the non-governmental sector with two challenges: the challenge of spending substantially more, and the challenge of spending it effectively. Linked to these questions is the issue of whether growth will cause NGOs to lose some of the attributes that have made them distinctive. There is, in particular, concern that, in growing, Dutch NGOs could lose their special capacity to work on a small scale, to take risks, and to respond quickly.

Coherence and Netherlands foreign policy

Following a review approved by Parliament in December 1995,[15] the Dutch government has pursued a policy of integrating development cooperation into the mainstream of foreign policy. NGOs have had mixed feelings on this. On one hand, they see potential for more coordination between departments, and thus the possibility of a more coherent Dutch approach towards poor countries. NGOs also see opportunities to exert greater influence on foreign policy. On the other hand, NGOs fear that the Netherlands' clear focus on development cooperation as a priority might be lost, and that the need for a Minister for Development Cooperation might even be challenged. Another concern has been that with a less clear cut division between development and other external relations, there might be a loss of transparency. Aid funds might be diverted to things such as peacekeeping operations. At the time of writing, the results of the foreign policy review were still evolving, and NGOs had not reached definitive conclusions about the positive and negative potentials.

The integrated approach to foreign policy does seem to have been a factor in encouraging the Netherlands to make coherence a key theme of its EU Presidency in the first part of 1997. It has been possible for NGOs and government to find common agendas around coherence on issues such as the poverty-related impact of EU fishing policies, beef dumping and cocoa imports.

On more politicized issues that carry a higher political and economic price (arms exports and human rights, for example) progress is much more difficult. In these areas, debate has tended to be left much more to parliamentarians and the media, while NGO advocacy has concentrated on 'back room' lobbying, based on their own experience and empirical research.

Decentralisation

An important outcome of the 1995 Dutch foreign policy review was the decision to devolve responsibility for much bilateral programming from The Hague to Dutch embassies in developing countries. By September 1996, some 1300 civil servants had changed jobs. One hundred of these changes involved a shift of posts to embassies overseas. Decentralisation has thus effectively shifted responsibility for many aid-related decisions to officials based in recipient countries.

Since January 1997, embassies and field offices have been able to take independent decisions regarding NGO funding, without having to refer back to DGIS. Funding decisions are based on perceptions of expertise and capacity and, generally, local NGOs have preference over Dutch organisations. For NGOs, the implications of this change were not clear at the time of writing. Some points can be made, however. While Dutch NGOs in principle welcome moving decision-making responsibility closer to people, NGOs and governments in developing countries, there is some unease that decentralisation could lead to fragmentation and a loss of coherence. It could make NGO monitoring of Dutch aid more difficult. Decentralised decision-making could mean greater control by southern governments, which could in turn mean less freedom for southern NGOs. There is an additional concern that decentralisation could lead to competition between embassies and Dutch NGOs for Southern partner organisations and projects.

In practical terms, since GOM will still be given a block grant to allocate between the CFOs, the 'big four' may be less affected by decentralisation than the other NGOs that will now have to develop a new funding relationship with overseas embassies and staff. NGOs, for example, are having to provide their overseas staff with new advice and training on grant procedures. While there are disadvantages to the new system, there may be advantages as well, if it means that the quality of NGO work on the ground is more clearly visible to people making funding decisions.

17 New Zealand

Ian Smillie with Michelle Auld[1]

SUMMARY

A Voluntary Agency Support Scheme (VASS) was established in 1974 to provide matching grant assistance to New Zealand NGOs. NGOs are funded either on a project-by-project basis, or through a block grant system. Emergency and disaster relief, reserved first for the South Pacific cyclone season and then made more widely available, totalled NZ$5 million in 1997/98. About 40 per cent of this is channelled through NGOs. In a limited number of cases, NZODA has contracted NGOs for the delivery of bilateral programmes.

In 1995, new evaluation procedures were elaborated with the aim of reviewing the overall work and management of block grant agencies. Unlike the one-off NGO evaluations that are done of, or by NGOs in other OECD member countries, an overall report drawing out generic lessons is widely circulated.

While the overall NGO share of NZODA still remains low in comparison to some OECD countries, it has increased significantly in recent years. Between 1993–4 and 1996–7, government support to NGOs through all delivery channels increased by 50 per cent, and between 1993–4 and 1997–8, the VASS alone increased by 83 per cent.

THE NEW ZEALAND NGO COMMUNITY

Background

New Zealand's international development outreach has its roots in 19th-century missionary efforts, primarily in the South Pacific. New Zealand assumed trusteeship responsibility, under the League of Nations and subsequently under the UN, for several former German and British colonies in the South Pacific. This, along with New Zealand's charter membership in the Colombo Plan, an obvious geographic rationale, and New Zealand's own origins as a Polynesian nation, helped to focus the country's later development efforts primarily within Asia and the Pacific.

Today, New Zealand's international development NGO community comprises a number of Church-based organisations affiliated with larger international bodies (eg Caritas, Christian World Service), a number of purely domestic organisations (such as CORSO and Volunteer Service Abroad), and several organisations affiliated with larger transnational charitable bodies (Oxfam, World Vision, Save the Children). Other mid-size organisations include TEAR Fund, the Salvation Army and the Leprosy Mission. Trade Aid Importers Ltd sells handicrafts and commodities through a network of 30 shops, each of which are independent charitable trusts.

In fundraising terms, the biggest NGOs are those affiliated with larger international organisations. World Vision is by far the biggest, raising four times more than the next largest NGO, and almost as much as all other NGOs combined.[2] Although the staff and trustees of the internationally-based organisations play an active role in the development of broad policies within the parent organisation, they are essentially fundraising bodies, channelling their income to programming organisations elsewhere. Many do not have significant programmes of their own overseas – either of a direct operational nature, or in partnership with local NGOs.

Volunteer Service Abroad (VSA) was established in 1962 as New Zealand's volunteer sending agency. Working primarily in the Pacific, South-east Asia and three countries in Africa, it has placed over 2000 volunteers since its inception and currently maintains about 100 individuals overseas at any one time.

A significant feature of the NGO scene in New Zealand is the preponderance of child sponsorship agencies. World Vision, with over 46,000 sponsorships, raises 70 per cent of its income in this way. TEAR Fund, another well-established NGO, raised over half of its NZ$2.2 million in 1996 on the basis of child sponsorships. About one fifth of Save the Children's income is based on sponsorships, and Christian Children's Fund, established in New Zealand in 1990, raised 85 per cent of its 1995 income through child sponsorship. (CCF's income increased by 40 per cent, to an estimated NZ$4.7 million in 1995.) CCF and World Vision New Zealand, in fact, have the highest number of sponsorships per capita in their respective international networks. In all, it is likely that at least half the income raised by NGOs in New Zealand is based on child sponsorship.

Another feature of the NGO community is the success of relative newcomers to New Zealand. CCF began in 1990, and by 1995 it had overtaken SCF for the position of second largest NGO in the country. Oxfam New Zealand, which began operations in 1991, had a respectable 1995–6 income of NZ$1.1 million. An attempt by Feed the Hungry to start a New Zealand operation, however, ended in 1994 with dramatic allegations of fraud and mismanagement (later found to have been without basis in an investigation conducted by the Serious Fraud Office).

Registration and regulation of NGOs

Most NGOs are registered under the Charitable Trusts Act of 1957 (as Amended, 1963). At least two, however (Christian Children's Fund and Trade Aid Importers Ltd), have registered as non-profit limited liability companies. In either case, the Department of Inland Revenue authorises the issuance of receipts for tax deduction purposes to organisations approved by Parliament.

The Council for International Development

The Council for International Development (CID) was established in 1985 as a national NGO umbrella organisation. Its objectives are to:

- act as a forum for discussion and cooperative action on international development issues;
- help coordinate and strengthen links between New Zealand NGOs and those in other parts of the world;
- encourage interaction and cooperation between NGOs and government;
- undertake a lobbying function on international development issues;
- increase public awareness of development issues.

Until 1990, when it received its first support from government, CID was operated on a voluntary staffing basis. Since 1994 it has had a full-time executive director and a part-time administrator. Its operations are still relatively modest, with a 1996 budget of just over NZ$100,000. In addition to its coordination and information functions, CID works with the Ministry of Foreign Affairs and Trade in organising the election of NGO members to the government's Project Selection Committee, and promotes NGO cooperation in responding to disasters through an NGO Disaster Relief Forum.

At the beginning of 1998, two prominent members of the NGO community were not members of CID: the Red Cross and CORSO. For the Red Cross, this is said to be a matter of independence. CORSO apparently believes that the NGO community as manifested thorough CID is overly cautious about important domestic and international political issues.

CID also hosts the secretariat for the Association of Non-Governmental Organisations of Aotearoa (ANGOA), an umbrella body founded in 1994 for organisations operating in the domestic social sector. (*Aotearoa* is the Maori name for New Zealand.) As of September 1997, CID had 38 member organisations and ANGOA had 48.

New Zealand's Official Development Assistance

In 1996, a 'Policy Framework of the New Zealand Official Development Assistance Programme' was approved. It describes the rationale for the programme as 'a contribution to peace, security and development in a global economy in which all countries are increasingly interdependent, but from which all countries and people do not yet benefit fully. It is an investment in a common future.' The principle purpose of NZODA 'is to achieve lasting improvements in the living conditions of present and future generations of people of developing countries, especially the poor'.[3]

Although not known then as such, New Zealand government aid programmes began in the 1920s with assistance and scholarship programmes in Western Samoa (which was administered by New Zealand as a United Nations Trust Territory until 1962) and other South Pacific dependencies (Cook Islands, Tokelau, Niue).

In recent years, NZODA has focused primarily on the South Pacific, with smaller programmes in ASEAN countries and very limited outreach to other parts of Asia, Africa and Latin America. Total NZODA spending in 1993–4 was NZ$146 million, or $92 million.

New Zealand's level of official development assistance was among the highest in the Commonwealth in the mid 1970s (0.6 per cent of GNP in 1976) but fell to 0.25 per cent in 1987, dropping even further, and then stabilizing in the early 1990s at something less than 0.25 per cent. In 1996, New Zealand's ODA was down by 8 per cent in real terms from the 1995 volume, corresponding with an ODA/GNP ratio of 0.21, down from 0.23 the year before. The decline was due to low bilateral expenditure during the first six months of the New Zealand fiscal year, and the timing of IFI promissory notes. NZODA appropriations continue to grow in real terms, and in the 1996–7 fiscal year amounted to an ODA/GNP ratio of 0.24 per cent.[4]

The New Zealand Official Development Assistance Programme (NZODA) is managed by the Development Cooperation Division (DEV) of the Ministry of Foreign Affairs and Trade.

Government Support to NGOs

VASS was established in 1974 to provide matching grant assistance to New Zealand NGOs. NGOs are funded either on a project-by-project basis, or through a block grant system. Applications are reviewed by a Project Selection Committee (PSC), which meets on a regular basis in Wellington. The PSC is made up of four NGO representatives elected by the NGO community at a ministry–NGO biannual meeting, and an appointee of the Minister of Foreign Affairs. (The NGO representatives do not necessarily come from the membership of CID.) Officials of the ministry attend the meetings in an advisory and service capacity.

The PSC makes recommendations to the minister on project and block grant funding. In recent years there have been few, if any, times when the minister has not accepted the recommendations. VASS criteria were last adjusted in 1994, when a new system of block grant funding on a three-year cycle was introduced. Each block grant agency is reviewed once during the cycle. As a result of the first round of reviews (not yet completed at the time of writing in January 1998), three agencies had their status downgraded, and two were declined block grant status. The reviews identified as key reasons poor understanding of the criteria, and project management issues. Concern over lack of clarity in the criteria has been expressed by NGOs, and policy papers were being produced on a variety of issues, including religious activity and development, and the relationship between social services and social development.

For NGOs eligible for project support, funding is available on a 2:1 matching basis with a maximum of NZ$100,000 for any project or programme in a given year. A concessionary ratio of 4:1 is available for projects aimed specifically at expanding opportunities for women. A special fund for small grants of up to NZ$10,000 is available to NGOs to expand their work relating to women in development and the environment.

Organisations with a successful record of meeting VASS objectives and requirements may be eligible for block grant funding, if they can provide a matching amount on a 2:1 basis. Projects within the block grant may not exceed NZ$100,000 of VASS funds. In 1997, six agencies had block grant status: Caritas, Christian World Service, Oxfam, TEAR Fund, Water for Survival and CORSO. Just as agencies may be added to the block grant system, so can they be removed.

Emergency and disaster relief, reserved first for the South Pacific cyclone season and then made more widely available, totalled NZ$2.9 million in 1993–4, increasing to NZ$5 million in 1997–8. In 1996–7, NZ$2 million, or 38 per cent of the total was channelled through NGOs.

In 1996/97 and again in 1997–8, NZODA provided special support of NZ$300,000 for the alternative trading activities of Oxfam New Zealand and Trade Aid. This allowed them to provide greater assistance – through product development and improved appraisal and monitoring – to community-based producer organisations.

In a limited number of cases, NZODA has contracted NGOs for the delivery of bilateral programmes (for example a maternal and child health programme operated by Save the Children in Papua New Guinea). VSA volunteers have been included in bilateral projects in Cambodia

Table 17.1: *NZODA Contributions to NGOs (NZ$,000)*

	1993/94	1996/97	1997/98
Voluntary Agency Support Scheme	3000	3800	5500
Volunteer Service Abroad	1913	3400	3400
Council for International Development	29	100	100
International Planned Parenthood Federation	*400*	*850*	*950*
IPPF Vision 2000 Fund			*200*
Population Council			*200*
ICRC	*400*	*500*	*500*
Intl Federation of Red Cross & Red Crescent			*100*
Development Resource Centre		140	n.a.
Development Education			200
Alternative Trade Organisations		300	300
Advisory Cttee on External Aid & Development		45	50
Emergency & Disaster Relief	1700	2000	n.a.
Bilateral Contracts	n.a.	n.a.	n.a.
Total	**7442**	**11,135**	**11,500**

Notes: NZ$1.00 = $0.62. Italics indicate international NGOs. The Development Resource Centre received NZ$100,000 ex-GST and its funding for 1997–8 is included in the general fund for development education. The Advisory Committee on External Aid and Development is not actually an NGO, but it lacks an ODA category.

and Vietnam, and a small New Africa Fund channels NZ$200,000 through NGOs. This does not appear to be part of a trend; rather it was a practical approach to the delivery of services that cannot be otherwise managed by government or the private sector. The scope for such activities is limited by the fact that few NGOs have an operational delivery capacity, although Government does hope to increase such activities in the future.

In 1996/97, the total for NGOs represented approximately 6 per cent of total NZODA expenditure, up from 5 per cent three years earlier. In 1997–8, overall ODA was expected to grow by 7 per cent, while NGO programmes were expected to grow by 26 per cent.

EVALUATION

Until the mid 1990s, external evaluation of NGOs was limited. Each NGO submitted reports to the Project Selection Committee of the VASS, which would then conduct the occasional field visit for an on-site inspection.

In 1995, new evaluation procedures were elaborated with the aim of reviewing the overall work and management of block grant agencies. A review team, appointed by the PSC and agreed by the Ministry of Foreign Affairs and Trade, reviews relevant ministry and NGO files, conducts NGO headquarters interviews and undertakes or commissions a field visit. Field visits aim to determine whether projects and programmes have met their stated objectives in a manner consistent with VASS criteria.

The 1996–7 Review studied three agencies – Caritas, Oxfam and World Vision – focusing on management issues and visiting three projects for each agency in either Papua New Guinea or Indonesia. The public report stated that the overseas field reviews are not intended to be 'detailed project evaluations'.

> *The purpose of the visits is to examine processes and practices of the agency's aid delivery. None the less an examination of projects is essential as they are the end product of the agency's philosophy, approach and skill in managing development projects. The field visits allow an assessment of an agency's reporting and monitoring ability, as well as other VASS accountability requirements and issues such as sustainability of inputs, and the impact on women. Management tools and processes are merely means to ensure good development. As the proof of the pudding is in the eating, so is the proof of a development agency's effectiveness in the evidence on the ground.*[5]

Unlike the one-off NGO evaluations that are done of, or by NGOs in other DAC member countries, an overall report drawing out generic lessons is widely circulated. Although it does not pinpoint the strengths or weaknesses in a particular project or agency, it does not mince words in its general findings. The 1996–7 Report, for example, raised several common management issues:

- insufficient attention was being given to the incorporation of women in development;
- project design was inadequate;
- there was inadequate monitoring;
- there was inadequate use of planning and management tools;
- there was uncertainty over the skill level of partner organisations.

NGOs in New Zealand are generally positive about the review process, agreeing that it has become more rigorous, encouraging greater accountability and effectiveness. Some feel that the evaluations may be too detailed, while others note that there is a blockage to transparency and the sharing of specific information because agencies are still reluctant to expose themselves to others.

Unlike many NGO-donor evaluation mechanisms, the New Zealand approach has sanctions in cases where an NGO does not meet expectations. For larger agencies, removal of block grant status is a real possibility. And in 1997 the VASS Project Selection Committee noted that it 'has the discretion to request the return of all or part of the VASS Grant or decline funding for future applications... on a case by case basis.' While such options exist for most official development agencies throughout the OECD/DAC, they are rarely stated as explicitly as this. The upshot is that content, process and findings of evaluations are likely to be taken very seriously, and recommendations – generic or specific – are likely be widely debated and incorporated into future NGO programming.

In addition to the annual VASS Review, a small Appraisal, Monitoring and Evaluation (AM&E) fund has been established, which individual NGOs may draw upon for their own monitoring and evaluation work. NGOs receiving block grants may use up to 7 per cent of their allocation for this purpose, and others may apply for a 7 per cent add-on to their project funds.

ISSUES

Absorptive capacity

A 1994 study conducted by the Minister's Advisory Committee on External Aid and Development examined the absorptive capacity of the NGO community under the prevailing criteria, and it was assumed that they could take on an extra NZ$2 million in support. Increased absorptive capacity, however, was essentially blocked by the existing funding ratios and criteria.

With the exception of emergency funding and women's projects, government support – whether on a project or block grant basis – had been on a one-to-one matching basis. The two largest fundraising NGOs, World Vision and SCF, were effectively 'capped' at much lower ratios, and in any case, VASS funding is not available for child sponsorship programmes. These restrictions, along with a NZ$50,000 per project ceiling, limited what agencies could draw from government. As a result, NZODA support to the NGO community was relatively low in comparison to other countries.

This changed in 1997. The standard matching ratio was raised from 1:1 to 2:1, and individual project limits were doubled to NZ$100,000. While the overall NGO share of NZODA still remains low in comparison to some OECD countries, it has increased significantly in recent years. Between 1993–4 and 1996–7, government support to NGOs through all delivery channels increased by 50 per cent, and between 1993–4 and 1997–8, the VASS alone increased by 83 per cent.

Disaster coordination

Efforts have been made by the NGO community to coordinate some of their fundraising efforts in disaster appeals. Problems began with uncoordinated and ineffective work following cyclones in Western Samoa in 1990 and 1991, and better coordination became a matter of urgency during the Rwanda crisis of 1994. In an effort to outdo others, some NGOs made exaggerated claims about how much of their funding was actually reaching the victims. Government support of NZ$1 million for a single NGO (Red Cross) and considerably less for others also fuelled antagonisms.

The NGO Disaster Relief Forum (NDRF) – formed in 1994 – is serviced by CID, and acts as an advisor to government in emergency situations. It therefore has influence over the types of messages used by NGOs. Early hopes of establishing joint fundraising campaigns in such situations have faded, and there is a consensus that joint fundraising is unlikely to take place any time in the near future. The NDRF encompasses organisations that are not currently members of CID, including CORSO, the Salvation Army and Engineers for Disaster Relief.

Table 17.2: *Spending on Development Education: Selected NGOs 1995–96 (NZ$)*

Agency	1995/96 Income	Number of Workers, Paid & Voluntary	Dev. Education Budget
Anglican Board of Missions	1,202,400	12 part-time	87,000
Caritas	1,812,500	1 half-time & 6 volunteers	80,000
Christian World Service	1,100,000	2 (4 days/week each)	90,000
Dev. Resource Centre	45,000	2.5 full-time equivalents	45,000
Save the Children	4,342,335	1 half time	70,000
Trade Aid	2,230,000	60 hrs/week	80,000
World Vision	20,600,000	3	300,000

Source: CID, Michelle Auld and Pat Webster, September 1997

Development education

Through the 1970s and 1980s there was a matching grant programme for development education, but it became a matter of considerable tension, not least because many of the organisations receiving government support for development education were highly critical of the government's development assistance policies. CORSO, one of New Zealand's earliest international NGOs, had its charitable status removed in the 1970s for its criticism of government policy,[6] and debates about effectiveness in ensuing years finally led the government to cancel all support for development education in 1990. In its last year (1990–91), support for development education totalled NZ$257,000.

With the assistance of CID and several NGOs, one of New Zealand's three development education centres, the Development Resource Centre in Wellington, was able to carry on some of the work of an earlier centre, providing a library function as well as specialised information, meeting and networking services. Other NGOs – notably Caritas, the New Zealand Committee for UNICEF and Christian World Service – have continued to carry out development education, although the size and scope of the overall effort is limited. One of the largest development education endeavours in New Zealand is carried out by World Vision, which devotes an estimated 1.5 per cent of its sizeable income to school-based development education programmes. In recent years it has developed a catalogue of publications and videos for primary and secondary schools. These are sold at competitive prices. One series of booklets developed by World Vision has been commercially published and marketed.[7] World Vision New Zealand believes it is the most active development education member of World Vision International, and its work in this field is praised by other New Zealand NGOs.

The DAC/OECD review of New Zealand's aid performance in 1992 commented on the absence of government funding for development education, and urged the government to review its position. A 1995 study, carried out on behalf of the ACEAD, 'Preparing New Zealand for International Cooperation in the 21st Century', recommended that the government should, inter alia:

- encourage the implementation of development education within enhanced national curricula;
- continue a public awareness and education programme with specialist and non-specialist NGOs or associations;
- help improve media coverage of international issues.[8]

As a result of this report, the minister announced funding of NZ$100,000 for the Development Resource Centre in the 1996–7 budget. The centre subsequently signed a three-year contract with the Ministry of Foreign Affairs to deliver in-service courses for school teachers, and to provide information and other services to NGOs and the business sector. Funding will decline over the three years, and the centre is required to earn an increasing amount of its own income, although in 1997–8 a small general development education fund of NZ$200,000 was established to support additional initiatives.

18 Norway

Judith Randel and Tony German[1]

SUMMARY

Norway has exceeded the UN target for aid since 1977. In 1996, ODA was $1.3 billion, up by 3 per cent in real terms from 1995, at an ODA/GNP ratio of 0.85 per cent.[2] Commitments to increase the ratio were reaffirmed. Norway's development assistance has been relatively free from commercial or foreign policy considerations, and as a small country it has sought to gain a reputation around its positive role in development cooperation, its support for the UN and its contribution to conflict resolution and democratic development. The focus of Norwegian aid on poor countries is still strong by DAC standards. The expansion of aid for emergency and humanitarian purposes and peace building resulted in Bosnia and the Palestinian Administrative Areas becoming part of Norway's largest recipients – in 1996, $45 million and $40 million respectively. Norway is particularly active in supporting donor follow-up of the Oslo peace process between Israel and the Palestinians.

Norwegian NGOs receive substantial funding from the State, although this is heavily concentrated on the larger organisations. Many rely on the State for at least two thirds of their income, and for some the figure is over 90 per cent. One quarter of Norwegian ODA is spent through NGOs.

The character of the NGO community has its origins in a strong national voluntary tradition, and the relationship with government is a product of this. The scale of funding and its relationship to NGO autonomy, the increasing role of NGOs in conflict resolution, and the development of appropriate relations with Southern NGOs are issues of common concern in the development community.

Norwegian development cooperation through NGOs has been extensively and seriously evaluated. Attention is now shifting to ways of learning from evaluation and applying the results.

VOLUNTARY TRADITIONS AND THE STATE

At a 1997 conference reviewing 35 years of NGOs in aid, a Norwegian academic, Per Selle, identified some key characteristics of the voluntary tradition and NGO government relationship:

- NGOs like political parties, have their historical roots in social movements, ranging from labour to temperance.
- NGOs are membership-based and democratically built, but there is a hierarchy in Norway that spans local level voluntary involvement and political engagement. Involvement in a

voluntary organisation brings with it access to, and engagement with the national political process;

- voluntary organisations are based on consensus and pragmatism;
- there is close contact between public authorities and NGOs, with an integrated approach to issues; as institutions, NGOs are brought into the process of public decision-making;
- there is a tradition of non interference by government in the organisational life of NGOs.

SCALE OF NGO ACTIVITY IN DEVELOPMENT COOPERATION

NGO activity in Norway has been a major growth area, and the Norwegian proportion of ODA spent through NGOs is one of the highest in the OECD.

In 1963 seven organisations got support for seven projects in seven countries. Thirty years later about 500 organisations in more than a hundred countries with thousands of projects were supported, and the funds amounted to 25 per cent of the bilateral aid budget. More than half of the Norwegian NGOs that were working in developing countries at the end of the 1980s had started their work there at the beginning of that decade. Between 80 per cent and 90 per cent of all the full time jobs in development aid work in the ten largest organisations in Norway in 1992 were established during the 1980s, most of them paid by the state.[3]

Support for NGOs falls into two categories. First, the Norwegian Agency for Development Cooperation (NORAD) has an 'NGO Allocation' and second, Norwegian ODA is spent through NGOs both for humanitarian assistance and to implement bilateral Norwegian aid programmes. In 1996 NORAD supported the projects of 95 Norwegian NGOs, in sectors ranging from organisational and institutional development to health, education, democracy and human rights, income generation, credit, agriculture and the environment.

Total development assistance via NGOs has been increasing steadily, from NKr683 million in 1987 to NKr1944 million ($306.8 million) in 1995. While the special allocation for NGOs has increased by 46 per cent over the past nine years, total ODA through NGOs has more than doubled.

The majority of NORAD's support to NGOs has been directed towards Africa – NKr273 million ($38.5 million) in 1996. The Latin American allocation has increased steadily from NKr114 million in 1993 to NKr147 million in 1996. The Asian allocation dipped in 1995 but recovered in 1996, reaching NKr172 million compared with NKr163 million in 1993.[4]

Table 18.1: *ODA Through NGOs, 1988–96 (NKr million)*

Year	Total ODA Through NGOs	Special Allocation for NGOs
1988	864	442
1989	1074	443
1990	1218	601
1991	1334	540
1992	1357	539
1993	1510	543
1994	1659	591
1995	1944	596
1996	1977	644

Source: NORAD Annual Report 1996, p.87; $1.00 = Nkr 7.083

The NGO scene has been dominated over time mainly by the same organisations. The top ten NGOs receive approximately 60 per cent of NORAD's NGO allocation. Within the group, the spread has become more even – around 40 per cent of the total goes to the top five, compared with 50 per cent in the mid 1980s. The concentration is more marked where humanitarian assistance is concerned. The top five organisations (all of which are among the top ten development recipients) received 79 per cent of the funding in 1993.[5]

Table 18.2: *Ten Largest Recipients from NORAD's Allocation to NGOs in 1996*

NGO	Nkr,000
Norwegian Church Aid	83,343
Redd Barna	76,288
Norwegian People's Aid	58,902
Norwegian International Disability Alliance	32,102
Norwegian Red Cross	22,813
Norwegian Confederation of Trade Unions	22,655
Norwegian Missionary Alliance	20,231
CARE Norway	17,889
Norwegian Lutheran Mission	17,362
Stromme Foundation	15,586

Source: NORAD Annual Report 1996

How Government Funding is Organised

Organisational structure

NGO matters are handled by a Department for Non-Governmental Organisations, which consists of a director, head of division, five advisers, four senior executive officers and two executive officers. The unit deals with Norwegian NGOs, Southern NGOs, and a few International NGOs focusing mainly on gender, environment and human rights issues. The NGO Department in NORAD is responsible for the NORAD portion of the NGO vote for development projects only; the Ministry of Foreign Affairs has a similar but smaller unit dealing with emergency relief.

Tax relief

The government provides limited tax benefits to NGOs. Donations are free of VAT but only donations to certain research programmes are deductible from income tax. In 1989 a special commission studying social development organisations proposed the introduction of an NGO tax-exempt status. This was not accepted, but in 1997 the issue of tax concessions was again under consideration.

Recognition

Although cooperation between NORAD and NGOs is based on trust, and on an understanding that organisations will maintain their own identity, independence and uniqueness, certain eligibility criteria apply:

- Norwegian NGOs must have an established set of activities and a stable financial base. They must be rooted in Norwegian society;
- the organisation must be an established legal entity with a properly elected executive committee, and it must have its own membership base or network of permanent contributors;
- the organisation must be of an idealistic and non-commercial character and must conduct its activity in a way that does not conflict with Norwegian development cooperation or foreign policies;
- NORAD will fund alliances of two or more independent organisations, and larger organisations can make applications and carry out contractual responsibility on behalf of local branches or smaller independent NGOs;
- organisations must have a stable financial base, as well as the administrative and human resources required to fulfil obligations toward the project for which funding is sought.

NGO matching funds are available on the basis of what is known as '*80 plus 20 plus 6*'. Eighty per cent of project costs are provided by the Norwegian government, and a further 6 per cent of NORAD's 80 per cent is usually given as an administrative overhead against costs in Norway. Project costs may include administration in the South. The NGO must raise 20 per cent of the costs itself in Norway. There is some flexibility in the system, particularly when an NGO project is seen as a tool in reaching common goals between a given country and Norway. In such cases an NGO may receive 100 per cent funding, plus 6 per cent for administration. Such projects are often financed outside the NGO vote.

For emergencies, the government will support 100 per cent of project costs with an additional 5 per cent for administration. There are three contractual instruments for NGO collaboration.

Individual agreements

These are multi-year contracts in support of a single initiative, such as a particular project, with an annual release of funds. In 1996, 77 NGOs had individual agreements with NORAD.

Framework agreements

These are arranged with organisations that fulfil certain minimum requirements and have several years of NORAD-supported experience, or are umbrella bodies. A framework agreement is based on established principles and clear statements of sectoral direction. It usually covers five years (sometimes three), with funding agreed on an annual basis and a budgetary plan for the following two years. In 1996, 17 NGOs had framework agreements.

Programme agreements

These are similar to framework agreements and are based on the submission by an NGO of a coherent programme of planning, activity and evaluation. Programme agreements were arranged with two NGOs in 1996.

Shifts to programmatic support

A number of NGOs in the domestic social sector receive a general non-project contribution from the government, sometimes based on the size of their membership. In the international sector, even within broader mechanisms such as framework agreements, funding is still based on projects. The 1995 Tvedt evaluation (see below) strongly recommended more strategic forward planning. NGOs would like to see a move towards more generalized support. NORAD's 1996 Annual Report suggests a modest shift in this direction:

> *The dialogue between NORAD and Norwegian NGOs has in recent years gained new content. From concentrating largely on individual projects, efforts are now being made to concentrate dialogue on the overriding strategic issues. On the basis of a dedicated strategy for cooperation with NGOs, NORAD has encouraged NGOs to clarify issues relating to the distribution of roles, the local support base, recipient responsibility and organisational development.*

In this vein, NORAD encourages umbrella bodies, such as the Norwegian Missionary Council, to take on capacity building and training of its members as part of its strategic role.

The programmatic approach is still in development, however. Even though several larger NGOs have made major efforts to develop a more strategic approach, the building blocks of their work are still individual projects. NGO objectives have, nevertheless, become broader, including development education, advocacy, institutional development, democracy and human rights, and these are more conducive to a strategic approach.[6]

Humanitarian assistance

Between the mid 1980s and the mid 1990s, Norwegian allocations for humanitarian assistance grew from 5 per cent to 15 per cent of ODA. NGOs have become deeply engaged in both the delivery of humanitarian assistance and in responding to complex emergencies. There has also been strong collaboration between NGOs, particularly Norwegian People's Aid and government on banning landmines, and on clearing landmines in countries such as Mozambique and Cambodia.

Mediation and conflict resolution have become important parts of Norwegian foreign policy, and the leading NGOs have become much more involved in establishing channels of communication between Norwegian mediators groups in conflict overseas. The scope and limitations of this type of NGO engagement are currently under discussion (see Issues section, below). Responsibility for humanitarian assistance will in future be shared with the Ministry of Foreign Affairs, as NORAD is to take on part of the budget and greater responsibility for human rights and democracy.

Volunteer programmes

The scale of volunteering has been declining – from 169 'volunteer-person years' in 1986 to 114 in 1995. The budget has also fallen, from NKr60 million in 1994 to NKr46 million ($6.5 million) in 1996. The drop in technical assistance personnel over the past ten years has been much sharper, falling from 208 person years to 40.[7]

The Norwegian Volunteer Service (NVS) strategy emphasises the poorest groups in programme countries, contributing to the acquisition of skills and leaving local employers with overall responsibility for making best use of NVS.[8]

Direct support to Southern NGOs

Norwegian funding of Southern NGOs is modest, but the number of NGOs being supported has grown dramatically – from zero in the 1970s, to approximately 300 in the early 1990s.[9] Support for Southern NGOs is country-specific, with guidelines drawn up by NORAD's local representative. These guidelines reflect the general country programme objectives.

Embassies with a NORAD administrative unit have responsibility for a local NGO budget allocation. The embassy has discretion over the choice of projects (with budgets of less than NKr15 million – $2.1 million) but it must send outlines of an NGO's strategy and annual work plan to Norway for general approval. Embassies in general fund only local NGOs, but in some cases this may extend to the local branch of an international NGO. Total direct funding to Southern NGOs amounted to NKr127 million ($18 million) in 1996 (compared with NKr130 million in 1993, NKr140 million in 1994 and NKr115 million in 1995).

DEVELOPMENT EDUCATION AND PUBLIC INFORMATION

The level of public support for aid in Norway has traditionally been high. In 1996, 84 per cent of Norwegians were in favour of Norway's development cooperation – much the same as ten years earlier. Human rights, UN involvement, and levels of development assistance have all been mainstream issues in Norway. In 1996, total government funds for information, public relations and development education amounted to NKr35 million ($4.9 million), making Norway's per capita spending one of the highest in the DAC.

In its relations with NGOs, NORAD places a high priority on information and development education. More than 100 voluntary organisations receive some form of support from NORAD for information and development education activities. Ninety per cent of this is for the long-term programmes of 24 NGOs that have four-year framework agreements with NORAD. These agreements often finance NGO information activities in full. Framework organisations range from political study groups (which receive support correlated to their electoral support) to umbrella bodies and operational NGOs. Individual projects tend to be small however, averaging approximately NKr25,000 ($3500).

The 'Tvedt Evaluation' urged NGOs to take a longer-term and more strategic view of their information work, focusing on actual results that might be achieved in 20 years, and resisting the easy conclusion that the high level of public support in Norway must be correlated to investments in public understanding.

Coherence of development education and information

The coherence of Norway's information programme is a recurring theme. It was the subject of talks seeking to build closer cooperation between NORAD and the big five NGOs in 1997. In addition, a new government Department for Information and Cultural Cooperation has been created in NORAD. Coherence is particularly important, as government responsibility is shared between the Ministry of Foreign Affairs and NORAD. The ministry is responsible for information on development policy, North–South issues, and multilateral cooperation, while NORAD keeps the public informed on its own activities.

The changing style of the government approach to development education and information has been criticised by Norwegian NGOs, and has been the subject of real controversy. In 1994, NORAD announced that its information activity would focus more on disseminating information about Norwegian government aid. At the same time, it attempted to ensure that NGOs receiving government support would also adopt a more systematic portrayal of NORAD . This was seen by NGOs as a clear and illegitimate use of public money to limit free debate. They also considered it likely to be counter-productive, arguing that Norway's high level of public support was in part due to the open and critical analysis of development assistance. As a result of NGO protest the the political leadership saw the danger of a conflict with a group of outspoken NGOs and the minister promised to respect their independence.[10]

ADVOCACY

Outspokenness on policy is not considered a barrier to funding. Indeed, it is argued that Norwegian NGOs have political engagement programmed into them. The process of influencing government reflects the integrated character of Norwegian aid. There is a great deal of personnel interchange between NORAD, the Ministry of Foreign Affairs and NGOs. The level of contact, trust and openness means that there is constant dialogue on issues of the day.

Since the 1980s there have been changes in the way influence is exercised. Individuals and bodies without a membership base are more visible in policy debate. There is also a much more positive attitude to the market.[11] Although there is diversity within the NGO sector, government funding is concentrated on a few large organisations. There are many smaller, single-sector bodies, and NGOs whose primary vocation lies in Norway but who undertake some development work. Smaller NGOs, perhaps with less to lose, have been more critical of NORAD's policy directions.[12]

NGOs are adept at using parliamentary lobbying and mobilisation. For instance a plan to withdraw the official aid programme from Mali had to be cancelled because of NGO political lobbying. Parliamentary concern was also mobilised to retain NGO independence in government-funded information work.

More formal arrangements for dialogue include quarterly seminars organised by NGOs to discuss priority issues. NORAD is often invited to these but does not set the agenda. NORAD has annual policy meetings with each individual Norwegian NGO. Similar meetings are held at more irregular intervals with international NGOs. Dialogue with Southern NGOs takes place through Norwegian embassies.

LEARNING FROM EVALUATION

In a case study on Norway written for the OECD/DAC NGO Evaluation Synthesis Study,[13] particular attention was paid to learning from evaluation. In November 1997, the University of Bergen and NORAD hosted a conference on 'NGOs in Aid: A Reappraisal of 35 years of NGO Assistance', which asked some fundamental questions about NGO comparative advantage and impact. This section is drawn from these two sources.

The case study highlights a change in NGO attitudes to evaluation from the mid 1980s, when,

> *'Every crown used on studies means less funds for the poor' captured maybe the sentiments of some NGO representatives… The emphasis was on action, not reflection, since organisations believe strongly in their mission to provide answers to development problems.*

Although the case study emphasised the glaring differences between and within organisations, and tensions between a critical-analytical approach and a more action-oriented culture, it concluded that real change had taken place.

> *These attitudes and evaluation practices started to change from the mid 1980s and have since then altered significantly. Evaluation guidelines and routines were introduced and institutionalized in most of the larger NGOs. The organisations recruited competent evaluators and increased their internal technical capacity. The number of evaluation studies carried out by the NGOs increased. New approaches were tried out and the perception of evaluation changed… to a useful tool for organisational learning and control.*

Another study[14] investigated the procedures used by Norwegian NGOs to enable evaluations, reviews and reporting to contribute to knowledge and learning. It concluded that:

- evaluations and reviews are perceived as sources of learning, but organisations find it problematic to integrate and link evaluations to planning;
- the need for information and knowledge is acknowledged but the time to process and integrate it is limited;
- evaluations are not the most important source of learning, but are a symbol of learning. Informal learning mechanisms are underestimated.

Evaluation as a tool for change

The OECD/DAC case study reported some clear instances of this:

> *NORAD played an active role vis-à-vis some of the mission organisations in the mid 1980s and made evaluation a condition for future funding. Evaluations became a powerful tool for introducing changes in projects which had been funded for years... and the NGOs were requested to evaluate and present plans for phasing out of external support.*

Following a major criticism in the early 1980s that evaluations were externally driven and were being forced on NGOs, NORAD effected a shift in policy:

> *[NORAD] made the first move, but later asked the NGOs to prepare and imple-ment the studies themselves (with funds from NORAD) and in due course present the findings from the reports... The NGOs adapted rapidly to the new require-ments and changed what was originally seen as a threat into an opportunity for themselves. Several organisations described how the evaluation medicine had hurt, but helped and induced positive reforms. Today, all the Norwegian NGOs interviewed for this study acknowledged the importance and usefulness of evalua-tions and described how they had built up and incorporated evaluation experience and practice into their planning and reporting systems.*

Today, most evaluations are initiated by NGOs rather than NORAD (except where there are specific problems or where NORAD is in doubt about future funding). While this is a good strat-egy for creating ownership of the results within an NGO, and for learning from findings, there are still problems with access to information. The integration of evaluation into planning, policy and practice remains more aspiration than fact.

Access to evaluation information

The case study gives reasons for problems of access to information:

> *Using informed estimates, the framework organisations may be involved in an average of 20 evaluations annually and the remaining 40 NGOs five reports each, which means that five hundred evaluations are prepared each year where Norwegian NGOs are involved directly or indirectly.*
>
> *The best and sometimes only source of information about [evaluation] reports is the desk officers, who may be able to retrieve one of the few available copies in his/her own file. It is exceptional to find evaluation reports registered in a database or easily available in a library or documentation centre, either for sale or for free*

distribution… evaluation reports are rarely used for broader dissemination of findings or as inputs to development education or fundraising.

Norwegian NGOs seem not to have the capacity and commitment to work systematically and professionally with evaluations in order to prepare and test new and innovative approaches to evaluations, or to fully utilize evaluations as inputs to policy development. NGOs have in principle accepted that evaluations are relevant and useful, but so far have not invested much in strengthening their own evaluation staff and competence.

NGOs which have both guidelines and procedures for how to prepare, implement and follow up evaluations and a board to whom findings are reported seem to benefit most from evaluations. Where there are no such organisational mechanisms, benefits depend more on individual initiatives and have less impact on institutional memory.

ISSUES

Dependence or synergy?

Norwegian NGOs could not operate on anything like their current scale without government funding. But the dependency issue cuts both ways. Observers ask if Norway would be able to spend its aid budget and maintain such high levels of public support without the substantial NGO involvement. But there is another question: has the lack of competition between government and NGOs led to complacency in both sectors, or has the open and undefensive relationship allowed mutual criticism, leading to more efficient and coordinated development cooperation?

One possible indicator of the degree of dependency is the extent to which NGOs work in the same countries and sectors as the official programme. Government supports NGO projects in over 80 developing countries, but almost two thirds of total funding goes to Norway's 13 programme countries. In 1981 only 37 per cent went to concentration countries.[15] The sectors prioritized by NGOs and NORAD, although different, have become much more congruent over the years.

The 'Tvedt Evaluation' pointed out sharply that NGO claims – that the quality of NGO work was superior to other forms of aid – could not be substantiated and that there was a gap between public images, expectations and actual achievements. These NGO propagandists included NORAD and the Foreign Ministry. Since NGOs are disbursing a quarter of the aid programme and are the most visible part of it, the government can hardly afford to be overly critical. Similarly for NGOs, there appears little incentive to bite the hand that feeds, not simply for reasons of financial dependency, but because of the integration of NGOs with official policy and practice, and because the people involved shift, apparently seamlessly, from one sector to the other.

Current circumstances do little to disturb the equilibrium between government and NGOs. While the limits are being tested in some areas, particularly around the NGO role in conflict resolution and government funding of Southern NGOs, there is little competition for funding either with government agencies or with other NGOs, and there appear to be few burning issues of policy dividing NGOs and government. With such a lack of competition in the development community as a whole, the role of evaluation and external critics in preventing complacency and raising standards becomes particularly important. The 1995 evaluation was critical of the lack of coordination arguing that, 'conflicting policy signals and unclear aims have made it difficult for NORAD (even if they had so wished) to create complementarity or coordination between Norwegian NGOs and NORAD's development policy in different countries.'

Similarly in emergency response and conflict resolution, the evaluation finds a gap between Norwegian aspirations to be a world leader in conflict resolution, the capacities of NGOs, and the ability of the government to use them.[16]

On the other hand, the development community has clearly responded to issues raised by external evaluation. The Tvedt study targeted both government and NGOs and, from an outsider's point of view, pulled no punches in its conclusions and recommendations. Within two years, specific action had taken place (such as the new shared responsibilities between NORAD and the Ministry of Foreign Affairs on emergencies and human rights, and the establishment of a new training institute). At a more general level, the call for NGOs to formulate longer-term strategies and to focus more on relations with partners, seems to have been heeded.

Cont(r)acting

There is a fine line between contracting and finding tasks of common interest with NORAD.[17] The major growth in Norwegian government support to NGOs has not been through the earmarked NGO allocation, but through activity funded by government for both humanitarian work and under special budget lines covering issues such as women in development, AIDS, the environment and certain specific countries. This provides incentives for NGOs that have priorities in common with NORAD and ensures their priority access to funds as a result.[18]

This large and growing engagement with the mainstream of Norwegian official aid has been accompanied by a growth in *contracting culture* in NORAD's relations with NGOs. This includes procedures (and more importantly their enforcement) requiring greater financial control and accountability, but also a change of style. While there is still a high degree of trust between NGOs and government, the structure is more formal and more open to government control.

The Ministry of Foreign Affairs has become very active in contracting NGOs to undertake work in areas where it considers it important that Norwegian organisations be present. The contract culture is particularly strong in relations between the MFA and the big five NGOs. The MFA point out that *contracting*, or maybe *contacting*, is a two-way relationship. Initiatives have in very many cases come from the NGOs themselves, which – through mobilisation of public and political support – put great pressure on the MFA to support activities in the remotest corners of the world, outside the normal sphere of Norway's foreign policy concerns.

Some people suggest that the extent to which contracting culture will govern NGO–government relations in Norway will be limited. The history of integration and interchange may result in relationships based on a more formal partnership, rather than contracts for services. However, questions are also raised about the consequences of this close dialogue, and the huge flow of money, for the internal democracy of NGOs. Has the mobilisation and participation of members become a redundant activity? Is it fostering an elite of NGO administrators, accountable only to themselves?

Development of relations with Southern NGOs

Direct government funding of Southern NGOs is a matter of debate in Norway. The effect of both direct and indirect support for Southern NGOs seems to have been significant. In Bangladesh, Ethiopia, Nicaragua and Zimbabwe, some 100 organisations have received official Norwegian assistance. Tvedt reports that,

> *Twelve of the NGOs funded by NORAD in 1992 as part of the local NGO grant in those four countries were established after 1990; 29 after 1980. Twelve of the organisations supported by Norwegian NGOs were also established after 1990. The organisations supported directly by NORAD and by the NGOs were not the same. A very significant part, therefore, of Norwegian cooperation in these countries was with very young organisations, established by donor money.*[19]

While Norwegian NGOs recognise that there is an element of self interest in their position, they also believe that there are matters of principle involved. At the heart of the issue is the role of the State and whether the government should concentrate on inter-governmental relations, leaving NGOs to their comparative advantage in relations with Southern civil society. Many Norwegian NGOs see themselves as having a key role in fostering civil society, and are investing in methods to improve their work with partners. One observer reports that,

> *Norwegian NGOs are increasingly calling themselves partner organisations and identify strengthening of organisations in the South as the new aid strategy. Several NGOs define their primary role as building the capacity of partnership organisations in the South, rather than providing support to programmes and projects.*[20]

Norwegian NGO partnerships with organisations in the South were, at the end of 1997, the subject of a major MFA evaluation exercise, also comprising relationships with business, consultants, State institutions and higher education and research bodies.

NGOs, foreign policy and conflict resolution

The Tvedt evaluation raised the question of whether NGOs can be neutral humanitarian development organisations and at the same time contracted for specific political purposes. Since then the debate has gone further. Questions have been raised about how far non-State actors can go politically in other countries, without compromising the Norwegian State, especially when they are largely funded by the State but not accountable to it.

NGOs and foreign policy interests have been intermingled for a long time and it is clear that in some countries NGOs have had a strong influence on Norwegian foreign policy. Looking at the Horn of Africa, Tvedt asks about the extent to which the Ministry of Foreign Affairs controlled developments, and the extent to which it became the captive of NGOs. His case study concludes that:

> *To the extent that anybody had a clear vision of the complexity of the situation they were involved in and what the outcome of these huge emergency operations could be, the NGOs and not the MFA were calling the tune. The MFA did not have a clear-cut strategy regarding the two big issues: the question of Eritrea's secession from Ethiopian and the unity of the Sudan. Neither did they have a clear idea of the complicated context in which the NGOs operated, while their 'humanitarian policy' was so broad that the NGOs could manoeuvre within it. The main reason why Norway became politically involved in these conflict areas (and not in other areas to the same extent) was not basic policy considerations or an assessment of the importance of these issues, but mainly because of the fact that Norwegian NGOs were working there.*

But the jury is still out on how much foreign policy can be determined by NGOs. In Mali, the detailed knowledge of Norwegian Church Aid (NCA) was described as an asset 'which funding from the Norwegian State permits NCA to exploit'.[21] NCA peacemaking in Mali, although constructive, was carried out entirely by NCA, with no policy direction from the MFA. Once an NGO starts to exploit its strengths for political action, it may leave official foreign policy with very little room for manoeuvre. After committed intervention in Mali by NCA, there have been calls for Norwegian championing of Malian causes with the IMF and the World Bank and for increased development assistance.

Tvedt argues that even if the State tries to distance itself and take a neutral view, it can have a political effect. He cites funding of three NGOs in Eritrea, all of which had markedly different views about the political actors there:

> *In discussion with the organisations, political issues were seldom mentioned. The State's role became more and more to assess the amount of money which should be channelled, rather than the political implications of support... [however] the map [of Eritrea] had been changed with Norwegian support, but not as a result of deliberate, long-term policies and without being followed up with either business investment or aid.*[22]

Engagement at this level is also changing those NGOs able to access funding from outside Norway, and this in turn makes them less accountable to the Norwegian State.

19 Portugal

Mário Ribeiro[1]

SUMMARY

The Portuguese development NGO movement evolved following the Revolution of 25 April 1974. The first modern development NGO, created in May of that year – Amílcar Cabral Information and Documentation Centre (CIDAC) – remained the only NGO until 1984. By 1997 there were 150 registered organisations, but only a few were in a position to play an active role in the Portuguese cooperation and development effort, and only 44 were members of the national 'Platform'.

Portuguese NGOs were strongly influenced from the outset by the anti-colonial struggle, by the Catholic Church, and by citizens motivated by humanitarian principles. The Portuguese NGO movement focuses heavily on projects in the five Portuguese-speaking African countries (the PALOPs) – Angola, Cape Verde, Guinea-Bissau, Mozambique and São Tomé e Príncipe. Though they lack professionalism, Portuguese NGOs have been able to remain independent and autonomous of government. Portuguese NGOs depend mainly on financing from multilateral sources, in particular the EU and, on a smaller scale, from government contributions and fundraising campaigns.

Portugal's development cooperation programme is closely linked to its history, language and culture. It is almost exclusively concentrated on the Portuguese-speaking countries of Africa. A large part of Portuguese aid consists of debt relief. Large annual fluctuations in the amount of debt relief have major repercussions for the volume of aid. ODA declined from $258 million in 1995, to $218 million in 1996, a decline in real terms of 17 per cent. As a share of GNP, ODA fell from 0.25 per cent in 1995 to 0.21 per cent in 1996. Portugal is beginning to diversify its aid effort somewhat beyond its former colonies, but helping these five countries evolve into well-functioning states remains a fundamental foreign policy objective. The development challenges are particularly formidable in Mozambique and Angola, where the question is how to consolidate the new governments formed after years of civil war.[2]

Portuguese NGOs play only a marginal role in Portuguese official development assistance. Despite mounting recognition of their work and growing financial support from government in recent years, their relationship with the administration is not yet fully institutionalized. There is neither a set government budget for them, nor a project funding policy. Dialogue between NGOs and government is growing. The government is introducing procedures governing the application by NGOs for public funds, and this should significantly facilitate future cooperation.[3]

Given the tentative position of government, the Platform has emphasised lobbying activities and the building of a wider movement, bringing together different partners (universities, local developmental associations and civil society organisations) in order to educate the public and to bring pressure to bear on government.

HISTORICAL BACKGROUND[4]

Before 1974, three non-governmental institutions carried out humanitarian assistance activities: the Portuguese Red Cross Society, the Portuguese Caritas and the Calouste Gulbenkian Foundation. Though non-governmental, none of these organisations could be considered a development NGO, as their activities and institutional characteristics are significantly different from the development organisations discussed in this chapter.

The Portuguese NGO movement was born out of the Revolution of 25 April 1974. In May that year, a group of four political militants – bound up with the anti-colonial struggle during the dictatorship period – launched the Anti-Colonial Information and Documentation Centre (CIDA-C). It was a political project, committed to the struggle for colonial independence, and claiming solidarity with the liberation movements. This was the starting point for the first Portuguese NGO, CIDAC – Amílcar Cabral Information and Documentation Centre

For a decade between 1974 and 1984, CIDAC remained virtually the only Portuguese NGO committed to international developmental activities, though during the same period other organisations started to emerge with similar objectives.

Table 19.1: *Number and Age of Portuguese NGOs*

Decade	Number	%
Up to 1949	2	10
1950s	1	5
1960s	–	–
1970s	9	20
1980s	18	40
1990s	14	25
Total	44	100

In February 1984, when Portugal was about to make its entry into the European Community, the European Community Commission Bureau promoted a seminar on co-financing and cooperation between Portuguese and other European NGOs, on the subject of development projects in Portuguese-speaking countries. By then, 19 organisations had begun to form. Later that year, other meetings were held in order to prepare the 'First General Meeting of the Portuguese Non-Governmental Organisations'. On that occasion, the attributes of an NGO were established:

* it must be formally recognised as an association in juridical terms;
* it must be non-profit making;
* it must have national representatives;
* it must have as part of its regular activity, solidarity activities with the South.

The first meeting of the national Platform took place in March 1985 and included three organisations. The following October, the first representatives of Portuguese NGOs were elected to take their place in European NGO bodies, as part of Portugal's entry into the European Community.

In the next ten years, there were lengthy negotiations with government, and in 1994 the Portuguese Parliament passed a law recognising the importance of NGOs in the development cooperation effort, and creating a statute for these organisations. In the eyes of the law, NGOs are considered 'collective individuals of private law, without profitable ends', their objectives being 'cooperation and intercultural dialogue as well as the effective and direct support of programmes and projects in developing countries', through 'actions towards development, humanitarian assistance, the protection and promotion of human rights, emergency assistance and public opinion-building activities'. At the end of 1997, this law was being revised, under pressure from the NGO Platform.

In 1997, there were 150 organisations registered with the Institute for Portuguese Cooperation (ICP) which considered themselves eligible for development cooperation support. The national Platform was the only representative structure for NGOs, with 44 member organisations. The majority were based in Lisbon with the balance concentrated mainly in Oporto.

In a 1994 study on the potential of Portuguese NGOs, it was found that only half had development cooperation activities in 1993, and among those only ten had started projects in the South, with the remainder planning to do so in the future. Portuguese NGOs are mainly active in the areas of education, vocational training, health, social welfare and human rights, and these activities are deeply rooted in the motivations and in the political environment from which they have emerged – namely a humanitarian ethic, participation in civil society, the anti-colonial movement prior to 1974, a commitment to the principles of action of the Catholic Church and, on a smaller scale, the influence of political parties. Most Portuguese NGOs focus their activities on projects in the Portuguese-speaking African countries. There is a three-generation typology of NGOs – emergency, rehabilitation and development. Portuguese NGOs have showed little competitiveness and, despite weak professionalism, they have been able to remain autonomous and independent of government.

In recent years, interaction between Portuguese NGOs and their counterparts in the South, particularly those operating in the PALOPs, has been growing. The total project disbursement through Southern NGOs in 1995 was Esc18.5 million ($124,000). 1996 examples include support to the Luanda *Patriarchal* of Esc15 million ($95,000) for a street children project in Angola, and NGOs in Cape Verde and Guinea-Bissau, funded to assist cattle breeding and poverty reduction projects.

CO-FINANCING MECHANISMS

Portuguese development cooperation is managed and coordinated by the ICP, which in administrative terms depends on the Foreign Affairs and Cooperation State Secretary. This is, in turn, an authority dependent on the Ministry of Foreign Affairs. In an effort to improve the coordination and management of its aid programme, in 1994 the government merged two departments working on development cooperation (the Directorate-General for Cooperation – DGC, and the former Institute for Economic Cooperation – IEC). The resulting structure, the ICP, has been charged with the planning, coordination, follow up and evaluation of development cooperation activities, which are seen as an integrated part of Portuguese foreign policy. Within the ICP, NGO support is provided by a Humanitarian Assistance Unit entrusted with 'the promotion, coordination, follow up and accomplishment of rehabilitation assistance, food or emergency aid, in the area of bilateral, communitarian or multilateral relations' (DL60/94, art° 23).

In recent years, greater importance has been given to the creation of a service specially committed to the planning, analysis and the inter-ministerial coordination of Official Development Assistance, and to giving it greater public visibility. Despite these improvements, the cooperation budget is not included in formal State budgets. Moreover, several ministries contribute funds to development cooperation activities, but these are not specified in their budgets either, making financial coordination very difficult and precluding a global perspective and political visibility.

Portuguese NGOs play a marginal role in ODA. Although there is awareness of the growing importance of NGOs in development, their relationship with government lacks institutionalisation and formal budget allocations. The Portuguese authorities do, however, envisage the creation of an Advisory Council for Cooperation composed of representatives of NGO, business and official bodies.

Volume

According to a 1995 study on Portuguese development cooperation, there was a decrease in the amount that year in funds available for NGOs (Esc56 million – $350,000) but there were no arrangements for the distribution of the funds. Exceptionally that year, four organisations were assisted with Esc95.5 million ($600,000) by the Fund for Economic Cooperation (FCE), an official body whose main objective is to 'promote the entrepreneurial spirit as one [part of] Portuguese cooperation policy' (DL 162/91).

According to DAC statistics on Portuguese ODA, government contributions to NGOs rose from Esc21 million ($130,000) in 1994, to Esc217 million ($1.45 million) in 1995, and $2 million in 1996.[5] Of this amount, the ICP contributed Esc185 million ($1.23 million), supporting 11 NGOs belonging to the national Platform, as well as other institutions that have occasional development activities (religious institutions, associations for the handicapped, student associations, women's entrepreneurial confederations, Southern NGOs). These disbursements co-financed projects in areas such as health, education, social integration, agriculture and humanitarian assistance. In that year the FCE supported one Platform NGO and two cooperation associations with Esc32 million ($210,000).

In 1996, total funding for non-governmental cooperation was about Esc322 million ($2.1 million). Provisional data supplied by the Institute for Portuguese Cooperation shows that about Esc271 million was for Portuguese NGO emergency and development projects in Africa, the strengthening of local NGOs in the PALOPs, religious and handicapped organisations, and one private company. About Esc97 million was shared by 15 NGOs with projects in the PALOPs, 10 of which were affiliated with the national Platform. The remaining Esc174 million was for emergency relief. The FCE disbursements, Esc51 million ($300,000), were granted to five institutions, three of them belonging to the national Platform.

The official support granted to foreign NGOs in 1995 – Esc46.5 million – went to the Red Cross International Committee for humanitarian aid.

Eligibility criteria

Government support has focused on proposals that concentrate in the PALOPs, in areas such as health, education and professional training. In 1995, NGO projects concentrated on the following areas:

- projects in the PALOPs in social development;
- projects focusing on citizens from the PALOPs admitted for settlement in Portugal;
- projects in the area of technical assistance and relief in the PALOPs, namely through the sending of medicine, books, equipment, school materials;
- humanitarian and emergency assistance.

Government has established the following eligibility criteria for NGOs:

- independence and financial stability (the NGO should raise sufficient funds in order to enable it to function as an autonomous institution);
- a good financial reputation and recognised leadership;
- efficient management of revenues.

Most NGOs are not aware of these criteria.

Co-financing

In duration and type, government co-financing is irregular, the principle being one of annual project grants rather than contributions to programmes. The sums involved in 1995–6 represented approximately 30 per cent of a project submission. Portuguese co-financing does not make any reference to overheads for project administration. There is no experience of Portuguese NGO involvement in bilateral projects and programmes.

Although a larger contribution has been allocated in recent years, the major source of NGO co-financing continues to be the EU. Beyond those NGOs that are members of the national Platform, only four or five Portuguese organisations have had access to European co-financing, since the eligibility criteria are quite difficult (for example, three years experience in the field), a fact that hampers the participation of many new NGOs.

NGO Fundraising

Most Portuguese NGOs suffer from a weak financial position since there is no fundraising tradition in Portugal and no tax incentives have been introduced so far. In addition to this, there is no public awareness of NGOs or their work, and consequently, there is little recognition of their contribution to society. This makes fundraising difficult. The self-financing capacity of Portuguese NGOs is therefore very small (estimated at 5 to 10 per cent of total revenues), and most contributions are in the form of membership dues, scattered donations (especially from churches), sporadic fundraising campaigns, and revenues obtained from rent, the sale of tropical products, and shows or concerts.

Public Opinion and Development Education

The aid programme enjoys broad support from all political parties. No public opinion polls have been carried out in recent years regarding public attitudes towards development cooperation, but it is believed that there is widespread support for aiding the PALOPs.[6] Government further states that 'many public and private [development education] initiatives have been taking place and that a number of institutional courses, at a higher level, about development education have been launched'. NGOs take a different position, holding that the public lacks information, involvement and participation in activities that could build knowledge about development issues (such as aid, underdevelopment, North–South dialogue, debt relief, migration, racism). In that regard, several NGO-sponsored initiatives have taken place throughout the country, in most cases with municipal authorities and local schools as their partners.

Where government support is concerned, eligibility criteria for development education funding are similar to those applied for NGO projects: there is no specific mechanism or budget committed to this type of activity.

Policy Dialogue and Advocacy: Mechanisms and Problems

In the 1994 study of NGOs in Portugal, the national Platform organisations were considered to be 'political protagonists' in development cooperation. This suggests that NGOs are, or should be, active political partners in the politics of development cooperation, committed to a collaborative approach towards official policy, but preserving their autonomy and independence from government. So far, however, the lobbying and advocacy work of Portuguese NGOs, especially as they relate to the main areas of political power (The Presidency of the Republic, Parliament and Government) have been incipient in scope and intensity. Nevertheless, growing attention is being paid by NGOs to this type of work.

Where dialogue between NGOs and government is concerned, government has announced its intention to improve relationships between NGOs and the Institute for Portuguese Cooperation and the Secretary of State for Cooperation. In recent years there have been several formal meetings to discuss various aspects of NGO–government relations.

There is no government support for NGO research activities, which are carried out by the NGOs in collaboration with Portuguese universities and research centres. In addition, government has not shown any interest in supporting the advocacy projects of southern NGOs.

ACTIVITIES OF NGOS IN THE DOMESTIC CONTEXT

As noted above, in addition to development education activities, Portuguese NGOs carry out several other types of activity at the national level:

*   technical cooperation, aimed at the professional training of personnel going to work in the PALOPs;
*   information and documentation centres about African issues and development cooperation;
*   technical assistance in the form of training centres for African students, giving courses and social support to scholarship-holders;
*   day centres aiming at facilitating the integration of foreigners and fighting against social exclusion;
*   refugee emergency assistance, especially to East Timor nationals, where the population has been fighting for human rights and self-determination.

ISSUES

The role of NGOs

In Portugal as elsewhere, it is commonly held among NGOs that the role of the Northern NGO is changing. Globalisation, the threatened marginalisation of Africa in the process, the new Lomé framework, a multipolar world, and the role of the media are some of the things forcing NGOs to explore new paths and strategies, or to attempt more specialised areas of work, such as work in lobbying and advocacy. Financial realities are also forcing change. In Portugal, many feel that these new realities are pushing NGOs more towards emergency and humanitarian projects, and to new geographical areas – Eastern Europe, for instance, where 100 per cent financing is available for projects. In Portugal, one can see a trend towards emergency and humanitarian relief.

At the organisational level, Northern NGOs (including the Portuguese) are going through a process of professionalisation. Old ideas of NGOs being cheap and efficient no longer hold true, as costs are growing exponentially. The development of consortia is an attempt to answer this problem, although such partnerships are so far very new. Portuguese participation in European NGO networks has been more successful and they have facilitated lobbying work as well.

In the area of fundraising, Portuguese NGO performance is very weak. With the exception of one NGO devoted almost exclusively to emergency aid, few have any serious fundraising capacity. There has been little interaction between Portuguese NGOs and the private sector.

NGOs have been critical of the ways in which ODA is structured. They have criticised the categorisation of debt forgiveness as ODA, and have called for 'fresh money' and the adoption of more flexible and transparent funding mechanisms. Dialogue between NGOs and government is growing. The government is introducing procedures governing the application by NGOs for public funds, and this should significantly facilitate future cooperation.[7]

Emergency assistance

Generally speaking, Portuguese NGOs do not envisage emergency assistance as part of an integrated cycle encompassing emergency, rehabilitation and development. To Portuguese NGOs, emergency assistance can create a dependency among the targeted population, and puts obstacles in the way of emergent development initiatives. On the other hand, the NGOs acknowledge the enormous constraints on their capacity in Africa, and are attempting to become more specialised in their approach.

Volunteers

Volunteers are an intrinsic feature of NGO activity in Portugal. Volunteer work is present in every non-governmental organisation, but the contribution can be sporadic: associates and members participate in reflection groups, they help to prepare events and they collaborate in professional training and other projects in the PALOPs. Nowadays, like other changing aspects of the NGO movement, volunteer work is going through a process of restructuring. In fact, with professionalisation, volunteer work may become something performed by professional personnel. As an outcome of this process, there is an overlapping of two types of volunteer work: the more 'traditional' volunteer connected with start of the NGOs movement, and another type, more modern in character and less voluntaristic, but with better insight into development problems.

Management issues

Project management, especially monitoring and evaluation, has not been given a great deal of attention by Portuguese NGOs, especially in the implementation of projects in the South. In the 1995 study, one quarter of those interviewed considered evaluation and assessment an unexplored field. In that study, NGOs identified two main components in the evaluation process: first, the internal aspects of the organisation (motivation, creativity, working relations), and second, external aspects that translate into NGO efficiency and impact in relation to project objectives.

Since then there have been some changes, in part because of NGO initiatives, but more because of pressure exerted by donors, especially the EU and the Portuguese Institute for Cooperation. Up to now this has been not conclusive, and a new approach is being developed under the auspices of a public university. This is compelling NGOs to give special attention to evaluation in a project's early stages, although it is still too early to judge what this will mean in practice.

Dialogue between NGOs and government

The NGO movement in Portugal is still young and fragile, and there is still a limited consciousness of them and their work in Portuguese society. The problems include:

- the lack of a strategy for sustainability and autonomy in relation to donors;
- poor definition of organisational models, and weak comparative advantage;
- a fragile affirmation of the national Platform at the level of both government and public opinion.

It is a common feeling among NGOs that government has ignored them as partners in development cooperation, although this has been changing in recent years. Where government policy is concerned, there is something of a paradox. On one hand, official discourse praises the role of development cooperation as a Portuguese value-added in the international arena. The recent founding of the Community of Portuguese Speaking Countries – CPLP, is one example. The government believes that the creation of this structure is of great importance to the development dialogue between Portugal and its partners. It promotes mutual learning and cooperation among them. On the other hand, government does not have a clear cooperation policy, a fact that leads some to conclude that this aspect of foreign affairs is not a priority.

In the opinion of most non-governmental organisations, the relationship between government and NGOs is still in a preliminary phase. Although the dialogue has improved since the 1995 election, ideas have not been translated into visible change where the most important questions are concerned – support and transparency in the co-financing of projects, and revision of the official status of NGOs.

20 Spain

Christian L Freres

SUMMARY

As a group, Spanish NGOs are reaching maturity, although only a small number have significant programmes and only a few are relatively independent in financial terms. In recent years, Spanish NGOs have become increasingly dependent on public funds. A particularly noteworthy fact in Spain is the growing importance of regional and municipal governments as aid donors, and these channel most of their funds through NGOs.

NGO relations with government have been complex. The socialist governments (1982–96) began the co-financing programme and expressed views in common with the NGO community. But in the end they were not very responsive to attempts by these organisations to institute serious reforms in the aid programme, or to increase ODA levels. The post-1996 conservative government began with a rather confrontational posture towards NGOs, because it felt they needed much closer supervision. After initial tensions subsided, some channels for dialogue opened, and there are now regular discussions on a number of issues. However, NGOs have not been able to influence the Development Cooperation Law to a great extent, nor have they succeeded in making the government reverse aid cuts.

BACKGROUND AND HISTORY

Evolution of Spanish ODA and Spanish NGOs

One of the defining characteristics of NGOs in Spain is the relative youth of the sector; well over half of the NGOs active in the development field today were created in the 1990s. There are two explanations for this recent and rapid growth. First, during the 40 years of the Franco regime, civil society could not develop as in most other OECD countries. Second, Spain itself was a net recipient of ODA until 1981, and only established a sizeable development assistance programme at the end of that decade.

Because the Spanish NGO community grew up alongside the official aid programme, it may be useful to review the factors that stimulated its rise. Perhaps the most important was that the government during the 1980s, formed by the *Partido Socialista Obrero Español/PSOE* (Spanish Socialist Workers' Party), felt that to truly 'belong' to the group of rich countries, Spain needed to increase its international presence. This included taking an active role in multilateral peace-keeping missions, the founding of the Iberoamerican Community of Nations, and joining the DAC in 1991.

Spain's 1986 entry into the European Economic Community led to a four-fold increase in its aid programme by 1990. And finally, the full spectrum of political parties showed their determination – through a Senate motion in 1984 – that Spain should have a modern aid programme. This was later formalised in a government document establishing overall policy guidelines for Spanish ODA, in the absence of a law on foreign aid.

The fact that Spanish NGOs grew alongside the country's aid structure is not in itself extraordinary, except that in Spain both NGOs and government have had to undergo a rapid 'catch-up' process at the same time. This factor marks the development field in Spain, and has had direct implications for NGO–government relations.

The first review of the Spanish aid programme by the DAC in April 1994 had an impact on Spanish aid policy and its relationship with civil society. In particular, Spanish NGOs have frequently drawn the attention of the aid administration to the DAC conclusions. Development NGOs are very active, and have mobilised a large part of Spanish civil society and parliamentarians in the cause of development. There is strong interest in development cooperation in both houses of parliament. All political parties support the idea of a larger and improved aid programme. In 1996, Spanish ODA was $1251 million, a reduction from $1348 million in 1995, reducing the amount in real terms by 9 per cent. The ODA/GNP ratio fell from 0.24 to 0.22 between 1995 and 1996. In Spain, regional and local authorities contribute increasingly to aid programmes.[1]

Size of the Spanish NGO community

In the past few years it has become increasingly difficult to determine the size of the Spanish NGO community, although estimates place the number at about 300. Until fairly recently over two thirds had their headquarters in Madrid or Barcelona, and were members of the national platform or umbrella group, the *Coordinadora de ONG para el Desarrollo* (Coordinator of Development NGOs), which was created in 1983. In 1997, the *Coordinadora* had 93 NGO members, up from 72 in 1994. In the European context it is one of the most inclusive and formal of NGO umbrella organisations.

The number of NGOs that are not members of the *Coordinadora* and that have central offices outside the two main urban centres has mushroomed. This parallels the growing importance of 'decentralised cooperation' in Spain, as all the 17 Autonomous Communities, along with dozens of municipalities and provincial governments have created their own aid programmes, mostly in the past few years. Some of these, however, including those in Catalonia and the Basque Country, and in the city of Vitoria, are at least as old as the modern bilateral aid programme. With expanded possibilities of funding, many new NGOs have emerged in these regions and have created additional coordinating bodies. Over 200 NGOs are members of these nascent *coordinadoras*; the NGO Federation of Catalonia alone has over 50 members. Inevitably there is some overlapping with the national *Coordinadora* since a number of local members are nominated by national NGOs.

A limited number of small NGOs remains outside the *Coordinadora* structure. Of particular significance is the '0.7% Platform', which managed to mobilise public interest through the organisation of solidarity camps across Spain in the autumn of 1994, followed by hunger strikes and other campaigns. The movement obtained 500,000 signatures in favour of raising ODA to 0.7 per cent of GNP, and obtained signatures of the political parties on the National Agreement for Solidarity. These campaigns led the government to increase significantly the grant aid budget and the subsidy programme for NGOs in 1995. Private donations to NGOs also rose substantially, doubling between 1991 and 1995, when they reached $137 million.

Historically, most NGOs grew directly or indirectly out of organisations of the Catholic Church. This, however, is changing. The 1996 directory of *Coordinadora* members notes that the largest 'social sector' of origin for NGOs is among the professions (especially medicine, but also economics and the law). NGOs in this category account for one quarter of the

Coordinadora's current members, compared with slightly under 20 per cent that identify themselves as confessional.[2] Over two thirds of Spanish NGOs are registered as associations, and close to one fifth as foundations.

THE CHARACTER OF NGO–GOVERNMENT RELATIONS

Relations between NGOs and government have been complex since the early 1980s. In addition, Spanish NGOs are generally inexperienced in relating to official organisations on broad policy issues, so once dialogue goes beyond technical project funding issues, tensions often arise, leading to dissatisfaction on both sides.

NGO funding: public and private

Within the bilateral aid programme, NGO co-financing remained at relatively low levels until 1995. In 1993, according to Spanish government figures provided to the DAC, support from the bilateral programme to NGOs was nearly Ptas3.2 billion in 1994. In 1995 the figure grew to a little more than Ptas10 billion ($81 million), and in 1996 it reached almost Ptas11 billion (approximately $87 million).[3]

In 1987 the government formalised the first Ministry of Foreign Affairs support programme for NGOs. The *Secretario de Estado para la Cooperación Internacional y para Iberoamérica* (SECIPI/Secretary of State for International Cooperation and for Iberoamerica) established a series of annual *convocatorias* (roughly translated as 'calls for tenders') for NGOs. This was complemented in 1988 by another arrangement, the *Convocatoria del IRPF* (*Impuesto sobre la Renta de Personas Físicas*/Personal Income Tax).This is funded through voluntary contributions on annual income tax returns, allowing people to apportion part of their taxes to activities 'with a social objective'. The government then allocates part of this to the Catholic Church and part to civic organisations engaged in social activities in both Spain and developing countries.

Both of these channels for NGO co-financing are responsive funds that were managed by SECIPI until July 1996, when the Spanish Agency for International Cooperation (*AECI/Agencia Española de Cooperacion Internacional*) took responsibility. The only other way NGOs can obtain funds from SECIPI for development-related activities is through the *Convocatoria Abierta y Permanente* (Open and Permanent Call for Proposals), through which most emergency and humanitarian aid projects are funded. There is no specific fund for volunteers in NGO projects. The two SECIPI *convocatorias* have been the main source of government financial support to NGOs.

Table 20.1 shows the general evolution of the co-financing programme over the period 1993–6. Having stabilized at an annual total of around 3000 million pesetas (about $24 million) in the early 1990s, the programme trebled in 1995. Table 20.1 also illustrates the heavy emphasis on Latin America (close to 60 per cent of co-financed projects), reflecting both government priorities and the limited experience of Spanish NGOs in other regions of the world.

The sudden rise in 1995 was a direct result of the 1994 '0.7%' campaigns mentioned above. One result of the increase has been a growing NGO dependence on public funds. In 1995, 56 per cent of the income raised by members of the *Coordinadora* came from public sources, two thirds of which were covered by SECIPI and the European Commission.[4]

The third largest public source of funds are the Autonomous Communities and municipalities (15 per cent of the total). Their contribution to *Coordinadora* NGOs doubled between 1992 and 1995, rising to a total of close to 3000 million pesetas (about $24 million) according to NGO sources, largely as a result of numerous decentralised administrations deciding to dedicate 0.7 per cent of their budgets to international development activities. In 1996, NGOs received over $110 million from regional authorities.

Table 20.1: *Spanish Government Co-Financing of NGO Projects, 1993–96*
(Millions of Pesetas)

| | 1993 | | 1994 | | 1995 | | 1996 | | 1993–96 | |
	Amount	%	Amount	%	Amount	%	Amount	%	Amount	%
Projects in Developing Countries	3032	99.1	3155	98.9	9859	97.7	10,734	97.7	26,780	98
Latin America	2125	69.4	1797	56.4	5811	57.6	6341	57.7	16,075	58.8
Africa, total	654	21.4	951	29.8	3067	30.4	3086	28.1	7757	28.4
Of which, sub-Saharan	505	16.5	540	16.9	2256	22.4	2254	20.5	5556	20.3
North Africa	149	4.9	411	12.9	811	8.0	831	7.6	2202	8.1
Asia	218	7.1	407	12.8	980	9.7	1191	10.8	2796	10.2
Europe	35	1.2	0	0	0	0	117	1.1	152	0.6
Development Education	29	0.9	34	1.1	229	2.3	250	2.3	541	2.0
TOTAL	3061	100	3189	100	10,087	100	10,984	100	27,321	100

Source: Based on data from CIDOB, *Anuario Internacional*, various years.
Barcelona. $1.00 = 127 Pesetas

During the period 1991–95, members of the *Coordinadora* obtained an annual average of 12,000 million pesetas (about US$ 95 million) from the general public, a large proportion of which was concentrated in less than 10 large NGOs. Since 1993, private sources of funds for NGO projects have not grown dramatically, although there was rapid growth in 1994 due to enormous public response to the humanitarian tragedy in Rwanda. (According to one study, the Spanish public gave more per capita than any other European country for this emergency).[5] The stagnation in private funds is a further factor explaining the increasing dependence of NGOs on public funds. Only a small number of NGOs – mainly those with large humanitarian aid programmes – have built an extensive network of regular donors that can assure greater autonomy.

Government strategy towards NGOs

Government strategy towards Spanish NGOs is based on at least three considerations:

Political: NGOs have a certain amount of public support and for this reason it is important to assist them. This was apparent after the '0.7%' demonstrations of 1994, when government rushed to increase the NGO co-financing programme. Increasingly, government seeks to gain political mileage from NGO-managed projects. This is done, for example, by requiring the prominent use of the Spanish aid logo in co-financed projects. All governments have tended to politicise their relations with NGOs, often favouring – with information and resources – those that are directly or indirectly linked to the party in power. Governments, however, have rarely counted on NGOs as allies in policy debates, or for defending ODA budgets.

Instrumental: NGOs are useful in achieving broad policy goals. Spanish governments have taken this to mean that in principle NGOs should serve state interests, particularly if their activities are co-financed. There is a difference between the approach of PSOE governments (1982–96) and the subsequent conservative Popular Party (PP) government. The socialists saw NGOs as an important expression of Spanish international solidarity, serving the state's general interests simply through their existence. The PP sees NGOs as contributing simultaneously to the struggle against poverty in developing countries and to resolving – directly or indirectly – domestic problems, such as unemployment (through the purchase and use of Spanish products in their projects). There is also a strong emphasis on the concept of NGOs as private actors that should not have to depend too heavily on government subsidies.

As a proxy for reducing poverty: NGOs are generally regarded as being more capable than bilateral donors of reaching the poor in developing countries (even though this assumption has not been tested in Spain). Some government officials believe that co-financing NGOs enables government to affirm that it is doing something to reduce poverty, freeing it to concentrate on programmes that may not have poverty reduction as their main or overarching goal.

None of this means that there is a clear and formalised government strategy towards NGOs. It has more to do with the lack of an overall development assistance strategy than with particular government views about NGOs – regardless of the party in power. In fact government views are quite varied. Under the PP Government, for instance, the AECI (Spanish Agency for International Cooperation) has had a tense relationship with the Coordinadora, while the SECIPI (the Secretary of State for International Cooperation, which overseas the AECI) has developed a fairly fluid dialogue with NGOs. NGOs have been hostile towards the Ministry of Finance, as this department is in charge of international lending, which is seen to only benefit Spanish businesses.

The unit in charge of NGO co-financing formed part of SECIPI's Office for Planning and Evaluation (OPE) until the PP government restructured the aid programme in mid-1996, placing it within AECI. Its role in both cases, however, has always been technical (reviewing proposals and relating with NGOs on specific projects) and not political. Policy-making on NGOs has been centred in the SECIPI Cabinet and Secretariat.

Currently there are no special tax benefits for most NGOs, although both the PSOE and PP governments expressed interest in changing this. Only those NGOs registered as foundations receive partial tax relief.[6] The government proposal for a development cooperation law (which was presented in Congress in July 1997) mentioned this issue, but was not specific. Included in the proposed legislation was provision for a register of NGOs that can apply for co-financing, specifying certain minimum requirements such as years of experience, demonstrated ability to manage funds, and external audits. If the law is approved, these provisions will go into effect almost immediately.

DEVELOPMENT EDUCATION AND PUBLIC INFORMATION

NGOs have grown rapidly over the past decade, and they have become increasingly concerned that the Spanish public remains relatively uninformed both about developing countries, and about the vast divide between the North and the South. This has led most NGOs to initiate development education activities, often directly related to their projects in the South. These efforts can be divided into three types. The first includes comprehensive public campaigns based on a simple theme such as *No to Poverty*. Such campaigns include extensive supporting material and sometimes television advertisements soliciting donations. They are carried out mostly by the largest NGOs, although smaller NGOs that stress development education may participate. The second are campaigns that are narrowly focused on schools and universities, with a strong emphasis on education and aiming to produce results over the long-term. The third approach consists of focused campaigns seeking contributions for specific emergencies.

There is no independent evaluation of Spanish development education efforts. NGOs claim that favourable public attitudes towards NGOs and development assistance result from their efforts, but evidence of this is slim.

For its part, the government has no strategy on development education. It has supported NGO efforts and has even run its own campaigns, but it does not have a clear notion of the utility of development education. Moreover, it has not provided much funding for development education (see Table 20.1, above). The main NGO funding mechanism allows for up to 5 per cent to be spent on development education, but between 1993 and 1996, development education averaged only 2 per cent of total co-financing. This represented an average of 135 million pesetas (about US$1.1 million) per annum. The fact that development education is lumped together with development projects, and that there is no special unit in charge of these activities, attests to the limited attention it receives in the government.

Autonomous communities and municipalities have given considerably more attention to development education in their NGO support programmes. In a number of cases they require that NGOs receiving funds dedicate a part of the subsidy to educational activities in the community where they are located.

NGO DIALOGUE WITH GOVERNMENT

The heterogeneity of the NGO community

With respect to NGO–government dialogue in Spain, the heterogeneity of organisations is a factor in both tone and effectiveness. There is a wide spectrum of ideological perspectives, and NGOs differ very much in size, affecting their relative ability to participate in collective efforts. Dialogue with government, therefore, is not always unified. The more political the issue, the more likely it is that splits will occur between different groups of NGOs. In addition, NGOs may have political affinities with the political party in power, and this can add to the problem of developing common positions.

The most problematic issue, however, has more to do with the division between the few NGOs that actively contribute to the *Coordinadora* (or to regional umbrellas), and the majority that are more passive members. There is a growing feeling among this latter group that important decisions are being taken by a small and unrepresentative group of NGOs.

In addition, there is a significant difference in approach between the *Coordinadora* and the *0.7% Platform*, which has implications for how each views dialogue with the government. This is most clearly illustrated by the way each focused their 1994 campaigns on the issue of increasing Spanish ODA. The *Coordinadora* had as its theme, a non-confrontational 'Yes to 0.7%'. Their campaign consisted of press conferences, a symbolic act in the Congress, and the distribution of stickers and brochures. The Platform's theme, however, '0.7% Now!' made a specific demand for immediate action. Its campaign was dramatic, with camp-outs in front of government ministries, hunger strikes and vigils. The Platform mobilised thousands of citizens throughout the country in highly visible activities.

This initial experience set the tone for the Platform, which focuses on pressuring government through annual Autumn 'mobilisations'. The Platform sees the *Coordinadora* as excessively focused on technical issues, such as the percentage of project costs NGOs must cover privately in order to receive co-financing. Refusing to accept government funding itself, it views the *Coordinadora* as too dependent on public funds to be able to take an aggressive posture towards government.

Despite these differences in vision and approach, both the Platform and the *Coordinadora* have maintained contacts, exchanging information and views on key issues, such as the pending development cooperation law. They have also occasionally organised joint activities.

Channels to the central government

There are two basic channels through which NGOs relate to government. The formal channel is through the *Coordinadora* structure, involving regular meetings between top *Coordinadora* representatives and government officials. Meetings may discuss general or specific issues. For instance, in 1995, the *Coordinadora* attempted to get the PSOE Government to commit itself to a 'Solidarity Pact' (which among other things, called for dedicating 0.7 per cent of Spain's GNP to ODA). Representatives of the 0.7% Platform have separate meetings with government, although the Platform has joined the *Coordinadora* on various campaigns.

The Council on Development Cooperation was created in 1995 (another result of the 0.7 per cent demonstrations), to debate general development policy. It comprises the President of the *Coordinadora*, four member NGOs, a representative of the 0.7% Platform, representatives from government trade unions, universities, business interests, independent experts and decentralised administrations. Although this forum has proven rather sterile – since it mostly consists of institutional representations and little real dialogue – at least it serves to present the various viewpoints in a formal way. Since government has over half the members of the Council, however, there is no possibility of a consensus different from the official position.

There is considerably more informal contact between government and individual NGOs – particularly the larger ones with institutional relations departments – both on issues of particular interest (such as a specific project proposal) or broader concern (such as ideas for improving the text of the development cooperation law).

NGOs also relate to government in other ways. In the past five years the *Coordinadora* has shifted from a service-oriented role to one giving greater emphasis to lobbying and communications. This reflects a maturing of Spanish NGOs as well as improved cohesiveness on the *Coordinadora*'s executive committee and board. It has led NGOs to initiate and develop channels to both Parliament and to political party organisations, discovering in the process that these contacts are often a more effective way of influencing government than the more direct approaches. In addition, the *Coordinadora* scaled up its communications department, holding more and better-organised press conferences, making board members and secretariat staff available for print and radio interviews, and improving its information materials.

Spanish NGOs have found, in fact, that their knowledge and their access to international sources of information – through NGO networks and their monitoring of multilateral organisations – have made them invaluable to parliamentarians (particularly those in opposition parties) and to journalists, many of whom have limited understanding of the issues under debate. It is not uncommon for members of parliament to call on the *Coordinadora* for advice, especially during the annual budget debates, opening new possibilities for influencing the policy process.

The *Coordinadora* is now trying to limit its lobbying efforts to a small number of issues around which there is a reasonable consensus amongst NGOs. This leaves room for other lobbying initiatives by smaller groups of NGOs. For instance, *Intermón*, one of the largest and best organised NGOs in Spain (which has recently joined the Oxfam group), has engaged in an informational and lobbying campaign with several other Spanish NGOs on land mines. It also conducts its own efforts on fair trade, and on aid levels through the Spanish version of *The Reality of Aid*. Finally, Spanish NGOs are increasingly active in international lobbying campaigns, often through networks such as EUROSTEP, Cáritas International, and the EU Liaison Committee of Development NGOs.

21 Sweden

Judith Randel and Tony German[1]

SUMMARY

International development NGOs have a strong popular base in Swedish society, reflecting in different ways the concerns and values held by organisations such as the Free Church, the cooperative and temperance movements, and the labour movement. They are also strongly integrated into official Swedish development assistance. Both NGOs and Sida recognise their mutual interdependence. Sida looks to NGOs for public support and a grassroots approach to development; NGOs benefit from funding and from the opportunity to influence Sida policy and programmes.

NGOs receive funding mainly through 13 framework NGOs, from Church-based organisations, to NGOs focused specifically on Africa, to *Forum Syd*, through which a large number of smaller organisations access official funds. Other official funding mechanisms include support for central and eastern Europe, humanitarian funding, volunteer programmes and – increasingly – bilateral contracting.

A major reorganisation of Sida – including the amalgamation of agencies concerned with the commercial aspects of development cooperation – has not diminished the closeness of relations between government and NGOs. In fact it has presented new opportunities for NGO dialogue with the private sector. The challenges of responding to Swedish EU membership and to budget cuts have reinforced an agenda that NGOs and Sida tend to share. Both have redoubled their respective attempts to increase public awareness and to bolster political enthusiasm for development assistance following aid cutbacks and the appearance of opinion polls showing a slump in public support.

A greater emphasis on accountability has increased Sida's scrutiny of NGO activities, giving new importance to NGO coordination. A major 1995 evaluation of NGO efforts suggested that immediate project outcomes were generally met but that greater focus on strategic impact was needed. This has led to more realistic perceptions of what NGOs can achieve, and has reinforced dialogue between NGOs and Sida on the NGO contribution to key Swedish aid priorities such as poverty, gender, human rights and the environment.

BACKGROUND AND HISTORY

Swedish overseas NGO activity began in Africa and Asia with Swedish church missionary activities in the 19th century. The 1960s saw a rapid expansion of NGOs, many of which are member-based organisations with a strong popular appeal. NGOs are seen less as a sector of Swedish society than a manifestation of popular movements and social concern. These popular movements – labour, the Free Church, cooperative and temperance movements – are the basis for the overall 'Swedish Model' of governance; hence a strong integration of the NGO movement into Swedish development cooperation.

Framework NGOs

The main form of funding for NGOs is via 13 'framework organisations'. These differ in character – some of them process and approve grants, some are implementing organisations that have projects of their own, while others do both.[2] Until recently, smaller NGOs applied for official funding through a framework organisation known as BIFO (Assistance and Information through Voluntary Organisations). But a new organisation, Forum Syd, has been formed by merging BIFO with the Swedish Volunteer Service.[3]

Table 21.1: *Swedish NGOs with Sida Framework Agreements (Funding in SKr million)*

Framework Agreement NGOs	1996 Sida Funding
The Africa Groups	28
DIAKONIA (Free Church Aid)	59
Swedish Organisation of Handicapped International Aid Foundation (SHIA)	26
LO/TCO Council of International Trade Union Co-operation	58
Olof Palme International Centre (OPC)	28
PMU Interlife	103
Swedish Save the Children (RB)	97
Church of Sweden Mission/Church of Sweden Aid	65
Swedish Missionary Council (SMR)	143
Swedish Red Cross (SRK)	42
Forum Syd	112
Swedish Co-operative Centre (SCC)	57
Training for Development Assistance (UBV)	15

In 1995, a new programme was started to allow funding for aid through political parties. In 1996, this programme was allocated SKr10 million (about $1.5 million). Youth organisations also received an allocation of around the same amount.

THE CHARACTER OF NGO–GOVERNMENT RELATIONS

Overall trends in government support to NGOs

A number of important changes have taken place since 1992, affecting both the entire Swedish aid programme and more specifically, NGOs. The most important development was the amalgamation of the five principal development cooperation agencies into the new-look Sida. These were the Swedish International Development Authority (SIDA), the Swedish Agency for Research Cooperation in the Developing Countries (SAREC), the Swedish Agency for International Technical and Economic Cooperation (BITS), the Swedish International Enterprise Development Corporation (SwedeCorp) and the Swedish Centre for Education in International Development (Sand). The new body is known as 'Sida', but this is no longer an acronym. The merger was intended to increase the flexibility, efficiency and clarity of Swedish aid programmes.[4]

Sweden's development cooperation programme has been consolidated behind the overall objectives of contributing to poverty reduction, democracy and sustainable development. As a new member of the European Union, Sweden is pushing for improved coordination, coherence and quality in EU aid. Sweden's historic commitment to 1 per cent of GNP for ODA was achieved in 1992. But for the period up to the millennium at least, it has been replaced with a standard of 0.7 per cent. Swedish ODA fell in volume during the early 1990s, reflecting a general national concern over public spending. However in 1996, ODA grew by 9 per cent over 1995, and the ODA/GNP ratio rose from 0.77 to 0.84. Bilateral aid maintained its share of Swedish ODA up to 1995. In both 1995 and 1996, however, it fell from 75 to 70 per cent.[5] 1995 marked Sweden's first payment of $100 million to the European Union.

Allocations to Swedish NGOs account for a substantial proportion of the aid programme. Throughout the 1990s, this has hovered around 12 per cent. In 1994–5 there was a sharp drop, particularly in emergency funding, reflecting a general aid decline and new demands on the aid budget as a result of Sweden joining the EU. In 1997, funding for NGO programmes and block grants was expected to be around SKr900 million (about $135 million). In general, support to NGOs is expected to follow the same pattern as the aid budget: support will be maintained if the aid budget is stable or declining, but it will increase in volume and percentage terms if the aid budget increases.

Support from the public for voluntary organisations as a whole, both domestic and international, has followed an almost identical trend to State funding, rising steadily from 1989 to 1994, but with a decline in 1995.

Table 21.2: *Trends in Government And Public Support To All Voluntary Organisations, Domestic and International (Billion SKr)*

	1989	1994	1995
Total Swedish NGO income	3.2	6.5	6.0
Of which, from the public	1.0	2.5	2.3

Table 21.3: *Trends in Sida Support to Development NGOs (SKr million)*

	1993/4	1994/5	1995/6
Private Funding	800 (approx)	850 (approx)	
Sida funding for humanitarian projects	892	477	547
Sida Programme Funding	915	999	852
Contracts to NGOs for Bilateral Programming	n/a	n/a	214

Note: The financial year in Sweden changed in 1996, so figures for the period 1995/6 have been pro-rated from eighteen month data.
Sources: Sida Questionnaire.

Organisation of government funding

A major evaluation of Swedish government support to NGOs[6] and a number of sectoral studies have led to a reorientation of the rules governing relations between government and NGOs. As a result, the guidelines referred to here were being revised at the end of 1997. The general purpose was to make the arrangements more explicit and more rigorous, in order to allow for better accountability.

Sida support for NGOs falls into two categories: programme funding through the framework organisations, and humanitarian assistance through Swedish NGOs. These are administered by two separate divisions within the Department for Cooperation with NGOs and Humanitarian Assistance (SEKA) which, at the time of writing, consisted of approximately 30 people in two divisions plus an administrative section. The NGO Division has six professional staff, one assistant and one head.

There is no facility for funding outside central government. Embassies usually have to refer back to Stockholm if they receive any requests for funding.

Programme funding through framework organisations

Sida provides 80 per cent of project costs or programme/block grant costs. Until 1998, a grant was negotiated annually with each framework organisation towards the administrative costs for all Sida-funded programmes (programme/block grants, humanitarian assistance, contracts). Further, implementation NGOs accessing funds through their framework organisation, or applying for humanitarian funds directly from Sida, were normally allowed to use 5 per cent of Sida's contribution for administration in Sweden. A new system was to be introduced in 1998, with each of Sida's funding windows establishing its own criteria for meeting administrative costs. For the NGO Division a fixed percentage (around 8 to 9 per cent) of programme/block grant costs was to be introduced.

The framework organisations are responsible to Sida for checking and assessing applications for grants on the basis of Sida's guidelines and their own criteria. Each central organisation then submits a summary budget request for development and information programmes to the NGO division at Sida. Those organisations with a number of projects or programmes, a proven track record in development and sound administrative back-up can apply for 'annual grants' for their activities.[7]

Central and Eastern Europe

There is a special facility for funding development within Central and Eastern Europe, and a framework agreement has been established with six organisations:

- LO/TCO Council of International Trade Union Cooperation;
- The Olof Palme International Centre;
- The Swedish Society for Nature Conservation;
- Swedish Farmer's Assistance;
- Swedish Save the Children;
- East Europe Committee of the National Board of Health and Welfare.

This facility will also fund partnership organisations in Central and Eastern European countries.[8]

Humanitarian assistance through Swedish NGOs

Humanitarian assistance projects are 100 per cent funded by Sida and are covered by separate guidelines for both conflict situations and natural disasters. Any organisation classified by Sida as an NGO can apply for humanitarian assistance funding. If the project is to be implemented by a partner organisation in a developing or transitional country, that organisation is also subject to assessment by Sida. These organisations may be local or international NGOs, or they may be a national or regional authority.[9]

The Sida definition of humanitarian assistance is wide, covering prevention, preparedness, projects during the acute stages of a disaster, and reconstruction. Strong emphasis is placed on the input of local communities and organisations in the implementation of humanitarian assistance.

Although funding for humanitarian programmes has several different channels, grants for UN organisations and NGOs predominate. Unless a particular NGO, such as the Life and Peace Institute, has a specific mandate to involve itself in the political side of conflict and conflict resolution, Swedish NGOs as a whole have tended to stay away from this aspect, and have no formal *modus operandi* with the military in such situations.

Contracting NGOs through the bilateral programme

Contracting through the bilateral programme is relatively new, with figures for 1995–6 showing that SKr214 million (about $32 million) was spent through NGOs. This represents about a quarter of the funding NGOs received through co-financing – not an insignificant amount. This type of funding provides 100 per cent of project costs, and administrative costs are negotiated on a case-by-case basis.

The scope within bilateral programmes for working directly with Southern NGOs is being expanded, with a transfer of funding from the NGO Division to regional budgets starting in 1998 (see also below).

Volunteer programmes

The Swedish volunteer programme aims to strengthen the development projects of different organisations. It is funded by the NGO division, which sets criteria and conditions, and it is executed by NGOs, who apply for volunteer funding. Allocations of ODA have been around SKr100 million (about $15 million) a year through the 1990s.

As a consequence of their work on a project, volunteers are expected to take part in infor-mation dissemination activities when they return to Sweden. The grant for each volunteer is usually approved in the first instance for 24–28 months. This allows for a two-year period overseas plus time for information activities on return.

Aid to political parties

A pilot project allowing political parties to receive development cooperation funds for interna-tional projects was under review in 1997. In 1995, SKr10 million was allocated to Swedish political parties from the Human Rights, Democracy and CEEC budget lines, on a formula relat-ing to the size of each party's mandate. Projects are run by organisations affiliated to the party, not the party itself. Guidelines are issued by government and the programme is administered by Sida in coordination with the Ministry of Foreign Affairs.

The goal of the programme is to offer training and support that will enable organisations in developing countries to learn more about the role of political parties. The NGO Unit is not involved in project selection because it would be difficult for a government agency to take decisions on funding via political parties. There is, deliberately, no coordination with Sida's human rights and democracy work, and efforts are made to explain that the two activities are quite separate.

Regulation and fiscal benefits

The Swedish public does not receive a tax concession on charitable donations, and NGOs do not receive any form of tax relief.

NGO eligibility for Sida funding is based on criteria that are widely regarded as overly vague. These were expected to be significantly tightened in 1998. At the time of writing, NGOs were required to:

- be democratic, have active members, an elected board, a constitution and regular meetings;
- have a registered address in Sweden;
- be non-profit;
- have been established in Sweden for at least two years, and to have documented activities in an annual report and final accounts;
- have worked with an organisation or institution in a developing country for at least one year;
- run activities and information programmes in Sweden related to its overseas work;
- have the capacity to carry out the planned development project – administration, personnel and/or active, experienced members, and a sound financial base.

NGOs are also accredited through a private monitoring body, *Stiftelsen for Insamlingskontroll* (Foundation for Fund Raising Control). Membership entitles NGOs to use a postal account number for donations. NGOs are dropped from the list if they do not conform with standards. The *Stiftelsen for Insamlingskontroll* publishes an annual set of NGO data, and requires NGOs to submit copies of their annual accounts. It also sets standards for ethical marketing and for appropriate levels of administrative costs. The new Sida guidelines will use a similar formula for reporting on administrative costs.

Government strategy towards NGOs

In Sweden, it seems less appropriate than in most other countries to talk of a 'government strategy towards NGOs'. The integration of Swedish NGOs into the political scene and civil society is long-standing and strong. There is considerable interchange of personnel between the government and non-government sectors. Swedish NGOs are heavily dependent on the government for funding, and the government explicitly states that it is dependent on NGOs, and on the relations developed by NGOs with their partners in the South.

NGOs sit on the Sida Board of Directors and they say that Sida wants to listen to them and to involve them in developing policy and strategies. This relationship, characterised by strong trust and mutual respect, does not appear to have been seriously undermined by pressures on spending, or by questions about the efficacy of Swedish aid.

When NGO support was cut in 1994–5, there was a strong political reaction, reflecting keen parliamentary support for NGO activity. In the reduced 1997 budget, it was explicitly stated that NGO support would be maintained at its previous level. The budget lines for parts of the Africa programme, democracy and human rights were also protected. However, while NGO co-financing was not threatened, Sida is now taking a larger share of areas that were previously spent to a great extent through NGOs. This includes sectors such as democracy and the environment, and some aspects of country programmes. Spending through NGOs also declined in South Africa when bilateral governmental assistance became possible.

Traditionally, Swedish NGOs have had a great deal of freedom in project implementation. The government's primary interest was in results, and it left it to the NGO to decide how to get there. Increasingly now, however, the NGO community perceives a change. Sida has developed a greater interest in the content of project proposals, and it is exercising more control as pressures on government spending demand greater accountability for public money.

The effect of this is felt most strongly by smaller NGOs who find it difficult to meet the project proposal standards that are now demanded. They also suffer disproportionately from the decline in public support. *Forum Syd*, an umbrella body with membership made up predominantly of smaller NGOs, reports that at its peak, 350 of its members would apply for Sida project funding. In 1997, the figure was nearer 200.

DEVELOPMENT EDUCATION AND PUBLIC INFORMATION

Public support for development cooperation has been declining. The annual Sida poll showed an all-time low in 1996. Only 44 per cent of the respondents to an annual survey were in favour of increasing or maintaining the aid levels – compared with 85 per cent in 1975. Forty two per cent were in favour of reducing or abolishing aid – compared with only 15 per cent in 1975. This change has gone hand in hand with a decreased commitment from politicians.

The response to this decline has been far from passive. Already the biggest per capita spender in the DAC on development education, Sida decided to intensify its work, increasing spending in 1997 by over 37 per cent from SKr24 million ($14 million) in 1996 to SKr33 million ($20 million) in 1997 and allocating SKr45 million ($27 million) in 1998. Combined with government funds to NGOs for information work the total Sida expenditure in this area, excluding salaries, was around SKr100 million ($60 million) in 1996.

Table 21.4: *ODA Spent on Development Education and Information (SKr million)*

	1993/4	1994/5	1995/6	1997
Sida spending on PR, & Dev. Ed.	18	25	23.0	32
Sida Spending through NGOs on				
PR & Development Education	60	70	62.6	69
Total Sida Spending on PR & Dev. Ed.	78	95	85.7	101

Note: Figures for 1995/6 have been pro-rated from 18 month totals; $1 = SKr6.7

Allocations to NGOs are shared between development NGOs, adult education organisations and trade unions. The latter two categories are generally regarded as more professional in their communication techniques, but because their membership or audiences do not start with a strong interest in development, impact may be harder to achieve.

Sweden's policy is to undertake extensive and comprehensive domestic information campaigns in order to create understanding and interest in developing countries. Information about other countries and cultures is seen as a way of counteracting xenophobia and racism within Swedish society. Sida will fund 100 per cent of project costs for information activities in Sweden, and for the administration of activities in Sweden.

While no radical changes are anticipated in Sweden's development education, there is a strong new focus on impact. A common communications strategy and joint campaigns – not necessarily with Sida, but between NGOs themselves – are seen as critical to this. An example is an initiative by six NGOs to publish *Globen*, a magazine aimed at ten to twelve year olds.

Volunteers and development education

The Swedish volunteer programme has been very demanding where professional and technical qualifications are concerned. As a result, the number of volunteers has been decreasing. It is now expected that there will be two programmes. One will be focused on technical assistance; the other will be much more flexible and aimed at youth. This will offer opportunities for different tasks – South–South volunteering, scholarships and other forms of exchange – without compromising the quality of the traditional technical assistance offered by Swedish volunteers.

A major evaluation of volunteering was undertaken in 1997 and, at the time of writing, Sida was examining the results. Early indications were that a major shift might take place. The evaluation is one of the very few areas where it is possible to see some light between the positions taken by Sida and by NGOs. Sida evaluators looked only at the development impact of volunteers in the South. Despite the fact that development education is built into the funding and that the value to Sweden of returned volunteers is recognised, Sida did not take this into account in assessing the contribution of the programme. Many NGOs regard the development education opportunity and prospect of life-long impact as more important than the services offered overseas.

Advocacy and engagement

There are a number of fora in which Swedish NGOs can engage the government. Sida's Director General meets with the framework organisations at least twice a year to discuss general policy, and many NGOs are involved in consultations on country strategies. However, most policy dialogue takes place at an informal level, among the networks that have built up between Sida and specific NGOs.

The effect of joining the EU

With such a collaborative climate in the Swedish development community, now reinforced by the 'new Sida', lobbying may seem somewhat redundant or unnecessary. However, with accession to the EU, NGOs and Sida are having to move to a more contentious style. There is, for example, a widespread Swedish sense of frustration with EU development cooperation. There is a lack of trust between Swedish NGOs and ECHO. The EU is perceived as lacking transparency, and NGOs find it difficult to cope with EU co-financing mechanisms. A widely reported government instruction to NGOs, to go Brussels and 'get Sweden's aid money back', has not resulted in substantial changes in funding, despite support from Sida to help NGOs understand the EU systems, and a staff secondment to Brussels jointly funded by Sweden and Finland.

There is a recognition that NGOs must become engaged in EU development policy and that the government must also try to influence EU development policy. Nevertheless, few NGOs have given priority to EU issues. New advocacy styles and tactics are likely to become an important feature for Swedish NGOs if they want to assert their voice in EU development policies and activities.

Paradoxically, if NGOs can develop a new advocacy style, it may reinforce their collaborative relationship with Sida, an organisation struggling with new structures and a smaller budget, in part because of its contributions to the EU. This situation is exacerbated by the lack of capacity in the European Commission for aid management in the social sectors, particularly in issues of special interest to Sweden: gender and poverty.

EVALUATION

Promoting development by proxy

Throughout the 1980s and 1990s, budget allocations for NGOs increased, but there was little in the way of substantive evaluation. In 1995, Sida's NGO Division and its Evaluations Unit commissioned the British Overseas Development Institute to undertake a comprehensive evaluation. The report of the evaluation, *Promoting Development by Proxy: the Development Impact of Swedish Government Support to NGOs*, was published the same year. It was a landmark event. The key findings found strong resonance among both NGOs and Sida. Its basic conclusions were that:

- immediate project objectives were, on the whole, met;
- project activities and outputs were consistent with the proposals made to Sida; but,

- development impact was much less clear, and there was too little strategic development thinking.

Presentation of the evaluation

A proactive approach to the findings was taken by both Sida and NGOs. There was widespread awareness and intensive discussion of the main findings and issues. NGOs organised an immediate three-day feedback session, and Sida held seminars and field workshops in Kenya, Tanzania, Zimbabwe, India and Bolivia to discuss the results.

NGOs have held conferences on the results, geared towards making recommendations for change. NGOs are reported to be focusing more on project follow-up, improving the quality and evaluation of impact, rather than on directing resources into new projects. It was noted that the new guidelines, expected in 1998, should include criteria for development impact. However, the main ideas discussed in response to the evaluation were first, relations with Southern partner organisations, and capacity building and, second, the role of information sharing and knowledge.

A Red Cross Seminar for example, held in April 1995 in Stockholm, came to a number of conclusions on the way forward for Swedish NGOs. Among these were that,

- more resources are needed for spreading knowledge and information;
- there are dangers for NGOs if they are perceived as just another channel for Sida support;
- Swedish NGOs need to set their own agendas for image-creating activities directed towards both the public and Parliament.[10]

A subsequent seminar in June 1995 concluded that,

- more guidelines are required for some of the Sida funding windows and improved coordination of existing budget lines;
- NGOs need to have more involvement at earlier stages of country strategy development planning;
- more interest must be taken by NGOs in the EU in Brussels;
- a logical framework analysis should be incorporated into project/programme design.

What has changed as a result of the evaluation?

People report that attitudes have changed. In debunking some of the exaggerated claims about NGO impact, the evaluation created greater acceptance among NGOs of Sida legitimacy. As a result, it reinforced a trend towards greater dialogue at policy level between Sida and NGOs on the key issues of Swedish aid: poverty, gender, environment, human rights, democracy, conflict.

NGOs have used the findings as a starting point, not just for debate but for reform and change. In the annual consultations between Sida and the framework NGOs for instance, both parties have gone back to the evaluation to establish what progress has been made in responding to its findings. The evaluation is seen to have created a climate of openness to self criticism and a real learning process.

At the time of writing, Sida was revising its general conditions and guidelines for relations with NGOs in an attempt to use its funding procedures to achieve greater development impact. This too is a product of the evaluation.

There is no doubt that this evaluation has had a significant influence on Swedish NGOs and on their relationship with government. It is taken extremely seriously and is perceived to have resulted not just in specific and procedural changes, but in changes to the mind set with which both NGOs and government officials approach their work.

KEY DEVELOPMENTS AND ISSUES

Dependency, competition and coordination

Some Swedish NGOs reject the contention that their funding relationship with Sida inevitably makes them subservient to government. They argue that Sida does not wish to influence their policies, and that NGOs are not fearful of speaking out. Swedish government policy is often similar, in fact, to policies that NGOs in other countries advocate, so perhaps it is not surprising that NGOs and Sida have much in common.

Some NGOs, however, do have a formal policy to limit the proportion of government funding. Church of Sweden Aid, for instance, has a formal limit of 50 per cent on government income. This is not so much out of fear of possible Sida domination; it reflects a concern that over-reliance on one source of support would make the organisation structurally dependent. Official funding for Church of Sweden Aid has so far never exceeded 35 per cent.

Sida sees a benefit in its public association with NGOs, not least because the Swedish public rate NGO development work much more highly than Sida's. From the NGO side, however, it is a commonly held view that the public is unaware of the proportion of NGO income that comes from the public purse, and that increased awareness could reduce voluntary support.

The issue of coordination, raised in the 1995 evaluation[11] came into sharper focus with the aid cuts and Swedish membership in the EU. Traditionally, framework NGOs have maintained separate identities. There was little sense of competition for funds, but even so, each NGO had its own independent relationship with Sida, and was responsible for its own public statements and campaigns. With the cuts, there was need for a more coordinated NGO response. Similarly, the EU NGO Liaison Committee requires a national body with a chair, in order to develop co-ordinated NGO positions on EU policy. The Swedish response has so far been for *Forum Syd*, representing the smaller NGOs, to take the lead on advocacy coordination, both in Sweden and in NGO relations with the EU.

There is some ambivalence in the NGO community about the need for coordination, particularly when it extends to programming. Some maintain that different NGOs have different programming constituencies and capacities, and that to coordinate them all together would result in reduced scope for participatory work. On information exchange and activity within Sweden, however, there is greater coordination – both through a 'One Per Cent' campaign to maintain ODA levels, and in informal and regular discussions between various agencies. (See also Development education, above.)

Side by side by Sida

The new Sida, combining traditional development assistance with bodies that focused on research, technical assistance and the private sector, was greeted originally with some concern by NGOs. Many anticipated a less intimate relationship with the new Sida, especially because it incorporated the more business-oriented agencies, BITS and SwedeCorp. This anxiety was fuelled by the coincidence of the first-ever cuts in government support to NGOs.[12] In fact, however, the experience has been very different. NGOs report that the new Sida is open and transparent, and that it enjoys strong leadership. There is greater outreach to a broader range of actors and to the media.

The greater representation of business interests is seen as beneficial by many in the NGO community. Swedish companies, like NGOs, are represented on the board of Sida, and relations with the private sector are now more transparent and open. Mention in the Sida mission statement of the jobs and contracts generated by aid is positively viewed by NGO leaders who are only too aware of sharply declining public support for aid. Some NGOs are increasingly keen to see Swedish long-term self-interest highlighted in development cooperation, moving away from a charitable or welfare paradigm. While a joint campaign between industry and NGOs on, say, fair trade, may still be some way off, dialogue is beginning to take place. A 1997 Uppsala University Seminar on India, for example, included corporations as well as NGOs, Sida and the research community.

This approach to building partnerships with stakeholders in the aid programme extends into development education and advocacy. There is a recognised need to collaborate in order to shape public opinion – for example the joint NGO–Sida campaign, '*Sida vid sida*' ('Side by Side') on assistance to countries of the former Yugoslavia.

Some Swedish NGOs talk about the need to move beyond the discussion of aid, to questions of coherence between other Swedish policies – particularly agriculture – and development cooperation objectives. There may eventually be scope for greater collaboration on the impact of non-aid policies between government and larger NGOs that have a policy capacity. Sida, however, remains focused at present on its own goals of poverty reduction, gender equality, environment and partnerships in Africa.

Development of relations with Southern NGOs

In the mid 1990s, Southern NGOs were receiving about SKr30 million annually (about \$4.5 million) directly from Sida. Southern NGOs apply for grants under 'Partner in Cooperation' criteria. These funds are open to local non-profit NGOs working on democracy and participation, which have run activities for at least one year, documenting them in some form. In exceptional cases, Swedish organisations working in cooperation with a central government or a local government agency can also receive support from this programme.[13]

The approach to Southern NGOs by Sida is one of strengthening local cooperative partners to take over the full responsibility, once the Swedish NGO has gone. Great stress is laid on transparency between parties as a key to achieving financial and environmental sustainability.[14]

Until 1996, this programme was part of the NGO budget allocation, but from 1997, allocations to Southern NGOs became part of Sida's regional budget lines, thus releasing a little more funding for Swedish NGOs and adding to the absorptive capacity of the regional programmes.

One conclusion of the Promoting Development by Proxy evaluation was the need for more dialogue between local participants, local NGOs and Swedish representatives in country (whether embassy officials or Swedish NGOs). The project approach was considered too limiting under the newer, more flexible mandate of Swedish aid as a whole. Greater emphasis on programme funding, or support for local institutions was considered to be more appropriate.

Competition between Swedish NGOs and those in the South and East?

There is some concern in the Swedish NGO community that their political space and access to resources may be challenged by the development of direct relations between Sida and Southern NGOs. They see a key role for themselves in taking responsibility for NGO relations in developing countries and for the spread of democratic values. They also point to an inconsistency between a strategy designed to strengthen Swedish NGOs and then a failure to use them. The model operating in Sweden, whereby umbrella organisations validate and act as an intermediary between smaller NGOs and Sida is, they argue, ready-made for application in recipient countries.

Sida appears to support this view – at least to some extent. It sees value in supporting Swedish NGOs because of their role in promoting positive public attitudes in Sweden, in addition to their work in development assistance. While Sida is happy to work through Swedish NGOs – Diakonia's work in South Africa is an example – in other areas such as Bangladesh it has a strong direct relationship with local NGOs. The new funding arrangements, it feels, should facilitate this double-pronged approach.

In Central and Eastern Europe there has been a much more proactive programme by Swedish NGOs to build up the capacity of the voluntary sector and the specific role of Northern NGOs in developing and supporting NGOs in the South is now under review.

22 Switzerland

Judith Randel and Tony German[1]

SUMMARY

Switzerland's NGO community, comprising 30 large and 150 smaller agencies, maintains a long tradition of voluntary and charitable activities, and is well regarded for its overseas work as well as for its contribution to democracy and to Swiss international relations.

The Swiss Agency for Development and Cooperation (SDC) has a clear NGO strategy, concentrating resources on larger organisations in order to support their capacity building, their professionalism and their ability to develop coherent programmes. Twelve of these NGOs received responsive programme funding of SF50 million in 1995, with government requiring clear priorities, a strategic approach, and high standards in programme planning, implementation, monitoring and evaluation. Smaller NGOs are eligible for project funding and for advice on management and design.

Emergency funding is highly concentrated on six NGOs. SDC supports the full costs of volunteers working through UNITE, a volunteer programme operated by a pool of NGOs. *En régie* funds are SDC projects contracted out to NGOs. *Helvetas, Swisscontact and Intercoopération* – an NGO consortium set up specifically for the purpose – receive over 80 per cent of en régie funds, which totalled SF60 million ($47 million) in 1996. In addition to Swiss Confederation support from SDC, Swiss NGOs receive about 5 per cent of their income from Switzerland's 26 cantons.

There is no single umbrella for NGOs, although there are a number of federations – the Swiss Coalition, comprising five large NGOs, being the most influential. Formal and informal dialogue between NGOs and SDC reflect the high priority placed on identifying synergies and learning from experience. A constructive relationship between SDC and NGOs means that there is now a shared approach to improving the quality of Swiss assistance. The government is anxious to work with all NGOs to build public constituencies that are supportive of development cooperation. A new foundation, for example, 70 per cent funded by SDC, has been established to promote development education in schools.

SDC has cooperated with southern NGOs for two decades, but the amount of funding involved is unclear. Both SDC and Swiss NGOs are aware of the possible pitfalls. Some NGOs have been active in Eastern Europe, however the development of new SDC strategies in the region leaves the future role of Swiss NGOs uncertain.

BACKGROUND AND HISTORY

Switzerland's development cooperation policy emphasises local participation and ownership. Swiss ODA policy has four main themes: safeguarding and promoting peace and security; commitment to human rights, democracy and the rule of law; promotion of general prosperity, promoting welfare, and social justice (notably relating to women); and protecting the natural environment.

Swiss ODA is financed through Framework Credits. Framework Credits are voted after a budget process during which policies are defined and approved. They sanction operations by the aid administration over periods of several years, allowing for sound development programming. Framework Credits cover policy areas such as technical and financial cooperation, economic and trade policy measures, Bretton Woods institutions and so on. In 1996, two new Framework Credits were approved by the Federal Assembly, one for humanitarian aid and the other for economic and trade policy.

In 1996, Swiss ODA declined by 1 per cent in real terms, to $1026 million, although the ODA/GNP ratio remained the same at 0.34 per cent. In its last 'Aid Review' of Switzerland (November 1996), the DAC noted the strong intellectual leadership and high quality of staff in the aid administration. The DAC stated that the active community of NGOs in Switzerland makes an important contribution.[2]

Switzerland's development cooperation is managed by the Swiss Agency for Development and Cooperation (SDC) in the Federal Department of Foreign Affairs (DFAE), which controls 90 per cent of aid spending. Ten per cent of ODA is the responsibility of the Federal Office for External Economic Affairs (OFAEE) in the Federal Department for the Public Economy.[3]

Support to NGOs is managed by SDC. In addition to federal funds, Swiss NGOs receive financial support from some of the 26 Swiss cantons. In May 1996, Rudolf Dannecker, Director of Operations for SDC, spoke about the role of Swiss NGOs in society:

> *In Switzerland, voluntary and charitable activities have a long tradition. It is no coincidence that an organisation like the International Red Cross has its origins in this country. Today Switzerland has about 30 large development NGOs active on a national level, and around 150 smaller NGOs active on a regional or national level.*

He went on to say that it was not only in development that NGOs were playing an important role, but also in other sectors, especially social fields such as health, support to disabled, older and poorer people, often taking over public functions in these areas. This warrants public support. 'In Switzerland, therefore, cooperation between the State (federal, cantonal or communal) and non-profit organisations has a long tradition and is a common feature of our life.'[4]

Others value NGOs for their contribution to democracy and international relations. Federal Councillor Flavio Cotti, Minister for Foreign Affairs, has talked of NGOs as the cement in the Swiss system of pluralist and federalist democracy, and of the positive contribution they bring to long-term Swiss international relations.[5]

Relations between development NGOs and the Swiss government are characterised by a clear SDC policy on the strategic role of NGOs, an emphasis on information-sharing, and a long-term view on institutional development and complementarity. There is a strong commitment within SDC and the NGO community to fostering public and political understanding of development cooperation. This is reflected in many areas of Swiss development assistance, including the legislation that governs it. A collaborative dialogue has developed between NGOs and government, with a significant convergence of agendas between SDC and the NGO community.

The Earth Summit is seen by many as an important point in the relationship between Swiss NGOs and government. Since 1992, consultation and engagement between the two have become routine on international negotiations, and NGOs are now regularly part of Swiss delegations to international summits.

NGO umbrella bodies

There is no overall representative body for development NGOs in Switzerland. There are a number of federated NGOs, as well as Geneva-based NGOs that have little to do with the Swiss NGO scene. One Geneva-based federation, *La Fédération Genevoise de Coopération* includes small, local organisations as well as international bodies. A similar body is based in Lausanne. They are funded by SDC to the tune of SF2 million annually, and take responsibility for the technical management of project proposals from their members, ensuring that they comply with government criteria and guidelines.

Within the national context, the most influential body and principal interlocutor with government is the Swiss Coalition, comprising five large Swiss NGOs. Collaboration among NGOs with common interests has been described as 'the order of the day'.[6] In the area of environment and sustainable development, like-minded NGOs have formed the Kontakstelle Umwelt to provide a platform for their political activities.[7]

Table 22.1: *Sources of Swiss NGO Funding in 1995*

	Voluntary	Confederation	Cantons & Communes	Total
Volume (SF millions)	219	163	19	401
% of Total NGO Income	55%	41%	5%	100%

Source: Aide Suisse aux Pays en Developpement et aux Pays de l'Europe Orientale 1995, IUED, Geneva.

Fiscal policies and regulation

There is no federal regulation of NGOs. There is a private agency – ZEWO – to which NGOs can belong, which requires strict standards of accountability and probity. Cantons will decide which organisations are eligible to offer tax relief to their donors, and the system for doing so appears far from transparent. There are no taxation schemes that particularly benefit NGOs. Some umbrella bodies do set standards for their own members. For instance the Common Board of the agencies of the Protestant Church and *Fastenopfer* of the Catholic Church have set standards for project implementation, monitoring and evaluation.

SOURCES OF NGO INCOME

In 1995, total Swiss development NGO income was reported at SF401 million (about $326 million). Just over half of this (55 per cent) was derived from voluntary donations; 41 per cent came from the Confederation and 4 per cent from the cantons and the communes. Total Swiss NGO income, including contributions from government and the public, represented the equivalent of 27 per cent of Swiss ODA.

While the shares from different sectors have remained stable over time, support from all sources declined in 1995, and support from the Confederation continued that trend in 1996.

GOVERNMENT SUPPORT TO NGOS

Criteria for funding

The NGO service within SDC has been working to improve transparency and the consistency of funding conditions and criteria for Swiss NGOs. It defines its NGO partners as those which are:

- well established in the eyes of the Swiss population, and provide information on North–South issues;
- use Swiss development statutes as a basis for their work;
- have a clear development policy, operational capacity and experience;
- are interested in cooperation and coordination.

Projects with missionary or pastoral aims cannot be financed from the public purse.

Actions propre – responsive funds

Responsive funds are divided into two categories – three-year programme support, and single project support. SDC distinguishes between 'bigger NGOs' and 'smaller NGOs'. The work of bigger NGOs is well known to SDC. Each one implements over a dozen co-financed projects and receives 'programme' contributions over three years. Smaller NGOs receive project funding. Both programme and project funds are normally provided on a 50:50 basis, although the four largest NGOs, having the longest experience in development cooperation, receive government support for 67 per cent of their programmes. Other terms differ marginally. Emergency grants cover up to 100 per cent of project costs, but are normally given on a 50:50 basis.

For project funds, 10 per cent may be charged as an administrative overhead, rising to 13 per cent for programmes and 15 per cent for emergencies. However, no allocations may be made to development education from project funds, and only 1 per cent for information in the case of block grants. This seems to contradict the official focus on public information and development education.

Programme funding

Twelve Swiss NGOs received programme funding, totalling approximately SF50 million (about $40 million) in 1995. The expectations of these NGOs are higher than those for project organisations. SDC requires and encourages:

- long-term implementation and planning;
- a programme orientation;
- professional planning, evaluation and monitoring, and the use of sustainability criteria in projects;
- clear priorities and policies;
- operational audit systems.

NGOs were originally cautious about the conditions and expectations attached to programme funding. Now, however, SDC reports that the demands for programme funding are increasing.

Project funding

Smaller NGOs such as solidarity groups qualify for single project financing. This is based on clear selection criteria – the extent of the NGO's constituency, its policy transparency, its administrative ability and its implementation capacity. NGOs are expected to work with local partners in developing countries.

EN REGIE FUNDS – BILATERAL PROGRAMME CONTRACTS

In 1976, the Swiss civil service was capped. At the same time and for several years thereafter, funding for development cooperation increased. SDC was therefore obliged to implement more projects with fewer staff. As a partial solution, it delegated the implementation of certain projects to NGOs. These are known as *en régie* projects. Because most NGOs could not, or would not take on a large number of bilateral projects (partly for fear of losing their non-governmental identity), seven of the largest NGOs created a consortium known as *Intercoopération*, in order to implement bilateral projects that are fully financed by SDC. *Intercoopération* is barred from public fundraising, and although regularly included in lists of NGOs, some question whether it should be classified as a voluntary organisation.

Projects *en régie* are essentially SDC projects implemented by NGOs, and are therefore funded 100 per cent by SDC. However, there is a slight ambivalence in the way these projects come about. The level of dialogue between NGOs and SDC means that, in practice, *en régie* projects may result from NGO suggestions. The NGO role, therefore, goes beyond acting as a neutral instrument in the delivery of government policy or projects.

While the volume of funds disbursed through *en régie* programmes quadrupled between 1980 and 1991,[8] it declined quite sharply in the early 1990s, falling to SF58.5 million (about $47.33) in 1996, from SF80.5 million ($65 million) in 1993. This was mainly due to reduced activities in Rwanda and a consequent reduction in funding for *Intercoopération.*

En régie funds are heavily concentrated on three NGOs – *Helvetas, Swisscontact* and *Intercoopération*, which between them have received over 80 per cent of *en régie* funding between 1993 and 1996. Some NGOs, such as Swissaid, do not on the whole think it appropriate to take *en régie* funds. A guiding principle for their work is that the initiative for an activity should come from the people they work with, and they do not believe that the *en régie* system is consistent with this. Others, such as Helvetas, also restrict themselves to certain types of project. While three quarters of Helvetas' budget comes from federal resources, only part is for projects *en régie*. The bulk is for Helvetas-initiated work.

In the past there was little competition between NGOs and the private sector for the implementation of *en régie* projects. Each sector was perceived to have different geographical and technical advantages. Now, the combination of a decline in resources and WTO rules that open *en régie* projects to international competition are likely to result in changes. Some NGOs are

Table 22.2: *NGO Humanitarian Income 1992–95 (SF,000)*

	1992	%	1993	%	1994	%	1995	%
Voluntary Income	62,82	60	55,317	58	54,909	58	47,039	55
Official Grants	42,441	40	39,900	42	40,400	42	38,100	45
Total Humanitarian Income	105,266		95,217		95,309		85,139	

Source: IUED

considering expanding the scope of their activities to enable them to engage more widely in development assistance. In 1997, for the first time, NGOs and the private sector were competitors on bids for SDC contracts.

Some officials in SDC foresee serious implications in this for the Swiss NGO sector. Others note the NGO comparative advantage – based on their relationships with government in Switzerland and with officials overseas, and on an increasing professionalism (fostered deliberately by SDC – see below). They believe that NGOs will therefore be well placed to make high-quality bids for project implementation. Collaboration with the private sector is also expected, with a new emphasis on complementarity between different actors in the public, private and not-for-profit communities. Such collaboration would be an extension of the emphasis on complementarity and synergy that already exists in SDC.

EMERGENCIES

Giving from the public for humanitarian emergencies has fluctuated over the past four years, but forms around a fifth to a quarter of voluntary donations. Just under 60 per cent of NGO income for emergencies comes from the public. About a quarter of total NGO income comes from official sources, however it is highly concentrated in a small number of NGOs. In 1996, just under 60 per cent of official humanitarian funding for NGOs went to six NGOs. In public donations, it is also highly concentrated: 85 per cent of humanitarian giving in 1995 went to 18 NGOs. Of this, SF27.5 million (about $22 million) went to just five NGOs: Caritas, *Kroatisches Humanitares Forum*, *Médecins sans Frontières*, the Swiss Red Cross and *Terres des Hommes Lausanne.*

Table 22.3: *Public Giving for Emergencies to the Top Five NGOs in 1993 (SF,000)*

	Private Income	As a % of the NGO's total income
Caritas	10,901	54.7
Kroatisches Humanitares Forum	3,898	100
Médecins sans Frontières	3107	100
Swiss Red Cross	7323	58.0
Terres des Hommes Lausanne	2345	13.3

Source: IUED 1995; $1.00 = SF1.24

Until 1995, Swiss humanitarian aid was managed under two mechanisms, one for the implementation of their own projects, and one for the funding of NGOs and multilateral agencies. Now there are desk officers responsible for geographical areas; they control their own budgets and can fund NGOs directly. This puts NGOs in a much more competitive environment. Desk officers may now choose between the private sector, SDC consultants, Southern NGOs or Swiss NGOs.

This organisational change coincided with a change of attitude in SDC. SDC has become more critical of NGO performance in the humanitarian sector, and is defining much more clearly what it expects from NGO partners. There is much greater focus on impact, and expectations of the partnership go beyond the funding relationship to a relationship based on mutual learning through the implementation of projects together.

The focus on complementarity is reflected in a debate about the degree to which the *Direction du Droit International Public* (the department responsible for humanitarian assistance) should define the procedures, scope and role of NGOs in humanitarian situations. What the humanitarian office would like to see is a matrix of geographical and regional competencies, with NGOs specialising in areas of comparative advantage. This would complement SDC's own changed approach to defining priorities in prevention, emergency response, reconstruction and social assistance.

VOLUNTEER PROGRAMMES

The volunteer programme, *Unité*, is run by a pool of NGOs. SDC meets the full costs of volunteers. Real value is placed on the contribution that they can make overseas, and on the resulting attitudes and experience which they bring back to Switzerland. In recognition of this, *Unité* changed its name from *Programme des Volontaires* to reflect the priority of North–South exchange.

In 1995, financial support for volunteers increased from SF8 million to SF9 million, and most of the increase was maintained in 1996. This increase was designed to enable *Unité* to implement innovative activities and to strengthen its own institutional capacity. New developments include South–South volunteering, short-term assignments, and seminars on fundraising methods for Southern project holders. There is no volunteer programme for Eastern Europe.

FINANCIAL BREAKDOWN OF OFFICIAL SUPPORT FOR NGOS

In 1996, 11 per cent of federal government expenditure on aid was channelled through NGOs. This included programmes run by NGOs, humanitarian assistance, and contracts with NGOs as executing agents. This figure compares with 19 per cent in 1985 and 18 per cent in 1990. This reflects an increase in Swiss ODA, resulting from the country's decision to join the Bretton Woods institutions in 1990. The volume of ODA available to NGOs has remained steady.

Table 22.4: *Allocation of Confederation Funding by Volume (SF,000)*

Year	En régie Funding	Responsive Funding	Volunteers	Humanitarian	Total
1992	75.4	48.3	7.5	42.4	173.6
1993	80.5	46.0	7.4	39.9	173.8
1994	78.8	56.7	7.7	40.4	183.6
1995	65.0	45.1	14.3	38.1	162.5
1996	58.5	42.6	11.2	31.5	143.8

Source: IUED Table 4.3 for 1992–5, SDC Annual Report, 1996

Table 22.5: *Allocation of Confederation Funding by Share*

Year	En régie Funding	Responsive Funding	Volunteers	Humanitarian
1992	43.4%	27.8%	4.3%	24.4%
1993	46.3%	26.5%	4.3%	23.0%
1994	42.9%	30.9%	4.2%	22.0%
1995	40.0%	27.8%	8.8%	23.5%
1996	40.7%	29.6%	7.8%	21.9%

Source: IUED Table 4.3 for 1992–95, SDC Annual Report, 1996

Official support for NGOs declined in 1995 and 1996, both in volume and as a share of total ODA, partly because of reduced activity in Rwanda. The only categories to show an increase were support for the programme funding of the 12 big NGOs and the volunteer programme. Between 1993 and 1996, responsive funding increased its share of the declining resources available to NGOs, in comparison with *en régie* funding, which suffered the sharpest fall.

Table 22.6: *Trends in ODA to NGOs, 1989–96 (SF,000)*

	1989	1993	1994	1995	1996
Responsive Funding to NGOs	46,496	53,400	64,400	52,900	52,297
En régie Funding to NGOs	53,629	80,500	78,800	65,000	58,469
Humanitarian Assistance via NGOs	34,433	39,900	40,400	38,100	38,200
En régie Funds via Intercoopération	20,429	39,200	38,900	34,200	28,300
Via the 12 Programme Funding NGOs	38,255	45,800	49,800	46,600	50,073

NGO EVALUATION

There are very different NGO views about evaluation. The agencies of the Protestant Church (HEKS, *Brot für Alle* and the French and German-speaking missions) have established a common board. One of its first actions was to set clear standards for project design and monitoring, with one member, *Brot für Alle*, taking responsibility for evaluation. The focus is more on project design than impact assessment, but there is a strong sense of the need to become more professional about planning, monitoring and evaluation.

At the same time there is reluctance among many NGOs to address the issue seriously. One of the obstacles is a perceived tension between evaluation and partnership. How does evaluation fit in a relationship that is supposed to be between equal partners? NGO discussions on the subject have noted the need for transparency, and the need to be able to report adequately to donors. For many NGOs their work hinges on choosing the right partner, and outcomes must be seen within the context of processes of community change and empowerment. Trust, personal judgement and time are seen as critical parts of the process. The evaluation style of SDC is seen as antithetical to this holistic and anti-technocratic approach.

In Eastern Europe, evaluation is only just starting, the impetus arising from the integration of Eastern European affairs within SDC. Learning from experience in Eastern Europe is perceived to have so far been too little and far too informal. A HEKS agricultural programme and a hospital partnership were both slated for evaluation during 1997–8.

SWISS STRATEGY TOWARDS NGOS

SDC has a policy of concentrating its resources on bigger NGOs in order to build capacity and professionalism. In practice this has meant a focus on 12 NGOs concerned with long-term development (15 including humanitarian NGOs). SDC has tried to use its support to encourage internally coherent programmes. It does not focus only on regions or sectors that are priorities for official Swiss aid. Three-year programmes are negotiated on the basis of both programme content and funding. The needs of smaller NGOs are catered through funds for small projects and local initiatives. SDC will offer these NGOs guidance on project design and management.

Developing dialogue and synergies: learning from experience

Developing understanding and dialogue has been a key aspect of the relationship between Swiss NGOs and SDC. In addition to significant levels of informal dialogue, there are regular formal meetings between SDC and different categories of NGO. These includes twice yearly discussion with

- NGOs that receive programme funds, and with *Unité*;
- development cooperation project managers (i.e. *en régie* contractors);
- Church-based NGOs.

The NGO Service has the job of transmitting information about NGOs to other parts of SDC. In future, information sharing is expected to extend to sector policies, political initiatives, trends in development policy, OECD/DAC publications, public relations and development education.

This focus on dialogue is a longstanding characteristic of Swiss development cooperation, and is reflected in the 1976 law by which it is governed. Article 28, for example, requires the organisation of an annual conference, open to all those interested in international development, in order to exchange views and to promote public understanding.

The development of relations with Southern NGOs

SDC started working with Southern NGOs 20 years ago. Relationships are governed by a set of principles that distinguish the roles of governments and of civil society. SDC takes the view that its programmes should be socially viable and it sees a critical role for NGOs in achieving this. The focus on complementarity between different development actors – which runs like a thread through much of Swiss development cooperation – is reflected in the development of private/non profit/public partnerships.

An example of direct funding of Southern NGOs can be found in India, in a programme to improve milk cattle production through artificial insemination and improved fodder production. The project extension work is carried out by Indian NGOs, especially in remote areas. Another example can be found in Bolivia, where SDC support to government decentralisation efforts is matched by support for NGOs at municipal level.

Swiss country coordination offices now have a significant advisory role on the allocation of aid funds and on country strategies. Although the amount of discretionary funds available to these field offices for Southern NGOs is very small, the influence of field staff on larger amounts is not insignificant. Where Southern NGOs receive money as partners in a wider programme, as in the Bolivian example, allocations may not be readily visible, but officials estimate that this type of funding of Southern NGOs is now quite significant – estimated by the Swiss Coalition at SF20 million.

There is some anxiety among Swiss NGOs about the growing trend in SDC towards direct funding. This anxiety is not simply about protecting their own sources of funding, although budget cuts do have to be taken into account. Swissaid argues that while it sees the attraction for SDC in funding Southern NGOs, the importance of official aid in helping to maintain a functioning state should not be neglected. It notes situations in countries such as Guinea Bissau where officials are leaving government departments in order to set up NGOs and access bilateral aid money. Swiss NGOs have also noted the creation of 'honey pot' NGOs that simply lose their voluntary ethic. With donor pressure to disburse large amounts of money, there is a risk that direct funding will undermine and overwhelm indigenous NGOs.

Proposals have been made by the Swiss Coalition for government to encourage Southern NGO participation in discussions on country strategies, and for building up Southern NGO advocacy capacities. These have been treated with interest by SDC. SDC's own view of its role with regard to Southern NGOs is based on a well-articulated policy that recognises many of the potential dangers highlighted by Swiss NGOs. SDC places value on learning from Southern NGOs, stressing the importance of transparency and of taking a long-term view.

Eastern Europe

Since 1992, there has been real public enthusiasm for assisting Eastern Europe. Pre-1989 village links between Switzerland and Romania have survived, and have been a mechanism for direct aid, for *ad hoc* technical assistance, and for stimulating political interest in, and support for aid to Eastern Europe. Historically, there has been a closer relationship between the Swiss government and Eastern European NGOs, than with NGOs in the South, because in Eastern Europe, NGOs were seen as the main interlocutors for development assistance. NGOs in Eastern Europe are not only an instrument of aid delivery, they are one of the goals of the aid programme itself – a contribution to building civil society.

Development cooperation with Eastern Europe began as a discrete programme managed by diplomats, but where technical cooperation is concerned, it has now been integrated with the mainstream in SDC. Balance of payments support is the responsibility of OFAEE, and humanitarian aid comes under the aegis of the *Direction du Droit International Publique* (Humanitarian Aid Office). Despite the growing integration, aid to Eastern Europe is still perceived as being 'different'.

Unlike the South, aid to Eastern Europe is provided on a project-by-project basis. Before 1995, it was managed on a sectoral basis, but with the opening of coordination offices in Bulgaria, Romania, the Former Yugoslav Republic of Macedonia and Albania, the sectoral emphasis has declined. Some coordination offices – such as the one in Romania – have contacted both Swiss and local NGOs, and it is anticipated that funding for local NGOs will increase.

In the early 1990s, before aid programmes had developed, NGO funding proposals were welcomed and, on the whole, funded. Now, however, not all NGO proposals for funding can be met, and SDC is setting more explicit and higher standards for NGO engagement. Specialised NGOs for Eastern Europe, such as *Inter Assist*, have grown up and some larger Swiss NGOs, such as HEKS, have built on previous links in Eastern Europe. Others, like Caritas, set up special Eastern European divisions, partly in response to the financial incentives in the early 1990s. It is these organisations that are now the most vulnerable to funding reductions arising out of the evolution of official aid strategies and increased government engagement with local NGOs.

DEVELOPMENT EDUCATION AND PUBLIC INFORMATION

According to the DAC, Swiss public opinion – in the form of popular referenda – is a powerful force in Switzerland. It is therefore important that the policies and programmes of Swiss aid maintain a high public reputation.[9] The 1976 Swiss ODA legislation sets out a provision for SDC to play a role in building understanding and sensitizing the public. Article 27 requires that,

> *Les offices féderaux compétents informent l'opinion publique sur la coopération au développement et l'aide humanitaire internationales en generale, et sur la contribution Suisse.*
>
> *Ils entretiennent des relations avec les cantons, les communes, les universités, ainsi qu'avec les organisations Suisses et les milieux privés, dans la mesure ou ces rapports servent à promouvoir la coopération au développement et l'aide humanitaire.*[10]

Funding for development education has been increasing in recent years, reaching over SF4 million ($3.2 million) in 1996. However, this still represents less than 1 per cent of bilateral ODA. Around a quarter of the total is spent through NGOs.

Table 22.7: *Swiss ODA Spending on Development Education (SF millions)*

	1993	1994	1995	1996
Total ODA spent on Information, public relations and development education	3.50	3.50	3.80	4.03
% of ODA on development education	0.88	0.88	1.16	1.27
% of ODA spent through NGOs on development education	0.68	0.68	1.00	0.97

Note: US$1.00 = SF1.236

The focus of Swiss development education is on schools, and on links between development and the environment. A distinction is made between development education, which seeks to sensitize young people on global issues, and public information, which is guided much more by a public relations perspective. Distinguishing between development education and information, however, is difficult because definitions are vague and there is a close link between the two.

NGOs put a lot of emphasis on outreach to the public. Protestant and Catholic Church organisations distribute information through their parishes to every household in Switzerland each Lent. This outreach is supported by media coverage and campaigns. The Swiss Coalition, among others, funds *InfoSud* for the provision of a development news service to the German language press. SDC itself has an annual development education 'theme' each year, a recent successful effort being based on Women's World Music.

There is a strong focus on youth in Swiss development education, with recognition of swiftly changing attitudes among young people. Officials comment, however, that effective ways of getting a development message across to 'the Benetton generation' have yet to be found. Many NGOs see development education and information as a mainstream activity, of equal importance to their project work. In practice, however, it is hard to know what this means, since development education funding, and the human resources devoted to it, are nowhere near the investment in projects.

ADVOCACY AND ENGAGEMENT

In addition to informal meetings, which take place between the Swiss Coalition and SDC's Policy and Research section, a formal Consultative Commission on Development Cooperation exists in order to report to the Federal Council. This has NGO representation as well as parliamentarians and private sector representatives. It meets five times a year, with SDC acting as its secretariat. It comments on proposed legislation, major policies, country strategies and sector strategies.

For NGOs outside the Swiss Coalition, there is an annual conference organised by SDC. Seminars and workshops also take place on particular issues such as the rule of law and human rights, public opinion, coherence and elaboration of a ten-year report on Swiss development cooperation. At a policy level the Swiss Coalition represents the major players in the NGO sector. Issues that have dominated discussions with SDC include:

Box 22.1 The Foundation for Education and Development

A recent evaluation of NGO development education found that work was not being properly implemented for two reasons: teachers were overburdened, and development education was not sufficiently integrated into the curriculum. Following the evaluation, a new approach was introduced. The 26 cantons of Switzerland each have their own curriculum, but they do have an umbrella body, *la Conférence des Directeurs Cantonaux de l'Instruction Publique* (CDIP). SDC took the initiative in establishing links with the Cantonal Directors of Education, and with teachers' associations and NGOs. In 1997, the CDIP, the *Direction du Developpement et de la Cooperation* (DDC), and NGO members of *l'Ecole pour un Seul Monde* announced the creation of the Foundation for Education and Development.

The aim of the Foundation is to encourage a global vision in schools, and to build a solid approach to understanding concepts of sustainable development. Seventy per cent of the costs will be met by SDC – money that is additional to existing funding for development education. Canton and educational executives, publishers and teachers have all expressed interest in the programme, which was to begin in 1998.

- the role of civil society in both Switzerland and developing countries;
- dialogue on a North–South document produced in 1994;
- multilateral debt;
- parliamentary discussion of legislation on issues such as aid, military expenditure and migration issues.

While SDC and NGOs sometimes work together on advocacy, this has its limits. NGOs have higher expectations of change, and will be more demanding of government action than a government department. None the less there is currently a high degree of consensus between SDC and the NGO community – consensus that is strengthened by an interchange of staff between the two sectors.

It is not therefore surprising that Swiss NGO advocacy has focused more on the quantity than the quality of aid. The Swiss Coalition is adamant about not arguing against a particular aid instrument, and while it might oppose mixed credits or structural adjustment programmes, the Coalition argues that development cooperation should be increased, and that it should be spent in ways they think best.

Some suggest that this collaborative style arises from the lack of difference between official and NGO projects, and from the significant level of government funding for NGOs. NGOs do employ parliamentary questions in order to get actions from SDC. But much of what NGOs advocate requires action by other departments, and is actually matched by less visible and more subtle work by SDC working with other ministries.

There is considerable sensitivity in both SDC and among NGOs about the limited but vocal parliamentary criticism of public funds being used to support government critics. As a result, the primary advocacy body, the Swiss Coalition, receives no core funding from government. Until the formation of the Foundation for Education and Development, it received funding only for the Schools Service for Development Education. General public awareness campaigns, such as the North–South Campaign, are also funded by SDC, but it is ensured that public money is not financing any controversial activities.

Convergence of agendas

There is open acknowledgment that SDC and NGOs are now in basic agreement – the NGO case for improving the quality of aid is seen to have been agreed by the government and now discussion is focused more on how to deliver good quality aid, than on differences over what the aid programme should be. SDC describes the relationship between itself and NGOs as constructive and open, and quotes examples of effective advocacy by NGOs.

Another area of convergence is the issue of the legitimacy of Swiss interests in the aid programme. SDC recently commissioned a study that demonstrated the returns to Switzerland – in terms of contracts and jobs – from the aid programme. NGOs have not criticised this study, but accept that it is legitimate to take Swiss interests into account at some stage in the aid process, although they, like SDC, would argue that Swiss interests cannot lead the aid programme. This may go some way to defusing private sector criticisms of NGOs. NGO criticism of the private sector (and some parts of government) continues, however, around issues of human rights and the environment.

23 United Kingdom

Judith Randel and Tony German[1]

SUMMARY

The British NGO community is one of the largest and most developed worldwide. There are some 400 NGOs engaged in a wide variety of development work and awareness raising. Some, such as Oxfam and Save the Children, are prominent at an international level.

The UK's Department for International Development (DFID) provides support to NGOs through a Joint Funding Scheme, through block grants for the largest NGOs, through emergency funding and with support for volunteering. NGOs also have new opportunities to work with funding from bilateral desks or decentralised aid management offices. Since 1997, a new national lottery has provided a significant source of additional funding for overseas projects.

The UK has a wide range of NGO networks, reflecting an increasing emphasis on issues-based work. The establishment of an overall umbrella – British Overseas NGOs for Development (BOND) – has provided new opportunities, particularly for smaller and medium-sized NGOs, to share information and to engage with DFID on policy issues. The rules regarding charitable status do not significantly inhibit British NGOs from engaging in advocacy, which is seen by many as an increasingly important aspect of their work.

At the programme level, NGOs are increasing their efforts to become more professional. Evaluation has become more important, not least because it is a priority for DFID. In 1997, NGOs were having to adapt to the challenges and opportunities presented by a new government with a new development agenda.

In 1996, British ODA dropped by 2 per cent in real terms. The ODA/GNP ratio fell from 0.29 in 1995, to 0.27 in 1996. A new government was elected in May 1997. Its policy, outlined in the White Paper, *Eliminating World Poverty: A Challenge for the 21st Century*, commits Britain to reversing this decline, and reaffirms a commitment to 0.7 per cent of GNP.[2]

BACKGROUND: NGOS AND THE LABOUR GOVERNMENT

This chapter was researched and written at the end of 1997, a time of considerable change and uncertainty in the British international development community. Following a General Election in May 1997, a Labour Government replaced the Conservative administration which had been in power for 18 years – more than the professional lifetime of many who work for British NGOs. The new government acted quickly to replace the Overseas Development Administration (ODA) – the department of the Foreign Office concerned with aid administration – with a new, independent Department for International Development (DFID). DFID was given a Cabinet seat and a broader development cooperation mandate.

Whilst NGOs had established a good relationship with the previous Aid Minister, there is no doubt that the NGO community as a whole had not been sympathetic to the broad thrust of Conservative Government policy as it affected development cooperation, particularly its adherence to World Bank and IMF policies, and its emphasis on market solutions. The virtual abolition of development education funding, the substantial cuts to aid in the early 1980s, and disagreement on links between aid and trade were major issues over which NGOs and the government had clashed.

With the change of government, NGOs welcomed DFID's enhanced status and its strong focus on poverty. But they were concerned that the incoming government's stated preference to work with states (because states have the potential to deliver universal benefits), and its heavy emphasis on the DAC's *21st Century Partnership Strategy*, might reduce the scope for responsive funding, for NGO innovation and for recognition of their broader role in civil society.[3]

At the time of writing, the implications of this change for British aid and for British NGOs in particular, were not entirely clear, though in November 1997 the new government outlined the approach it planned to take in the first White Paper on international development presented to Parliament in over two decades (see box, below). A key future issue for NGOs, used to taking a watchdog role, will be how to relate to a government that came to power with a development manifesto, large parts of which NGOs themselves might have written.

For purposes of clarity, the term DFID will be used throughout the chapter, even though prior to 1997 the official name for the British aid administration was ODA.

THE SIZE AND SHAPE OF THE BRITISH NGO COMMUNITY

Britain has a well developed voluntary sector, with a total of 200,000 registered charities in 1995. In 1996 the voluntary income of Britain's top 500 charities reached almost £2 billion (about $3billion).[4] Development NGOs feature prominently within the sector, receiving about one fifth of all British donations. Oxfam is the UK's largest charity.[5] Twelve of Britain's 50 largest charities are principally concerned with overseas aid, and several other large British NGOs (such as Help the Aged and WWF UK) are significantly involved in aid and sustainable development.

The development NGO community in the UK is one of the oldest , largest and most diverse worldwide. According to a survey carried out in 1996, UK aid agencies employed almost 68,000 people, of whom 14 per cent (8915) were expatriates, 58 per cent indigenous staff, 22 per cent UK staff and 6 per cent UK volunteers.[6] One directory lists almost 400 UK voluntary organisations concerned with sustainable development.[7]

The work of British NGOs varies greatly. Organisations such as Afghanaid and the UK Foundation for the South Pacific have a geographical focus. Agencies such as Sightsavers, Send a Cow, Book Aid International or the Pesticides Trust – as their names suggest – focus on particular activities. Others, such as AHRTAG (Appropriate Health Resources and Technologies Action Group) and WaterAid are defined with reference to particular technical expertise. Some organisations such as Save the Children Fund and ACTIONAID are operational, while others such as Christian Aid act largely as funding agencies, channelling money to Southern church organisations, affiliates and grassroots organisations.

In addition to these NGOs, there is a wide range of organisations such as development education centres (DECs) and local 'linking organisations' that may not have formal charitable status (and which do not necessarily see themselves as NGOs), but which none the less contribute to the richly varied British development community. Amongst them are pressure groups such as Tapol (the Indonesia Human Rights campaign), information organisations such as the Latin America Bureau, specialist agencies concerned with NGO development and training such as INTRAC (International NGO Training and Research Centre), and NGOs such as the International Broadcasting Trust that are concerned with the media.

Box 23.1 Key Points from the 1997 White Paper

A White Paper, entitled *Eliminating World Poverty: A Challenge for the 21st Century* (Cm 3789), was released in November 1997. The points below are not meant to give an overview, but to reflect issues of relevance to NGOs.
   The UK will:

- refocus international development efforts on the elimination of poverty and the promotion of sustainable economic growth that benefits the poor – measuring progress against targets established for poverty reduction by 2015;
- work to increase public understanding of mutual dependence and of the need for international development – and to mobilise the political will to achieve international development targets;
- start to reverse the decline in British aid;
- ensure that the range of British government policies take account of development objectives;
- give particular attention to human rights, transparency, and ethical approaches to international relations, and to the need for political stability, social cohesion and effective response to conflict;
- pursue new ways of working with the private and voluntary sectors towards the development targets.

The new ways of working with the voluntary sector envisage working with NGOs in partnership countries and supporting their efforts in non-partnership countries. Partnership countries are those 'committed to the elimination of poverty and perusing sensible policies to bring that about'. Such countries will receive a longer-term commitment, enhanced resources and greater flexibility. Britain will assist non-partnership countries through alternative channels, including NGOs, focusing on the victims of neglect and oppression.

   In addition to the large number of organisations whose main focus is international development, many other groups within British civil society devote considerable attention to development issues, including churches, schools and a wide range of local organisations such as the Rotary and Women's Institutes.

Umbrella organisations

Prior to the 1993 establishment of BOND, Britain had no overall umbrella group for NGOs comparable to ACFOA in Australia or InterAction in the USA. Rather Britain has had – and continues to have – a variety of groupings and networks reflecting particular interests and attributes.[8] Under the banner of the Disasters Emergency Committee, the largest NGOs (including Oxfam, Christian Aid, SCF, the British Red Cross, CAFOD – the Catholic Fund for Overseas Development – and ACTIONAID) coordinate their emergency appeals in association with the media. Most of these organisations also belong to the British Overseas Agencies Group (BOAG), which provides an informal mechanism for the heads of the major NGOs to meet and consider issues of common concern.
   The Aid and Environment Group (AEG) was formed prior to the 1992 Earth Summit to bring together environment and development NGOs. The British Volunteer Agencies Liaison Group provides a mechanism for exchange between Voluntary Service Overseas (VSO), International Cooperation for Development, UNAIS and Skillshare Africa.

For larger NGOs with specialist staff focused on particular issues, it is possible to participate actively in several networks: for example the UK Food Group, or the Joint Agency Group on Aid (JAGA), which mounts regular campaigns to ward off aid cuts. Smaller NGOs that are less well resourced often have to choose carefully which groups to contribute to. In some cases, the networks have developed a 'sign-on' system that enables agencies to be identified with a position – even though they have not been able to play an active part in the detailed work of the network.

The UK has a very active National Platform of the EU/NGO Liaison Committee, with over 100 member agencies. The UK Platform aims to provide members with a flow of information on EU policy and EU funding opportunities. It also enables members to work together to influence the Commission and the British government on issues such as the future of the Lomé Convention.

The establishment of BOND

In the early 1990s, DFID (then ODA) initiated a dialogue with NGO representatives on a range of funding issues. During the discussions, the need for an umbrella body to act as the link between NGOs and government on areas of common importance was identified. BOND was established by interested NGOs in 1993, with financial support from ODA. By mid 1997 its membership had grown to over 150 UK NGOs. Both ODA and its successor, DFID, have taken care to respect BOND's independence.

Initially BOND was concerned with the practicalities of funding and reporting, but it has slowly broadened its mandate to include advocacy. For instance it produced, on behalf of its membership, a memorandum on the role of NGOs for the 1997 White Paper, which was expected to shape UK development cooperation into the new millennium. In 1997, NGOs under the BOND umbrella met with the DAC team working on the UK Aid Review.

BOND has had to develop its advocacy role carefully, working out a relationship with other bodies and establishing appropriate procedures for consulting and representing its members. Most of the larger NGOs already had established relationships with officials and politicians, and did not need the help of an umbrella body to establish either communications or credibility. But smaller NGOs, with very limited resources for advocacy, looked to BOND for information and access that they probably could not achieve on their own.

A key part of BOND's work is to act as a channel between DFID and NGOs on issues ranging from how DFID can best provide social development advice to NGOs, to how DFID should revise its Joint Funding Scheme (JFS) Guidelines. BOND also runs a range of workshops and training sessions for members, on practicalities such as monitoring and evaluation, the use of logical frameworks, participatory rural analysis, project budgeting and accounting and measuring impact.

In 1997, BOND and the UK platform of the EU NGO Liaison Committee co-hosted a European Union UK Presidency Project.

Academic links

In recent years, engagements between NGOs and the academic community have substantially increased. NGOs now participate regularly in the activities of the Development Studies Association (the key development academic umbrella), and they also play an important role in networks – such as the Structural Adjustment Forum – that are often based on research programmes funded by DFID. NGOs frequently draw on academic expertise for assistance with programme design or evaluation, and a number of academics sit on NGO boards of trustees. Academics also draw fairly extensively on NGO experience in their work. DFID's recent strong emphasis on strengthening NGO programme design, monitoring and evaluation – and on the dissemination of research to users – reinforces pressure on both NGOs and academics to share their experiences.

OFFICIAL FUNDING

The joint funding scheme

In 1995–6 the British government spent almost £180 million (about $280 million) through UK NGOs (9.3 per cent of total aid to developing countries). Of this total, one fifth was allocated to the JFS (responsive funding), one third was spent on emergencies and 14 per cent on volunteer-sending agencies. The remaining third was mainly spent through NGO work that was part of bilateral country programmes.

Table 23.1: *Official Funding for NGOs (UK£ million)*

	1993/4	1994/5	1995/6	1996/7
Total Funding	159	185	179	167
Of which, emergencies	65	85	59	30
Joint Funding Scheme (responsive)	32	34	36	40
Volunteers	21	23	25	28
Other, Including Bilateral Desk Funding	41	42	59	69
Total Number of NGOs Funded	*208*	*223*	*244*	*233*

Note: US$1.00 = £0.641

While the UK aid budget declined substantially between 1979 and 1997 under the Conservative Government, the Joint Funding Scheme for NGOs increased steadily. Between 1991–2 and 1995–6 the JFS rose by 61 per cent, from £23 million to over £37 million (from about $36m to $58 million) compared to a 7 per cent increase in UK aid to developing countries during the same period. Even so, by 1997 the JFS represented a smaller proportion of government funding for NGOs than it had been five years earlier. Over this period, funding for NGOs from bilateral desks has increased by 44 per cent. Whereas the JFS is a responsive mechanism, NGO activities funded from bilateral desks are intended to reflect government policy priorities as outlined in DFID Country Strategy Papers. The substantial increase in funding for NGOs, particularly from bilateral desks, reflects the evolving relationship between government and NGOs, and government recognition of increasing NGO effectiveness in delivering grass roots assistance.

During the early 1990s and subsequently, a key concern of NGOs has been that their independence and their own policy priorities should be recognised by government. This concern was reiterated by NGOs in a 1997 BOND submission to the new government's White Paper:

> *NGOs do not see themselves primarily as contractors for the delivery of DFID objectives using DFID cash, but as organisations with similar objectives to DFID but with different strengths.*

British NGOs have tended to draw a clear distinction between responsive funding from the JFS and other official support, which explicitly follows DFID policy. But the distinction may be more apparent than real. In most instances, the funding that NGOs receive from bilateral desks is actually for projects conceived and designed by NGOs themselves. These projects are attractive to DFID staff because they happen to fit in with country strategies.

While other forms of funding for NGOs have increased rapidly, NGOs place particular value on the JFS because of the explicit importance it places on NGOs' own dynamics and initiatives, because of the mutual learning it fosters between NGOs and DFID, and because of the flexibility it offers. The JFS, for example, will fund poverty-focused projects that do not fall within the confines of DFID's own country strategies.

Under the JFS, NGOs are allowed 10 per cent for UK administration costs. Costs of overseas administration are acceptable and are assessed during appraisal.

On funding issues, the NGO Unit is DFID's central point of contact with NGOs. But as funding from the bilateral programme for NGOs increases, NGOs are developing links with bilateral desks based in Britain, and with the five regional Development Divisions, and the Aid Management Offices in India and Bangladesh.

Extending block grant support for NGOs

In common with all other government departments, DFID (then ODA) conducted a Fundamental Expenditure Review in 1995. One of the findings was that government should take stock of its relations with NGOs and draw up a triennial strategy paper for the Joint Funding Scheme. It recommended that the block grant system should be extended at least to NGOs receiving JFS grants of over £750,000 (about $1.2 million), provided they could satisfy DFID criteria on competence and the use of funds.[9]

Although work was started on the strategy paper, its completion was overtaken by the election of a new government and the production of DFID's White Paper. At the time of writing, only one of the five block grant agencies – Save the Children Fund – had been reviewed. Reviews of the other agencies were postponed, pending publication of the White Paper.

Volunteers

There are four volunteer-sending agencies in Britain, but the scene is dominated by the largest, Voluntary Service Overseas. The degree to which volunteer-sending agencies follow the priorities of British official aid is the subject of discussion. Support to volunteer-sending NGOs is handled by DFID's NGO Unit. VSO's relationship is governed by a formal agreement, and a DFID official is an *ex officio* trustee on the VSO Executive Committee. VSO receives an annual core grant that may not exceed 90 per cent of its total income.

For volunteers in Central and Eastern Europe, the situation has been different. As transitional countries, they came under the ambit of a joint department of the diplomatic and aid wings of the Foreign and Commonwealth Office – the Joint Assistance Department. Here, the terms of support were very different, with VSO having to seek funding on the basis of project proposals which, with the exception of Russia, itemized individual volunteers. Since the creation of DFID, responsibilities for development policy and activities in these countries has been transferred to DFID. At the time of writing the future for volunteers in Central and Eastern Europe was not known.

The main issue of debate for volunteer-sending agencies is the degree to which they should follow British aid priorities, and in particular how strongly they should focus on poverty reduc-

Table 23.2: *DFID Support to Volunteer-sending Organisations 1995–96*

Agency	(UK£,000)	Programme Share
Skillshare Africa	1381	5%
Overseas Development Institute	669	3%
Catholic Institute for International Relations	1914	8%
British Executive Service Overseas	1087	4%
United Nations Association	929	4%
Voluntary Service Overseas	19,483	77%

Note: US$1 : £0.641

tion as their objective. As elsewhere in the volunteer-sending community, there is a perceived tension between achieving direct impact overseas and achieving indirect impact through the changed attitudes and values of returned volunteers in Britain. An evaluation of VSO, for example, commissioned by DFID and completed in 1997, focused very much on the need for direct poverty impact. While goals may be prioritized differently, this should not be an either/or situation. Making placements with the greatest potential to reduce poverty does not preclude a broader range of volunteers who can contribute to broader development goals as well.

Direct funding of Southern NGOs

In recent years, DFID's bilateral programmes have increasingly been funding Southern NGOs directly, through a variety of mechanisms. Perhaps the best known of these is the Direct Funding Initiative (DFI), launched by DFID's East Africa Development Division in 1994. The aim was to improve impact on the poor by supporting more local NGO-initiated poverty reduction and capacity-building projects.

By early 1997, the DFI had committed £6 million (about $9 million) to 15 NGO projects (both local and UK-based). An early review of the DFI suggested that it was enhancing the poverty focus of the British Development Division, East Africa (BDDEA) in Kenya and Uganda, though making less progress in Tanzania because of weakness in the local NGO community and the consequent difficulty in identifying partners. The review noted closer links between BDDEA and NGOs, allowing BDDEA to gain exposure to participatory planning and management. NGOs felt the relationship had enhanced their capacity in project design and planning. The review recommended a more structured approach to mutual lesson learning, and more work with NGO partners in order to assess their impact on poor people. It also recommended that further consideration be given to a DFI conceptual framework for capacity-building with NGOs and community based organisations.

DFID has a number of specific windows open to NGOs (and others) for the funding of particular programmes. For example the Conflict Policy Unit and the Health and Population Unit both have 'seedcorn funds' relating to conflict, and to sexual and reproductive health. These can be accessed by NGOs for innovative work in these fields. In both cases, specific guidelines explain procedures and requirements.

British embassies have limited discretionary funds at their disposal that can be allocated to NGOs under the British Partnership Scheme (BPS). The BPS supports projects costing up to £40,000 (about $62,000) a year, and each country has an annual ceiling of 250,000. Funds available under the BPS have been increasing substantially, to a 1997 figure of just over £9 million (about $14 million).

EVALUATION

Twelve joint studies conducted by British NGOs and the ODA/DFID Evaluation Department were undertaken between 1992 and 1994. The UK case study for the DAC NGO Evaluation Synthesis Study[10] comments on the results and methods of NGO evaluation, and on learning and dissemination. It talks of a sea change in NGO attitudes to evaluation, and estimates that over a thousand evaluations of development projects and programmes have been undertaken or commissioned by British NGOs in the last ten years.

Today, there is little dispute among the vast majority of the big UK NGOs about knowing about impact. As a recent review of ITDG (Intermediate Technology Development Group) projects begins, 'If we don't know what works we can't disseminate it; if we don't know what does not work we might disseminate it. And in either case, we need to know why'.[11]

Although there is widespread recognition among NGOs of the need to learn from evaluation, in practice there are serious obstacles. First, the majority of evaluations are not in the public domain. Second, the purpose of evaluation – both NGO and donor-initiated – often has much more to do with accountability than with learning. The DAC study notes that UK evaluations:

> *Have been instituted largely as part of a narrow concern to ensure merely that funds provided have been well spent. Thus, it is argued that the motivation for undertaking and commissioning evaluations is accountability... largely upwards to the donor, Parliament and the (increasingly sceptical) tax payer.*[12]

The contradictions between evaluation for accountability and an environment that enables learning to take place are apparent to NGOs. The demand for success and results is not easy to reconcile with an approach that puts learning and the application of findings at the top of the agenda.

One attempt to overcome this has been the formation of a group called REMAPP – a network of evaluation staff in NGOs, sharing information on methods and approaches. REMAPP is complemented by BOND for its work on evaluation training. While information has been shared, however, REMAPP is not able to overcome the real institutional problems in applying the lessons learned from evaluation. These often imply changes in approach, a reassessment of activities, and sometimes serious 'boat rocking'. Evaluation units are usually modestly resourced and staffed, and are not in a strong position to push for major change within an organisation. It is therefore helpful when external pressures, especially from donors, can reinforce the learning aspect.

Another initiative for learning is *MandE* – an Internet-based news service supported by Oxfam, SCF, ITDG and ACTIONAID. *MandE NEWS* encourages documentation of new monitoring and evaluation methods, no matter how small, and without regard to academic style or content.[13]

DFID's Joint Funding Scheme has put considerable emphasis on evaluation. In 1994, *Project Evaluation: A Guide for NGOs*, was published.[14] NGOs are now advised of the importance of on-time reporting and its relationship to their future funding. While some of this focuses on procedures, it also reflects a concern that the content of reports be used to improve the quality of projects. This also reflects an NGOs view reported in the DAC study: enhancing impact requires that attention go beyond evaluation and that it include appraisal and monitoring.

In a climate of frozen aid resources, the NGO Unit – like other parts of DFID – has been under pressure to demonstrate that the money it spends through British NGOs is achieving results. This pressure is passed on to NGOs, although there is a recognition of the real difficulty that NGOs (and others) have in demonstrating clear impact. While new JFS guidelines were on hold pending the publication of the 1997 White Paper, procedures were under discussion that encouraged NGOs to comment on the way project objectives had changed.

Openness is another precondition for learning, and NGOs have long been frustrated at the lack of direct and regular access to advisers in the British academic community who are contracted by DFID to comment on NGO reports and proposals. This adds to the problem of learning from evaluation, but it can also result in poor judgement when reports do not do justice to the reality of a project. DFID's view is that it is unrealistic to make advisers routinely available to the 150 or more NGOs that have contracts with the JFS. 'Lesson learning' was the subject of a 1997 DFID/BOND/NGO workshop, attended by NGOs and DFID staff and advisers. A number of proposals emerged to ensure that lessons are learned and disseminated.

DEVELOPMENT EDUCATION

Through the 1980s and 1990s, the British government provided extremely limited funding for development education. As a result, NGOs have had to rely on their own resources and on assistance from the EU to fund development education and advocacy. The Labour Government, however, pledged to strengthen DFID's contribution to public awareness, and on taking office in 1997, began to discuss with NGOs the establishment of a development education programme.

A key partner for DFID in establishing such a programme is the Development Education Association, established in 1993 to promote and support the work of those involved in building public understanding of global issues. Among the DEA's 250 member organisations are NGOs, Development Education Centres, local education authorities, youth groups, universities and media organisations. Among the recommendations made by the DEA are that DFID should aim to spend £4 million (about $6 million) a year on development education, compared with £0.7 million ($1.1 million) in 1996. It also recommended that an advisory council on development education should be established. In 1997 the DEA obtained National Lottery funding to initiate a research programme on the evaluation of development education.

Joint campaigning to build public commitment to development cooperation

The UK NGO community has undertaken joint campaigns on issues such as aid cuts, but despite several attempts, it has never managed to find common ground on which to base a major campaign that might substantially raise public and political interest in, and commitment to, development cooperation. In 1994 and 1995 the largest NGOs (members of the British Overseas Aid Group – BOAG) made considerable progress in identifying the elements of a common campaign, but in the absence of a fully shared agenda, were unable to get as far as implementation. It is possible that the Labour Government, which is attempting to raise development cooperation on both public and political agendas, will give added impetus to NGO efforts to build a broad-based, lasting public awareness campaign.

INFORMATION AND ADVOCACY

Increasingly, UK NGOs see information and advocacy activities as important aspects of their mandate. Many larger agencies such as CAFOD (Catholic Action for Overseas Development) or World Vision have departments focused entirely on policy advocacy. In smaller NGOs, however, lack of resources usually means people combining an advocacy role with other responsibilities. Some organisations, such as the International Institute for Environment and Development (IIED), the Catholic Institute for International Relations (CIIR) and the World Development Movement (WDM), are almost exclusively concerned with achieving change through research, information and advocacy.

NGO policy work in Britain tends to fall into two parts. In one, NGOs try to encourage others (including official agencies) to adopt particular approaches or techniques – such as participatory rural appraisal (PRA) or micro credit. In the other, NGOs try to influence broader aspects of government policy such as governance, structural adjustment or trade policies.

Charitable status and NGO advocacy

The role of NGOs in piloting new approaches and encouraging others to emulate their approach is familiar and uncontroversial in Britain, but the right of NGOs to contribute to wider policy discussions is less clear cut under UK charity law. Acts of Parliament in 1953, 1960, 1985 and 1992 defined and refined which activities are charitable and which are not, and the Charity Commissioners for England and Wales are responsible for monitoring and regulating charities.

Charitable status brings significant benefits, particularly tax advantages, and it confers a mark of legitimacy and respectability that is significant in the public mind. But charitable status also imposes obligations such as the need for regular reporting and accounting. It also entails some restrictions, perhaps the most significant being one on political activity. In the past, NGOs such as Oxfam have been censured by the Charity Commission for taking sides in foreign political controversies, or for attempting to influence UK aid policy. On other occasions, however, NGOs have been able to mount high-profile campaigns – for example against cuts in the aid budget – without repercussion.

Under British law 'an organisation established for political purposes can never be a charity, but trustees of a charity may do some things of a political nature as a means of achieving the purposes of the charity'. What this means in practice is that any political activity must be 'in furtherance of, and ancillary to' the main aims of the organisation. Political activities must not dominate the organisation. Trustees must be able to show a reasonable expectation that the activities will eventually assist the charity's beneficiaries. The views expressed by charities must be based on a 'well-founded and reasoned case and expressed in a responsible way', and trustees must take steps to control and evaluate these activities.

While the rules are complex and charities need to be careful, the latest version of the Charity Commission Guidelines[15] stresses the need for flexible interpretation. The guidelines stress that it is legitimate for charities to engage in campaigning, and that charities are well placed to play a part in public debate on important issues of the day. They also leave substantial room for interpretation on which advocacy and campaigning activities are permissible. This lack of clarity leaves NGO staff (and trustees – who are legally responsible for charities' actions) having to make difficult judgements. Some argue that clarification of the law would be helpful. Others feel that clarification could restrict charities further and that, as things stand, NGOs have a large degree of freedom to address issues that are highly sensitive for government – provided that a 'reasoned' case is made and that charities do not take an overtly party political approach.

Controversy over the Pergau Dam in Malaysia provides an interesting illustration. In November 1994, following a high-profile legal challenge by the pressure group World Development Movement (WDM), the High Court found that the British government had acted illegally in allocating aid to the Pergau Dam in Malaysia. The court case followed a report by the UK's National Audit Office and an enquiry by Parliament's Foreign Affairs Committee (FAC) into the 'entanglement' of aid and arms sales. The FAC concluded that a 1988 protocol between the UK and Malaysia had breached a UK policy proscribing 'conditional linkage' between defence exports and the provision of aid.

WDM itself is not a registered charity, and therefore not subject to restrictions on political activity, but many large charitable NGOs (most of whom receive substantial government funding) also joined in the criticism of government's misuse of aid, its trade policy towards Malaysia and its approach to arms exports.

In 1997 a group of non-charitable NGOs including WDM, the Campaign against the Arms Trade (CAAT) and Tapol (the Indonesia Human Rights Campaign) took the government to court to challenge its arms export policy, claiming that it was breaking its own guidelines. The action was unsuccessful, but it illustrated the sophistication and growing determination of NGOs to use all available instruments in their lobbying and advocacy.

As issues of aid, trade, foreign policy and humanitarian action become increasingly connected, the British government has clearly signalled that NGOs have an important role to play on policy issues. The Foreign Office, for example, has invited NGOs to attend meetings to discuss human rights issues, and DFID routinely consults NGOs on a range of issues. It has also included NGO representatives on official delegations to UN conferences. So while the rules on political activity by charities have not changed, in practice British NGOs have substantial freedom to say what they want, and it now seems that an NGO would have to take a highly controversial approach to risk serious reprimand.

The larger UK NGOs, and those established with a particular emphasis on policy, tend to be most prominent and active in advocacy work. The emergence of BOND, however, is enabling smaller NGOs with fewer resources to keep abreast of issues and to make some contribution on policy. Larger NGOs have specific staff – sometimes specific departments – focused on policy and advocacy. There are also advocacy networks such as the UK Working Group on Landmines, which has around 50 members.

In recent years, NGOs have built up a substantial range of contacts within the media, Parliament, and the Civil Service. Some larger NGOs have invested in understanding how to get their case across to appropriate audiences. Many stories about aid and development in the media are either furnished, or are at least inspired by the NGO community. NGOs regularly submit evidence to the Foreign Affairs Committee and the new International Development Committee.[16] Regular dialogue with parliamentarians, civil servants and researchers is well established within the major NGOs – though many would admit that their range of contacts could be extended to include more policy and opinion makers.

NEW ISSUES: NEW DIALOGUE

Before 1990, British development NGOs focused their attention mainly on the Overseas Development Administration – the wing of the Foreign Office concerned with aid. Few contacts were established with other government departments. But since 1990, a range of factors has encouraged NGOs to broaden their contacts. The Earth Summit process encouraged new links with the Department of the Environment. The blurring of distinctions between foreign policy and development policy – and the importance of issues such as governance, human rights and the role of civil society – have led to a new engagement with the Foreign Office and the Department of Trade and Industry. A series of complex emergencies has meant some dialogue between NGOs and the Defence Ministry.

Inevitably, along with new opportunities to contribute to policy, comes new scrutiny and sometimes criticism. In Rwanda for example, NGO judgement and their capacity to comment was called into question by the media. The issue of NGO accountability for policy statements is real, and it is not likely to go away.[17]

In recent years, there has been a noticeable thawing in relations between UK NGOs and the private sector. Several factors have contributed to this, including recognition of a common interest in promoting socially responsible management practices overseas. Reports commissioned by BOAG have urged the NGO community to build wider alliances. There is a growing acceptance amongst NGOs of the need to work with, rather than against, the grain of the market. And it is dawning on some companies such as Shell Oil, that the priorities advocated by NGOs are often not fringe preoccupations, and that they are of significant concern to many of their customers and shareholders. There are other factors as well:

- NGOs see the impact of globalisation and the role of trade and the market as critical to the prospects of developing countries;
- involvement in a range of activities from micro credit to fair trade initiatives have encouraged NGOs to look more closely at the role of the private sector;
- DFID has encouraged NGO–private sector dialogue, and organisations such as Worldaware and the Prince of Wales Business Leaders' Forum have provided opportunities for NGOs and the private sector to exchange ideas;

- reports commissioned by the NGO community have urged NGOs to broaden the base of public support for aid and to engage with the private sector on matters of shared interest;[18]
- the corporate sector itself has become more open to dialogue: both Shell and British Petroleum have made significant efforts to understand the role of NGOs in civil society; companies such as the Bodyshop have championed environmental issues, and some are taking a greater interest in social auditing. NGOs and the private sector are starting to find common ground.

Devolution

At the time of writing, referenda had approved the establishment of a Parliament in Scotland and an Assembly in Wales. While foreign affairs remains firmly within the purview of the British Parliament, there have been proposals in the past for a Scottish development cooperation programme, and the devolution of some aid activities in due course cannot be ruled out.[19] NGOs with strong Welsh and Scottish identities are already well established, for example *Dolen Cymru*, a Wales–Lesotho link, and SEAD – Scottish Education and Action for Development. Devolution may encourage UK-wide NGOs to focus more closely on their Scottish and Welsh constituencies.

The emergence of a National Lottery

In May 1997, the first grants to development NGOs from Britain's new National Lottery Charities Board were announced. Grants totalling £25 million (about $39 million) were given to 130 organisations. The grants ranged from £7000 ($10,000) to over £1 million ($1.5 million). (The NLCB had received over 755 applications requesting grants totalling £182 million – $284 million.)

The £25 million grants represented less than 5 per cent of the £500 million ($780 million) lottery proceeds distributed to charitable causes by May 1997. A second distribution by NLCB to organisations concerned with international development was planned for 1998. While the amount of money available to development organisations from the NLCB is uncertain, particularly in view of the incoming government's decision to review the operation of the entire lottery, it seems likely that the lottery will provide a significant source of additional funding, despite concerns that ordinary fundraising could suffer because of the impact of lottery ticket sales on charitable giving.

24 United States[1]

Ian Smillie

SUMMARY

In the United States, NGOs – or 'PVOs' – range from very small organisations to some of the largest NGOs in the world. In 1995, 14 US PVOs raised more than $100 million dollars each in cash and kind from all sources, including government. A 1997 report on the relationship between USAID and the PVO community observed that the nature of the partnership had changed significantly over the years, and that 'USAID and the PVO community now share a more common development agenda, have engaged in constructive dialogue on foreign assistance programs, and have worked together to resolve administrative barriers to a more collaborative relationship'.

According to the US Budget Office, the total funding of PVOs and NGOs in 1996, excluding food aid, was $927.7 million. This represents approximately 10.1 per cent of ODA. Of non-emergency Title II food aid, PVOs programmed over 70 per cent of the total between 1993 and 1997. In 1993, PVOs programmed over half of all emergency food, but by 1996 the PVO share had dropped to 23 per cent. The USAID budget for disasters has increased dramatically in recent years to an estimated $200 million in 1997, not including food aid. Of this, over 60 per cent is programmed through US PVOs. USAID's development education programme, the focus of negative attention within the Republican-dominated Congress after 1993, was capped at $500,000 for 1998.

Despite the growing levels of PVO evaluation activity, a 1997 report was critical: 'Lack of baseline data, an emphasis on outputs and effect indicators, and inadequate monitoring arrangement, have led to reports focusing on implementation issues rather than impact.'

The dependency question remains more substantive in the US than in other countries because of the importance placed by government on US strategic and programmatic objectives of development assistance. Dependency, of course, can be seen as a two-way street. USAID is heavily dependent on US PVOs for the effective delivery of food aid and for a high proportion of its emergency assistance. And PVOs are also increasingly recognised as an important window on, and channel to, the development of pluralism in countries where the development of democratic institutions is a priority.

INTRODUCTION

In this chapter, 'PVO', or Private Voluntary Organisation, refers to US NGOs. Where the term 'NGO' is used, it usually refers to Southern NGOs. USAID defines PVOs as 'tax-exempt, non-profit organisations working in international development that receive some portion of their annual revenue from the private sector (demonstrating their private nature) and receive volun-tary contributions of money, staff time or in-kind support from the general public (a demonstration of their voluntary nature). Not all non-profit organisations are necessarily PVOs'.[2]

THE FOREIGN AID POLICY ENVIRONMENT

In recent years, the policy context in which US official development assistance operates has changed dramatically. US foreign assistance started officially with President Truman's inaugural address in 1949, but the United States Agency for International Development (USAID) was not created until 1961 under the Kennedy Administration. An independent government agency, its administrator reports directly to the President of the United States, however at the end of 1997, legislation was pending that would continue USAID as a distinct agency under the authority of the Secretary of State.

With the end of the cold war, US foreign aid changed. Old policies based on the containment of Communism gave way to a policy of 'inclusion', the promotion of democracy and free market economic systems. Plans for a more de-politicized foreign assistance legislation were derailed in 1994 by two factors. The first was a tightly-knit web of both vested and parochial interests, protected by a complex and arcane legislative process. A 1988–9 Congressional Task Force examining the aid programme found that 'scattered through the Foreign Assistance Act are 33 objectives... Foreign Aid legislation contains 288 individual reporting requirements... Earmarks have increased to unprecedented levels... Congress receives upwards of 700 notifications of project changes each year... In addition there are numerous directives, restrictions, conditions and prohibitions in the foreign aid legislation... The result is an aid program that is driven by process rather than by content and substance.'[3] A 1992 report from the Overseas Development Council echoed these views: 'USAID is dominated by short-term concerns rather than long-term planning, and it has only a minor voice in setting US development policy priorities. In addition, the agency is hobbled by too much specific congressional direction on how and where to use its funds.'[4]

A second factor working against legislative change was the advent of a Republican-dominated Congress after 1994. Unlike a Republican *administration*, a Republican-controlled Congress had little to lose from its insistence on significant changes to US foreign aid, not least of which was severe down-sizing. In his Congressional Presentation on the 1997 USAID budget, the Administrator laid out the dramatic changes that had taken place over the previous four years. USAID, he said, 'faces the cumulative impact of years of budget cuts. It is no longer able to 'do more with less'. US foreign aid levels are at their lowest ebb, in real dollar terms, since before World War II. In fiscal year 1996 alone, Development Assistance was cut by 23.1 per cent from the year before.' In addition, by 1997 USAID had closed more than two dozen overseas missions and laid off one third of its staff.

Although the middle years of the decade were dominated by budget reductions, USAID also introduced a number of major changes in the way it did business. It was one of the lead agencies in a programme for the 're-invention' of government, focusing its work much more squarely on results than on activities (described below). Many of its contracting and procurement procedures and regulations were dramatically streamlined, and strong efforts were made to improve the relationship between USAID and the US PVO community (also described below).

Legislation that would effect a major reorganisation of the US foreign affairs agencies became stalled during 1997 in the US Congress. The effort was likely to be pursued in 1998. The Executive and Legislative branches had agreed, however, that USAID would remain a distinct agency under the direct authority and foreign policy guidance of the Secretary of State. This arrangement is similar to what existed before 1979 when, with the creation of the International Development Cooperation Agency, the USAID Administrator reported directly to the President.

THE US PVO COMMUNITY

Alexis de Tocqueville's famous 1835 book *Democracy in America* saw the strength of the new nation's democracy in the multiplicity of its voluntary associations. In the post-Civil War era, the foundation of the concept of private responsibility for public good shifted from religious grounds to new ideas about the role of the elite, and about enhanced private sector responsibilities. Before the turn of the century, big business and private philanthropists were heavily underwriting the growth of universities, hospitals and professional organisations. During the same period, there was rapid development of labour unions, savings and loan societies, cooperatives and other community-based organisations.

Fear of socialism and a fundamental mistrust of governmental action, in particular in the social field, encouraged wealthy industrialists in the first three decades of the 20th century to build on these initiatives, and to establish philanthropic foundations as an alternative to government. The Carnegie, Sage and Rockefeller Foundations emerged at this time (before the advent of personal and corporate income tax in 1913), and helped form a concept of 'Welfare Capitalism', which maintained a high degree of legitimacy and influence until the depression of the 1930s.

The growth of the welfare state in the 1930s stimulated the non-profit sector. This occurred in part because the 1936 Tax Act allowed corporations and individuals, for the first time, to deduct charitable donations from their income tax, and because the government made a conscious decision to work *with*, and to provide financial support to, the non-profit sector, rather than to set up full-scale alternatives itself. It is estimated that in 1993, 79.5 per cent of private giving to US voluntary organisations was derived from individuals, 8 per cent from foundations, 7 per cent from bequests and 5 per cent from corporations.[5]

The international development PVO community emerged, as in other countries, from a missionary and humanitarian tradition, and as a response to the enormous needs following World War I and World War II. Further growth took place in the 1960s and 1970s, stimulated in part by operations such as the Peace Corps and by a vision of development brought home by returning volunteers. The size of the US international development PVO community is relatively small *per capita*, in comparison with its counterparts in other DAC countries. The Independent Sector counts 1515 nonprofit organisations under the rubric of 'international and foreign affairs' but this casts the net much wider than the standard PVO definition. At the beginning of 1997, about 420 PVOs were registered with USAID's Office of Private and Voluntary Cooperation (PVC) while InterAction, the US PVO umbrella organisation, had 152 member agencies.

These range from very small organisations to some of the largest NGOs in the world. In 1995, 14 US PVOs raised more than $100 million dollars each in cash and kind from all sources, including government. Among these were CARE ($460m), Catholic Relief Services ($270m), the Institute of International Education ($140m), Christian Children's Fund ($111m) and Project Hope ($120m).[6] In addition, 21 PVOs had total cash and in-kind income in excess of $50 million, including the Adventist Development and Relief Agency ($60m), Children International ($53m), the International Executive Service Corps ($70m) and the International Rescue Committee ($82m).

Some of these undisaggregated numbers are misleading. USAID, for example, calculated the total 1995 support and revenue of all the PVOs that are registered with its Office of Private and Voluntary Cooperation at $7.2 billion. Some of the registered PVOs, however, devote a relatively small proportion of their income to work overseas. The Nature Conservancy, with a total 1995 income of $323 million, committed only 7 per cent of this amount to overseas programming. The American National Red Cross, with an income of $561 million, spent only $23 million overseas. Of the total support and revenue from all sources for the PVOs registered with USAID, an impressive $4.22 billion was devoted to overseas programmes.

The degree of PVO dependency on USAID varies widely. For example, CARE's 1995 private contributions, at $50 million, represented only 11 per cent of the gross. Forty two per cent of the total was food and freight, and another 6 per cent was in-kind contributions. Private

Table 24.1: *Total PVO Income By Source ($,000)*

	FY 90	FY 95	Change
USAID Freight	2324	2787	+20%
PL480 Freight	96,275	127,402	+32%
PL480 Donated Food	255,370	278,668	+9%
USAID Grants	382,332	802,736	+110%
USAID Contracts	107,761	229,325	+114%
Other USG Grants	219,929	364,355	+66%
Other USG Contracts	33,041	86,621	+162%
Other Govt & Intl Orgs	179,918	488,362	+171%
In-kind Contributions	566,000	1,200,139	+112%
Private Contributions	2,109,000	2,405,946	+14%
Private Revenue	792 648	1,236,127	+56%
Total Support & Revenue	4,744,053	7,222,472	+52%

Source: Report of American Voluntary Agencies Engaged in Overseas Relief and Development Registered with USAID, USAID Office of Private & Voluntary Cooperation, 1992 and 1997

donations represent only 17 per cent of the income of Catholic Relief Services. Twenty six per cent of its income was in the form of US government grants and contracts, and 46 per cent represented USAID food and freight. Christian Children's Fund, on the other hand, received very little US government support, and no food aid. Almost 95 per cent of the organisation's income was derived from private contributions and private revenue.

Until the mid-1960s, most PVO efforts concentrated on emergency relief and refugee assistance, and some US PVOs remain among the world's biggest and most professional relief organisations. During the 1970s, there was a major shift towards the inclusion of development programming. Several of the largest PVOs — CARE, Catholic Relief Services, World Vision, Save the Children, Childreach (formerly Foster Parents Plan) — are directly operational, and some of them have been slower than other Northern NGOs in the general move towards support for Southern NGOs. USAID's Advisory Committee on Voluntary Foreign Aid observes, however, that the context in which PVOs work has changed dramatically in recent years, and that programming must now be based upon new concepts. 'There is probably no single issue which more dominates discussions within the US PVO community today than its changing relationship with indigenous or Southern NGOs.'[7] For its centrally administered grants, USAID's Office of Private and Voluntary Cooperation requires US PVOs to identify local NGO partners.

FISCAL POLICY AND REGULATION OF THE US PVO COMMUNITY

Fiscal policies and regulation

Donations to PVOs holding an Internal Revenue Service (IRS) tax exemption certificate are tax deductible. As noted above, the introduction of this facility in 1936 proved to be a major stimulus to the domestic voluntary sector in the US. Although the decision to donate is not usually made on the basis of tax policy, studies have shown that the *amount* donated is influenced by tax policy, and that tax rates have a clear impact on the overall volume of giving. In 1981, when the highest tax rate was 70 per cent, a one dollar donation actually cost the giver only 30 cents. Changes to the tax rate in 1986 increased the cost of a one dollar donation to 72 cents. The number of individuals claiming a tax deduction in that year dropped from 39 per cent to 29 per cent.[8]

Incorporation of PVOs as not-for-profit organisations is a state, rather than a federal responsibility, and requirements vary from jurisdiction to jurisdiction. There is no requirement that an organisation be headquartered in the state of registration. In order to issue tax receipts, however, an organisation must be registered with the Federal Government's Internal Revenue Service under Section 501 of the Internal Revenue Code. To maintain tax exemption, an information return, known as Form 990, must be submitted annually.

In order to receive government support for international development work, an organisation must also be registered with USAID's Private and Voluntary Cooperation branch within the Bureau for Humanitarian Response.

InterAction

Formed in 1984, InterAction is a broadly based coordinating and advocacy coalition of 152 PVOs. Its purpose is 'to enhance the effectiveness and professional capacities of its members engaged in international humanitarian efforts. InterAction exists to foster partnership, collaboration, leadership and the power of this community to speak as one voice as we strive to achieve a world of self-reliance, justice and peace'. To these ends, InterAction maintains a number of committees and task forces dealing with advocacy and development education, development policy and practice, the advancement of women, disaster response and resources, and migration and refugee affairs. It has developed a Code of Ethics for its membership, and a PVO Standards Committee 'works to promote the highest level of standards for InterAction member agencies in the areas of governance, finance, communication with the public' and general management practices.

InterAction has Category I status in UN-ECOSOC and participates on the UN Inter-Agency Steering Committee, which coordinates humanitarian response. InterAction publishes a regular newsletter, a bi-annual directory of members, and it maintains a comprehensive and informative website. Much of the organisation's work in recent years has focused on dialogue with USAID over its programmes, its budget, and changes in its structure. Based in Washington, InterAction has better access to the World Bank than many other voluntary organisations, and in recent years it has worked to promote participatory sustainable development through monthly meetings of a World Bank Working Group.

The Advisory Committee on Voluntary Foreign Aid

The Advisory Committee on Voluntary Foreign Aid (ACVFA) began in 1946 as a Presidential Committee related to the Marshall Plan in Europe. Members are private citizens with experience in cooperative and business development, health, education, finance, law, relief and community development. It reports to the Administrator of USAID and is housed in the Office of Private and Voluntary Cooperation of USAID.

In 1997, it completed an assessment of the relationship between US PVOs and government, and produced a frank and comprehensive report, *An Assessment of the USAID/PVO Partnership*. The report found that the partnership was 'significantly stronger than it was four years ago', a noteworthy achievement, 'given the stresses on the relationship and the entire development community resulting from the greatest pullback in US foreign assistance since the Marshall Plan'. This improved relationship resulted in part from the new administration in Washington and from a sweeping set of changes in the way USAID dealt with PVOs.[9] The report noted the changes within USAID, and the growing capacity of both US PVOs and Southern NGOs. And it described some of the changes that had occurred in the government–PVO relationship over the previous four years:

- increased and more productive consultations;
- revision of the overall policy guiding government–PVO relations;

- new policies on grants and cooperative agreements;
- simplification and streamlining of procedures, including the PVO and NGO registration processes.

The report noted that some reforms were still not being implemented consistently, in part because of different interpretations of policy by USAID missions abroad. Further work was needed, the report said, in the area of results-based management, the need for local NGO strengthening, and dissemination of information about 'best practices'. It recommended that education and outreach to the US public on international development and foreign assistance should assume greater pre-eminence in the USAID–PVO relationship, although in the absence of a meaningful budget, few recommendations were made as to how this might be achieved.

GOVERNMENT SUPPORT TO PVOS

Background

Total US ODA to developing countries fell from $16 billion in 1989, to less than $12 billion in 1990. In 1995 it reached a low of $7.4 billion. In 1996, ODA grew by 25 per cent to $9.4 billion, bringing the US into second place after Japan in total ODA, but with an ODA/GNP ratio of only 0.12 per cent (up from 0.10 per cent the year before).[10] The estimated 1997 ODA figure represents about 0.1 per cent of GNP, the lowest figure in a decade and the lowest among the 20 most industrialized countries. The 1995 DAC Review of US development cooperation noted that 'the ODA concept does not play a role in the US aid budget process... The various elements which make up ODA are funded mostly under the so-called 150 Account covering International Affairs, a sub-section of which is Multilateral and Bilateral Assistance for Development'. Some of the elements of this 150 Account are ODA, and some are not. Some ODA is funded under appropriations from the Department of Agriculture. Within the ODA category, some expenditures stand out. The most striking is the level of assistance to Israel and Egypt. These two countries alone absorbed 50.8 per cent of all bilateral expenditures in 1992–3.

Government support to PVOs began with contributions to relief and disaster efforts during World War II, and grew during the 1950s and 1960s. The Office of Private and Voluntary Cooperation was established in 1974 as the focal point for contact between USAID, PVOs and cooperative development organisations (CDOs). The 1997 ACVFA report on the relationship between USAID and the PVO community observed that the nature of the partnership had changed significantly over the years, but that 'USAID and the PVO community now share a more common development agenda, have engaged in constructive dialogue on foreign assistance programs, and have worked together to resolve administrative barriers to a more collaborative relationship'.[11]

The relationship is based on a number of policy principles articulated in 1995.[12] These include:

- *consultation:* 'The congruence of objectives between USAID and the PVO community can be deepened, sustained and better defined through a structured process of consultation and dialogue, both in Washington and the field... from matters of policy and program strategy to activity design';
- *participation:* 'Broad-based, equitable participation is vital to sustainability and to the success of development efforts... It is USAID policy to build opportunities for participation by host country organisations and peoples into the development processes in which the Agency and its PVO partners are involved';
- *programme integration and managing for results* (see also below);
- *independence:* 'A PVO's relationship with USAID must not result in a loss of the PVO's private and independent character.' This relates to a legislated 'privateness requirement',

which stipulates that US PVOs must receive at least 20 per cent of their financial support for overseas activities from non-US government sources.

Statistics on the volume of USAID support to PVOs are somewhat difficult to understand. At the 1995 Copenhagen Social Summit, Vice President Gore made a commitment to channel up to 40 per cent of USAID development assistance through PVOs and NGOs. The USAID Budget Office estimated the 1996 obligations as having already reached 33.9 per cent, a jump from 27.7 per cent two years earlier. These percentages, much cited by NGOs in other countries, are misleading, however.

In actual fact, the 33.9 per cent figure is a percentage of what is called the 'Development Assistance Program' (DAP), which represented only 20 per cent of ODA in 1996. As a percentage of ODA, therefore, the PVO/NGO share (using the DAP figures) was only 6.6 per cent. To this can be added contributions and contracts for PVOs/NGOs that fall under a category known as the Economic Support Fund (ESF), which is not part of the DAP. The ESF is essentially a cash transfer programme, much of it balance of payment support to Egypt and Israel. According to the US Budget Office, the total funding of PVOs and NGOs in 1996, including DAP and ESF, was $927.7 million, out of a total ODA figure of $9.12 billion. This represents approximately 10.1 per cent, a slight increase over the previous year. Food and freight chanelled through PVOs totalled US$408.8 million in 1995, representing an additional 5.6 per cent of ODA.[13]

USAID registration of PVOs

The registration of PVOs began during World War II and has continued since then as a means of vetting organisations for the receipt of government funds and food aid. The form of registration has changed over the years. Since 1977, registration has been a prerequisite for any PVO wishing to apply for most forms of USAID assistance. The registration procedure is handled by the Office of Private and Voluntary Cooperation in the Bureau for Humanitarian Assistance.

Registration does not confer any official status or approval. Once a lengthy and cumbersome procedure, registration was significantly simplified in 1995. A simplified procedure for the registration of non-US NGOs was introduced in 1996, in English, French, Spanish and Arabic. To maintain its registration, a PVO must submit a number of documents annually, including audited financial statements, annual report, annual budget using USAID forms, Internal Revenue Service reporting documents and a 'privateness percentage report'.

USAID Resources Available to Registered PVOs

General

There are two basic forms of agreement between USAID and the non-governmental sector, contracts and 'assistance instruments', and there are two types of assistance instrument – grants and cooperative agreements. Grants are much like government grants to NGOs elsewhere, in that they are largely responsive to the organisation making the request, and as long as they fit within overall government priorities, there are few strings attached. Usually there is a matching requirement. Matching may be as high as 50 per cent, and may be calculated in cash or kind, according to the programme requirements. The most common requirement is 25 per cent, and although there are debates about the way the figure is applied, USAID intends the amount to be flexible and illustrative, with an overall PVO match of 25 per cent, rather than a strict match on each and every project. Cooperative agreements, which may also require a matching component, tend to be much more like contracts, and until recently were so controlling that details such as the travel of PVO staff required prior USAID approval. Many of the restrictions have now been lifted, although USAID still retains the right to approve the workplan and the hiring of key personnel under such agreements.

By far the largest proportion of government funding to PVOs is determined overseas by individual USAID missions. This is usually done through a competitive process, as are 'awards' made from the central bureaus in Washington.

Mission-funded Program Grants

These grants comprise the major form of development assistance support for PVO/NGO programmes. Program Grants are typically multi-year grants made by USAID missions overseas, usually requiring a 25 per cent match from the PVO. Funds are made available for projects and programmes that fit within the USAID country framework and programme. In some cases projects are identified by the PVO and taken to USAID for support, while in other cases USAID will approach the PVO with a programming initiative. The size and nature of the PVO portfolio will be determined by the mission in question. There is no pre-set allocation.

'Co-financing' or 'umbrella' grants are an increasingly used variant. Umbrella grants are administered by a PVO, a contractor, or a USAID mission, which in turn approves and manages sub-grants to PVOs and NGOs operating in-country in accordance with agreed criteria.

Matching Grants

The Matching Grant Program supports competitive, multi-country agreements that link strategic, capacity-building approaches and sustainable development methodologies. Emphasis is placed on the development of formal partnerships between US PVOs and local NGOs. At the end of 1997 there were 38 agreements, including programmes to strengthen micro-enterprise, health delivery systems, the environment, civil society and sustainable agriculture. Awards are made competitively for three or five years, depending on programme complexity and the maturity of the applicant. Applications are judged in relation to published guidelines that are designed to assist PVOs in the implementation of strategic approaches to international development. The programmes require a cash match of at least 50 per cent, although many applicants exceed that amount. Agreements in place at the end of 1997 totalled $176.7 million in combined USAID/PVO funding, covering three to five years.

Child Survival Grants

Child Survival Grants are intended to address the special health needs of infants, children and mothers, with emphasis on immunisation, nutrition, oral rehydration therapy and HIV/AIDS, and on capacity-building for US PVOs and their local partners. Grants are made on a competitive basis by USAID in Washington. In 1997 18 four-year grants and two 'entry level' two-year grants were made. Most new programmes are up to $1 million, with a 25 per cent cost-sharing requirement. At the end of 1997, USAID was supporting 64 programmes in 30 countries, through 26 PVOs, with a portfolio value of $55.8 million.

Farmer to Farmer Program

The Farmer to Farmer Program, initiated in 1995, is intended to provide short-term technical assistance to, and people-to-people contact with, farmers, cooperatives, agribusiness and agricultural training institutions in developing countries and the former Soviet Union, through US volunteer farmers and agricultural professionals. Funded under the Farm Bill, the programme fields about 600 volunteers each year. The programme had a 1997 budget of about $10 million.

The Cooperative Development Program

The aim of this centrally funded USAID/Washington programme is to foster and expand cooperative development in the South (and more recently in Eastern Europe and the former Soviet Union). The major component is a portfolio of core grants designed to enable US cooperative development organisations to maintain international departments that develop, assist and evaluate the work of cooperatives overseas. The programme has a five-year budget of $25 million, and the average grant is approximately $600,000.

New Partnership Initiative

USAID's New Partnership Initiative (NPI) began in 1995 and went through an experiment and design phase in 1996. Its Resource Guide (available on the USAID website) describes it as 'an integrated approach to sustainable development that uses strategic partnering and an active engagement of civil society, the business community, and institutions of local governance to bolster the ability of local communities to play a lead role in their own development'.[14] This formal description may obscure what could become an important development initiative, based on a recognition that national governments, regardless of the policy environment and regardless of the quality of their governance, often have limited impact at the community level. Conversely, many of a nation's most intractable problems – poverty, environmental degradation – have their roots and their most destructive manifestation at the local level.

Taking its cue from a recognition that community development in industrialized countries involves an often intimate working relationship between civil society organisations (eg the local Rotary Club), local government (eg the mayor and town council) and business (eg the local bank that finances an addition to the hospital and makes loans to small enterprise), the NPI sought similar connections in the 15 countries that it studied. These included countries as diverse and as far afield as Guinea, Sri Lanka, Russia, South Africa, Indonesia and Ecuador. What emerged was a realisation that the three sets of actors rarely interact in a positive way, and that in many countries they are antagonistic towards each other.

The challenge posed by the NPI, therefore, is how to foster, nurture and sustain partnerships among local government, the private sector and civil society. If the NPI premise is accepted by PVOs and NGOs, they could have an important role to play in its evolution. At the time of writing, the NPI secretariat was in the process of disseminating its findings. It had no programming budget, but it seemed to be generating solid support from the US PVO community. Although it is too early to say where the initiative may go, it is an interesting and rare example of practical development research within a bilateral development assistance agency.

Development Education Grants

Development Education Grants were originally aimed to 'facilitate public discussion within the United States on hunger and related issues. Programmes are intended to increase US public awareness of political, economic, technical and social factors relating to hunger and poverty in less developed countries.' The programme, which was budgeted at $2.5 million in the early 1990s, became the focus of negative attention within Congress after 1993, and was capped at $500,000 for 1998. Each grantee must sign an agreement that states that no advocacy work or lobbying will be done with the grant funds. The tiny budget and its restrictions mean that effectiveness can only be achieved through a high degree of leveraging. PVOs are therefore being encouraged to work with domestic organisations with parallel interests and in-built dissemination networks. Current programmes include linkages between PVOs and farmers' associations, the American Library Association and the National Geographic Society.

Food aid

US support for worldwide food aid was formalised in the Agricultural Trade Development and Assistance Act of 1954, also known as Public Law 480 (PL 480). Since its inception, about 375 million metric tons with a commodity value of more than $50 billion have been distributed. The US remains a major provider of food and development assistance. In fiscal year 1997, over 2.5 million tons of commodities valued at $1.1 billion were delivered.

PL 480 has three major 'titles' – Title I, managed by the US Department of Agriculture, provides for the sale of agricultural commodities to developing countries and private entities for dollars on favourable credit terms. Title I funding approved for fiscal year 1998 totalled $245 million. Title II, managed by USAID, includes both emergency and development assistance programmes in donated commodities, and is programmed through PVOs, cooperative development organisations, Southern NGOs and international organisations such as the World Food Program. Title II fiscal year 1998 approval levels totalled $837 million. Title III, managed by USAID Regional Bureaus, provides grant-financed commodities to least developed countries (LDCs) for policy reforms related to food security. The fiscal year 1998 Title III approval level was $30 million.

In 1996, Title II development and emergency grants were made to 21 PVOs and NGOs in 27 countries. Of non-emergency food aid, PVOs programmed over 70 per cent of the total between 1993 and 1997, with most of the balance going to the World Food Programme. In emergency food there has been a significant shift away from the use of PVOs in recent years. In 1993, PVOs programmed over half of the total, but by 1996 the PVO share had dropped to only 23 per cent, with a concomitant growth in the proportion programmed by WFP.

In 1995, half of the US food aid channelled through US PVOs went to CARE, and 93 per cent of the total went to four PVOs: CARE, Adventist Development and Relief Agency, Catholic Relief Services and World Vision Relief and Development.

Emergencies

The USAID budget for disasters, administered by the Office of Foreign Disaster Assistance, has increased dramatically in recent years, from approximately $50 million in 1989–90 to an estimated $200 million in 1992–3, and roughly the same through 1997, not including food aid. More than 60 per cent of this funding was programmed through US PVOs.

This has created new demands on both USAID and the PVO community, to find increasing numbers of people to work in emergency situations, to develop new capacities in new countries such as the former Yugoslavia and Central Asia, and to engage in a new type of work — on-going military situations and 'failed states'. In many cases PVOs have had the motivation to deal with these new challenges, but not the skills; and several have had to review and re-think their mandates. A basic problem for USAID is the lack of consistency in the technical competence of PVOs. A highly professional operation by a PVO in one country does not necessarily mean the same level of effectiveness by the same organisation elsewhere. Part of the difficulty has been the increase in the number and the intensity of emergencies, and part has to do with the usually unaffordable cost for PVOs of keeping a stable of professional emergency programmers available on short notice.

In 1997, USAID introduced an idea that may improve effectiveness and efficiency in PVO delivery – the Indefinite Quantity Contract (IQC). A competition was held in 1997 for contracts that would require the organisation to mobilise an emergency response at USAID request, anywhere in the world, on 72 hours notice. At the time of writing, four awards had been granted (two food and two non-food), but they had not been activated.

In recent years, USAID has worked increasingly in 'transition' situations (for example, Bosnia, Haiti, Angola) and has relied heavily on US and local nonprofit organisations in the process. USAID has established an Office of Transition Initiatives (OTI), which at the time of writing was growing rapidly, and was providing substantial funding to PVOs.

Overheads

USAID calculates a separate overhead formula for each of the organisations it deals with. This formula, known as the Negotiated Indirect Cost Rate Agreement (NICRA), then covers all grants made by USAID until or unless it is reviewed and altered. Both NGOs and USAID officials are generally satisfied that the approach — although time-consuming in the first instance — is fair and that it is practised consistently.

Trends in funding

The proportion of USAID contracts as opposed to grants and cooperative agreements has not changed appreciably in recent years. Contracts represented 42.5 per cent of the total in both 1992 and 1996, while there was a slight increase in grants and cooperative agreements from 53.9 per cent to 55.9 per cent.

There have been shifts, however, in the share of USAID funding to the top PVO recipients. In 1996, the top 20 recipients received 70 per cent of the funding, down from 85 per cent five years earlier.

Table 24.2: *Share of USAID Funding to All PVOs by Top Recipients (000)*

	FY 92	FY 94	FY 96
$ to top 20	$665,063	$813,116	$476,866
% to top 20	85%	75%	70%
$ to top 5	$379,023	$479,516	$228,884
% to top 5	48%	44%	33%

Source: ACVFA, 1997 (These figures represent the 'total estimated cost' amounts of the awards issued in the year, rather than actual expenditure.)

Direct funding of Southern NGOs

Direct funding of Southern NGOs has long been a common practice of the United States Government, primarily through its USAID missions overseas. A major limiting factor has been USAID's registration and reporting requirements, which, onerous enough for US PVOs, have been beyond the capacity of most smaller Southern organisations. For example, all USAID grants and contracts must be audited by one of five major accounting firms. The primary Southern beneficiaries of USAID grants and contracts, therefore, have tended to be larger organisations that have programming and institutional capacity, and that can cope with the paperwork.

Ironically, and despite this limitation, USAID has outpaced many of the largest US PVOs in developing relationships with Southern NGOs, and for many years, the Advisory Committee on Voluntary Foreign Aid (ACVFA), and more recently USAID's PVC Office, have urged greater cooperation between US and Southern organisations.The 1997 ACVFA report noted that while 'there was unanimity on the key importance of strengthening local NGOs... institutional weaknesses on both [the USAID and PVO] sides constrain progress'. Many of the larger US PVOs have made their reputation on the basis of direct programming overseas, much of it food and emergency-related. This does not lend itself to an easy transition to a supportive, rather than an operational role. Given the growth in size and professionalism of the Southern NGO community, however, this is likely to remain a thorny issue as US PVOs struggle to catch up with their counterparts in other DAC countries.

EVALUATION AND RESULTS

One of the Clinton Administration's first efforts was a National Performance Review, which led to the passage by Congress in 1993 of a far-reaching Government Performance and Results Act (GPRA). As part of USAID's 're-engineering', a new system of planning, implementation, monitoring and evaluation was initiated in 1995. USAID is no longer concerned about projects per se; instead, it aims to achieve strategic objectives – strategic development results that can be achieved over five to eight years. Along with these are intermediate results that can be measured in two to five years. In this context, evaluation is being given a new role. According to the Director of USAID's Center for Development Information and Evaluation (CDIE),

> *Evaluations are seen as a way of learning about experience: what is happening, what are the intended and unintended impacts of USAID's activities, why things happened the way they did. To be effective learning tools, evaluations must involve managers, contractors, counterparts, beneficiaries. They must be participatory. This view of evaluation contrasts, however, with another view – perhaps more prevalent in the agency and the donor community generally – that evaluations should be independent, objective, rigorous, and be instruments to hold managers and contractors accountable for the results for which they are responsible. The shift to a more participatory, learning role for evaluation will not occur overnight and is by no means assured. It will require a change in USAID's institutional culture and system of incentives.*[15]

This new approach raises a number of issues for US PVOs, although it may be useful first to review the record of PVO evaluation over the past decade or so. In a 1982 USAID study – *Turning PVOs Into Development Agencies: Questions for Evaluation* – Judith Tendler challenged many 'articles of faith' regarding PVO effectiveness, and said that far too little impact evaluation was being done. She further suggested that impact evaluation of social programmes and processes was not as difficult a proposition as had once been thought. This report, which received mixed reviews, opened the way for other efforts to think about, and to re-think the way PVOs are evaluated.

All PVO projects and programmes funded by USAID are technically required to have an evaluation. At the beginning of 1997, the CDIE database in Washington, which dates back to the 1970s, contained 1471 evaluations of PVO or PVO-related projects, although given the decentralised nature of the agency, this number probably represented about half of the PVO evaluations that had been carried out by USAID. In addition to these evaluations, perhaps as many have been carried out by PVOs themselves. USAID's PVC Office has placed increasing emphasis on evaluation in its grants programme, with the objective of strengthening a PVO's own evaluation capacity. Funding is included in grants for this purpose.

There is also a growing number of PVO-related evaluation networks. InterAction members have created a Committee on Development Policy and Practice which, inter alia, examines development issues facing its members. Fourteen PVO evaluators held their third annual round-table meeting in 1997 to discuss questions of impact, the role of the evaluator and partcipatory evaluation. A network of PVOs involved in micro-enterprise development – SEEP – has an evaluation committee, and others exist within the fields of health, population and education. A number of overview or synthesis studies have also been prepared in recent years – of country programmes (DAI's *The Development Impact of PVOs: Kenya and Niger*), or sectoral areas (*Management Systems International's Overview Studies on the Impact of Microenterprise Credit*).

Despite the growing levels of evaluation activity, a 1997 synthesis report, carried out as a background study for a larger report to the OECD/DAC Expert Group on Aid Evaluation, was critical:

> *Lack of baseline data, an emphasis on outputs and effect indicators, and inadequate monitoring arrangement, have led to reports focusing on implementation issues rather than impact. Where impact has been addressed it tends to be impressionistic based on observation and the recall of project staff and beneficiaries. Systematic impact assessment, based on baseline data, disaggregated by gender, socio-economic status and ethnic group is particularly rare, but becoming more common in child survival and microenterprise interventions... The [1995] General Audit Office synthesis study of PVO interventions is indicative of this type of evaluation. Despite projects whose objectives largely targetted improvements in the lives and livelihoods of beneficiaries, the evaluation focused on the achievement of output and effects rather than impact... Similarly, CDIE's efforts in 1994 to determine the factors that contributed to the success of PVO initiatives were hampered by an inadequate sample of quality reports and insufficient detail of project impact.*[16]

While the conclusions of the 1997 synthesis study are not very positive, they do not say that there is no impact; they only say that the impact is not being evaluated or recorded in a way that is accessible to external observers. This poses a challenge for PVOs and for USAID, the same one posed by Judith Tendler in 1982. Obviously there is a greater need than ever before to provide evidence of impact. Reduced levels of financial support make this necessary, as does USAID's new emphasis on results. The question that remains is how this evidence will be gathered: by a growing insistence on external evaluation of short-term results, or through something more akin to the way evaluation was described above by the Director of USAID's CDIE.

POLICY DIALOGUE AND CAMPAIGNS

In 1993, *Stakeholders for Development*[17] observed

> *that the United States PVO community has a mixed record on policy dialogue and campaigning. To the dismay of US activists in the development field, many of the largest PVOs are quiescent on questions relating to the quality of US ODA. This is not to say that these organisations are uninterested in policy dialogue. Many maintain Washington offices for the purpose of keeping in touch with events and making representations on their organisation's behalf. Many of these offices, however, are intended primarily to support and bolster the organisation's funding position and political profile with both USAID and Congress.*

While there is still truth in this statement, there have also been changes. In 1995, a bill was drafted by a Member of Congress aimed at stopping charities from their alleged use of federal government grants for 'political advocacy'.The proposed legislation, however, went further. It would have prevented charities in receipt of government funding from writing a letter to the editor of a newspaper; it would have tied the hands of organisations such as Mothers Against Drunk Driving, and would have prevented international development organisations from speaking out on a wide range of international issues. A coalition of domestic and international organisations, joined by a chorus of politicians and journalists defeated the legislation, but it served, in a sense, as a wake-up call, and as a signal that PVOs could, and perhaps should, engage much more actively in certain types of advocacy work.

A growing political focus on domestic rather than international issues, the re-engineering of USAID, and the severe cutbacks in official development assistance have created both dangers and opportunities for policy dialogue and advocacy. On the one hand, much advocacy work has been defensive, marked by intensive lobbying to preserve and increase the aid budget. While there has been general agreement that USAID was in need of reform, most members of the PVO community have had serious reservations about the possibility that if it were merged with the Department of State, the commitment to long-term development would suffer, and funding decisions would become politicized. For much of the mid 1990s, the pages of InterAction's *Monday Developments* were filled with stories on these two subjects. Much of its work was taken up with Capitol Hill briefings, press conferences, legislative updates posted on its website, letter-writing campaigns and the like.

Regarding the quality of aid, PVOs have worked more closely with USAID in recent years on issues relating to transparency and sustainable development. An Aid Reform Working Group has acted as a forum for discussion on USAID's re-engineering and competition guidelines for assistance instruments. A major activity in 1996 and 1997 was an effort by InterAction and its members to educate policy-makers on how little the US actually spends on development assistance. The 'Just One Per cent' message has been widely disseminated throughout the country, and InterAction takes credit for the fact that both the President and the Secretary of State have used the figure in speeches defending development assistance.

In 1997, 18 PVOs created a Committee to Stop Famine in North Korea, lobbying congress and criticising the government for the use of food aid as a political tool. Led by World Vision and some of the largest US NGOs, the committee paid for, among other things, six weeks of television advertisements on the subject.

Being geographically closer to the World Bank than other NGO communities, US PVOs have access that others do not enjoy. This was the primary reason for the 1995 opening of a Washington office by Oxfam International, to act as a listening post among the international financial institutions, and to press for changes in policies with which it disagrees. InterAction has created a 'World Bank Project' aimed at promoting popular participation and gender concerns in Bank policy, project design, implementation and evaluation. Monthly meetings are held on these and other reform agenda topics.

Enhanced PVO access to the corridors of USAID and the World Bank has resulted in part from greater PVO pressure for entry, and perhaps from a more sophisticated approach to negotiation and lobbying than prevailed in the past. PVO support for development assistance and for the independence of USAID has served the agency well and PVO support for IDA replenishment is not unimportant to the World Bank. In a sense, both institutions need PVOs. But improved PVO access and credibility are also due, perhaps in equal measure, to a willingness and to the pro-active engagement of PVOs by USAID Administrator Brian Atwood and World Bank President James Wolfensohn. There is a general recognition among leaders of the US PVO community that the openness and accessibility of these two individuals has led to a significant change in the way their institutions do business with the voluntary sector.

ISSUES

Statistics

At several points in this report, the question of statistics has arisen. There are difficulties in comparing US figures with those of other countries because of the way ODA is calculated, and because such a large proportion of what is reported as 'income' has to do with food, freight and other in-kind contributions. A further problem, as in other countries, has to do with inconsistency in the way PVOs present their financial statements to the public. Reports vary from organisation to organisation, and from year to year. Some give detailed breakdown on the sources of income, while others do not distinguish between government grants and contracts, or between government and private donor support.

Official bureaucracy

In 1993, *Stakeholders for Development* noted that official bureaucratic reporting and accounting requirements, and a lengthy project cycle had made the obtaining and implementation of grants a highly complex and time-consuming procedure for many PVOs. With the re-engineering of the mid 1990s, much of this has been streamlined and improved, and many of the more onerous conditions imposed by USAID on the PVO relationship have been removed.

It remains to be seen, however, how the reforms will be put into practice. USAID's own 1996 assessment noted that 'a pervasive problem affects USAID's management of PVO/NGO activities. It is the inconsistency of USAID staff's management of grants and cooperative agreements. Staff appear knowledgeable about technical differences between funding instruments, but in practice these differences are often ignored. Preferences of individual officers, rather than requirements of specific funding instruments, seem to determine how activities are managed'.[18] The 1997 ACVFA Report observes that reform is a long-term process. 'Attempts to institutionalize fundamental change in the relationship between an embattled government agency stretched across the globe, and more than 400 PVOs of different sizes, interests and capabilities, will take longer than four years. The unevenness within USAID and the lack of full awareness and impact of agency reforms within the PVO community suggest that USAID should continue to communicate the reforms... and focus on removing barriers to their effective implementation'.

Evaluation and results

Following close on the heels of this issue is the question of USAID's new results orientation and the changes that are implied in the evaluation function. 'Embattled government agencies' that are being closely watched by politicians for the results of their work can be more controlling. They can focus more on the short-term results for which they will be held most accountable, at the expense of the longer-term results that so often characterise good development. A PVO community that has so far paid little attention to impact evaluation is thus vulnerable to the swings of a USAID pendulum that in 1997 might have been at the height of an arc stressing participation, consultation and sustainable development. The challenge for PVOs to demonstrate impact is therefore likely to become more, rather than less important, and failure to do so could damage the improvements that were made in the government–PVO relationship in the middle years of the decade.

Cost-sharing and dependency

The dependency question remains more substantive in the US than in other countries, simply because of the importance placed by the government on US strategic and programmatic objectives of development assistance. The availability of increasing amounts of public money for US PVOs through the 1970s and 1980s and the complexities of the funding and evaluation procedures have made many increasingly reliant on USAID. This has, in the view of some, 'cut them off from their natural and original constituencies and broad-based support in the United States and made many of them less responsive and less accountable to the poor. The erosion of PVO independence in the 1980s has been the inevitable result of the significant PVO relationships with AID during the 1970s and the subsequent rapid growth in PVO budgets, staff and operations. In recent years this independence has been further compromised as a result of decisions by PVOs to package projects specifically for AID'.[19] The danger in over-dependence has also been noted regularly by Congress, which, in an addition to the 1978 Foreign Assistance Act, warned PVOs against compromising their 'private and independent nature'.

USAID's own 1995 Policy Guidance on the USAID–PVO Partnership states that 'While an organisation's ability to maintain its independence depends on a variety of factors, undue dependence on a single source of funding can jeopardize the role of PVOs, not just as independent entities, but also as intermediaries for USAID programmes. The 'privateness requirement' legislated by Congress is designed to address this potential problem by establishing that US PVOs must receive at least 20 per cent of their financial support for overseas activities from non-USG sources'.

The interpretation of this requirement is broad, and there are anomalies. Some organisations receive no funding from the US government, and therefore have a 100 per cent privateness rating. Among them are organisations like the American Friends Service Committee and the Catholic Medical Mission Board. Catholic Relief Services, however, which received 77 per cent of its 1995 income (in cash and kind) from US government sources, had an 82 per cent privateness rating because USAID removes contracts, Title II food and other government-initiated activities from the calculation. Overall, PVO dependency on government increased between 1990 and 1995. Private contributions and revenue declined from 61.1 per cent to 50.4 per cent of the total income of PVOs registered with USAID over the five year period.[20] (See Table 24.2 for details.)

Dependency, of course, can be seen as a two-way street. USAID is heavily dependent upon US PVOs for the effective delivery of food aid and for a high proportion of its emergency assistance. PVOs are also increasingly recognised as an important window on, and channel to, the development of pluralism in countries where the development of democratic institutions is a priority.

25 European Union[1]

Judith Randel and Tony German

SUMMARY

The EU provides support for NGOs on a large scale – over ECU800 million in 1995 (more than $1 billion) – well over 20 per cent of the EU development budget. A 50 per cent match is generally available for both projects and for development education activities. NGOs must provide 15 per cent of their contribution from private sources. EU co-financing rules are in the process of being changed, with more flexible financial terms and a simplification of procedures that in the past have been regarded as onerous and bureaucratic. About 65 per cent of EU assistance in 1995 was for humanitarian work – half the budget of the European Community Humanitarian Office (ECHO) being spent through NGOs.

The NGDO–EU Liaison Committee (generally known by its French acronym, CLONG) is the main point for information and representation between NGOs and the Commission, Parliament and Council. Other networks provide advocacy platforms for Catholic, Protestant and non-confessional NGOs, and there are NGO coalitions on issues such as debt, women in development and emergencies.

EU discussions with NGOs are shifting from finance and administrative issues to policy-related discussions. The EU has strongly supported NGO development education efforts – particularly important in countries such as Britain and France where national government support for development education has in the past been negligible. NGOs have invested heavily in EU level advocacy and are perceived to have had some success in raising issues of coherence (such as EU beef dumping). Recently the Commission has been keen to explore the potential for dialogue on broader issues such as micro credit and problems in the Great Lakes region.

There is pressure within the Commission for a clearer definition of what it means to be an NGO. NGOs, however – reluctant to produce a definition that might inhibit traditional flexibility – have produced a Charter that is a minimum set of standards to which the sector is expected to subscribe. Increased openness, additional resources and a single evaluation unit increase the potential for real learning from evaluation. Evaluations suggest, however, that a more strategic NGO approach to development education is needed.

Direct funding of Southern NGOs has been possible since 1988, but it has been slow to develop. EU NGOs are ambivalent about direct funding, but it is becoming a priority for the Commission. Potentially such cooperation will involve work with town councils, schools and professional bodies.

BOX 25.1 THE EUROPEAN UNION, THE COMMISSION AND PARLIAMENT

The European Union comprises 15 member states: Austria, Belgium, Denmark, Finland, France, Germany, Greece, Ireland, Italy, Luxembourg, Netherlands, Portugal, Spain, Sweden, United Kingdom. Together, they provide almost 57 per cent of DAC official development assistance. As well as providing aid bilaterally, EU members contribute to the EU's own aid programme, which at $4.8 billion in 1996, was the DAC s fifth largest. EU aid is divided into two parts. The European Development Fund (EDF) finances activities in African, Caribbean and Pacific (ACP) countries under the Lomé Convention. Countries not covered by Lomé (Asia, Latin America, southern Mediterranean and the Middle East, and countries in Eastern Europe and the former Soviet Union) receive aid from the EU budget.

The European Commission is responsible for the development of policy and legislation, the guardianship of legislation and treaty obligations, and the execution of policies – including management of the budget. The Commission comprises 20 commissioners drawn from member states and its 15,000 staff are organised within 26 directorates general (DG) and 15 specialised services. Management of EU aid is divided between the Commission's directorates general. DG VIII manages Lomé, non-emergency food aid and NGO financing. DG I-B is responsible for Asia, Latin America, the Mediterranean and Middle East. DG I-A manages Eastern Europe and the former Soviet Union. The European Community Humanitarian Office (ECHO) deals with humanitarian aid, including relations with, and financing for, NGOs on emergency issues. Five different European commissioners have responsibility for aspects of EU aid management. The Council of Ministers (the Development Council and Council on Foreign Affairs) has political responsibility for decision-making. The presidency of the council rotates every six months between member states.

BACKGROUND AND HISTORY

Member countries of the EU channelled 17 per cent of their ODA programmes through the European Commission's development cooperation instruments in 1996. EC net ODA rose in 1996 by 3 per cent in real terms over 1995, to $5537 billion.[2]

The EU has a strong record of support for NGOs. Between 1976 and 1995, the EU co-financed over 7420 projects carried out by 650 NGOs in 133 countries. In 1995, EU funding for NGO projects reached over ECU800 million (about $1015 million) per annum, excluding direct funding of NGO activities through the European Development Fund (EDF) or DG 1. Altogether well over 20 per cent of the European Community development budget was managed by NGOs in the mid 1990s.[3]

The main institutional responsibility for relations with NGOs lies with DG VIII, in the Directorate General for Development Cooperation, Unit B2. This NGO unit has a staff of 17, and three secretarial staff. It is responsible for the management of NGO co-financing globally, and plays a facilitating role on NGO policy issues in relation to the Commission. However, DG VIII does not have responsibility for development cooperation with Asian, Latin American and Mediterranean countries. These are the responsibility of DG 1. Humanitarian assistance, half of which is spent through NGOs, is managed by ECHO, falling under the management of yet another commissioner.

The European NGO community is represented to the EU through a number of coalition and liaison bodies, and the Commission also relates directly to individual NGOs, some of which have placed officers in Brussels in order to interface with the Commission, the Council and Parliament. Some NGOs have stronger links with the EU than with their own governments.

Portuguese NGOs, for example, receive very little co-financing from their government, but they can access EU co-financing. British NGOs relied heavily on EU support for development education during the 1980s and early 1990s, when the British government had a virtual embargo on support for such activity.

NGO LIAISON AND UMBRELLA BODIES

The main interface for NGOs is through the NGDO–EU Liaison Committee (CLONG). CLONG represents European NGOs to EU institutions (not only the Commission itself but also the Parliament and the Council) and provides an important channel for dialogue on both policy issues and practical matters such as co-financing.

CLONG represents some 800 member organisations, grouped within 15 National 'Platforms' in member states. It has a General Assembly that meets annually to determine an overall programme and to provide guidance on its implementation. The Liaison Committee, which meets five times a year, comprises a representative from each of the National Platforms. CLONG has a Brussels-based Secretariat headed by an executive secretary and guided by a bureau (comprising the CLONG president, vice president, treasurer and executive secretary). The Secretariat's staff services CLONG's various working groups, undertakes the day-to-day work of monitoring the Commission, feeds information to NGOs, provides logistical support for CLONG activities, and follows through on issues such as the Elewijt Process (discussed below). The Secretariat organises quarterly information meetings and produces ten issues a year of Liaison News. All CLONG materials are produced in French and English, and a large number are translated into German, Italian and Spanish. These give detailed updates on such matters as the EU budget, progress on enlargement, the Intergovernmental Conference (IGC), and issues relating to the Lomé Convention. CLONG also hosts a coordination meeting every other month, enabling EU networks to discuss and coordinate their work on policy issues.

Other networks include:

*   VOICE: Voluntary Organisations in Cooperation in Emergencies. A sub-committee of the Liaison Committee, VOICE offers member organisations involved in emergency operations a focus for information, consultation and dialogue with the Commission, and especially ECHO.
*   APRODEV: Association of World Council of Churches-related Development Organisations in Europe – the lobby organisation through which Protestant Church Agencies in Europe lobby and access EU institutions and resources. APRODEV has 16 members.
*   EURO-CIDSE: Represents the justice and development interests of 12 Catholic development agencies based in member states.
*   EUROSTEP: Aims to coordinate the advocacy activities of its 22 member agencies on the official development cooperation policies of multilateral institutions and to improve the quality of aid offered by NGOs.

Table 25.1: *EU Co-financing of NGOs 1993–96 (ECU million)*

	1993	1994	1995	1996
Total Responsive Funding for NGOs	135	145	175	174
Percentage Increase		+ 6.9%	+20.7%	- 0.6%
Total Allocation for Block Grants	21.9	21.5	23.7	21.9
Share of NGO Responsive Funding	16.2%	14.8%	13.5%	12.7

Note: US$1.00 = ECU0.78.
Source: EU DG VIII Unit, Decentralized Cooperation and Co-financing with NGOs

- WIDE: Network Women and Development Europe – a network of national platforms which works to build European and international awareness of gender and development issues. It represents groups in 12 European countries.
- EURODAD: The European Network on Debt and Development – a consortium of European NGOs working on debt issues.
- SOLIDAR: An alliance of NGOs, trade unions and campaigning groups with links to social democratic and socialist parties and trades unions. It has NGO representatives from 11 EU countries.

OVERALL TRENDS IN EU SUPPORT TO NGOS

In 1995, ECU833 million (about $1057 million) was contributed by the EU to various NGO activities, compared with ECU803 million (about $1019 million) in 1994 and ECU702 million (about $891 million) in 1993. Of this, more than ECU500 million (about $635 million) was for non-emergency aid, an increase of 85 per cent in cash terms over 1990.

The total non-emergency and non-food aid responsive funding programme for NGOs grew steadily between 1993 and 1995, but remained the same in cash terms in 1996.

In 1996, 824 projects were co-financed; 90 per cent of the funding was for 639 projects in developing countries. One hundred and seventy-nine projects on awareness raising in Europe were also co-financed. Funding was concentrated in Sub-Saharan Africa and Latin America, each of which took 34 per cent of community co-financing. Nineteen per cent was allocated to projects in Asia, 5 per cent to the Caribbean and 6 per cent to the Mediterranean.

Co-financed operations (projects and development education) are oversubscribed on a ratio of roughly two to one, both for the number of applications and their total value.

THE TERMS OF EU CO-FINANCING

At the time of writing, EU co-financing was governed by the 1988 General Conditions for the Co-financing of Projects undertaken in Developing Countries by NGOs.[4] However these guidelines were being revised during 1997, with the expectation that new ones would be published in 1998 and made operational by 1999. Some of the likely changes are noted in this section.

Under the 1988 guidelines, the Commission funds 50 per cent of project costs and 50 per cent of development education or information costs. In exceptional circumstances the Commission will fund 75 per cent of the costs. Six per cent of the EU contribution may be charged as an overhead for administration. This does not have to be justified in proposals or reports and is considered a flat rate charge. Five-year co-financing covers costs ranging from a minimum of ECU12,000 (about $15,000) to a ceiling of ECU150,000 (about $190,000) per year, or ECU500,000 (about $635,000) over the lifetime of the project. For public awareness projects there is a ceiling of ECU80,000 (about $101,000) per year, and ECU240,000 (about $304,000) over the lifetime of the project. Where NGOs collaborate on projects, these figures can be doubled, and the EU looks particularly favourably on consortia involving NGOs from more than one member state. The NGO is expected to provide 15 per cent of project costs from private sources (in cash or in kind) and the remainder can come from official funding and from local partners, and may include in-kind contributions.

Annual block grants are offered to NGOs if they 'have cooperated satisfactorily with the Commission for a number of years'. This offers more flexible financing for smaller, process-based projects, often in conjunction with larger projects. In 1996 the Commission issued 164 block grants with a total value of ECU21.9 million (about $28 million), much the same level as 1993 and 1994.

Changes expected in the new guidelines include an extension of the co-financing element to 75 per cent, increases in ceilings, and an increase in the administration charge to 10 per cent. Since 1988 the budget for co-financing has increased dramatically, but the ceilings for block grants and project co-financing have not changed. This has led to an inevitable increase in the number of projects, and fails to recognise the scale of NGO activity. There is also an expectation that support will move from projects to support for NGO programmes, and there is a strong hope on all sides that procedures – currently onerous – will be simpler and more flexible. Consideration may be given to four-year framework agreements based on concrete programmes.

In its 1996 annual report on co-financing, the Commission noted the outcome of the May 1996 seminar held with Northern and Southern NGOs:

> *Institutional support demands long-term moral, political and financial commit-*
> *ment which requires both the NGOs and the Commission itself to move from its*
> *present project-based approach to a longer term programme approach. This is a*
> *rapidly developing area of NGO reflection and change in practice which the*
> *Commission is actively supporting and will accommodate on revising its General*
> *Conditions for Co-financing.*

Changes are also expected in the terms of co-financing. It is possible that NGOs will no longer be able to include in-kind donations. For Italian NGOs, for example, which rely heavily on volunteer staffing, and for Southern NGOs benefiting from local labour, this would have serious implications. The impact would be mitigated, however, if the expected increase in the Commission contribution from half to three quarters of activity costs were to take place.

The 1988 eligibility conditions focus on the status of the NGO within an EU member state – the bulk of its human and financial resources must be there, along with its decision-making authority. Similarly, while there are conditions concerning competence and experience, the ability to mobilise solidarity and private resources within the EU is the first in a list of factors that are taken into account. Eligibility and the definition of NGOs has become a key issue, and is discussed later in this chapter.

HUMANITARIAN ASSISTANCE

The lion's share of EU assistance to NGOs is for humanitarian work and food aid, which together represented 65 per cent of all assistance to NGOs in 1995. Total Community support for humanitarian operations amounted to ECU656 million in 1995 (about $832 million). Approximately half of all ECHO funding went through NGOs. In other budget heads relating to emergencies, NGOs are also prominent. For example, 44 out of 69 projects for refugees, returnees and displaced persons were implemented by NGOs, and 91 per cent of aid for refugees under the Lomé Convention was managed by NGOs.

A wider role for ECHO?

ECHO was set up in 1992 to oversee and coordinate the EU's humanitarian operations in non-member countries. In four years ECHO had become a giant on the world humanitarian aid stage, accounting for a quarter of all international assistance. This figure rises to over 50 per cent for the EU as a whole when member state contributions are added in. It currently operates in over 60 countries with aid varying from basics such as food and clothing to regional mine clearance programmes. It works in partnership with NGOs, the UN and others such as the ICRC, and has signed a number of framework agreements designed to speed up response time.

Discussions between ECHO and NGOs have emphasised administrative issues and financial reporting. NGOs argue that more discussion is needed on objectives and on the quality of work. Consultations on a new Framework Partnership Agreement are an example of this. NGOs note the relationship of trust and dialogue, but discussion has focused on technical issues such as administrative costs and the implementation of contracts. While the EU recognises that political solutions are essential in complex humanitarian emergencies, ECHO draws a clear line in its own work between political processes and humanitarian relief. Nevertheless, NGO engagement has been increasing at the policy level as well as in operations on the ground. In 1996, gender and emergencies, and ethics in humanitarian aid were major subjects of dialogue, and the Commission acknowledges that NGOs have acquired a 'conceptual role' in rehabilitation.

ECHO has taken on outreach and capacity building activities, visiting capitals to meet NGOs, holding training sessions, financing technology transfer between NGOs in different EU countries, and developing relations with NGOs. Through its Network on Humanitarian Assistance, it also seeks to build human resources in specific areas such as law, logistics or epidemiology, so that skills will be available, as required, to both NGO and official humanitarian agencies.

There is EU–NGO dialogue on the linking of emergency, rehabilitation and development work. Haiti is given as an example of good collaboration on the transfer of responsibility for programmes moving from emergency to rehabilitation, and then to long-term development. Discussion on this topic takes place through task forces set up in 1996 to enable liaison between Commission agencies on rehabilitation and longer term development. These task forces are not open to NGOs.

FOOD AID

In 1996, the EU contribution of food aid through NGOs fell to ECU107 million (about $136 million) – half the previous year's amount, but still representing 21 per cent of the total, and 45 per cent of indirect food aid (that is, food aid channelled through international organisations).

The food aid programme is run by EURONAID – a service agency set up and managed by the 24 European and international NGOs that are the main users of food aid. Whether EURONAID should continue, or whether NGOs should relate directly and individually to the Commission has been a matter of debate. There is a marked difference between large and small NGOs, with smaller NGOs relying on the EURONAID service, and larger ones feeling that they could do better by themselves.[5] In 1996, for the first time NGOs were free to choose whether to implement their food aid operations through EURONAID or directly through the Commission. The majority was still undertaken by EURONAID.

In 1996, through a working group of the Liaison Committee, NGOs were actively engaged in discussions on the reform of EU food aid, aimed at influencing a new policy framework for food aid and food security due for launch late in 1997.

The EU has been the third largest food aid donor to Ethiopia since 1984; 75 per cent of the food has been supplied through NGOs and the number has, unsurprisingly, grown from fewer than 25 in 1984 to over a hundred in the mid 1990s. Over this period, NGOs were seen as a means of delivering food aid with a minimum of wastage or diversion to the military. A 1996 evaluation found that as a body, the EU had not been actively engaged in policy discussions on food aid, despite its engagement in other areas of policy development. NGOs in Ethiopia would have welcomed a more active role in the management of food aid, including support from the EU Delegation to help maximise benefits.[6] EU flexibility, however, and the decentralisation of decision-making to a local technical committee in the late 1990s, were seen as highly appropriate for achieving the best use of assistance through NGOs.

THE EUROPEAN VOLUNTEER SERVICE (EVS)

Launched in 1996, the EVS[7] aims primarily to offer young people a learning experience that broadens their horizons and familiarizes them with different social and cultural environments. At the same time, the scheme offers young people an opportunity to make a contribution to development projects. Initiatives may come from any EU organisation with a partner in a developing country, although it is also hoped in time that EU delegations will seek opportunities for volunteers in EU-supported projects. This forms a very small part – perhaps 5 per cent – of the wider initiative to engage young Europeans in volunteering throughout the Union.

Despite EVS's strong focus on solidarity, and the importance of engagement with the European public that underscores relations between DG VIII and NGOs, there has been little attempt to take advantage of this programme. The explicit priority on volunteer learning and the emphasis on youth make the programme difficult to access for many NGOs and for the Commission itself, where the main priority is the effective use of technical cooperation for sustainable development.

THE EU STRATEGY TOWARDS NGOS

There is a plethora of EU financial instruments for supporting NGO activities. The 1997 digest of these resources runs to 89 pages and covers 27 subjects, making any overall strategy difficult to ascertain.[8] The basic EU co-financing approach to NGOs is set out in its annual reports and in the preamble to its general conditions. As these are now ten years old, the degree to which they represent current EU strategy is uncertain. The stated purpose of co-financing, however, is 'to facilitate and strengthen action by European NGOs aimed at improving, on a durable basis, the living conditions and development prospects of beneficiaries'. The statement refers specifically to the commitment and support of the European public to solidarity at a non-governmental level, and to the hope that European NGOs will 'bear the message of the solidarity of the European public and of the Community as an entity to their partners and beneficiaries'. The policy is phrased in terms of mutual respect and responsibilities:

> *In its cooperation with NGOs, the Community undertakes to respect their pluralism, their independence and the specific nature of their operations, which are both an act of solidarity with the poorest, responding directly to their basic needs, and one of support for their self development.*[9]

The Commission places great emphasis on respect for the 'specificity of NGOs', and supports organisations that are innovative and flexible. It does seek coherence with EU policy, but this is applied in terms of best practice in sectoral approaches rather than to particular themes or sectors.

Annual Reports also stress the distinctive contribution of NGOs: participation, contributions to the basic democratic fabric of developing countries, and their ability to mobilise European public opinion and political leaders.[10] This is seen as complementary to other EU development assistance; for example: 'It is very important that NGDOs should complement the EU's efforts in the official cooperation programmes with developing countries.'[11]

The role of the EU Delegations

In achieving complementarity between the EU's development efforts and those of NGOs, both in long-term development and in emergency relief, the role of the Delegations is crucial. One of the findings of the Evaluation of Development Cooperation between the European Union and

Ethiopia was a lack of coherence between EU and NGO assistance, largely because of the lack of involvement of EU Delegation staff in co-financing.

For example, the evaluation found that an NGO co-financed rural conservation projects was located in the same zone as a large rural conservation project, also funded by the EC/EU but with no communication between the two. There has also been some evidence of incoherence between co-financed projects and government policy.[12]

On the issue of decentralised cooperation, discussed below, the absence of an understanding of NGOs by EU Delegations was noted as early as 1993.[13] A 1996 CLONG seminar on decentralised EU cooperation reported the need for new capacities and training in EU Delegations to ensure coherence and to prevent the possibility of deadline and disbursement pressures undermining development goals.

Increasing liaison between Northern and Southern NGOs, and between member states and Brussels, increases the potential for bringing incoherent policies and practices to light. The role of NGOs in monitoring the application of a policy such as decentralised cooperation can therefore be expected to have some positive effect.

DEVELOPMENT EDUCATION AND PUBLIC INFORMATION

The EU has been a significant source of development education support for NGOs. It has been particularly significant for countries like France and Britain, where official funding for development education has not, in recent years, been available from government.

The conditions governing co-financing of development education activities were established in 1988[14] and were aimed at improving solidarity between peoples of Europe and the 'Third World':

> *Only when the public is fully aware of these [development] problems can it play*
> *an active part in the search for appropriate responses to the problems themselves,*
> *and to the dangers they represent for peace and for economic and social progress*
> *throughout the world.*

The rationale also stresses the importance of avoiding false images of the South, which are 'sometimes hostile, often passive and almost always [show people] in distress, with all the consequences such images have on people's everyday behaviour and attitudes'. These last two points reflect preoccupations at the end of the 1980s, in contrast to more recent concerns about globalisation and mutual self-interest in development cooperation.

The EU supports development education with matching grants for 50 per cent of project costs, and 6 per cent of the EU share may be charged as a flat-rate contribution to administration. Fifteen per cent must come from private contributions, but the rest may come from public financing or from other partners. The EU will allow the value of human and other in-kind resources to be counted in the calculation. Project evaluation costs may be built into a proposal.

In 1995 a process emphasising strategy development and evaluation was started, with the establishment of a Development Education Forum. The Forum, which meets annually, debates improvements in strategy, and the diversification of NGO themes and target groups. An evaluation of development education projects in schools was initiated by the European Commission in 1995, in order to provide an assessment of the relevance, quality and results of 20 co-financed projects, the capacity of the promoting bodies, and the adequacy of Commission management and procedures.[15]

Evaluations of EU-supported development education suggest the need for NGOs to take a more strategic and longer-term approach – working, for example, with trade unions, or working more on the inclusion of development issues in school curricula.

EU guidelines have allowed NGOs to use a percentage of project budgets for development education. But in 1997 the Commission proposed an end to this option on the grounds that less

Table 25.2: *EU Funds for Development Education and Public Awareness, 1995*

Country	Number of Projects	Amount (ECU,000)	Share of EU Development Education Funds
Austria	5	333	2.1%
Belgium	22	1919	11.9%
Denmark	5	564	3.5%
France	15	1477	9.2%
Germany	27	2888	18.0%
Greece	3	213	1.3%
Ireland	8	674	4.2%
Italy	31	2141	13.3%
Luxembourg	1	74	0.5%
Netherlands	17	1637	10.2%
Portugal	3	337	2.1%
Spain	14	1254	7.8%
Sweden	1	56	0.4%
United Kingdom	22	2 265	14.1%
Total	**174**	**15,832**	

than 1.25 per cent of the funds available had been used for this purpose. According to the Commission, much of it seemed to have been spent on self-promotion by NGOs, rather than on raising public understanding of development issues. The Commission argued that NGOs wanting to undertake project-based development education should apply for standard development education co-financing in future. This would mean that all development education activities would be scrutinized under the same criteria. At the time of writing, no final decision had been reached. NGOs were not enthusiastic about this proposal.

ADVOCACY AND ENGAGEMENT

NGOs have invested heavily in building knowledge of EU institutions and mechanisms. To this end, some have placed staff in Brussels. Others are part of coalitions doing similar tasks. NGOs have coordinated their advocacy programmes to take account of the changing EU presidency every six months.

As is the case within many EU member states, there is a sense of common interest between the EU NGO Unit and NGO umbrella bodies, especially the Liaison Committee. Put crudely, Unit B2 needs to disburse funds, and the CLONG needs to ensure that its members can access them. It is in both of their interests to enable this to happen as painlessly as possible.

Increasingly, NGO advocacy focuses on the relationship between member states and the EU, not just on the Commission or on the quality of EU development cooperation per se. Serious attempts are being made to get members to take proper responsibility for EU aid. In the mid 1990s, some NGOs also worked on member state unwillingness to allow the Commission to take on extra staff while at the same time criticising its lack of capacity in critical areas such as social development. A policy focus within the EU on the 'three Cs' – complementarity, coherence and coordination – has aided this approach.[16]

NGO campaigns on coherence have become one of the success stories of the sector. Applying coordinated pressure on EU institutions in Brussels and Strasbourg, along with pressure on member state governments in their capitals, has proven extremely effective. The most frequently cited example is a campaign on beef dumping, which sought to end the negative impact of subsidised European beef exports on Sahelian pastoralists – who were at the same time being supported by EU development cooperation. The campaign took the form of a Europe-wide lobby at both national and international levels, making use of already established networks. It drew on detailed empirical research carried out in West Africa by NOVIB (Netherlands), Solagral (France) and Christian Aid (UK). It also employed political contacts in Belgium and the EU, courtesy of the Belgian Presidency.

After initial success, the campaign extended its geographical focus, looking at South Africa and Namibia. It also spawned a series of additional coherence campaigns on fisheries, chocolate, the arms trade and bananas. The focus on policy coherence has strengthened EU relationships with NGO units, both in Brussels and in member states, as such campaigns look outwards, seeking support from other ministries and departments rather than simply criticising aid policy and practice. Thus, NGOs and NGO units in member states find themselves on the same side of an issue.

Another priority area for advocacy, one of concern to the CLONG, is the role of development cooperation after the expiry of the Lomé Convention that governs relations between the EU and African, Caribbean and Pacific States (ACP).

EVALUATION

In addition to many project evaluations, DG VIII/B2 has in recent years commissioned four thematic NGO evaluations:

- evaluation of EU–NGO co-financing in relation to institutional support for grassroots organisations in developing countries (1993);
- evaluation of vocational training projects (1994);
- evaluation of integrated development projects (1994);
- evaluation of NGO credit and savings projects (1994).

An evaluation on decentralised cooperation was in progress at the time of writing. A full list of evaluations is maintained by and available from DG VIII.

Structurally, the management of evaluation has improved, with one unit in DG VIII now responsible for all evaluations, regardless of whether they lie in countries covered by DG I or DG VIII. There is also a perceived change in style, with more resources and greater openness. The NGO Unit encourages discussion and learning from evaluation, and has a strong wish to apply evaluation findings in guidelines for appraisal and project approval.

ECHO evaluation unit

ECHO began its evaluation activities in 1993. Initially it only evaluated specific operations, but latterly it has moved into evaluation of programmes, sectors and disaster preparedness. ECHO considers evaluation as a tool closely linked to its operational work, providing it with independent information that can facilitate decision-making and improvement of working methods.

The evaluation unit is independent of the operational services. It deals with requests for evaluation, selects consultants on the basis of sound field experience and objectivity, gathers data, works on logistics and monitors methodology. Evaluations are aimed primarily at ECHO itself and its partners. ECHO operational services and partners (international organisations and NGOs) receive terms of reference and consultants' CVs. Evaluations start with a preliminary briefing in ECHO and end with a debriefing session at which evaluators discuss their draft report with representatives of the evaluation unit, operational services and, sometimes, other parts of the European Commission. The partner agency is invited to discuss the evaluation results with ECHO. During 1996 and 1997, 91 evaluation reports were drawn up.

ECHO has stated its keenness to improve its working methods and share its experience with all those involved in the field of humanitarian aid. To this end, two seminars on evaluation have been organised – one for member states and one for ECHO partners. Participants believe that the level of dialogue could be deepened and such seminars made more productive. A manual of evaluation of humanitarian aid was published in 1996 and outlines basic methodology. At the beginning of 1998, it was being revised, and a new edition was expected to be completed later in the year.

The evaluation unit is very modestly resourced (four professional staff, two of whom are on short-term contracts, and one secretary), and partly for this reason, access to evaluations and dissemination of findings is not extensive. For instance, while the manual states that an annual report on activities will be produced, there was no prospect of one as of early 1998. As a result, there is scope for improvement in the opportunities for learning from evaluation.

Lessons from evaluation

The 1996 evaluation of EU development cooperation in Ethiopia produced some interesting findings on NGOs from a developing country perspective:

- NGO co-financing as an instrument had proven highly relevant in Ethiopia;
- its focus on poverty alleviation reflected the needs of Ethiopian people;
- it was able to reach populations inaccessible via official aid;
- there was beneficiary engagement and a process approach;
- projects were given the flexibility by Brussels to reallocate unspent funds and to change direction;
- objectives were often unclear, and were not output-oriented;
- effectiveness was generally positive, particularly in social dimensions;
- the Commission's criteria for eligibility encouraged participation in project design;
- there were some weaknesses – particularly around issues of gender and participation – in assessment, monitoring and evaluation;
- sustainability was mixed, and not enough was done to involve local government structures in planning and implementation.

The evaluation highlighted two issues – the first was a *laissez faire* approach by the EU Delegation. It was seen as inappropriate for the EU to be involved in project planning. As a result, NGO autonomy was left unchallenged, but limitations in the NGO approach were not addressed. The centralised EU co-financing process meant that the delegation had little responsibility for NGO matters, and the weight of the overall workload encouraged the lack of attention to NGOs. This limited EU capacity to ensure coherence with its own official aid programmes, and to address issues such as geographical spread or local capacity-building in NGO projects.

NGOs in Ethiopia were complimentary about the clarity of EU procedures, multi-year funding, block grants that enabled rapid disbursement, and the minimal reporting requirements. Areas of criticism included slow response to project proposals, and the centralised decision making in Brussels. While the advantages to NGOs of working this way are clear, achieving the best possible results for poverty reduction depend on the effectiveness and maturity of the NGOs in the first place.

KEY DEVELOPMENTS AND ISSUES

Two opposing forces shape the current state of relations between the Commission and NGOs. On the one hand, the Commission is called upon by member states to be more accountable, and to avoid waste. Examples of misspending are eagerly reported by the media. In particular, the special treatment given to NGOs under co-financing agreements has to be justified on the basis of special NGO attributes. On the other hand, the Commission is also accused by governments and the media of being cumbersome and bureaucratic, and is told to cut red tape.

These two forces produced the so-called 'Elewijt Process' (see below), under which NGOs are being asked to define themselves and to clarify their status, competence and legitimacy. It has also encouraged the Commission to revisit its General Conditions for Co-financing, with a view to streamlining procedures.

Defining NGOs: the Elewijt process and the NGO Charter

At a 1994 meeting at Elewijt in Belgium, it was noted that NGOs were receiving more than a billion ECU a year from over 40 different EU budget lines. Since then, the Commission has been pressing for NGOs to define themselves, arguing that a clearer concept of what it means to be an NGO would ensure better understanding, and therefore better dialogue between officials and the NGO community. It would also lead to more straightforward financial and administrative procedures. Within the Commission, officials deal with many external partner organisations, and many want to know what is special about NGOs, and why NGOs should be treated differently from other organisations.

Since the Elewijt Meeting, extensive dialogue has taken place between the Commission and NGOs on the structure of EU–NGO relations, with both parties conducting research and consultation on the issues involved. On behalf of the NGOs, CLONG drafted position papers in 1996 that aimed to clarify questions of NGO identity and added value. Meetings between NGOs and the Commission discussed the NGO approach to development, and NGO links with civil society – both in the EU and in the South. A key issue for NGOs has been how to define NGOs in a way that would assist the Commission without unduly restricting the scope and dynamism of the NGO movement. In 1996, the Commission reassured CLONG that it would be flexible in its interpretation of any NGO definition, so that NGOs that do not fully satisfy the criteria will not be automatically excluded from official support.

NGOs find themselves in a dilemma. They do not welcome the idea of extending the range of organisations eligible for co-financing, but they do not want to set hard and fast definitions of what counts as an NGO. This issue is likely to become more pressing with the accession of new members with different views on NGOs. The accession of Austria, for example, where NGOs are responsible for implementing very large parts of the aid programme under a national principle of subsidiarity, has raised real difficulties around definition and eligibility. Prior to accession, Austrian NGOs thought they would receive significant funding from Brussels. They quickly became frustrated, however, with a process that required them to 'fight against the prejudice that they were not proper NGOs because their income did not include a high enough proportion of private donations'.[17]

By mid 1997, the Elewijt process had reached an important stage, with the publication by CLONG of an NGO Charter. This identifies basic principles to which development and humanitarian aid NGOs are expected to adhere. It does not attempt to define NGOs in terms of structure, approach or values. Rather it identifies some basic characteristics to which most NGOs can subscribe. NGO National Platforms – for instance in Italy – are already using the charter as part of their own membership criteria. It remains to be seen, however, whether the charter will do enough to satisfy the Commission's desire for clarity in its relationship with NGOs.

Reform of the General Conditions for Co-financing

An update of the EU's 1988 General Conditions for Co-financing is long overdue and, at the time of writing, was a major topic of discussion between the Commission and NGOs. Both

NGOs and the Commission saw the revision as an opportunity to improve technical aspects of the relationship, such as the administrative percentage that NGOs can add to project proposals. The revision was also an opportunity to take account of the overall NGO role within EU development cooperation.

During the first half of 1997, the Commission outlined some of the principles underlying its approach to revising co-financing conditions. These included the need to ensure coherence and complementarity between NGO and EU development approaches, the Commission's wish to support initiatives emerging from EU civil society, and its desire to strengthen the professional capacities of NGOs. Under the proposed new conditions, the Commission has suggested the possibility of financing through framework contracts with networks of operational NGOs.

The reduction of co-financing bottlenecks

A major issue for NGOs in recent years has been the lack of capacity within the Commission. A recruitment freeze has meant that staff numbers have not kept pace with the increased workload. The result has been long delays in the processing of applications and reports.

A direct response to this problem was the 1997 establishment of the Co-financing Support Programme (CSP), under the auspices of CLONG. Under the CSP, a team of advisers based in CLONG and member states, and responsible to National Platforms, has been established.[18] The advisers will monitor and advise on the presentation of co-financing documents, reviewing proposals and reports to ensure that they follow procedures and contain the necessary information. The idea is to strengthen NGOs, identifying difficulties and training needs, and then to offer support and training to overcome problems. A likely consequence will be that officials in DG VIII/B2 will be able to focus their expertise on content, increasing the speed with which the Commission can respond.

Broad policy dialogue

In 1996, the Commission and CLONG began to explore the potential for increased dialogue on specific geographical and sectoral policies, such as the EU's approach to micro credit, decentralised cooperation, issues in the Great Lakes, Angola and Haiti, and questions such as the relief-rehabilitation-development 'continuum'.

The Commission has spoken of its wish to tap NGO expertise in areas such as capacity-building and has suggested that it might be possible to identify joint implementation guidelines for areas where both NGOs and the EU are active. The Commission has stressed the need to respect each others' autonomy and capacities, as well as the need to learn from each others' successes and failures.

Development NGOs have not yet been involved by DG VIII in EU Delegations to UN summit meetings, something that is common practice for many donors. This is clearly possible, however, within the EU system. DG XI has been assiduous, for example, in involving NGOs in the Rio process.

Decentralised cooperation

'Decentralised cooperation' covers a wide swathe of activity. In many countries, the term is used to include initiatives by towns, cities, partnership organisations and direct cooperation relationships (a marked trend in Italy). It also supports greater involvement of grassroots civil society organisations in the South. To quote the Commission:

> *Decentralized cooperation is now one of the priorities of EU aid and development policy. Its aim is to create a form of cooperation more in line with the needs of the people concerned, the social and economic agents, by granting more room for manoeuvre and more autonomy and responsibilities to the active forces in civil society.*[19]

This has raised many issues for European NGOs and for the Commission in its development of direct relations with Southern NGOs (see role of EU Delegations, above).

Southern NGOs have been enthusiastic about the development of decentralised cooperation. It offers them both a source of funding and a source of influence. Some have seen it as an opportunity to raise questions concerning the quality of EU cooperation, and an opportunity to engage in debate. The response among European NGOs is more differentiated. Some are concerned about the possibility of direct funding, citing the lack of experience of Southern NGOs in liaising with official bodies, and expressing concern about undermining their participatory values. A less charitable interpretation of their concern would be simple fear of competition over resources. There has been little welcome for the idea that fire brigades or city councils might become competitors in the delivery of development services.

This, combined with a fear that decentralised cooperation may undermine the role of developing country governments, has meant less enthusiasm from some NGOs than might have been expected. However, it is one of the key focuses of NGOs in CLONG – as evidenced in a pilot project on NGO involvement in decentralised cooperation, and in the quarterly publication, Liaison South. European NGOs support the concept of local participatory development that is embodied in decentralised cooperation, but have preferred to delegate the role of policy dialogue with the Commission to the Liaison Committee and collaborating networks.

Decentralised cooperation is a challenge to European NGOs to develop new roles for themselves, and it comes at the same time as pressure from the Commission for greater NGO accountability and definition. Nevertheless, there are real opportunities for NGOs – in capacity-building with Southern NGOs, for example, and with EU Delegations. Decentralised cooperation is also encouraging new approaches. The Lomé Convention has formed the centrepiece of EU aid for over two decades, but it is only since the 1995 Mid-term Review of Lomé IV that greater emphasis on decentralised cooperation has encouraged close NGO involvement. As some people see it, this shifted Lomé from being essentially a government-to-government agreement to one that also stresses the participation of civil society.

The role of NGOs in difficult political situations

South Africa and Ethiopia are examples of countries where relationships with the EU and NGOs have had to change radically in response to a changing external environment. The 1996 *Evaluation of Development Cooperation with Ethiopia* found that during the Mengistu regime, NGOs were a valuable channel of assistance:

> *During the Derg, co-financing provided an alternative aid channel to projects financed under the Lomé framework, which enabled more marginal regions of the country to be reached by European aid. And during the civil war, NGO co-financed projects were implemented in areas under the control of the Tigrayan and Eritrean liberation movements, which would not have been reached through EDF-funded projects.*

However, as the situation changed, NGOs became subject to much tighter national regulation by the Ethiopian Relief and Rehabilitation Commission, and the process of regionalisation changed the nature of NGO–government relations. NGOs reportedly took the view that the EU should have used its intermediary position much more in order to mediate the dispute, and to use its influence with government to improve relations. The evaluation noted a lack of engagement by EU Delegation staff on NGO co-financing, but pointed out interesting situational differences. Under the Derg, for example, there was a lack of coherence between NGO projects and government policy – probably a good thing. However, under more enlightened economic policies, this is considered a weakness, and closer involvement of the EU Delegation could have facilitated better NGO–government cooperation.

Similarly, in South Africa the Commission Annual Report noted that in 1995 there was a major shift away from NGOs as the main implementing agents in the European Programme for Reconstruction and Development in South Africa (EPRD). The South African Government is now the main implementing agent, with EU aid focused on a small number of programmes that dovetail with government priorities. NGO involvement has been maintained, but on a different scale and with different relations. NGOs, for example, will be responsible for the human rights programme and the Transitional National Development Trust (TNDT), created in 1995 to ensure the continuation of financial support to local NGOs.

26 The World Bank[1]

Ian Smillie

SUMMARY

Relations between the World Bank and NGOs were limited through the 1960s and 1970s, grew somewhat during the 1980s, and began to expand dramatically in the 1990s. Contacts have ranged from collaborative arrangements on project planning and delivery, to policy dialogue and some of the most vituperative criticism in the history of development assistance. This chapter attempts to describe the evolution and maturation of the relationship, the growing number of collaborative contacts, as well as the extent and nature of 'policy dialogue' between the Bank and NGOs.

THE BANK

The World Bank and the International Monetary Fund (IMF) emerged from deliberations that took place at Bretton Woods, New Hampshire, in 1944. The aim was to establish a blueprint for global economic governance that would prevent a recurrence of the great depression of the 1930s and the fascism and war that it spawned. The primary concerns of the 400 delegates from 44 countries who attended the Bretton Woods meeting were full employment and improved human welfare, based on an international system that could monitor and regulate the international trading arena, and assist national financial systems in times of crisis.

The World Bank aimed to create long-term conditions for growth and, according to John Maynard Keynes, its broad purpose was 'to develop the resources and productive capacity of the world, with special attention to the less developed countries, [and] to raise the standard of life and conditions of labour everywhere'.[2] This 1944 description is not significantly different from one used in 1997 to describe the Bank's new 'Strategic Compact': 'The objective of the Strategic Compact is to achieve greater effectiveness in the World Bank's basic mission – reducing poverty – through the delivery of better products and services for our clients. In so doing, the Bank will reaffirm its position as the premier global development institution – a respected leader and partner in the business of catalysing knowledge and financial resources in the fight against poverty'.[3]

Technically a specialised agency of the United Nations, the World Bank Group comprises a number of institutions, including the International Finance Corporation (IFC), the Multilateral Investment Guarantee Agency (MIGA), and the International Centre for Settlement of Investment Disputes (ICSID). The term 'World Bank', however, normally refers to the two main institutions, the International Bank for Reconstruction and Development (IBRD), and the International Development Association (IDA). The IBRD works primarily in middle-income countries, financing its lending operations mainly through international capital markets. This enables the Bank to lend to developing countries at more favourable terms that would be available on the open market. Most IBRD loans are repayable over 15 to 20 years, with a five-year grace period.

The International Development Agency, established in 1958, shares staff and facilities with the IBRD, and lends to the poorest countries on concessional terms. These include 35–40 year repayment periods, no interest, and a ten-year grace period. IDA is supported through contributions, known as 'replenishments', from wealthier member countries. Loans are made to member governments, which in turn pass them on to public or private agencies. The Bank is supervised by a Board of Governors, comprising one representative from each member country. A 24-member Board of Executive Directors meets more frequently to decide Bank policy and approve loans and credit proposals. Voting rights are allocated in accordance with the proportion of a member's financial contribution. The United States, for example, casts over 15 per cent of the votes. In 1997, Japan had 6.1 per cent of the votes, China 2.89 per cent and Australia 1.42 per cent.

THE BANK'S DEFINITION OF NGOS

A 1989 Operational Directive on NGO collaboration observed that the diversity of NGOs strains any simple definition or classification. 'NGOs include a wide variety of groups and institutions that are entirely or largely independent of government and characterized primarily by humanitarian or cooperative, rather than commercial, objectives'. These organisations engage in activities 'to relieve suffering, promote the interests of the poor, protect the environment, provide basic social services, or undertake community development... While most of the NGOs with which the Bank works are implementation organisations, some NGOs focus primarily on the advocacy of specific changes in policies or approaches to development'.[4] Operational NGOs have been subdivided by the Bank into three further categories: community-based organisations (CBOs), national organisations working in one country, and international organisations, usually based in a developed country and working in several countries in the South. A revised 'good practice' directive on NGOs was under discussion in 1997.

THE BANK AND NGOS IN THE 1970S AND 1980S

Formal relations between the World Bank and NGOs began slowly, with little meaningful contact before 1970. Between 1972 and 1979, there was NGO involvement in a handful of Bank-supported projects, but these represented less than 5 per cent of the total. Dialogue on the possibility of direct funding to NGOs began in 1979, a dialogue that would continue without much result for the next two decades. In 1982 an NGO–World Bank Committee was formed to examine ways in which the Bank could enhance the involvement of NGOs in Bank-supported projects. At the time, many Northern NGOs suspected that the Bank's interest in the non-profit sector was a public relations move, and from the outset they pushed for more substantive involvement. In 1984, Southern NGOs were added to the committee, which now represents all geographic regions. There are five members each from Africa, Asia, Latin America/Caribbean and Europe (one of them from Eastern Europe), four from North America/Pacific, one each from Central Asia and the Middle East, and two additional international members. In recent years, committee interests have tended to focus primarily on policy dialogue, with emphasis on structural adjustment and popular participation.

NGO members of the World Bank Committee collectively form the NGO Working Group on the World Bank (NGOWG), which meets independently and maintains a rotating secretariat housed in the offices of one of the member agencies. In the mid 1990s, a decentralisation of the consultation process began, with one annual meeting in Washington and a second meeting in each of the three major Southern regions in order to enable wider participation.

Through the 1980s, NGO involvement in Bank projects increased to an average of 8 per cent of all projects, although by 1989, the total had risen to 21 per cent. During this period the Bank employed one or two individuals to broaden the dialogue with NGOs, but it was not until 1988 that a full-fledged 'NGO Unit' was established, with four high-level staff and the occasional consultant, sometimes seconded from an NGO. The unit has had various homes over the years, first in External Affairs, reinforcing an NGO suspicion that it was a public relations issue for the Bank. Then it moved to Human Resources and in 1997 fell within the Bank's environmental ambit. Expanded collaboration with NGOs was mandated by the 1989 Operational Directive mentioned above, with emphasis on NGO involvement in project design. An NGO data base was established, training courses on NGOs were run for Bank staff, and discussions on direct funding continued.

During this latter period, policy dialogue between the Bank and NGOs continued apace, with NGOs becoming more stridently critical of Bank policies on structural adjustment and calling for greater transparency and popular participation in Bank decision-making.

THE BANK AND NGOS IN THE 1990S

Operational collaboration

Operational collaboration between NGOs and the Bank increased dramatically in the 1990s, with some form of NGO involvement in an estimated 48 per cent of Bank projects approved in 1996.[5] The Bank's NGO Unit and members of the NGO Working Group suggest that this number should be treated with caution, as in some cases the involvement may be minor. The highest levels of collaboration took place in South Asia (76 per cent of all projects) and Sub-Saharan Africa (56 per cent), with sectoral involvement most prominent in agriculture (92 per cent of the projects) and the social sector (88 per cent of the projects). There was an overlap in the types of NGOs involved, although by far the most prominent involvement was among national in-country NGOs (74 per cent of the NGO-related projects) and CBOs (53 per cent). International NGOs figured in only 15 per cent of the NGO-related projects, a significant downturn over the early years of Bank–NGO collaboration.

'Operational collaboration' can mean different things, ranging from informal consultation to consultancies and contracts for project execution. At the participation end of the spectrum, in the late 1980s, in response to members of the NGO–World Bank Committee, the Bank began a 'participation learning process'. This involved the formation of a Participatory Development Learning Group of Bank staff who eventually prepared *The World Bank and Participation* (1994), with an action plan to mainstream participation into the Bank's work.

At the consultation end of the spectrum, NGOs are increasingly involved in a variety of Bank planning processes, from poverty assessments through to national environmental action plans. NGOs participated, for example, in workshops to discuss the *Forest Strategy Paper for Sub-Saharan Africa*, the *India Family Planning Strategy*, and the *Morocco Women in Development Strategy Paper*. NGOs may be involved in project identification and project design, and in a few cases, they may contribute their own resources to project implementation. The most frequent form of collaboration, however, is in the implementation stage, where NGOs have sometimes been contracted for project management services, service delivery, training and community development work.

As a general rule, the Bank does not directly fund NGOs. There are, however, some exceptions that fall under the general rubric of the Special Grants Program. In fiscal year 1996, approximately $5.34 million was disbursed to NGOs through a variety of mechanisms:

The World Bank Small Grants Program

Established in 1983 to promote dialogue on development issues of interest to the Bank, this programme supports conferences, seminars, publications and other forms of networking. Grants range in size from $10,000 to $15,000, with a total outlay in 1996 of $600,000. Since 1997, the programme has focused exclusively on developing country organisations.

The Safe Motherhood Special Grants Program

Initiated in 1988, this fund promotes reduction in maternal mortality and morbidity, focusing on maternal health advocacy, research and project interventions. In fiscal year 1996, $800,000 was disbursed through international organisations and NGOs.

Consultative Group to Assist the Poorest (CGAP)

CGAP is a multi-donor initiative, started in 1995 to increase the resources available for micro-finance lending. A Policy Advisory Group includes a number of leading micro-finance NGOs, although much of the $200 million pledged by donor countries is administered directly by themselves. The Bank's $30 million three-year core fund is being administered by a CGAP Secretariat, with $3.3 million disbursed in FY96.

Social Funds

Between 1986 and 1996, the Bank channelled over $1.3 billion into more than 30 Social Funds (SF) in Asia, Africa, Latin America and Eastern Europe. Social Funds are designed to be 'rapid, demand-driven funding mechanisms which channel resources to community-level development projects according to a set of predetermined selection criteria. They do not implement projects themselves, but finance subprojects proposed by other public, private and voluntary (formal and informal) organisations'.[6] In some cases, NGOs have been critical of both the concept and the impact of social funds. In several cases, however, they have played an important role in the design and delivery of the funds. The Bank estimates that NGOs have sponsored and/or implemented between 15 and 20 per cent of the total SF subprojects, and that about 15 per cent of total SF disbursements have been channelled through NGOs. At a more informal level, NGOs and CBOs may have been involved in one way or another in 45 to 50 per cent of the subprojects.

Other

Other funds include the *Population NGOs Special Grants Program* ($850,000 in fiscal year 1996) and a new programme established in 1996, the *Mutilation and Adolescent Reproductive Health Special Grants Program*, which disbursed $450,000 in fiscal year 1996 to NGOs and others working on female genital mutilation and adolescent reproductive health. NGOs may also receive support through an *Institutional Development Fund*. This is intended primarily for public sector capacity building projects, but governments have, on occasion, taken IDF grants and channelled them on the NGOs. Approval was expected in fiscal year 1997 for a $10 million multi-donor project in support of NGOs in the West Bank and Gaza.

Contracts

More than half the Bank's funds are disbursed from Washington to suppliers and contractors, mainly in the private sector. The Bank is reputed to be the single largest source of work for the international consulting industry. Contracts may be of interest to some NGOs, but the Bank's preferred method of procuring services, through competitive bidding, effectively excludes most NGOs because of the large size of most contracts. There are exceptions, usually invoked under 'special circumstances'. Among these are 'local competitive bidding', a simplified process for national NGOs and other local organisations. 'Local shopping' (three competitive bids) and sole-source contracts may also be used in special cases where projects are small, scattered or are carried out in remote areas.

Capacity building

Much of the Bank's work with NGOs during the mid 1990s has focused on building the capacity of both the Bank and NGOs for more mutually beneficial collaboration. In recent years, NGO Liaison Officers have been appointed in resident Bank missions overseas to serve as a point of contact for NGOs and other civil society organisations, to gather and maintain information about the NGO sector, to facilitate policy dialogue and to support NGO involvement in Bank activities. By mid 1996, there were full-time NGO liaison officers in 34 resident missions, and 15 part-timers.

Capacity-building workshops and training programmes have become a common feature of the NGO–Bank relationship. The Economic Development Institute (EDI), which is the Bank's training and learning branch, has worked with FICONG (*Fortalecimiento Institucional y Capacitacion para Organizaciones non Gubernamentales*) in Latin America on workshops and seminars dealing with the legal framework for the NGO sector, reform of urban policies and decentralisation. Between 1991 and 1997, some 100 NGOs in 13 countries were involved. In West Africa the Bank has supported IRED, an NGO network and training organisation, to develop training manuals on planning and management for NGOs in several Francophone countries. In 1997, EDI was developing a programme known as *Learning and Action to Mainstream Participation* (LAMP) to strengthen partnerships between government, donors and NGOs on gender-sensitive participatory approaches to the design and implementation of development programmes.

Research and analysis

Over the years, the World Bank has conducted wide-ranging research into economic, social and other issues aimed at providing information and advice on its lending portfolio. In recent years, NGOs have become a more active part of this work, both as participants and as subjects. NGOs, for example, are becoming a more regular source of information and advice in the preparation of Country Assistance Strategies, the documents that set out the overall framework for Bank activities in a given country. The Bank undertakes a number of Poverty Assessments each year, and these frequently draw on NGOs for information, advice and background research. The Bank also involves NGOs in sectoral studies. In 1996, for example, a Dutch NGO worked with the Bank on an evaluation of policy options for improving primary education in Kenya.

A Bank Operational Directive requires that affected communities, including NGOs where appropriate, be consulted during environmental assessments in projects likely to have a significant environmental impact. In some cases, NGOs have been more actively involved. CARE, for example, was engaged to carry out a socio-economic and cultural survey in connection with the *Nam Theun 2 Hydroelectric Project* in Laos which planned, *inter alia*, to displace 21 communities.

The Bank has also initiated work in recent years on the subject of NGO–state relations. Three studies had been completed by 1997: Uganda (1994), West Bank/Gaza (1995) and Bangladesh (1996). The Bank has also begun to examine the overall question of the legal framework for NGOs. In recent years, the legislation under which NGOs operate has, in many countries, been tightened, with arbitrary and unpredictable decisions causing considerable disruption for both organisations and their projects. In 1995 the International Center for Non-Profit Law (ICNL) was engaged by the Bank to carry out a study of existing practice and to offer lessons and recommendations for good practice. A discussion draft, *Handbook on Good Practises for Laws Relating to Non-Governmental Organisations*, was published in 1997, with a planned revision and updating in 1998.

Policy dialogue

A Bank report notes that 'in addition to collaborating with the Bank in operations and research, NGOs play an important role as advocates for policy change and institutional reform'.[7] From the NGO perspective, the aim is to change or influence Bank policies and procedures. As noted elsewhere, the 'dialogue' has often been acrimonious, and has sometimes been carried out in the form of street demonstrations and angry NGO denunciations of Bank policies and programmes. With the arrival of James Wolfensohn as Bank President in 1995, this began to change.

The new approach to policy dialogue has taken several forms. The President took a personal role in holding meetings with NGO groups and leaders in many different countries, often on particular environmental, poverty or gender issues, and on structural adjustment. In addition, a number of new structural arrangements have been made to enhance dialogue around key developmental issues. In 1996 an *External Gender Consultative Group*, comprising 14 gender experts and NGO leaders, was constituted to meet with the Bank on a regular basis to exchange information and views on gender programmes and policies. An NGO Focus Group was formed in 1996 to advise a newly appointed *Social Strategy Task Force* aimed at examining and improving the Bank's work in social development. An *Interagency Group on Participation*, formed in 1995, includes representatives of NGOs, bilateral and multilateral agencies and aims to promote information-sharing and learning on issues related to participatory development. Twenty Bank projects have been designated as 'participation flagships' and have been marked for closer monitoring and reporting.

For more than a decade, a great deal of NGO attention has been devoted to the structural adjustment programmes promoted by the World Bank. Structural adjustment has been a key feature in Bank lending programmes, and has been based on the idea that the short-term social and economic distress of the adjustment process is far outweighed by the long-term economic gains that will be achieved.

Many NGOs have argued, on the other hand, that structural adjustment programmes have hurt the poorest in society, have undermined essential social services, and have not delivered the promised longer-term benefits. This debate, at times bitter and acrimonious, has characterised many Bank–NGO meetings, and has been a feature of discussion at the NGO World Bank Committee for many years. In 1995, a group of NGOs, coordinated by the US Development Group for Alternative Policies (DGAP), proposed a series of public meetings in developing countries to examine the impact of structural adjustment lending over the previous decade. The President of the Bank asked Bank staff and the NGOs to refine the proposal, and as a result, a plan for a joint, participatory review of structural adjustment was agreed, with a start-up in mid 1997. The Structural Adjustment Participatory Review Initiative (SAPRI) is managed by a joint steering committee with responsibility for objectives, approach, methodology and country selection criteria.

The Bank, of course, is an inter-governmental organisation, and policy dialogue between NGOs and the Bank will always be affected by the level of government involvement. Some governments were, for example, reluctant participants in the SAPRI process, while others simply rejected it.

Evaluation

A planning paper produced by the Bank's Operations Evaluation Department (OED) notes that progress in the operational relationship with NGOs has not been simple.

> *First, the Bank rarely lends directly to NGOs, and must operate through governments and in conformity with governments' policies towards NGOs. Second, NGOs and the Bank may, at times, appear not to share the same organisational values, missions or objectives... Third, Bank and borrower procedures may create obstacles to efficient working relations with NGOs. Fourth, while a small number of NGOs have grown to become large and professional organisations, most remain small and work at a scale that is smaller than the Bank's. Lastly, the Bank itself may have been slow to respond to the new policy agenda [on NGOs]. Whereas some Bank task managers have been quick to involve NGOs in their work, others have not.*[8]

Although there have been claims of widespread NGO involvement in Bank projects in recent years, this has not been systematically quantified and, although there is some evidence of improved quality in programmes that have involved NGOs, none of this has been seriously evaluated in a systematic way.

As a result, in 1997, the Bank began an evaluation process aimed at answering the following question: Does NGO involvement improve the performance of projects supported by the Bank? A sub-set of questions follows:

- If NGO involvement improves the performance of Bank-supported projects, where, how, and under what circumstances is this achieved? What can the Bank do to strengthen the performance further?
- If NGO involvement does not improve the performance of Bank-supported projects, or if improvement is achieved only at a high cost, what constrains NGO effectiveness? And what can the Bank do to relieve these constraints?
- When should NGO involvement in Bank-supported projects not be sought because it is ineffective or disadvantageous for the stakeholders involved?

The results of this study, expected in 1998, are likely to have an important role in shaping the future directions of Bank–NGO operational collaboration.

ISSUES

In its guide to operational collaboration with NGOs, the Bank's *Working with NGOs* spells out a number of 'key issues in working with NGOs'.[9]

Identifying an appropriate NGO partner

The Bank outlines three areas of concern in identifying an NGO partner. The first is gathering good information about the NGO sector in a given country; the second has to do with the establishment of selection criteria; and the third has to do with the selection process. At issue are the credibility, the specific competencies and track record, and the representivity of a particular NGO. The issue of representivity is a thorny one, spanning the spectrum of organisations from grassroots CBO to the NGOs sitting on the NGO–World Bank Committee. There has been a feeling in recent years that this committee, which is self-selecting, is not always representative of either NGOs or NGO views. There are plans to decentralise it to country and regional levels, and to spell out more clearly what its rights and responsibilities are, in an effort to make it more attractive to a broader cross-section of NGO leaders. There is a sentiment within the Bank that it may have been listening to the wrong NGOs – the loudest, and those in, or closest to, Washington.

One change that has taken place in recent years is a much greater reliance on the views and services of CBOs and national NGOs, rather than the international NGOs that once dominated the relationship.

Time and flexibility

Working with NGOs cites NGO comments about the bureaucratic procedures and delays involved in working with the Bank, and notes that delay can be particularly detrimental to schemes that promote participatory projects. For example if NGOs are obliged to use the Bank's competitive bidding procedures for procurement, they may be locked into a lengthy process (of up to 34 steps) for the purchase of any item over $1000. Similarly, flexibility – an NGO hallmark – is often difficult if not impossible within a standard Bank loan agreement.

Financial issues

Many NGOs approach the Bank and participate in Bank-initiated programmes in the hope that funding will become available. There are Bank grant mechanisms for small amounts (described above), and the Bank can negotiate or encourage a contracting relationship. Often, however, Bank officials are simply interested in learning from the NGO experience, or want the legitimation that may come with widespread consultation. There may, in fact, be no money for NGOs at all. The lack of resources for NGOs has caused some confusion, with an expectation of free services on the part of some Bank officials, and the expectation of some kind of remuneration on the part of NGOs.

Whether NGOs come to the Bank for money or dialogue, there is a cost involved, one which most smaller NGOs simply cannot afford. As a result, much of the Bank's interaction over the years has been with larger NGOs, and more especially with American NGOs that are based in Washington or have an office there.

Where a contract *has* been negotiated, a further issue can arise: overheads. *Working with NGOs* takes an approach all too rare among donor agencies in recognising that overhead costs can vary dramatically, depending on the activity and the organisation involved. 'It is important for Task Managers to ensure that NGOs understand what constitutes legitimate overhead costs for the Bank and how various fees and costs should be categorized... Local NGOs with limited experience in dealing with donors sometimes fail to include any overhead costs in their initial proposals and, as a result, find it difficult to satisfactorily fulfill project commitments'.

Delays in disbursement can be problematic in two ways. Delays in payment from the Bank side (perhaps because of delays within a government agency) can be damaging to a project and, in some cases, to the financial health of an NGO, most of which have little or no liquidity. On the other hand, pressure from the Bank to disburse against preset targets that have become inappropriate with time can also cause problems within a project.

NGO–government relations

An inter-governmental organisation, the Bank works first and foremost with governments. In some countries, relations between NGOs and government are excellent, and there are few problems in establishing working relationships on Bank-supported projects. In many countries, however, the relationship is antagonistic, with NGOs (or at least some NGOs) refusing to work with government, and vice versa. Making NGO involvement a requirement in project develop-ment, therefore, does not always make sense. *Working with NGOs* describes the problems that arose between government and NGOs in a 1986 Guatemala social fund. Attempts to involve Ghanaian NGOs in a similar fund were unsuccessful because of government heavy-handedness. Sri Lankan NGOs refused to become involved in a Sri Lanka fund until a widely-feared govern-ment commission of inquiry into NGO activities was completed. In Ghana, government was mistrustful of NGOs, and in Sri Lanka, the opposite was the case. There are other issues in addition to those identified by the Bank.

Advocacy

One Bank official has commented that the relationship between the Bank and NGOs is perhaps more honest than the relationship between NGOs and other donor organisations, because it is almost completely unleavened by money. Whereas most Swedish NGOs, for example, have a financial relationship with SIDA, few have any financial dealings with the World Bank, and so are less constrained in stating a point of view than might otherwise be the case.

The Structural Adjustment Participatory Review Initiative (SAPRI) will likely be a testing ground for the kind of relationship that will develop in the future. There is a feeling in some quarters that this may be 'yesterday's issue' in the sense that structural adjustment programmes have evolved over the years to take into account many of the criticisms made by NGOs. Other issues, however, loom. Among them are transparency, participation, debt, and trade-offs between industrial development and the environment. The pivot of these debates – the Bank's focus on economic growth and the private sector – may become the new central point of contention between it and activist NGOs.

'NGO-creep'

Among some NGOs there is a feeling that the leopard cannot change its spots. Long-time critic, Bruce Rich, uses the environment to make a point. He quotes then Bank President Robert McNamara speaking at the 1972 Stockholm Environment Conference about how the Bank's environmental office reviewed 'each project processed by the Bank' and conducted 'careful in-house studies' of the ecological components, using comprehensive environmental criteria embodied in checklists that 'encompass the entire spectrum of development'. But, Rich says, 'the statements had no basis in reality. In 1972, the environmental office consisted of one senior advisor and a recently hired assistant. The environmental review of every project and 'success-ful implementation' of 'safeguards' were, in any meaningful sense of the words, non-existent'. The subsequent experience of environmentalists with Bank lending for large dam projects, forced resettlement and coal-fired power generation tended to vindicate what Rich said, and to build support for his position: 'Fifty years of the Bank as we know it is enough. If, indeed, the role of multilateral institutions is an important one in the new world order, the World Bank must liter-ally remake itself, open its files, end its secret ways and document and learn from its mistakes – not merely on projects, but in the foundations of its economic policy prescriptions.'[10]

Within the Bank there is a contrary view, that there has been a kind of 'NGO-creep' – a gradual insinuation of NGOs at all levels of planning and policy, without a clear idea in the Bank, or among NGOs, about where this is leading. In fact general donor fascination with NGOs and with the larger construct of civil society may be fuelling some of the backlash that now exists among borrowers on the whole issue of 'good governance'.

There are several reasons why NGOs have become important to the Bank. Some of the reasons are given in *Working with NGOs*: the innovative and experimental nature of NGOs can provide useful development lessons. NGOs have a great deal to teach the Bank about the impor-tance and techniques of participatory development. NGOs can enhance project uptake and can extend project benefits to people and to areas where government and larger donors cannot reach. Working with CBOs can enhance sustainability, and by working with NGOs, the Bank can gain alternative perspectives. Even the watchdog role that NGOs play, although sometimes politically painful, can be useful.

But there are other reasons, some not very far removed from the critique offered by Bruce Rich. One is an acknowledged crisis for the Bank and an urgent need for institutional renewal. The 1997 Strategic Compact gives two basic reasons for this:

- the spectacular increase in net long-term private capital flows has meant that much of the Bank's traditional clientele now has an alternative source of funding;
- a recognition that there is a broader development paradigm than the one traditionally supported by the Bank. Today there is greater emphasis on social and environmental sustainability, local capacity building and improved governance.

The technological revolution has speeded up processes, requiring changes in decision-making, improvements in quality and reductions in cost. 'In many respects,' the Strategic Compact observes, 'the Bank has failed to keep up with these trends... This has resulted over time in a severe deterioration – indeed a crisis – in our effectiveness'. Indications of this crisis include reductions in lending, the loss of important knowledge, a lack of expertise in key areas, and the fact that many of the Bank's potential partners have become competitors and critics. The Bank itself cites the vociferous NGO campaign, '50 Years is Enough' as an example of how poorly it has managed the relationship with NGOs. The success of American NGOs in gaining the ear of Congress during negotiations on the 11th IDA replenishment in 1995 underlined this point in red ink.

Much of what the Bank has done to engage the NGO sector during the 1990s has, despite the planning and care that has gone into it, been somewhat *ad hoc*. Many observers inside and outside the Bank believe, however, that the engagement of NGOs can have a valuable impact on the work of the Bank – not just in service provision, but in the advancement of the development agenda. Less confrontation and more negotiation on some of the thorniest points of contention could, it is believed, benefit both sides in the more difficult debates. The Bank, after all, is intimately involved in the evolution of relationships between the State, the market and society. That alone is sufficient reason for the Bank and representatives of civil society to be on close speaking terms.

Appendix

Stakeholders for Development: Government–NGO Dialogue on the 21st Century Development Partnerships Strategy,

organized by the Development Assistance Committee
and the OECD Development Centre
Paris, 13–14 January 1998, OECD, Château de la Muette

PROGRAMME

13 January 1998

Opening Session: Objectives for the 21st Century Development Partnerships Strategy

Chair: Jean Bonvin, President, OECD Development Centre, welcome and introduction.

Introductions by:
- George Foulkes, Parliamentary Under-Secretary of State of International Development, United Kingdom
- Ambassador James Michel, Chair, OECD Development Assistance Committee
- Greetje Lubbi, Advocacy Director, NOVIB, the Netherlands

Session I: Stakeholders: the Global Dialogue

Chair: Ambassador Peter Jankowitsch, Permanent Representative of Austria to the OECD and President of the Advisory Board of the OECD Development Centre
- The 21st Century Partnership Strategy: The State of Play: Bernard Wood, Director, OECD Development Co-operation Directorate
- Major Issues of Non-Governmental Actors in Developing Regions: Roberto Bissio, representing the NGOs of the Social Watch Report, Uruguay
- Issues in partnership between NGOs in developing regions and NGOs in DAC countries: Mamadou Cissokho, Président du (CNCRS) Comité national de coordination des ruraux du Sénégal

Discussion

Session II Stakeholders: the OECD Dialogue

Chair: Ambassador James Michel, Chair, OECD Development Assistance Committee

- Government objectives for the 21st Century Partnership Strategy: Ambassador Walter Fust, General Director, Swiss Agency for Development Co-operation, Bern
- NGO Objectives for the 21st Century Partnership Strategy: Simon Stocker, Executive Secretary, Eurostep
- Major issues resulting from the analysis of the Reality of Aid Group: Judith Randel, Editor of the Reality of Aid reports 1993–1997

Discussion

14 January 1998

Session III: Stakeholders: the Dialogue within DAC Countries

Chair: Simon Stocker, Executive Secretary, Eurostep

- Major issues resulting from the Development Centre analysis on Government–NGO Relationships: Ian Smillie, Co-editor of the Development Centre report
- Major issues resulting from the Development Centre analysis on Public Attitudes for and International Development Co-operation: Henny Helmich, OECD Development Centre

Discussion

Concluding Remarks

Rapporteurs:

Colm Foy, OECD Development Centre
Richard Gerster, Swiss Coalition of Development Organisations, Switzerland
Diana Mitlin, International Institute for Environment & Development, United Kingdom
Aye Aye Win, North-South Centre, Council of Europe

Conference Organiser:

Jody Kaylor, OECD Development Centre

List of Participants * (in addition to those mentioned in the programme and the rapporteurs)*

Kirsti Aarnio	Delegation of Finland to the OECD
Charles Abbey	African Development Programme, Ghana
Christine Atkinson	Department for International Development, United Kingdom
Chihiro Atsumi	Delegation of Japan to the OECD
Michèle Bailly	The World Bank, Office in Paris
Sophie Bascoulart	Caisse française de Développement, France
John Batten	ACTIONAID,United Kingdom
Anders Bengtcén	Delegation of Sweden to the OECD
José-Luis Bernal	Delegation of Mexico to the OECD
Christoffer Bertelsen	Delegation of Denmark to the OECD
Olivier Berthoud	Service ONG, Swiss Agency for Development Cooperation, Switzerland

---

* Participants in the Dialogue were invited to participate in their personal expert capacity.

Doris Bertrand	Delegation of Austria to the OECD
Sophie Bessis	Enda/Vivre autrement, France
Barbara Brouwer	Club du Sahel
Giovanni Celiento	North South Centre, Council of Europe
John Clark	NGO Programme, The World Bank
Nicola Crawhall	Reality of Aid, c/o ACTIONAID, United Kingdom
Patricia Cullen	Delegation of Ireland to the OECD
Magdalena Diaz	Delegation of Mexico to the OECD
Jean-Marc Dupeux	Service oecuménique d'Entraide, CIMADE (for APRODEV), France
Jan Dybfest	Delegation of Norway to the OECD
Paloma Escudero	Interóm of Norway
Michel Faucon	CRID – Centre de Recherche et d'information pour le développement, France
Jef Felix	CIDSE – Coopération internationale pour le Développement et la Solidarité
Giulio Fossi	OECD Development Centre
Christian Freres	AIETI, Spain
Paul Frix	Delegation of Belgium to the OECD
Gunnar Garbo	Norwegian Peoples Aid, Norway
Tony German	Development Initiatives, United Kingdom
Robert Gibson	Delegation of the United Kingdom to the OECD
John P. Grant	USAID, Office of Private and Voluntary Cooperation, USA
Vicky Harris	Department for International Development, United Kingdom
Mats Hårsmar	The Swedish Mission Council, Sweden
Ulrich Hiemenz	Director, OECD Development Centre
Tony Hill	United Nations-NGLS
Birthe Horn	NGO Division, Sida, Sweden
Antero Järstä	Ministry for Foreign Affairs, Finland
Miho Kawahatsu	Delegation of Japan to the OECD
Seung-Ho Kim	Delegation of Korea to the OECD
Carol Lancaster	School of Foreign Service, Georgetown University, USA
Guido La Tella	Delegation of Italy to the OECD
Jean Ledem	European Office, International Monetary Fund
Carolyn Long	InterAction, USA
James Mackie	Liaison Committee of Development NGOs to the European Union
Sawako Matsuo	Delegation of Japan to the OECD
Jim McAlpine	NGO Unit, Department for International Development, United Kingdom
Hunter McGill	Delegation of Canada to the OECD
Fritz Meijndert	OECD Development Co-operation Directorate
Jim Moody	InterAction, USA
Renaud-François Moulinier	Delegation of the EC to the OECD
Kristen Neymarc	OECD Development Centre
Clodagh O'Brien	NGO Unit, DG VIII, European Commission
Paul Obrist	Delegation of Switzerland to the OECD
Yann Pradeau	Ministère des Affaires étrangères, France
Jean-Marc Pradelle	Club du Sahel
Ana Maria Ribeiro da Silva	Delegation of Portugal to the OECD
Tie Roefs	Vredeseilanden, Belgium
Alex Rondos	The World Bank
Lee Roussel	Delegation of the United States to the OECD

Paul J. Sciarone	Delegation of the Netherlands to the OECD
Kazuo Takahashi	Fasid – IDRI, Japan /North-South Centre of the Council of Europe
Cesare Taviani	ASAL, Italy
Brian Tomlinson	CCIC – Canadian Council for International Cooperation, Canada
Mariano Valderrama	Centro Peruano de Estudios Sociales – CEPES, Peru
Nuno Vaz	Direction des Services d'Aide Humanitaire, Institut de la Coopération portugaise
Ambassador Peter Vereker	Delegation of the United Kingdom to the OECD
Pat Webster	Council for International Development – CID, New Zealand
Horst Wetzel	Delegation of Germany to the OECD
Dick Wentinck	Ministry of Foreign Affairs, the Netherlands
Adéle Woods	OECD Development Centre

Notes

NOTES TO CHAPTER 1: INTRODUCTION

1   In preparing this Introduction, I used reports by Colm Foy, Richard Gerster, Diana Mitlin and Aye Aye Win on the fourth Government–NGO Dialogue on the *21st Century Development Partnerships Strategy: Stakeholders for Development*. I thank Kristen Neymarc for her support in editing the summary report and other documentation for this Dialogue. A programme and list of participants can be found in the Appendix to this publication.

2   Over 90 participants active in development cooperation from governments, multilateral organisations and NGOs as well as experts from research institutes attended this 1998 Dialogue. These dialogues have become a unique forum for participants to gain a better understanding of each other's experiences and learn from the varied perspectives of people present. The keynote address was delivered by George Foulkes, Parliamentary Under-Secretary of State for International Development of the United Kingdom. Other speakers were Jean Bonvin, President of the OECD Development Centre, Ambassador James Michel, DAC Chair and Ambassador Walter Fust, General Director of the Swiss Agency for Development Cooperation, Simon Stocker of Eurostep, Roberto Bissio of Social Watch and Greetje Lubbi of NOVIB. The main objective of the meeting was to identify and analyse areas where both governments and NGOs could improve their own approaches in order to carry out more effectively the overall goal of poverty reduction. A second objective was to build public and political support for international development cooperation. This dialogue, being an informal one, did not aim to establish a consensus on conclusions or recommendations. However, participants proposed two follow up activities:

   a)   For the OECD Development Centre: In order to avoid overlap with other international fora, participants suggested the formation of a joint steering group with a mandate for identifying a more specific focus and themes for future dialogues.

   b)   For the Development Assistance Committee: The present inputs of NGOs and civil society from the North and from the South in the OECD–DAC peer review processes were acknowledged as being very useful. Some participants wished to see this involvement expanded in future.

3   Over the past 35 years, the Development Centre worked closely with many NGOs and other organisations in the civil society of OECD countries. It closely monitored this evolution and published, jointly with several key partner organisations, a series of NGO Directories. These directories each focused on a different aspect of development, such as the environment, human rights and refugees, population and urban development and habitat. They provide detailed NGO profiles country by country, with a description of their principal activities. The 'master' database on NGOs now includes some 6000 NGOs, as against 2900 listed in our first directory, published in 1989.

4   The terms 'civil society' and 'non-governmental organisations' are often and incorrectly used interchangeably. The *21st Century Partnership Strategy* highlights the *strategic* role of civil society in inducing positive social change. There is much to be gained, by both governments and NGOs, through more considered interactions between them and other civil society groups committed to poverty reduction. In recent years, 'civil society' has come to describe a broad range of voluntary or non-profit associations, including both NGOs and a diverse collection of other citizens groups. However, a critical distinction needs to be made in referring to organisations for the poor. For example, the *Club du Sahel* developed an innovative programme which involves Sahelian farmers' associations in a forum that provided an opportunity for them to speak directly to development policy-makers. The vision they presented was then passed on to Sahelian governments and played a significant role in the further planning process. The OECD Development Centre and the North South Centre of the Council of Europe organised on 3–4 July 1997 an informal experts' workshop on practical ways in which external actors and donors could support civil society in developing regions. This is the subject of a separate 1998 joint publication, *Civil Society and International Cooperation*, edited by Amanda Bernard, Henny Helmich and Percy B. Lehning.

5   As can be seen if the present publication is compared with the first Stakeholders publication: Smillie, I and Helmich H (eds), *Government–NGO Relationships, Stakeholders for Development*, 1992 and 1993, OECD Development Centre, Paris.

NOTES TO CHAPTER 2: AT SEA IN A SIEVE

1   The author is grateful to Judith Randel, Tony German and Henny Helmich, who offered helpful and constructive comments on an early draft.
2   Garth Nowlan-Foreman has outlined the evolution of government funding in New Zealand: 'Neither Mendicant Nor Deal-Makers: Contracting, Government Funding and Voluntary Organisations', New Zealand Council of Christian Social Services, 1995.
3   Osborne, D and Gaebler, T, *Reinventing Government: How the Entrepreneurial Spirit is Transforming the Public Sector*, 1992, Addison-Wesley, Reading, Mass. The Clinton quotation is taken from the cover of the 1993 Plume edition.
4   DAC, *Development Cooperation 1994*, 1995, OECD, Paris.
5   USAID, 'Enhancing AID's Ability to Manage for Results',1994, mimeo, Washington.
6   Smith, S and Lipsky, M, *Nonprofits for Hire: The Welfare State in the Age of Contracting*, 1993, Harvard University Press, Cambridge, Mass, p45.
7   Information taken from the annual reports of the organisations mentioned.
8   EC/1995/SC.2/CRP.27, UNHCR, 4 September, 1995.
9   Maren, M, 'A Different Kind of Child Abuse', December 1995, Penthouse. Maren wrote subsequently about this in *The Road to Hell*, 1997, the Free Press, New York.
10 *Aide Suisse aux Pays en Développement at aux Pays de l'Europe Orientale,* produced for the *Direction du développement et de la coopération* by the *Intitut universitaire d'études du développement*, Geneva, 1996.
11 WFP: correspondence between CARE Canada and WFP, December 1997; UNHCR: 'Information Note', Funding and Donor Relations Service, February, 1997.
12 Statistics on Plan International are taken from *Plan International Worldwide Annual Report 1996*
13 World Vision statistics are derived from World Vision International *1996 Annual Report*, and from the 1996 Annual Reports of World Vision Australia, World Vision Canada and World Vision United States.
14 CARE International, *Annual Report*, 1995.
15 Information derived from *Oxfam International: Your Essential Guide to the 1996–1998 Plan*, 1996, Oxfam International, Oxford.
16 International Save the Children Alliance, *Annual Report*, 1996.
17 MSF *Activity Report* 1994–5.
18 MSF *Activity Reports* 1994–5, 1995–6, 1996–7.
19 Annual Reports, 1993 and 1996, Christian Children's Fund Inc.
20 SCF members in the South are independent members of the Save the Children Alliance, but most are very small and their formal relations with Northern Alliance members are tenuous.
21 World Vision United States, *Annual Report 1996.*
22 The 1982 figure is taken from the *New Internationalist*, May 1982; the 1996 figures are taken from the 1996 Annual Reports of the three organisations.
23 See the chapter on Australia in this volume.
24 In discussion with the author, 7 July 1997.
25 See the chapter on Canada in this volume.
26 *New Internationalist*, May, 1982.
27 McCullough, Margaret, 'Measuring the Impact of Relief and Development Through Child Sponsorship', 2 February 1998, *Monday Developments*, InterAction, Washington.
28 'About This Special Report', *Chicago Tribune*, 15 March 1998.
29 'Unprecedented? Charity's Own Probe Finds More Dead Children', *Chicago Tribune*, 15 March 1998.
30 *Monday Developments, op cit.*
31 The SCF Alliance saw a slight downturn (less than 3 per cent) in overall spending between 1993 and 1996, and MSF saw its income decline from $306 million – at the height of the Rwanda crisis – to $252 million in 1996.
32 Parts of this section are an updated and revised version of an unpublished paper prepared by the author for the OECD Development Centre in 1996.
33 Tendler, Judith, *Turning Private Voluntary Organisations Into Development Agencies: Questions for Evaluation*, 1982, USAID, Washington, p129.
34 Farrington, John and Bebbington, Anthony, *Reluctant Partners? NGOs, the State and Sustainable Agricultural Development*, 1993, Routledge, London, p180.

35   Riddell, R., Bebbington, A. and Peck, L., 'Promoting Development by Proxy: The Development Impact of Government Support to Swedish NGOs', 1995, ODI, London, ppix–x.
36   Marsden, David, 'The Meaning of Social Development', in Marsden, David, and Oakley, Peter, *Evaluating Social Development Projects*, 1990, Oxfam, Oxford, p27.
37   Beaudoux, E., de Crombrugghe, G., Douxchamps, F., Gueneau, M. and Nieukerk, M., *Supporting Development Action: From Identification to Action*, COTA/Macmillan, London/Brussels, 1992, p115.
38   Marsden and Oakley, *op cit*, p51.
39   *ibid*, p140.
40   'New Ethics Code is Just a Start', Toronto *Globe and Mail*, 9 September 1997.
41   'Open Trading; Options for Effective Monitoring of Corporate Codes of Conduct', New Economics Foundation and Catholic Institute for International relations, London, 1997.
42   In most OECD member countries, registered NGOs are required to submit audited financial statements to a government authority – in the US they must fill out a Form 990 for the IRS; in Canada, T3010. In Britain the Charity Commission for England and Wales examines a range of NGO reports. Given the huge numbers of charitable organisations, given the widespread disparity in the work they do domestically and internationally, and given the diversity in the way financial statements are constructed, there is virtually no possibility that these forms and the bodies that receive them can perform a serious watchdog function.
43   Minister for Development Cooperation, Australia, 'Code of Conduct for NGOs', Press Release, 31 August 1995.
44   Cleary, Paul, 'Where Does the Aid Dollar Go?', *Sydney Morning Herald*, 24 March 1997.
45   Maren, Michael, *The Road to Hell: The Ravaging Effects of Foreign Aid and International Charity*, 1997 Free Press, New York.
46   Stewart, Walter, *The Charity Game: Greed, Waste and Fraud in Canada's $86-Billion-a-Year Compassion Industry*, 1996, Douglas and McIntyre, Vancouver, pp115 and 120.
47   Sommer, John, *Beyond Charity: US Voluntary Aid for a Changing Third World*, Overseas Development Council, 1977, Washington, p80.
48   USAID, 'Development Effectiveness of Private Voluntary Organisations', 1986, Washington, pp4–5.
49   Riddell, Roger, *Judging Success: Evaluating NGO Approaches to Alleviating Poverty in Developing Countries*, 1990, ODI, London, p5.
50   Ministry of Foreign Affairs of Finland, for the OECD/DAC Expert Group on Aid Evaluation, Searching for Impact and Methods: NGO Evaluations Synthesis Study, (2 Vols), Helsinki, 1997.
51   See Foy, Colm and Helmich, Henny (eds) *Public Support for International Development*, 1996, OECD Development Centre, Paris.
52   UNDP, *Development Aid: What the Public Thinks*, Office of Development Studies, New York, December 1996.
53   For example, a 1995 University of Maryland poll found that 75 per cent of Americans believed the US to be spending 'too much' on foreign aid. Most thought that aid consumed about 18 per cent of the federal budget. When questioned further, they said that a reduction to 3 per cent – triple the actual figure – would be too severe. But when they were told the actual amount, many still stubbornly favoured a cut. Source: 'Americans and Foreign Aid: A Study of American Public Attitudes', January, 1995, University of Maryland. Michael Kinsley criticises the public ignorance revealed in this study – and the attachment of any political importance to it – in 'The Intellectual Free Lunch', *New Yorker*, 6 February 1995.
54   Bhasin, Kamla, 'Towards South–North NGO Partnership: Some Thoughts', Manchester University Conference on NGOs, June, 1994.
55   Ford-Smith, Honor, *Ring Ding in a Tight Corner: A Case Study in Funding and Organisational Democracy in Sistren, 1977–88*, 1989, International Council for Adult Education, Toronto, p100.
56   Tandon, Y. 'Foreign NGOs, Uses and Abuses: An African Perspective', *Associations Transnationales*, March, 1991.
57   Malena, Carmen, 'Relations between Northern and Southern Non-governmental Development Organisations', IDS, University of Sussex, 1992; also published in *Canadian Journal of Development Studies*, Vol XVI, No.1, 1995.
58   'South–North Linking for International Development', *Conference Proceedings*, November, 1990, quoted in Malena, op cit.
59   See Trebilock, Michael, 'Can Government be Reinvented?' in Boston, 1995 (pp1–35), and Paul Milgrom and John Roberts, 1992, *Economics, Organisation and Management*, Prentice Hall, New Jersey.

60   The problem of attribution is discussed at greater length in Howes, Mick, 'Linking Paradigms and practice: Key Issues in the Appraisal, Monitoring and Evaluation of British NGO Projects', *Journal of International Development*, Vol.4, No.4, 1992, and Fowler, Alan, 'Assessing NGO Performance: Difficulties, Dilemmas and a Way Ahead', in *Beyond the Magic Bullet: NGO Performance and Accountability in the Post-Cold War World*, 1995, Earthscan, London.
61   Michael Edwards has written extensively about how NGOs learn in 'Organisational Learning in NGOs: What Have We Learned?', *Public Administration and Development*, Vol. 17, 1997.
62   Marsden, David, Oakley, Peter, and Pratt, Brian, *Measuring the Process: Guidelines for Evaluating Social Development*, 1994, INTRAC, Oxford, p151.
63   Power, Michael, *The Audit Explosion*,1994, Demos, London, p34.
64   Saul, John Ralston, *The Unconscious Civilisation*, 1995, Anansi, Concord.

NOTES TO CHAPTER 3: AUSTRALIA

1   A great many individuals in the Government of Australia and the Australian NGO sector helped to make this chapter possible. Special thanks are due to Rima Das Pradhan, AusAID's NGO Program staff and the Australian Council for Overseas Aid.
2   Over five years, the big agencies have gradually taken a larger share of the funds. In 1991–2, the top five received 47.5 per cent of AusAID funds, while the bottom 68 received 2.8 per cent.
3   The 1994 figures are skewed by a major appeal for Rwanda that raised A$ 3.4 million.
4   When the CARE difficulties began, CARE was not a member of ACFOA. Under new management, it has since become a member.
5   OECD, *Development Cooperation Report 1997; Efforts and Policies of Members of the Development Assistance Committee*, 1998, Paris, p92.
6   An NGO's 'indicative planning figure' (IPF) is based on a complex formula that relates the organisation's 'recognized development expenditure' on a pro rata basis to the amount of money available in the overall pool. Until 1996, no agency was permitted to receive more than 25 per cent of the funds in the ANCP; the ceiling was raised to 33 per cent in 1996, effectively allowing the very largest NGOs a greater share of the fund.
7   'Australian NGOs and Overseas Development Assistance Program', L. Nicolau, September 1992.
8   'The 1996–7 Aid Budget: A sharper humanitarian focus', Thomson, Andrew *Development Bulletin*, October 1996, Vol 39.

NOTES TO CHAPTER 4: AUSTRIA

1   The OECD Development Centre and the *Österreichische Forschungsstiftung für Entwicklungshilfe* (ÖFSE) undertook, as part of the Stakeholders Project, a more extensive case study on Austria. This was published bilingually in German and English: Karin Kübelböck, 'NGOs – Stakeholders for Development, Case Study Austria', in Henny Helmich and Gerhard Bittner (eds), *Der dritte Sektor in der Entwicklungspolitrik; Zusammenarbeit zwischen Staat und Nict-Regierungsorganisationen*, NROS, Vienna, 1996, and Karin Kübelböck *NGOs in der Entwicklungszusammenarbeit*, in Austrian Journal of Development Studies, 4, 1996, Vienna, 1996, pp371–96. The current chapter refers to NGOs that receive co-financing from the government. Usually these NGOs do not receive official funding. They are included in order to provide a more complete picture of the Church-related NGO sector.
2   OECD, *Development Cooperation Report 1997; Efforts and Policies of the Members of the Development Assistance Committee*, 1998, Paris, p93.
3   For more detailed information about Austrian NGOs, see *Der Dritte Sektor in der Entwicklungspolitik*, ÖFSE Edition 4, 1996, Vienna.
4   *KommEnt* has published a comparative study by Susanne Höck on development education in Ireland, Austria, the Netherlands and Switzerland: *The Organisation and Funding of Development Education and Awareness Building on Development Issues in Four European Countries*, 1996, Vienna. The study is available on KommEnt's website: www.komment.sbg.ac.at.

5   OECD, *Austria*, Development Cooperation Review Series, No15, 1996, Paris, p16.
6   It would be against the Austrian constitution for the decisions of an advisory board to be binding upon a minister or state secretary. Normally, however, the administrative body would be obliged to justify a decision differing from the well-founded opinion of an Advisory Board.
7   OECD *Austria*, Development Cooperation Review Series, No.15, 1996, Paris, and DAC Aid Review of Austria, 1993.

NOTES TO CHAPTER 5: BELGIUM

1   As part of the Stakeholders Project, the OECD Development Centre and Coprogram undertook a more extensive case study on Belgium that was published in Dutch, French and English: Tie Roefs, 'NGOs and Governments: An Association for Development, Case Study Belgium', 1995, Brussels. Most interviews for this chapter took place in Brussels in September 1997. The chapter benefited from the reflections of distinguished academics with a long-term perspective on Belgian development cooperation, and from thoughtful and perceptive analyses from within the NGO sector itself. The authors are also grateful for discussions with the Belgian Administration for Development Cooperation. Particular thanks are due to Guy Bastiaensen, Jean Bossuyt, Robrecht Renard, Tie Roefs, Miek Roegiers and Melanie Schellens.
2   OECD, *Development Cooperation Report 1997; Efforts and Policies of the Members of the Development Assistance Committee*, 1998, Paris, p86.
3   See *Searching for Impact and Methods: NGO Evaluation Synthesis Study*, DAC Expert Group on Aid Evaluation, Ministry of Foreign Affairs, 1997, Finland.
4   See Douglas de Coninck, *Witte Olifanten* published in 1996. Some of the failures that were highlighted in this book and in the more sensational press stories were repetitions of press revelations over a long period of time. Both NGOs and government felt that many known and past errors were recounted again as 'new revelations'.
5   The provinces are the next level of government below the Flanders and Wallonie Community governments.

NOTES TO CHAPTER 6: CANADA

1   Background research for this chapter was ably carried out by Tony Rogge. Many individuals in CIDA and among Canadian NGOs provided invaluable assistance. The author is grateful for helpful comments offered by several readers of an early draft. CIDA's Canadian Partnership Branch took special pains to review and advise on all statistics in the chapter. These presented a particular problem because of differences in the way government reports on allocations and disbursements, and because of differences between the government financial year and that of many Canadian NGOs. A note on the general problem of NGO statistics is contained in Chapter 1.
2   *Au Courant*, CCIC, July, 1997.
3   CCIC *Annual Report*, 1996.
4   *Canada in the World*, Government of Canada, 1995, Ottawa, p43.
5   OECD News Release, 'DAC Aid Review of Canada', Paris, 26 January 1998.
6   '1997/98 Federal Budget and CIDA's 1997/98 Expenditure Plan Estimates', CCIC, Ottawa, 1997.
7   OECD News Release, *op cit.*
8   'Planned funding cuts to foreign aid are partly restored', *Globe and Mail*, Toronto, 25 February, 1998.
9   'Guide to the NGO Project Facility', CIDA/CPB, December, 1996.
10   There were three exceptions: two organisations were given increases and one was decreased.
11   Although not historically a volunteer-sending organisation, Oxfam Québec merged in 1993 with a much larger volunteer-sending organisation, *Organisation canadienne pour la solidatité et le développement*. CIDA funding for the volunteer activities represents about 80 per cent of its contribution.
12   Deciphering the financial statements of most volunteer-sending organisations is extremely difficult, because all assign a usually unexplained cash value to the voluntary contribution of personnel (this has been subtracted from the figures used here), and most do not disaggregate private donations from

'other income', which might include a contract from a foreign government or a UN agency, or even counterpart funds derived from the sale overseas of Canadian commodities.

13 All figures in this paragraph are derived from 'Should CIDA Allow Open Competition Between the Private and Non-profit Sectors?', CIDA/CPB, 1995.

14 Guide to the NGO Project Facility, *op cit.*

15 The figures are derived from CCIC's submission to the *Reality of Aid 1997*. They are based on CIDA's Annual Statistical Report on ODA and data on individual bilateral projects. Figures do not include universities, colleges or research institutions. Food aid is included. Figures may differ somewhat from others in this report because *actuals* as reported to the DAC are not the same as *allocations* made by CIDA in a given year.

16 Ministry of Foreign Affairs of Finland, *NGO Evaluation Synthesis Study*, for OECD/DAC Expert Group on Evaluation, Helsinki, 1997.

17 *NGO Evaluation Synthesis Study; Canada*, Ian Smillie and Brian Rowe, CIDA, June, 1997; much of this section is derived directly from this report.

18 Samuel Martin, *An Essential Grace*, McClelland and Stewart, 1985, Toronto.

19 Sources: 'Charity Facts 1993', Canadian Centre for Philanthropy, Toronto, 1993; *Portrait of Canada's Charities*, Canadian Centre for Philanthropy, Toronto, 1994.

20 Brian K. Murphy, 'Towards the 21st Century; Reflections on the Future of Canadian NGOs', Inter Pares, October 1993.

NOTES TO CHAPTER 7: DENMARK

1   The authors are grateful to Danida and to staff in Danish NGOs for their perceptions and analysis of the Danish NGO sector and its relations with government. The chapter has also benefited from evaluation material produced by Danida. Special thanks are due to Birte Hald, Bent Kristensen and Flemming Schultz.

2   The 1996 OECD *Directory of NGOs Active in Sustainable Development*, lists 191 NGOs in Denmark, suggesting that just under 200 is a reliable estimate of the size of the overall NGO community.

3   Note that this 0.5 per cent is in addition to allocating 0.15 per cent of GNI to aid.

4   OECD, *DAC Development Cooperation Review Series*, No10, 1995, Denmark, Paris.

5   *The Danish NGO Evaluation Non Governmental Actions: A Necessary and Growing Option*, CASA, November 1989.

6   *The Evaluation of the Framework Agreements between DANIDA and Four Danish NGOs* (Ref 104.N.90.3), by COWIconsult.

7   The consultants pointed out that given the short time frameworks had been in place, their report might lean towards criticism and might not bring out the positive benefits that could accrue over the longer term.

8   Act 265 approved by the Finance Committee of the *Folketinget* (parliament) also authorised framework agreements with four UN agencies.

9   These figures were plans at the time of writing.

10 For instance, see *Challenges for the Future: the Role of Danish Development NGOs, Mellemfolkeligt Samvirke*, November 1993.

11 Evaluation Report 1996/14, COWI, November 1996.

12 CEC Commission Report on Cooperation with European NGDOs in those Fields of Importance to Developing Countries (FY 1995).

NOTES TO CHAPTER 8: FINLAND

1   This chapter is based on a number of documents on Finnish NGOs and their relationship with government. These include an evaluation conducted by the London-based Overseas Development Institute (ODI), *Strengthening the Partnership: Evaluation of the Finnish NGO Support Programme*, 1994. Other important background documents are Timo Kyllonen's 1997 Case Study on NGO

Evaluation Policies and Practices, the Evaluation of Finnish Personnel as Volunteers in Development Cooperation, the 1996 Thematic Evaluation of Finnish Humanitarian Assistance, and the 1995 DAC Aid Review.

2   OECD, *Development Cooperation Report 1997: Efforts and Policies of the Members of the Development Assistance Committee*, 1998, Paris, p97.

3   OECD/DAC, *Development Cooperation Series* No. 11: Finland, OECD, 1995, Paris.

4   Ministry of Foreign Affairs of Finland, DIDC, 'Guidelines for Programme Design, Monitoring and Evaluation', Helsinki, 1997.

5   Overseas Development Institute (UK), *Strengthening the Partnership: Evaluation of the Finnish NGO Support Programme*, FINNIDA/MFA, 1994, Helsinki.

6   *ibid.*

7   OECD/DAC, *op cit.*

8   KEPA Progress Report 1–6/97 (unpublished).

9   ODI *op cit.*

10 Ministry of Foreign Affairs of Finland, DIDC, 'Thematic Evaluation of Finnish Humanitarian Assistance, July 1996.

11 ODI, *op cit.*

12 *ibid.*

13 ODI *op cit.*

14 Decision-in-Principle on Finnish Development Cooperation, Cabinet Paper 12.9.96.

15 Kyllonen, T, 'The Finnish Case Study: NGO Evaluation Policies and Practices', for DAC/OECD *NGO Evaluation Synthesis Study*, IDS, Helsinki, May 1997.

16 *ibid.*

17 OECD/DAC, *op cit.*

18 *ibid.*

19 ODI *op cit.*

20 *ibid.*

21 'Thematic Evaluation of Finnish Humanitarian Assistance', DIDC/MFA, July 1996.

22 *ibid.*

23 Decision-in-Principle, *op cit.*

24 'Evaluation of Finnish Personnel...' *op cit.*

25 *ibid.*

26 KEPA, *op cit.*

27 *ibid.*

28 Randel, J. and German, T. (eds), *The Reality of Aid 1997/8*, Earthscan, London.

29 Voipio, Timo (IDS, Helsinki), 'Coherence of Policies towards Developing Countries: The Case of Finland', paper prepared for an International Workshop on Policy Coherence towards Developing Countries, Geneva, April 1997.

30 Randel and German, *op cit*

31 ODI *op cit.*

32 Executive summary from Riddell, R. et al, *Strengthening the Partnership, Evaluation of the Finnish NGO Support Programme*, Finnida.

33 Ministry of Foreign Affairs of Finland, DIDC, *Searching for Impact and Methods: NGO Evaluation Synthesis Study* (2 vols), May 1997.

NOTES TO CHAPTER 9: FRANCE

1   The authors are most grateful to many individuals in both the Ministry of Foreign Affairs and the NGO sector for their provision of written material and their perceptions provided through interviews. Special thanks are due to Elena Borghese who added a perceptive commentary on recent developments in French cooperation and NGOs. We are very grateful to Michel Doucin, Head of the French government's *Mission de Liaison auprès des ONG* of the Ministry of Foreign Affairs for his critical review. Particular thanks are further due to Patrice Blanc, Sharon Courteau, Michel Faucon, and Philippe Ryfman.

2   Information from Coordination SUD (Solidarité, Urgence, Développement).

3   Vielajus, Jean-Louis, '*Etude de Case de la France, l'Evaluation des ONG, politiques et pratiques*' as

part of OECD/DAC, *Searching for Impact and Methods, NGO Evaluation Synthesis Study*, Ministry of Foreign Affairs, Helsinki, May 1997.

4   An exception is CCFD's network of branch organisations.
5   See OECD/DAC, Aid Review Series No. 21, France, OECD Paris 1997.
6   Letter to the authors from Michel Doucin, Head of *Mission de Liaison auprès des ONG* in the Ministry of Foreign Affairs.
7   See OECD/DAC, Aid Review Series No. 21, France, OECD, 1997, Paris.
8   OECD, *Development Cooperation Report 1997; Efforts and Policies of Members of the Development Assistance Committee*, 1998, Paris, p82.
9   Vielajus, *op cit* and MFA, *Lire et comprendre le Budget Français d'aide publique au développement*, 1996.
10 *Conditions Generales de Co-financement*, Ministry of Foreign Affairs and Ministry of Cooperation, May 1994, Paris.
11 ECHO, *Annual Report 1996*. The 13 French NGOs are: *Action Contre La Faim, Action Nord Sud France, Aide Médicale Intérnationale France, Croix Rouge Française, Equilibre France*, Handicap International, *Médecins du Monde, MSF, Pharmaciens Sans Frontières, Première Urgence, Secours Populaire Français, Solidarités.*
12 Vielajus, *op cit.*
13 CCD, *Argent et organisations de solidarité internationale*, June 1996.
14 *Conditions Générales de Co-financement*, Ministry of Foreign Affairs and Ministry of Cooperation, May 1994, Paris.
15 The FEP (*Fonds d'Etudes Préalables*), which supported feasibility studies and the FEE (*Fonds d'Etudes Evaluations*), which offered matching funds for evaluation.
16 F3E, *Principles and Objectives*, 1997.
17 Barbedette, L, *et al*, 'Charter for Evaluations Made During Development Work', *Fondation de France*, Paris, September 1995.
18 See Vielajus, *op cit.*
19 The 'ambit' countries, also known as *du champ*, are the countries with which France has cooperation agreements and which are therefore within the ambit of the Ministry of Cooperation.
20 See OECD/DAC, Aid Review Series No. 21, France, OECD, Paris, 1997.
21 *ibid.*

NOTES TO CHAPTER 10: GERMANY

1   Wiemann, J., German Development Aid in Cox, A., Healey, J. and Koning, A. *How European Aid Works: A Comparison of Management Systems and Effectiveness*, ODI, 1997, London.
2   Reported in OECD DAC Aid Review Series No 9, Germany. OECD Paris 1995.
3   OECD DAC Aid Review *op cit.*
4   BMZ budget.
5   OECD DAC Aid Review *op cit.*
6   Wiemann, J, *op cit.*
7   CEC, DG VIII, *Development Aid: Building the Future with Public Support*, Report by INRA Europe 8 January 1997.
8   The voluntary commitment made at the World Summit for Social Development that 20 per cent of ODA and 20 per cent of developing country public expenditure should be allocated to basic social services.
9   Fues, T., *Social Priorities in Development Cooperation: Implementing the 20/20 Initiative* for the Deutsches NRO-Forum Weltsozialgipfel, March 1996.

NOTES TO CHAPTER 11: GREECE

1   Ministry of National Economy and Ministry of Foreign Affairs, *The Aid Programme of Greece*, revised version, November 1996, p41.

2   *ibid*, p1.
3   In accordance with *Shaping the 21st Century: The Contribution of Development Co-operation*, OECD, May 1996, pp1 and 5.
4   *The Aid Programme of Greece, op cit*, pp2–3.
5   *ibid*, pp33–34.
6   *ibid*, pp45 and 47.
7   In 1996 US$160,000 was collected during the Sunday of the Orthodoxy celebration. The 1997 budget of the *Apostoliki Diakonia* was US$555,600. Source: interview with an *Apostoliki Diakonia* official, Athens, January 1997. For the seven year period 1985–1992, the income of the external missionary sector was US$1.7 million, and expenses were US$1.5 million. Source: *Apostoliki Diakonia tis Ekklissias tis Ellados*, 1985–1992 report, p40.
8   The Aid Programme of Greece, *op cit*, p1.

NOTES TO CHAPTER 12: IRELAND

1   As part of the Stakeholders Project, an earlier case study on Ireland was published in the *Trócaire Development Review*: Ian Smillie, 'Irish Development NGOs and Government: An OECD Case Study', Dublin, 1996. Many individuals in the Government of Ireland and the Irish NGO community helped in the production of that study, including Martin Greene of Irish Aid and Anna Farrell of Dóchas. That study and this chapter benefited from various studies of Irish Aid written in recent years by Prof. Helen O'Neill of University College Dublin. Maura Leen of Trócaire assisted greatly with new information and perspectives in bringing the 1996 study up to date.
2   'Remembering the Irish Famine', Pastoral Letter of the Bishops of Ireland, 24 September, 1995.
3   CONGOOD, 1992, p128.
4   OECD, *Directory of Non-governmental Organisations Active in Sustainable Development*, Part I: Europe, Paris, 1996.
5   Concern is becoming more widely known as 'Concern Worldwide', to distinguish it from the British organisation, 'Concern Universal'.
6   The scheme was made available only to international development NGOs because unlike domestic charities, they do not have access to proceeds from the national lottery.
7   Although a variety of names are used to describe Ireland's development assistance programme, the 1993 *Strategy Plan* stated that 'it is intended in future to adopt the standard description "Irish Aid".' This term will be used throughout this chapter.
8   OECD, *Development Co-operation Report 1997; Efforts and Policies of the Members of the Development Assistance Committee*, Paris, 1998, p99.
9   *Strategy Plan*, pp12–13.
10   'Irish Aid Co-Financing Scheme', Dept. of Foreign Affairs, 1995. In 1996, Trócaire and Concern each expected to receive block grants of £300,000, Goal expected to receive £250,000 and Christian Aid £75,000.
11   O'Neill, 1995b.
12   Trócaire reports that 'emergencies expenditure' is a broad category which includes rehabilitation, some support for human rights programmes and trauma counselling.
13   Irish Aid Annual Report, 1993.
14   OECD 1995, p12.
15   O'Neill, 1995a; Trócaire alone reported development education spending of Ir£1.2 million, and Concern, Ir£319,000.
16   *The Reality of Aid 1997–8*, Earthscan, London, 1997, p83.
17   Hanlon, Joseph, *Peace Without Profit: How the IMF Blocks Rebuilding in Mozambique*, James Curry, Oxford, 1996.
18   Government of Ireland, *Challenges and Opportunities Abroad: White Paper on Foreign Policy*, Dublin, 1996, p227.

NOTES TO CHAPTER 13: ITALY

1   As part of the OECD Stakeholders Project, the Italian NGO *ASAL*, with *L'Harmattan Italia*, published an Italian version of the 1993 *Stakeholders for Development* (see bibliography) with a special updated preface on Italy by Maria Stella Rognoni (*'Organizzazioni non governative e governi: un tandem per lo sviluppo'*, *ASAL/L'Harmattan-Italia*, Rome, 1995). Maria Stella Rognoni, who worked on the original Stakeholders project at the OECD Development Centre, also edited the complete Italian version. The editors are most grateful to many individuals in both the Ministry of Foreign Affairs and the NGO sector for their comments on a draft of this chapter. Special thanks are due to Maria Stella Rognoni and Cesare Taviani from ASAL, and Elena Borghese, the former NGO specialist working with the DAC Secretariat, and Guido La Tella of the Delegation of Italy to the OECD for their comments. Guido La Tella also provided very helpful documentation.

2   CLONG News No 13, December 1995.

3   For a detailed overview of this law and of the basic facts of the evolution of the Government-NGO relationship see; Marcello Cavalcaselle, Le Ong nella cooperazione allo sviluppo italiana; evoluzione storica, rapporti con la DGCS e caratteristichi essentiali, in: DIPCO, Bolletino della Cooperazione, No 8 of 4 March 1998, pp133–48.

4   This Charter identifies the basic principles to which development and humanitarian aid NGOs are expected to adhere. It does not attempt to define NGOs in terms of structure, approach or values – rather it identifies some basic characteristics to which most NGOs can subscribe.

5   OECD, *Development Cooperation Report 1997; Efforts and Policies of the Members of the Development Assistance Committee*, 1998, Paris, p100.

6   *ibid*, p78.

7   *ibid*, p100.

8   See OECD DAC Aid Review Series No 16, Italy, OECD, 1996, Paris, p18.

9   ICVA/Eurostep, *Reality of Aid 1994*, ActionAid, 1994, London, pp139–40.

NOTES TO CHAPTER 14: JAPAN

1   Research for this chapter was largely done through a visit to Tokyo in October 1997. The authors are extremely grateful to individuals in the Ministry for Foreign Affairs and in the NGO community for taking time to contribute to this study and for their perceptive analysis of the issues. Particular thanks are due to Akira Chiba, Masahiko Horie, Michio Ito, Kenzo Oshima, Mitsuhiro Saotome and Akio Takayanagi.

2   Survey by the Economic Planning Agency, published in 1993.

3   December 1993 Survey carried out by the Prime Minister's Office.

4   The DAC noted that 'This announcement constitutes an important change in the basic framework of Japan's ODA effort.' In 1996, Japan's ODA dropped by 24.7 per cent in real terms to $9.44 billion, with the ODA/GNP ratio falling from 0.28 per cent to 0.20 per cent. The 1996 fall reflected a temporary drop of 65 per cent in multilateral disbursements. See OECD, *Development Cooperation Report 1997; Efforts and Policies of Members of the Development Assistance Committee*, 1998, Paris, p101.

5   DAC, *Development Cooperation 1996*, Table 17, OECD, 1997, Paris.

6   Information supplied by JANIC.

7   Less structured that the *minashi hojin* is another category known as *nin'i dantai*. These may have little in the way of formal organisation, but they bring people together informally around a common theme or objective.

8   A 1994 estimate put the number of unincorporated organisations – *nin'i-dantai* – at 5000.

9   For example, case studies of four Nepal projects recommended greater efforts to combine grassroots projects with other aid schemes in order to emphasise local participation.

10   Companies argue that steps to reduce tied aid have reduced returns to Japan. Japanese companies that are said to have been winning two out of every three supply contracts under aid loans a decade ago, now win less than one in three.

Notes to Chapter 15: Luxembourg

1   OECD, *Development Cooperation Report 1997 'Efforts and Policies of the Members of the Development Assistance Committee'*, 1998, Paris, p102.
2   The figures LF450 million (1994) and LF500 million (1996) were obtained from the *Direction des Relations Economiques Internationales et de la Coopération*. They, however, and some NGOs believe that a large amount is actually retained in NGO bank accounts.
3   As there was virtually no surplus in these two budget lines at the end of 1996, no subventions for investment in administrative structures were assigned that year.
4   OECD, *Development Cooperation Report 1997, 'Efforts and Policies of the Members of the Development Assistance Committee'*, Paris, 1998.

Notes to Chapter 16: The Netherlands

1   This chapter has benefited from considerable depth of academic expertise on the NGO sector in the Netherlands and excellent background material. A wide range of NGO perspectives informed the chapter, and the authors are very grateful for the insights that were contributed. Particular thanks are due to Kees Biekart, Menno Gibson, Piet van Harn, David Sogge, Ton Waarts, Dick Wentinck and Henk Zomer.
2   In Dutch, the acronym for CFO (Co-financing Organisation) is MFO.
3   In Dutch, the acronym for CFP (Co-financing Programme) is MFP.
4   327 are listed in the *Directory of NGOs Active in Sustainable Development*, OECD Development Centre, Paris, 1996.
5   *New Directions*, GOM, April 1995.
6   See, Ministry of Foreign Affairs, *The Dutch Co-financing Programme*, undated, The Hague
7   OECD, *Development Cooperation Report 1997, 'Efforts and Policies of Members of the Development Assistance Committee'*, Paris, 1998, p88.
8   SNV is the largest single expert sending organisation.
9   *A World of Difference: A New Framework for Development Cooperation in the 1990s*, Ministry of Foreign Affairs, The Hague, 1991.
10 Jan Pronk was Minister for Development Cooperation between 1973 and 1977, and from 1989 to 1998.
11 OnzeWereld Survey, quoted in *The Reality of Aid 1995*, ICVA/EUROSTEP, Earthscan, London.
12 In 1994, 27 per cent of the Dutch public thought aid was well spent, compared with 38 per cent in 1986.
13 *Significance of the Co-Financing Programme: An Exploration, Gemeenschappelijk Overleg Medefinanciering* (GOM), 1991.
14 Schulpen, L., 'The Same Difference', PhD Thesis, quoted in *De Volkskrant*, 13 September 1997, '*Pronks hulp minstens zo goed als particuliere*'.
15 *The Foreign Policy of the Netherlands – A Review*, Ministry of Foreign Affairs, The Hague, 1995.

Notes to Chapter 17: New Zealand

1   In the framework of the Stakeholders Project, a more extensive case study of New Zealand was undertaken and published in 1996 (Ian Smillie, *NGOs and Governments: An Association for Development*, New Zealand Case Study, Wellington, 1996). This chapter is an updated and revised version of that study. Michelle Auld, under the auspices of the New Zealand Council for International Development provided new data and analysis. Pat Webster provided invaluable logistical support and insights.
2   The gross incomes of the three largest organisations in 1995–6 were: World Vision – NZ$ 20.6m; Save the Children – NZ$4.3m; Christian Children's Fund – NZ$4.7m.
3   NZODA, 'Investing in a Common Future; A Policy Framework of the New Zealand Official

Development Assistance Programme', NZODA, February, 1996.

4   OECD, *Development Cooperation Report 1997; Efforts and Policies of the Members of the Development Assistance Committee*, 1998, Paris, p103.

5   VASS Review 1996/97, Report to the NGO Community in New Zealand, Helen McNaught Consultancy Services, June 1997.

6   CORSO's charitable status was reinstated in 1984.

7   Titles include *On the Move* (about nomadic people), *Not in My Back Yard, Our Environment: To Change or Not to Change? Picking Up the Pieces, Our Town,* and *One Nation, Many Cultures,* Longman Paul, Auckland.

8   DAC, *New Zealand*, Development Cooperation Series, No17, OECD, Paris, 1996.

NOTES ON CHAPTER 18: NORWAY

1   This chapter benefits from extensive discussions on the Norwegian NGO community that took place in Bergen in November 1997 at a conference sponsored by the Royal Ministry of Foreign Affairs and NORAD on '35 Years of NGO Assistance, A Reappraisal'. The authors are most grateful to those in NORAD, the Royal Ministry of Foreign Affairs and in the NGO community for their contributions to the chapter. Particular thanks are due to Erik Berg, Marit Karlsen and Terje Tvedt.

2   OECD, *Development Cooperation Report 1997; Efforts and Policies of the Members of the Development Assistance Committee*, 1998, Paris, p104.

3   Tvedt, T., Development NGOs, – Actors in a New International Social System Draft paper for a conference on 'NGOs in Aid. A Reappraisal of 35 years of NGO Assistance', 3 –5 November 1997, University of Bergen, Norway, 1997a, supported by the Royal Ministry of Foreign Affairs and NORAD.

4   NORAD Annual Report 1996, p88.

5   Tvedt, T., *NGOs as a Channel in Development Aid. The Norwegian System*, Royal Norwegian Ministry of Foreign Affairs, Oslo, 1997b.

6   Kruse, Stein Erik, 'The Norwegian Case Study; NGO Evaluation Policies and Practices', in *Searching for Impact and Methods: NGO Evaluation Synthesis Study*, Ministry of Foreign Affairs of Finland for the OECD/DAC Expert Group on Evaluation, Helsinki, May 1997.

7   NORAD Annual Report 1995, p82.

8   NORAD Annual Report 1995.

9   Tvedt, *op cit.*

10 Garbo, G., Norway in ICVA/EUROSTEP, Reality of Aid 1995, Earthscan, 1995, London.

11 Per Selle, lecture at 'NGOs in Aid, A Reappraisal of 35 Years of NGO Assistance', 3–5 November 1997, University of Bergen.

12 Tvedt, 1997a, *op cit*, p78.

13 Ministry of Foreign Affairs of Finland for the OECD/DAC Expert Group on Evaluation, *Searching for Impact and Methods: NGO Evaluation Synthesis Study*, Helsinki, 1997.

14 Kjersti Morvik, *Kunnskapsutvikling og loering i fire norske private organisasjoner*, Sub report for Tvedt, T. *NGOs are a Channel in Development Aid*, 1995.

15 Tvedt, 1997a, *op cit*

16 *ibid*

17 Tvedt, T.,(2) NGOs as a Channel in Development Aid. The Norwegian System , Royal Norwegian Ministry of Foreign Affairs, August 1997, Oslo.

18 Tvedt quotes the example of Redd Barna and NORAD discussing rehabilitation of rural districts in Mozambique as a priority area for both. Tvedt (2), *op cit.*

19 Tvedt, T, 1997a *op cit.*

20 Kruse, *op cit.*

21 Royal Ministry of Foreign Affairs, *Norwegian Church Aid's Humanitarian and Peace making Work in Mali*, Evaluation Report 6.97 by International Peace Research Institute, Oslo, MFA, Oslo, October 1997.

22 Tvedt, 1997b, *op cit.*

NOTES ON CHAPTER 19: PORTUGAL

1   The author wishes to thank the Portuguese Platform for NGOs as well as the directors of several
    NGOs who assisted in the preparation of the document. Thanks are also due to the Planning,
    Programming and Evaluation Department of the Institute for Portuguese Cooperation (ICP), to the
    Fund for Economic Cooperation (FCE), and to Luísa Teotors of several NGOs who assisted in the
    preparation of the document.
2   OECD, *Development Cooperation Report 1997; Efforts and Policies of the Members of the
    Development Assistance Committee*, 1998, Paris, p84.
3   *ibid*, p85.
4   Among Portuguese NGOs it is difficult to pinpoint a definite pattern in activities. The facts and
    opinions in this chapter, therefore, represent mainstream organisations and issues. Statistics are based
    on the data available. With rare exceptions, documentation contains poor and incomplete information,
    making both data collection and analysis difficult.
5   OECD, *op cit*, pA33.
6   *ibid*, p85.
7   *ibid.*

NOTES ON CHAPTER 20: SPAIN

1   The author wishes to thank Roberto Monedo for his research assistance. He also greatly appreciates
    the time and information provided by those consulted or interviewed for this chapter. From the NGO
    community they are: Mercedes Alonso (*Prosalus*), Luis Arancibia (President, *Coordinadora*), Paloma
    Escudero (*Intermón*), Rafael Grasa (President, Catalonian Federation of NGDOs), Tomás Mallo
    (AIETI), José Mejias (0.7% Movement), Miguel Romero (ACSUR) and Maite Serrano (Secretary
    General, *Coordinadora*) who also gave useful suggestions on an early draft. From the Spanish
    Government, Carmen Arteaga (NGO Unit, AECI), Fransisco Montelban (Director, Office of Planning
    and Evaluation, SECIPI) and Jorge Orueta (Director, Technical Cabinet, AECI). The editors have
    updated some sections with the latest OECD/DAC information.
2   Coordinadora de ONG para el Desarrollo España, *Directorio Electronico, Organizaciones No
    Gubernamentales para el Desarrollo*, Madrid, 1996.
3   Senillosa, I. (ed.), *La Realidad de la Ayuda* 1994, Intermón, Barcelona. The largest component of the
    bilateral programme is the *Fondo de Ayuda al Desarrollo* (FAD/Development Assistance Fund),
    controlled by the Ministry of Finance.
4   Coordinadora, *op cit.*
5   Burgui, T., and Serrano, M. (1998) Chapter on Spain in: Smillie and Helmich, Public Attitudes and
    International Development Co-operation, Paris, OECD Development Centre, pp125–131.
6   Coordinadora de ONG para el Desarrollo España, *Estudio sobre la Fiscalidad y Régimen de Registro
    de las ONGD*, 1997, Madrid.

NOTES TO CHAPTER 21: SWEDEN

1   The authors are grateful to all those who contributed to this chapter. There was considerable reflec-
    tion on NGO–government relations following a 1995 evaluation, and this has provided a wealth of
    background material. Particular thanks are due to Magnus Lindell, Carin Norberg, Margareta
    Ringström and Svante Sandberg.
2   Sida, *Guidelines for Sida's support to the development programmes of Swedish NGOs*, 1993,
    Stockholm, p4.
3   Sida, *op cit.*
4   OECD, *Development Assistance Report 1996; Efforts and Policies of the Members of the
    Development Assistance Committee*, Paris, 1997.
5   OECD, *Development Assistance Report 1997; Efforts and Policies of the Members of the

Development Assistance Committee, 1998, Paris, p106.

6   Riddell, R.C., Bebbington, A. and Peck, L., *Promoting Development by Proxy: The Development Impact of the Swedish Government's Support to NGOs*, Evaluation Report 1995/2, SIDA, Stockholm.

7   Sida, *Guidelines, op cit*, p5.

8   Sida, *Guidelines for Sida's Support to the Development Programmes of Swedish NGOs in Central and Eastern Europe*, 1993, Stockholm.

9   Sida, *Humanitarian Assistance through Swedish NGOs*, Stockholm, 1997.

10 Westermark, P., 'Promoting Development By Proxy: Report on a Two Day Seminar with Swedish NGOs', June 1995, p4.

11 Riddell, *op cit*.

12 ICVA/EUROSTEP, *Reality of Aid* 1996, Earthscan, London, p177.

13 Sida, *Guidelines for Sida's Support to the Development Efforts Programmes of Swedish NGOs, op cit*, p6.

14 Westermark, P, *op cit*.

NOTES TO CHAPTER 22: SWITZERLAND

1   Research for this chapter was initiated during a study visit to Switzerland in April 1997 which provided a wide range of NGO and government perspectives. The chapter draws heavily on the annual analysis of Swiss development cooperation provided by the University of Geneva. Particular thanks are due to Olivier Berthoud, Richard Gerster and Beatrice Meyer. The authors are extremely grateful for the excellent materials made available by SDC, OFEEA, IUED, the Swiss Coalition and other NGOs.

2   OECD, *Development Cooperation Report 1997; Efforts and Policies of the Members of the Development Assistance Committee*, 1998, Paris, pp80–81.

3   See *La Confédération en Bref 1996*, Federal Chancellory, Berne, 1996.

4   Dannecker, Rudolf, 'Some Reflections on NGOs and Development Cooperation', Conference at the University of Dyiarbakar, East Anatolia, Turkey, 7 May 1996.

5   *La Suisse et Le Monde* 6, 1996.

6   See *Les ONG de Suisse, in La Suisse et le Monde 3*, 1996.

7   Members are *Fédération Suisse des Amis de la Nature* (FSAN), *La Ligue Suisse pour la Protection de l'Environment* (LSPN) *La Fondation Suisse de L'Energie* (FSE), *La Societé Suisse pour la Protection de l'Environment* (SPE), *L'Association transports et environmental* (ATE) and the World Wide Fund for Nature Suisse.

8   Dannecker, *op cit*.

9   OECD, *Development Cooperation Report 1997; Efforts and Policies of the Members of the Development Assistance Committee*, 1998, Paris, p81.

10 Translated as: 'The relevant federal departments build public opinion on development cooperation and humanitarian aid in general, and on the Swiss contribution. They maintain relations with cantons, communes, universities, and with Swiss organisations and the private sector, where these relations serve to promote development cooperation and humanitarian assistance'.

NOTES TO CHAPTER 23: UNITED KINGDOM

1   Research for this chapter took place after the election of a new government, which created a Department for International Development with Cabinet status, and which published the first White Paper on aid for twenty years. With such changes going on, the authors are particularly grateful to people within DFID and the NGO community for their comments on early drafts of the chapter, and for their insights into NGO–government relations. Particular thanks are due to Richard Bennett, Jim MacAlpine and Robin Russell.

2   OECD, *Development Cooperation Report 1997; Efforts and Policies of the Members of the Development Assistance Committee*, 1998, Paris, pp90–1.

3   See, for example, speech by Secretary of State Clare Short to IDPM, Manchester, 6 June, 1997.

4   Charities Aid Foundation, *Dimensions of the Voluntary Sector*, CAF, 1997, Tonbridge.

5   In terms of voluntary income; if income from rent and investments is included, Oxfam is second to The National Trust.

6   International Health Exchange and People in Aid, *The Human Face of Aid, 1996*.

7   OECD Development Centre, *Directory of NGOs Active in Sustainable Development*, 1996, Paris.

8   In 1995 BOND produced a register of 27 networks. While no up-to-date list of networks exists, it is likely that there are significantly more than these.

9   These were ACTIONAID, CARE, Concern, Wateraid and Marie Stopes, a family planning NGO.

10   OECD/DAC Expert Group on Aid Evaluation, *Searching for Impact and Methods: NGO Evaluation Synthesis Study*, Ministry of Foreign Affairs, Finland, 1997.

11   Barnett, A. and Bush, A., '*Case Proven? A review of the impact of ITDG's work as evidenced in evaluation and reports to major donors, 1993–5*', ITDG, Rugby, 1995, quoted in OECD/DAC, *op cit*.

12   Riddell, R., '*United Kingdom Case Study: NGO Evaluation Policies and Practices*' May 1997 in OECD/DAC *op cit*.

13   *MandE NEWS* is accessible by e-mail and web browser. The Internet website can be found at http//www.shimbir.demon.co.uk, or send an E-mail message to www@kfs.org.

14   Robinson, M. and Thin, N., *Project Evaluation, a Guide for NGOs, ODA*, 1994, London.

15   *Political Activities and Campaigning by Charities*, Charity Commission CC9, February 1997.

16   Both of these are Select Committees of the House of Commons. The committees comprise backbench MPs whose role is to scrutinize the activities of major departments of State. The new International Development Committee resulted from DFID being moved from the Foreign Office to become a separate department headed by its own cabinet minister.

17   See, for example, various articles by Alex de Waal (published by African Rights, London) on Rwanda during 1996, and Edward Mortimer in the *Financial Times*, 26 October, 1997.

18   Raven, Hugh, *Future Imperfect*, for BOAT, 1996; Development Initiatives, *Evaluation of NGO 1995 Aid Cuts Campaign*, for BOND, 1996.

19   See, for example, *Living in the Real World: An International Role for a Scottish Parliament*, Kevin Dunions, Scottish Education and Action for Development (SEAD), 1995.

NOTES TO CHAPTER 24: UNITED STATES

1   Data gathering for this chapter from 20 of the largest American PVOs was carried out by Tony Rogge. Interviews with a wide range of USAID officials and PVO leaders in the Washington and New York areas were carried out by the author in June and July 1997. Comments on an early draft were gratefully received from USAID and from InterAction.

2   USAID, The *AID–PVO Partnership*, 1992, Washington.

3   Craggier, Anne, *Economic Policies at Cross-purposes: The United States and Developing Countries*, Brookings Institute, 1993, Washington, p62.

4   Sewell, John, *et al*, *Challenges and Priorities for the 1990s*, Overseas Development Council, 1992, Washington, p44.

5   Nonprofit Sector, *Nonprofit Almanac 1996–7*, 1997, Washington, p59. Despite its small proportion of the total, US corporate philanthropy receives undue amounts of publicity. Reports, for example, of new forms of corporate philanthropy from 'techno millionaires' such as the founders of Microsoft, the Aldus Coporation and others – going mainly to domestic charities – give the impression of a generous private sector and suggest the possibility of a whole new approach to welfare.

6   USAID, *Report of American Voluntary Agencies Engaged in Overseas Relief and Development Registered with the U.S. Agency for International Development*, Bureau For Humanitarian Response (PVC), Washington, 1997a.

7   USAID, *An Assessment of the State of the USAID/PVO Partnership*, Advisory Committee on Voluntary Foreign Aid (ACVFA),Washington, 1997b.

8   *Nonprofit Almanac 1996–7, op cit*, p60.

9   See USAID, *Strengthening the Public-Private Partnership: An Assessment of USAID's Management of PVO and NGO Activities*, Program and Operations Assessment Report No. 13, 1996, Washington.

10   The sizeable 1996 increase highlights recent volatility in year-to-year flows. Multilateral ODA was unusually low in 1995 because of the timing of subscriptions to multilateral agencies, and the shortfall was made up in the 1996 data. Delays in approving the 1996 US budget for fiscal year 1996 also meant that two years' worth of grant disbursements to Israel were inlcuded in the 1996 data. Source:

OECD, *Development Cooperation Report 1997; Efforts and Policies of the Members of the Development Assistance Committee*, 1998, Paris, p107.

11 USAID 1997b, *op cit*, pvi.

12 USAID, *USAID–US PVO Partnership; Policy Guidance*, Washington, April 1995

13 These figures must be regarded as approximate. Non-food figures are derived from a statement of PVO funding obligations provided by the USAID Budget Office. Food and freight figures are taken from USAID's Bureau for Humanitarian Response 1997 Report. Both sets likely include grants, contracts and food for non-ODA countries and this would have the effect of inflating the percentage of ODA channelled through NGOs. Offsetting this, however, an additional $450 million is channelled through PVOs from other government departments in the form of grants and contracts. This amount has not been reflected in these calculations.

14 USAID, *NPI Resource Guide*, Vol 1., Washington, January 1997c.

15 Smith, Scott, 'Program Performance Monitoring and Evaluation at USAID', USAID, 1996, Washington.

16 Mansfield, David, 'NGO Evaluation Synthesis Study: United States', pp11–12, in *Searching for Impact and Methods: NGO Evaluation Synthesis Study*, Ministry of Foreign Affairs of Finland for the OECD/DAC Expert Group on Evaluation, Vol II, 1997.

17 Smillie, Ian and Helmich, Henny (eds), *Non-Governmental Organisations and Governments: Stakeholders for Development*, OECD, 1993, Paris.

18 USAID, *Strengthening the Public-Private Partnership*, *op cit*, pix.

19 Hellinger *et al*, *Aid for Just Development*, Lynne Rienner, 1988, Boulder, p103.

20 The decline is less dramatic when privately donated in-kind goods are included in the calculation. The total private income during the period, including in-kind donations, fell from 73 per cent of the total to 66 per cent.

NOTES TO CHAPTER 25: EUROPEAN UNION

1   Interviews for this chapter were carried out in September 1997. The authors are very grateful for the opportunity to draw on expertise both within DG VIII and ECHO, and from NGOs. Particular thanks are due to Karen Birchall, Andrew Bunbury, Genevieve de Crombrugge, Debjani Das, James Mackie, Clodagh O Brian, Xavier Ortegat, Giorgio Guaneri and Bernard Ryelandt.

2   OECD, *Development Cooperation Report 1997; Efforts and Policies of the Members of the Development Assistance Committee*, 1998, Paris, p96.

3   Bernard Ryelandt, Head of EU NGO Unit for Co-financing, DGVIII/B2, quoted in CLONG, *Liaison News*, No 30, September 1997.

4   European Commission Document VIII/764/87/EN.

5   IDS, University of Sussex, and IDS University of Addis Ababa, *Evaluation of Development Cooperation between the European Union and Ethiopia, 1976–1994*, IDS UK and Ethiopia, June 1996, p63.

6   *ibid*, p59.

7   See *European Voluntary Service for Young People: General Information and Third Countries*, European Commission DG XXII, Directorate C, info3cen.br.09.07.97.

8   These are: Aid by Country/Region; AIDS; Campaigns in Europe; Decentralized Cooperation; Democracy and Human Rights; Development Projects in Developing Countries; Drug Abuse; Environment/ecology; Family Planning; Fisheries; Food Aid; Health; Humanitarian Aid; Microenterprises; Migrants/immigrants; NGO development operations; Nutrition; PHARE programme; Population; Refugees/returnees/displaced persons; Rehabilitation/reconstruction; Research; Rural and Urban Development; Training; University; Women in Development; Youth.

9   European Commission Document VIII/764/87/EN, pp1–2.

10 Commission Annual report to the Development Council for 1995.

11 *ibid* p12.

12 IDS, University of Sussex and IDS University of Addis Ababa, Evaluation of Development Cooperation between the European Union and Ethiopia, 1976–1994, IDS UK and Ethiopia, June 1996.

13 See Crombrugghe, G., Douxchamps, F. and Stampa, N., *Evaluation of the EEC-NGO Co-financing in Relation to Institutional Support for Grassroots Organisations in Developing Countries*, Synthesis

Report, COTA, Brussels, 1993.

14 *General Conditions for the Co-financing of Projects to Raise Public Awareness of Development Issues Carried out by Non Governmental Organisations (NGOs) in the European Community*, VIII/271/87/EN.

15 Commission Annual report to the Development Council for 1995.

16 This refers to coherence between policies of the EU and member states so as not to undermine development cooperation objectives; complementarity between instruments and policies of EU and Member States; and coordination on implementation.

17 Hartmeyer, H. and Obrovsky, M., in ICVA/EUROSTEP, *Reality of Aid 1996*, Earthscan, 1996, London.

18 Austria, Belgium, Greece, Luxembourg and the Netherlands will share two Brussels-based advisers.

19 DGVII/B2, *Decentralized Cooperation*, Explanatory Sections, Introduction.

NOTES TO CHAPTER 26: WORLD BANK

1   The assistance of the World Bank's NGO Unit in the preparation of this chapter is gratefully acknowledged. Thanks are also due to other departments in the Bank, and to InterAction, Alan Fowler and Carmen Malena, who all commented on an early draft.

2   Quoted in the *Oxfam Poverty Report*, Oxfam, 1995, Oxford, p72.

3   'The Strategic Compact: renewing the Bank's Effectiveness to Fight Poverty', World Bank, 13 February, 1997.

4   Operational Directive 14.70, 'Involving Nongovernmental Organisations in Bank-Supported Activities', World Bank, August 1989.

5   Projects have an average life span of five years. About 36 per cent of the total portfolio of all active projects at the end of 1996 had some NGO involvement.

6   Malena, Carmen, *NGO Involvement in World Bank-Financed Social Funds: Lessons Learned*, World Bank, Washington, December 1996.

7   'Cooperation Between the World Bank and NGOs: FY 96 Progress Report', Participation and NGO Group, 1997.

8   'The Contribution of NGOs to Development Effectiveness in World Bank-supported Investment Projects: Study Design Paper', 1996, OED.

9   *Working with NGOs: A Practical Guide to Operational Collaboration between the World Bank and Non-governmental Organisations*, Operations Policy Department, March 1995.

Bibliography

BIBLIOGRAPHY TO CHAPTER 3: AUSTRALIA

Australian Agency for International Development, 'AusAID-NGO Co-operation; Annual Reports 1995–96 and 1996–97

Australian Agency for International Development, 'Review of the Effectiveness of NGO programs', July 1995

Australian Agency for International Development, 'Review of the Efficiency and Effectiveness of Australian Volunteer Programs', June 1996

Australian Council for Overseas Aid, Submission to the Review of Australia's Aid Program, December 1996

Australian Council for Overseas Aid, ACFOA Response to AusAID's Review of the Effectiveness of NGO Programs, December 1995

Australian National Audit Office, 'Accounting for Aid: The Management of Funding to NGOs', Australian Agency for International Development, August 1996

Development Bulletin, 'The Future of Australia's Aid programme', Volume 39, October 1996

Commonwealth of Australia, 'Australia's Overseas Aid Program 1992–3', Minister for Trade and Overseas Development, 1992

Commonwealth of Australia, 'Australia's Overseas Aid Program 1996–7', Minister for Foreign Affairs, August 1996

Commonwealth of Australia, 'One Clear Objective: Poverty Reduction through Sustainable Development', Report of the [Simons] Committee of Review, Canberra, 1997

Commonwealth of Australia, 'Australia's Overseas Aid Program 1997–98', Minister for Foreign Affairs, May, 1997

Interim Code of Conduct Committee, 'Report to the Minister for Foreign Affairs and ACFOA', August 1996

Kilby, Patrick (ed), *Australia's Aid Program: Mixed Messages and Conflicting Agendas*, Monash Asia Institute and Community Aid Abroad, Victoria, 1996

Parliament of the Commonwealth of Australia, 'The Australian Aid Program: Report on Proceedings of a Seminar, 31 July 1996, Canberra', Joint Standing Committee on Foreign Affairs, Defence and Trade, September 1996

Smillie, Ian and Helmich, Henny, *Nongovernmental Organizations and Governments: Stakeholders for Development*, OECD, Paris, 1993

BIBLIOGRAPHY TO CHAPTER 12: ITALY

AAVV, '*Teorie dello sviluppo e nuove forme di cooperazione*' Rome, 1997, Movimondo Cavalcaselle, Marcello '*Le Ong nella cooperazione allo sviluppo italiana; evoluzione storica, rapporti con la Dgcs e caratteristichi essentiali*', in: DIPCO, Bolletino della Cooperazione, Roma, No 8 of 4 March 1998, pp 133–48

Focà, Anna, 'Italy' in Ian Smillie and Henny Helmich (eds), *Stakeholders for Development: NGOs and Governments*, OECD, Paris, 1993

MAE–DGCS, '*Relazione Annuale sull'attuazione della politica di cooperazione allo sviluppo nel 1996*' DIPCO, Bollettino della Cooperazione, Roma, No38 of 5 November 1997, pp 12–19

BIBLIOGRAPHY TO CHAPTER 15: THE NETHERLANDS

Hoebink, P, *Coherence and Development Policy in the Netherlands*, draft, April 1997
OECD DAC, Aid Review of the Netherlands, 1994, No4
OECD DAC Press Release on Aid Review of the Netherlands, 3 October 1997, CLONG, *Liaison News*,
    October 1995, Brussels

BIBLIOGRAPHY TO CHAPTER 18: PORTUGAL

Afonso, Maria Manuela, 1995, Cooperação para o Desenvolvimento- características, evolução e perspecti-
    vas futuras, Lisboa, CIDAC (edições Nortisul-Investigação e Pesquisa 2)
Ministério dos Negela, 1995, Cooperação para o Desenvolvim 1995–10 *Anos de Política de Cooperação*,
    Lisboa
Ribeiro, Mário, 1995, *O Potencial das Organizações Não-Governamentais Portuguesas de
    Desenvolvimento* (ONGD), Lisboa, CIDAC (*edições Nortisul-Investigação e Pesquisa 1*)

BIBLIOGRAPHY TO CHAPTER 21: SWITZERLAND

Aide Suisse aux Pays en Developpement et aux Pays de L'Europe Orientale, 1995, 1994, 1993, 1994.
    IUED, Geneva
Education et Développement, press release, February 2 1997, Berne
Gerster, Richard, *In Gemeinsame Interessen Investieren Nationales Forschungsprogramm*, Einsiedeln,
    June 1995
Guidelines North South, SDC 1994
La Suisse et le Monde No3, 1996, ONG, *Partenaires de la politique étrangère fédérale,* DFAE, Berne
Local NGOs; A Working Guide, SDC, Berne 1995
Loi fédérale sur la coopération au développement et l'aide humanitaire internationales, 19 March 1976
SDC Annual Reports, 1993, 1994, 1995 and 1996
Swiss Coalition News, various editions
Wem soll ich spenden? Zentralstelle für Wohlfahrtsunternehmen (ZEWO), Zürich
'Principles for Successful Project Work', Swiss Protestant Aid Agencies and Missions, Bread for All,
    Département Missionaire, Swiss Interchurch Aid, Association of Protestant Churches and Missions
'Some Reflections on NGOs and Development Cooperation', Conference at the University of Dyiarbakar,
    East Anatolia, Turkey, 7 May 1996
NGO annual reports, statements, policies and other materials

BIBLIOGRAPHY TO CHAPTER 24: EUROPEAN UNION

Boulon-Lefevre, Anne, Evaluation of Vocational Training Projects, carried out by NGOs and co-financed
    by the EC, VIII/695/94/EN
Catholic University of Louvain, 'Evaluation of Integrated Development Projects Co-financed with
    NGOs', November 1994, VIII/451/95/EN
CEC, 'Digest of Community Resources Available for Financing the Activities of NGOs and other
    Governmental and/or decentralized bodies representing civil society in the fields of development
    cooperation and humanitarian aid', VIII/207/97 EN
CEC, *Annexes Statistiques au Rapport de la Commission sur la cooperation avec les organizations non-
    gouvernmentales de developpement europeennes dan des domaines interesant les pay en voie de
    developpement*, exercise 1995, VIII/1210/96
CEC, 'General Conditions for the Co-financing of Projects Undertaken in Developing Countries by
    NGOs', January 1988, VII 764 87 EN

CEC, *Liste indicative des ONGs en contact avec la direction generale due developpement (secteur ONG)*, VIII/1206/86

CLONG *Liaison News*, various issues

CLONG, 'Revision of the General Conditions of Co-financing, Submission by the NGDO–EC Liaison Committee to the NGO Unit (DGVIII/B2)', CEC, February 1996

CLONG, 'The Role of NGDOs in EU Decentralized Cooperation', Brussels, August 1997

CLONG, *Liaison South*. Various issues

CLONG, *NGO Handbook*, 1997

'Commission Annual Report on Cooperation with European Non Governmental Organizations in Those Fields of Importance to Developing Countries', DGVIII, B2, Various years

Cox, A., Healey, J. and Koning, A., *How European Aid Works*, ODI, 1996

Crombrugghe, G., Douxchamps, F. and Stampa, N., *Evaluation of the EEC-NGO Co-financing in Relation to Institutional Support for Grassroots Organizations in Developing Countries*, Synthesis Report, COTA, Brussels, 1993

DG VIII, *Partners in Development: The European Union and NGOs*, CEC, Luxembourg 1995

DGVII/B2, *Decentralized Cooperation*, Explanatory Sections, Introduction

Dhonte, R. et al, *Evaluation of Credit and Savings Projects Co-financed by the European Commission with NGOs*, VIII.597/95/EN

ECHO, *Operational Manual for the Evaluation of Humanitarian Aid*

ECHO, 'Annual Report 1996'

ECHO, *Disaster Preparedness*

'General Conditions for the Co-financing of Projects to Raise Public Awareness of Development Issues carried out by Non Governmental Organizations (NGOs) in the European Community', VIII/271/87/EN

IDS, University of Sussex, and IDS, University of Addis Ababa, *Evaluation of Development Cooperation between the European Union and Ethiopia, 1976–1994*, IDS UK and Ethiopia, June 1996

VOICE, 'Voluntary Organizations in Cooperation in Emergencies', CLONG, Brussels, July 1996

Index